Routledge Revivals

TENTS IN MONGOLIA

TENTS IN MONGOLIA
(YABONAH)

ADVENTURES AND EXPERIENCES AMONG
THE NOMADS OF CENTRAL ASIA

BY
HENNING HASLUND

First published in 1934 by Kegan Paul, Trench, Trubner & Co. Ltd.

This edition first published in 2018 by Routledge
2 Park Square, Milton Park, Abingdon, Oxon, OX14 4RN
and by Routledge
52 Vanderbilt Avenue, New York, NY 10017, USA

Routledge is an imprint of the Taylor & Francis Group, an informa business

© 1934 by Taylor and Francis

All rights reserved. No part of this book may be reprinted or reproduced or utilised in any form or by any electronic, mechanical, or other means, now known or hereafter invented, including photocopying and recording, or in any information storage or retrieval system, without permission in writing from the publishers.

Publisher's Note
The publisher has gone to great lengths to ensure the quality of this reprint but points out that some imperfections in the original copies may be apparent.

Disclaimer
The publisher has made every effort to trace copyright holders and welcomes correspondence from those they have been unable to contact.
A Library of Congress record exists under ISBN: 25007588

ISBN 13: 978-0-367-17587-0 (hbk)
ISBN 13: 978-0-367-17588-7 (pbk)
ISBN 13: 978-0-429-05749-6 (ebk)

TENTS IN MONGOLIA

The Author

[*frontispiece*

TENTS IN MONGOLIA
(YABONAH)
ADVENTURES AND EXPERIENCES AMONG THE NOMADS OF CENTRAL ASIA

By
HENNING HASLUND

WITH 64 PLATES
AND A MAP

LONDON
KEGAN PAUL, TRENCH, TRUBNER & CO., LTD.
BROADWAY HOUSE: 68–74 CARTER LANE, E.C.
1934

First published, April 1934
Reprinted, November 1934

Translated from the Swedish by
ELIZABETH SPRIGGE
and
CLAUDE NAPIER

DEDICATION

One of them had the soul of an artist. He loved music and understood the æsthetic value of all that is primeval and unspoilt. The other had accompanied Stanley on his arduous travels, and had been the first white man to gaze out over Lake Leopold II and many another panorama of the " Black Continent ".

Those were my childhood's great days on which I made a third in their circle and performed the journey from the knees of one of those storytellers to the other's ; and from their great fund of experience and appreciation I imbibed a longing for the same far horizons.

That is why I dedicate this book to

My father and his cousin, Albert Christophersen.

CONTENTS

BOOK I

CHAP.		PAGE
I	THE ORIGIN OF THE KREBS EXPEDITION	1
II	THE JOURNEY OUT	12
III	OUTSIDE THE WALL	27
IV	THE LAND OF MEMORIES	38
V	THE ROBBER PRINCESS	45
VI	THE DESERT	55
VII	THE CLOISTER OF GOD	66
VIII	ON TO THE NORTH-WEST	76

BOOK II

I	THE ARRIVAL AT BULGUN TAL	85
II	PIONEER LIFE, EXORCISM AND RUSSIAN BATHS	89
III	CHRISTMAS AT BULGUN TAL	101
IV	THE STEPPE BECOMES OUR HOME	106
V	FUR TRANSPORT UNDER DIFFICULTIES	116
VI	SPRING	129
VII	A RIDE TO THE POST	136
VIII	I BECOME A FATHER	143
IX	WE FILL OUR BARNS	147
X	THE LONG ARM OF THE SOVIET REVOLUTION	154
XI	A DIFFICULT ACT OF FRIENDSHIP	161
XII	THE JOURNEY HOME	168
XIII	CUSTOMS EXAMINATION AND CHRISTMAS TREE TINSEL	178
XIV	WINTER FUR CAMPAIGN	188

CONTENTS
BOOK III

CHAP.		PAGE
I	Journey's End—Kiăkt	199
II	Round the Camp-fire	206
III	The Trading Station, "Alpino Serai"	217
IV	Is there more between Heaven and Earth . . . ?	224
V	The Snowstorm. Sava Comes Back	232
VI	Peril to Northward	241
VII	In Captivity	254
VIII	Daily Life in the Prison at Shinkish	267
IX	On the Way to Freedom	275
X	Back in Mongolia	283
XI	The Shaman	294
XII	In Nature's Bosom	304
XIII	A Dangerous Travelling Companion	318
XIV	A Man's Way is only One—the Way preordained by Fate (*Mongolian Proverb*)	325
	Notes	337
	Index	341

LIST OF ILLUSTRATIONS

FACING PAGE

The Author . . . . . . *Frontispiece*
Dr. C. E. Krebs, leader of the expedition 6
I. In the villages through which we passed, the Chinese cultivators brought their tribute in the form of steaming green tea 24
II. Our Chinese caravan boys 24
I. The Falconer 25
II. A piece of the Great Wall of China 25
I. Poverty-stricken Mongols 30
II. Rest in Chahar, the lost land of the Mongols . . 30
The poor Mongolian Shepherd 36
Hunter on horseback (*from an old Mongolian painting*) . . 37
I. Free Mongolian soldiers, fully conscious of their descent from Jenghiz Khan's warriors 44
II. Irregular soldiers—or honest bandits ? 44
I. Mongolian Princess 45
II. Dambin Janzang, Mongolia's most notorious and dreaded bandit leader. He was executed in 1926 . . . 45
Mongolia's swift-footed antelope (*Gazella Subgutterosa*) . 56
I. The Desert 57
II. " The western sea—the desert " (*Mongolian song*) . . 57
I. Ox caravans crawl forward through the country . . 60
II. Camel caravans winding between the sand dunes on the way to distant goals 60
I. Summer 61
II. . . . and Winter 61
One of the Gobi Desert's " three trees " 64
Censer of hammered copper—on the front side of the censer are seen " the eight glorious symbols " (in Tibetan, *tashi dagai'ä*) which are regarded in the Lamaistic world as propitious emblems. From left to right these are : 1. The white baldaquin—unrestricted dominion. 2. The two auspicious golden fishes. 3. The vase containing the holy water that confers eternal Life. 4. The Lotos flower—purity and heavenly birth. 5. The spiral

LIST OF ILLUSTRATIONS

FACING PAGE

trumpet that announces victory. 6. The auspicious diagram representing Buddha's bowels. This symbolizes the endless series of rebirths in a sinful world. 7. The invincible banner. 8. The victorious wheel—a kingdom where the sun never sets. (The wheel of life or the sun) 65

I. Ungern-Sternberg, "the mad baron", who proclaimed himself a reincarnation of the Mongols' god of war and who held sway in Kalka-Mongolia in the beginning of "The iron bird's year", 1921 68
II. Women from Chahar in Mongolia 68
Woman of the Durbet-Khukhet tribe 69
Unmarried and married woman from Kalka-Mongolia. The married woman's headdress symbolizes cows' horns, and the wadded ornaments the cow's prominent shoulder blades 70
For many years the Kalka-Mongols were under the guardianship of the Tsar's Cossacks and the Mandarins of the Dragon Throne 71
The principal entrance to the Living Buddha's palace at Urga 72

I. Mongolian pilgrims on their toilsome way to Bogdo Kure (the Cloister of God) 73
II. Pilgrims on the way to Bogdo Kure 73
III. Having reached their goal, the pilgrims collapse exhausted outside the outer enclosure surrounding Bogdo Hutuktu Gegen's palace. Here they remain in prayer for days and weeks 73

Khans and Chiefs of Kalka-Mongolia in past times . . 74
Mongolian hutuktu (reincarnation of a divinity) . . . 75
I. Interior of Temple 80
II. Three high Lamas with their shabis 80
Temple painting illustrating the purifying and saving influence of Lamaism upon the unclean and intractable people. (The inscription reads: "A people without religion is like a horse without reins.") 81

I. My comrade on the steppe 108
II. Mother-love on the steppe. (A few minutes before this picture was taken a herd of several hundred half-wild horses was grazing on the spot, but they vanished at a gallop when we approached with the camera. A newborn foal caused the anxious mother to remain.) . 108

Bukha barildena. To the right, under the awning, sit the Chiefs and Noyans (nobles and officials). To the left the men of the people. In the background women of the people 109

xii

LIST OF ILLUSTRATIONS

FACING PAGE

Bukha barildena, the Mongolian wrestling match, is a favourite sport, and at the festivals arranged for the amusement of the Chiefs and people the bator (strong men) of the tribes meet to compete for victory and honour . 112

Our Mongolian house-girl, Surong 113

I. Jetom, our Mongolian first hand 128
II. Mongolian yak oxen, in home-made harness and yokes, drew our American ploughs through the virgin soil . 128

Waterwheels brought the river water to our fields day and night 129

I. Across the Sable Plateau at a gallop 136
II. " Buckjumping " 136

Silver Khurudu (prayer-mill) 143

By a method of my own for calling forth spirits, I drew out voices and tunes from a little box to the great astonishment—and subsequent delight—of the natives . . . 148

" The river with the willow-covered banks " (*Mongolian song*) 152

I. The first Mongolian postage stamps. Until 1923, in sending letters from Urga, either Chinese or Russian stamps were used according to which of the two powers had at the moment the greater influence in the land of the Mongols. In 1924 the " Young Mongols " issued the stamps depicted above. These were printed by a Western firm in China and were used in Mongolia until the end of 1925, when Soviet Russia introduced new stamps with Mongolian text 153

II. *Nighen* (one) *tugherik*. The first Mongolian coinage came into use in Urga in 1924. The coins were struck in Moscow. A tugherik, worth 0·78 Mexican dollar, was divided into 100 munggu. . . . Before this time trade was almost exclusively carried on by barter, and standards of value were arranged in different districts in respect of goods from which the district in question obtained its steady income. In Northern Mongolia the unit was nighen (one squirrel skin), and on the steppes a horse or a head of cattle was valued in proportion to how many pud shartos the animal was worth. (One pud shartos = 16·5 kilo of butter.) Officially taxation was assessed with the aid of silver value. A yamba was a lump of silver in the shape of a horse's hoof weighing 1·87 kilos. The yamba was divided into 50 Lahn (Chinese Liang) of ten chan (Chinese ch'ien) of 10 tung (Chinese fen). On the introduction from China of the Mexican dollar this was counted as the equivalent of 0·76 Lahn . 153

Lamas gathered at a temple festival in Urga . . . 161

LIST OF ILLUSTRATIONS

	FACING PAGE
I. Three distinguished Lamas on horseback	170
II. Bassoon-blowers in a Lamaistic procession	170
III. Courageous Lamas from Van Kure venture out on the Orchon river in a hollowed-out tree trunk	170
Acclimatized	182
Silver Yamba (Chinese yüan-pao)—natural size	192
The Gods	193
I. Shabi	198
II. The old Lama and his deaf servant at Dain Derchen Kure	198
Tsong Kapa (in Mongolian, Bogdo Lama) the reformer of Lamaism and founder of the yellow sect (1356–1418)	199
Mongol Chief with his suite	204
" The herdsman's call-note among the hills " (*Mongolian song*)	205
Bomberja	210
I. Old copper amulet with the twelve signs of the Zodiac. The Mongols indicate time with the aid of the twelve zodiacal beasts. In the case of a time more remote than twelve years they attach the name of the beast to one of the five elements of the Chinese : wood, fire, earth, metal and water. Each element in turn is assigned to two of the twelve beasts. The sixty-year periods thus arrived at are repeated, but are more closely determined by being numbered. In Northern Mongolia the day is divided into twelve hours, which are likewise named after the twelve beasts. 0–2, the hour of the Mouse ; 2–4, of the ox ; 4–6, of the tiger ; 6–8, of the hare ; 8–10, of the dragon ; 10–12, of the serpent ; 12–14, of the horse ; 14–16, of the sheep ; 16–18, of the ape ; 18–20, of the cock ; 20–22, of the dog ; 22–24, of the pig. 1923, the year our expedition arrived in Mongolia, was the " Water-pigs' " year, the fifty-seventh year in the Mongols' fifteenth period	216
II. *Chikherli bodena*, the skull bored from ear to ear, a typical example of the Mongols' skill in shooting	216
I. Dalachi, the sorcerer, who after long meditation and repetition of mystic formulas, can divine	217
II. By laying a sheep's shoulder-blade in the fire and then interpreting the cracks made by the heat	217
I. The wolf, the Mongols' hereditary enemy, alive	224
II. ... and dead	224
" Ole'en Lama "	225
The heavily laden horses made their way laboriously up the narrow valleys	240

LIST OF ILLUSTRATIONS

FACING PAGE

The two legendary antelopes, worshipping the purity and splendour of the sun 284

I. Soyote hunter 288
II. The happy child of nature 288

The Obo 296

Mongolian gurtum. A gurtum is a Lama who after prolonged prayers and other preparations can put himself into a state of ecstasy, during which he is able to answer questions concerning the future. In practice the gurtum is the same as the Shaman of the " black magic " who has been adopted by Lamaism 297

Maytreya (in Mongolian, Maidari) the Messiah of Lamaism . 304

Pilgrims on their way to the temple festival . . . 308

I. The Prior of the Monastery. 309
II. Lamas assembled in the temple courtyard to listen to the Prior's reading from the sacred books . . . 309

Mongolian Hunting Scene. The picture is painted on silk and is ascribed to the end of the fifteenth century. Noble Mongols and Manchus are taking part in the chase. The hunters are armed with bows and arrows, ancient muzzle-loaders and spears. They are employing both hounds and hawks. The original is in Consul Black's collection at Rungsted 314

I. Silver Soborok (in Tibetan, Chorten). The Soborok is a reliquary in which the relics of a deceased hutuktu or high Lama are preserved. Its form symbolizes the five elements into which the body is resolved after death 324
II. Lamas from the " Black Hat " community dance in the temple courtyard 324

Gold mining in Northern Mongolia 325

I. Buga (in Tibetan, Sa-ba), the companion of the god of death, is one of the chief figures in the tsam dance (devil dance). Opposite Buga dances " The Deaths-head ", who chases away the ravens that attack the sacrifice, " Zor " 328
II. The devil dance concludes with the breaking of the sacrifice to pieces. This is a clay figure and is presumably a substitute for the human sacrifice of former times . 328

Scouts of the Desert 332

Khara-khun (black people) is the term for male Mongols who do not belong to the priesthood. They wear a long pigtail, the longer the better 333

xv

ILLUSTRATIONS IN THE TEXT

	ON PAGE
Route of the Expedition from start to finish	14
Yabonah	33
Plan of the Iga Farm	151
Measurements used in the Mongolian Bazaars	209
Mongolian Bazaar Measurements	212
Mongolian Bazaar Measurements	213
Map of the Expedition's journey in Mongolia	*facing* 336

TENTS IN MONGOLIA
(YABONAH)
BOOK I

CHAPTER I

THE ORIGIN OF THE KREBS EXPEDITION

ON a wind-swept promontory outside the ancient mercantile city of Helsingör lies old Gothic Kronborg.

For many a long year the black, foam-crested waves of the Kattegat and the Sund have beaten against the walls of the fortress—but they stand.

The castle whispers of legends and adventure.

At the extreme point of the headland lies the " Flag Battery ", with patinated cannon that recall the time of greatness when the grim fortress exacted toll from vessels sailing by. The cannon lie silent and dreaming now, but from the battery's tall flagstaff the Danish colours flutter in the wind—they wave amicably to the neighbour across the sound and send glad greetings to the passing ships.

One grey November day in 1914 a hundred and thirty young Danish cadets of the thirtieth regiment arrived at Kronborg. I suppose we belonged to the last generation to be animated by the spirit which prevailed before the world war.

And we were very young.

With devout steps we trod the ancient castle courtyard and marched up in front of the cadet-school wing. From the long façade of the building there flashed to us in golden letters the legend : " For Ret at Byde, Laer først at Lyde." [1]

We were very young and, standing there, we remem-

[1] For the right to command learn first to obey.

bered H. C. Andersen's story of Kronborg, which our mothers had read to us not so long before.

Deep down in the dungeons of the castle sleeps old Ogier the Dane. With his mailed figure resting against the marble table he sits dreaming of all that happens in the land of Denmark. From time to time, half in dream, he stretches out his fist and presses the hand of Denmark's youth. If its grip be strong, its will firm and its eye clear, he returns to his dream-filled slumber. For Ogier the Dane will not awake until the day when danger is at hand.

In the school dining-hall hung a long row of photographs depicting youthful warriors. These were the heads of their respective years, and the name of the latest was Ove Krebs.

His brother Carl Krebs belonged to our year. They were sons of one of Denmark's Generals.

Carl was the eldest cadet in the school. He had qualified in medicine and thus was entitled to serve his time as an army surgeon with the rank and pay of an officer, but he had insisted on beginning as a private and proceeding through the ranks, in order to acquire the training which an officer ought to possess and which he regarded as useful to a man.

Another of the cadets at the school was named No. 2 Borgström, but by us he was called " Hassan ", " Baby ", or " Buffalo ".

When the curriculum did not demand our time, Buffalo was always surrounded by a large troop of comrades for whom he produced a never-failing stream of funny stories. He was, moreover, the strongest fellow in the school and could do the same rifle exercises with a twenty-four pound machine-gun as we performed with difficulty with a nine-pound rifle.

There were, besides, many pleasant and merry companions at the school. The only distinctive quality to which I myself could lay claim was that of being the Benjamin of the school.

So by degrees we got our pips and our swords, and were distributed over the country to the regiments to which we had been gazetted.

ORIGIN OF THE KREBS EXPEDITION

For several years the Danish army remained mobilized, The whole world around us was fighting, but we ourselves never were at war.

Occasionally we met old comrades on leave or in garrison and heard news of the two brothers Krebs, who had cut loose from this routine job and this uneventful life. They had gone out into the world and were already wrestling with great tasks. We constantly heard rumours of what they had accomplished and of missions that had been entrusted to them.

First they were both appointed to the Danish Legation in Moscow. Ove was later transferred to Peking, where he served as Chargé d'Affaires.

Carl was attached to the International Red Cross on whose account he travelled round inspecting the prison-camps in Russia and Siberia. He was entrusted with similar supervisory powers over the Austrian war prisons as were exercised by Elsa Brändström, among others, over the German.

But Carl had many other experiences. He assisted Maria Feodorovna, the mother of the murdered Tsar, who was a Danish Princess, by bringing her food, medicine and money when she was a fugitive in the Crimea, and later he laboured with the assistance of American money to alleviate the distress in the war-prisons of Siberia. When the Bolsheviks reached Irkutsk he bought a horse and rode away through the mountains southward of Lake Baikal. Thence he proceeded, riding by compass, till he reached remote Peking.

He travelled alone, without a caravan, and this ride was a feat which certainly few before him had performed. By day he rode across steppes and desert, guided only by the compass, and at night he slept in a sleeping sack, with no tent, in fifteen degrees of frost. During the journey he was bitten by a snake and lay in high fever for many days, but he recovered and went on. On his way he passed a place, Bulgun Tal or Sable Plateau, which was lovelier than anything he had seen, and he was greatly captivated by this idyllic scene, the memory of which persistently remained with him.

From Peking he returned home to Denmark by sea

ORIGIN OF THE KREBS EXPEDITION

and, on his arrival, eloquently described to us all the splendid things he had seen and done. When at last he told us that he was going to return one day to Sable Plateau to settle there, both Buffalo and I declared our intention of accompanying him, and the more we thought of it the more we longed for the day actually to arrive.

In 1919 and 1920 Krebs was again in Mongolia and Urianhai for the purpose of more closely studying the conditions of the country. Before leaving for home again he arranged with a family of Russian emigrés named Shishkin to establish themselves on the Sable Plateau and make preparations for our coming. When Krebs reached home he had much to tell us of the Sable Plateau and the country which had already strongly gripped our interest and stirred our imagination, about gold and asbestos discoveries and other things awaiting men who would come and take possession of it. For the land was ownerless, and tradition tells how it came to be without a lord.

One of the earliest agreements between Russia and China concerning the boundary in Asia places this along the mountain chain of Tannu Ola. This is the southernmost of the mountain chains which, as eastern offshoots of the Altai, divide and enclose Urianhai, and small pyramids of stone were erected on the summits as a sign that hither extended the kingdom of the Son of Heaven.

In the time of Catherine the Second it was desired to determine the extent of the Imperial dominions, and a Commission was despatched to ascertain the boundary. The members of the Commission travelled along the old road that was used for the exiles and then turned southward through the almost impenetrable *taigan*.[1] After many days difficult travel they saw from a pass a row of white pinnacles which disappeared to East and West behind the green tops of the larch forest. This was the Sayan range, the more northerly of the two chains that enclose Urianhai.

The Commission had never supposed that Siberia

[1] The great belt of primeval forest which extends through Southern Siberia.

ORIGIN OF THE KREBS EXPEDITION

extended so far south, and still less was it imagined that it could reach even farther. There were no boundary marks there, so as they felt these ought to exist, they built a row of stone pyramids upon the long chain of the Sayan Mountains.

Thus the Imperial Crown lost the precious jewel of Urianhai.

Krebs brought home with him a Russian General-Staff map embracing Northern Mongolia and Urianhai, and this we now studied zealously. We found on it two places with the indication " Russki dom " within the territory of Urianhai. The name simply means " Russian house " and was a relic from the time at the end of last century, when occasional Russian wayfarers traversed the country, noted the native names of mountains and rivers and recorded, as especially noteworthy, the existence of two Russian houses. These belonged to enterprising traders from the lower reaches of the Yenisei, who had built there for the purpose of buying sables and other furs from native trappers.

By and by immigrant Russian peasants came and settled just within the natural gate to Urianhai, namely where the Yenisei finds its way out of the country through the Sayan Mountains. Where the first log-houses had been built there were now whole villages, but the settlement did not extend beyond the district along the Yenisei. All the rest of the country lay undisturbed by the activities of white men, as it had done for no one knows how many hundred years. Only the nomads moved about it with their vast herds of horses, cattle and sheep, just as they had done in the days of Israel.

Until the time of the Russo-Japanese war, the Russians regarded Urianhai as an outlying territory which, if it were of any value, would in time be united to the slowly growing colossus. The Russian mining department at Irkutsk supported the enterprising gold prospectors to the extent of registering their claims, and extorted in return a duty on the gold panned out.

On the other hand they regarded the nomadic Mongol Princes living to the southward as their subjects in

ORIGIN OF THE KREBS EXPEDITION

respect of the sables which they were obliged to pay as tribute, until finally the Emperor of China asserted that, in consideration of a single black sable which was paid to him, the country properly appertained to him.

After the Russo-Japanese war Russia's prestige in Asia fell immensely, but with the Mongolian-Chinese conflict of 1912 the position was once more equalized, and Urianhai was now more than ever a lordless land.

There, far off in distant Asia, it lay and called to us —that land dreaming care-free within its encircling alps.

MEANWHILE Ove Krebs had left Peking and returned home.

But, as time went on and the plans for our Mongolian expedition took firmer shape, he was seized anew by the lust for travel. He took part in all the meetings at which we discussed and worked out details, and one fine day he informed his brother Carl that he had changed his mind and that, if the expedition took place, he wished to join it.

More and more people became interested and were initiated into our plans, and men of experience and insight, who sympathized with the idea, attended the discussions to give us good advice.

Mr. Riefestahl, who had lived thirty years in Transbaikalia and had worked gold mines in Urianhai, showed us specimens of the precious metal which he had succeeded in bringing with him to Denmark when the Bolsheviks drove him out of his property. He poured gold out of a leather bag on to the table in front of us and showed us on the map where it was to be found in the mountains out there. He would have liked to go with us, but he was too old and too ill, and we had to content ourselves with the abundant information he imparted to us.

It was decided that six men should take part in the first expedition with the object of investigating the possibilities for an eventual colonization on a larger scale.

The project later became public through a lecture which Carl Krebs delivered to the Royal Danish Geo-

Dr. C. E. Krebs, Leader of the Expedition

ORIGIN OF THE KREBS EXPEDITION

graphical Society, which aroused great attention in the press and interest in various circles.

Before the revolution there were in Siberia several thousand Danish dairy farmers and agriculturists. They had been organized, and until 1918 they led in butter production in Siberia. But the Bolsheviks had confiscated their farms, with the result that the colonists were workless and in most cases ruined. Instead of helping all these Danes, most of whom had been living out there for many years, to return home, the idea was mooted of transferring them to Mongolia, south of the district in which they had previously worked, where there seemed to be a chance of establishing a new dairy-farming country.

The conditions out there were really hopeless during the years 1920 and 1921. It was at this time that the crazy Baron von Ungern-Sternberg and his White Guards were fighting the Bolsheviks, and the struggle spread over the whole of Mongolia where both " Reds " and " Whites " ravaged the country of the Nomads.

But we believed in the future, and two excellent men out there, who were interested in the expedition and had supported it from the beginning, promised to keep us informed of events and to let us know when times became better. One of them was the head of the Great Northern Telegraph Company at Tientsin, Mr. S. Black, and the other the superintendent of Chinese Telegraphs, Mr. K. P. Albertsen, who in his capacity of inspector of telegraph lines across Mongolia from Kalgan to Kiachta was able to keep us constantly informed of the political developments in that country.

The large numbers of applications from persons wishing to take part in the intended colonization venture showed the interest which the scheme aroused in Denmark. Nearly four hundred applications came in from people in the most diverse positions. Officers, students and teachers were in the majority, but there were also many farmers, engineers, missionaries and sick-nurses among the applicants.

Krebs realized, however, that a primary condition of the expedition being able to survive the initial difficulties

ORIGIN OF THE KREBS EXPEDITION

and the pioneer life in the wilderness was harmony, and he chose the six who were to make the first attempt from among persons whom he knew well.

Borgström, the Krebs brothers and I had known one another from the Military School and life in the army. The Polytechnic teacher Tage Birck was chosen because the Krebs brothers knew him from many years work together in the Academic Protection Society. And they had taken part together as gymnasts in the Olympic Games at Stockholm. The sixth member, Erik Isager, was a doctor's son from Jylland, and none of us knew him personally, but he was selected on the ground of brilliant recommendations as a capable agriculturist, and perhaps, too, because Carl Krebs thought it advisable to have with us a phlegmatic Jyllander who might somewhat moderate our youthful enthusiasm.

An agreement was drawn up in writing, and the duties in the future expedition were allotted among us.

AGREEMENT

1. We the undersigned set out in fellowship under the leadership of Dr. C. I. Krebs, on an expedition to Northern Mongolia. The object of the expedition is to found a farm for corn, horse and cattle raising. The farm is intended to be situated on the tributary of the Selenga, Egin Gol (Iga). The farm is also to serve as a base for trading (Furs) and investigation of the district's mineral resources. (Obtaining of concessions.)

2. The members of the Expedition shall each subscribe five thousand crowns to the funds of the Expedition.

3. Dr. Krebs, as leader of the Expedition, is in charge of all financial and administrative matters.

4. Another member of the Expedition shall be its Book-keeper and a third its Treasurer.

5. Each member of the Expedition has for his part a claim to one part of the Expedition's assets and profits (1 " share ") and on payment of the 5,000 Kr. to another part. Dr. Krebs has however for his leadership a claim to two parts (thus, on payment, to three shares).

6. If a member wishes to leave the Expedition a valuation shall be made of the Expedition's property

ORIGIN OF THE KREBS EXPEDITION

at such time (two members to be valuers, one chosen by the Expedition and the other by the retiring member. Referee, Dr. Krebs). The share thus appertaining to the retiring member shall be paid off in yearly instalments in the course of five years, but without interest or profits.

7. Mineral discoveries made by a member belong to the finder as to 25 per cent and to the Expedition as to 75 per cent.

8. No member may without the consent of the Expedition start new activities apart from the Expedition in Mongolia or Urianhai for three years after his retirement from the Expedition.

OVE KREBS, who was an ex-engineers officer, was to be the one to investigate the possibilities of mining in the new country. He threw up his appointment and went to America, where he began to work as a miner in newly opened mines and mines in course of construction. People at home said he was mad.

Erik Isager was to specialize in dairy farming and took a job as bailiff on an estate in North Jylland. Birck went to Jylland to gain experience in agriculture, and I to England to work at cattle, sheep and horse breeding. Borgström was to train himself in commerce and to take care of our headquarters in Copenhagen.

Meanwhile we were to compile lists, each in his own department, of what ought to be taken with us. When in course of time these lists were completed, they were scrutinized by experts who altered them and made additions, so that in the end they embraced everything that could be thought of use for a period of five years. Among other things the lists included all necessary machinery for the conduct of a modern farm and all spare parts that might be required.

TIME went on and the years passed. Krebs was working with the Danish ambulance service in Poland and afterwards with the Red Cross Relief Expedition to Russia. This was during the famine of 1922, and in that year he made great efforts to secure the Soviet Government's permission for the expedition to travel across Russia and Siberia, but without success.

Thus there was only one course for us, to make the long sea voyage to China and thence to proceed by rail to Kalgan on the borders of Mongolia. From that town we must afterwards journey by caravan throughout the whole expanse of Mongolia before we should reach our distant goal on Sable Plateau. The length of the journey was no deterrent to ourselves, but the cost of transporting all our heavy machinery and other baggage would be very considerable and greater than our small subscribed capital would bear, after we had paid for all the material.

But Krebs succeeded in enlisting the support of the Geographical Society, the Carlsberg Fund and the East Asiatic Company; and one day in the beginning of March, 1923, I received in England a telegram which quite laconically informed me that the expedition was to start from Copenhagen on Sunday, March 18th, at 7.20 p.m.

I landed in Copenhagen a week before the departure and found Carl Krebs, Borgström and Birck in full swing with the preparations. Isager, whose contract in Jylland would not expire until the late autumn, and Ove Krebs, who was still working as a miner in America, were to join us later in Peking.

All our goods went off on March 12th on M.S. *Malaya*, and we ourselves were to join the same boat at Hamburg on the 20th. This gave us a few days rest in Copenhagen.

We took leave of all those who had prophesied that we should never get started. And we took leave of those who believed in our enterprise and trusted us and wished everything to go well with us. Those were unforgettable days.

Then came the last day of farewell, farewell to all and sundry who hitherto had meant much to us in life. But this day was by no means the end—it was the beginning of the story of our real life.

It was a sunny, early Spring Sunday and all the Royal City had put on its finest holiday clothes. We went

ORIGIN OF THE KREBS EXPEDITION

together, I and one that I was very fond of, to take leave of the many places rich in memories of childhood. We went to the old school by the lake over whose portal stood the grave words "Ora et labora". And we recalled the school song:

> ". . . Out where new duties call,
> Great after small,
> Leaving the little fane.
> Be it not asked in vain
> How each with hand and brain
> Will serve his land."

WE went out to Langelinie, past tarry-smelling frigates and into the old Citadel. We often had to stop to assure ourselves that the other recollected some happy memory attached to a particular spot.

At last we went into the old Citadel Church, our church, and we remembered the many Christmas Eves when we had sat there side by side. One of the earliest memories was the impression that the many gilded stars on the blue vaulted roof had made upon us. Surreptitiously we had tried to count them during divine service, but had never succeeded in getting our figures to tally. When later we came to hear that the stars of heaven are innumerable we were not at all surprised. When we grew bigger it was the faded old regimental colours that spoke their language to us. They hung in two long rows in the half darkness along the church walls, threadbare, but ever urging us to achievement.

We promised one another that in five years we would once more visit these places together, come here once again. Not until the last moment did we drive to the train. My three travelling companions were already there, surrounded by leave-taking friends and relatives.

The conductor was beginning to shut the doors and we had to tear ourselves away. Then the engine whistled and from the platform sounded three long and three short cheers—the farewell greeting of our friends.

The train began to move, brave smiles tried to hide the pain of parting—and we rushed out into the night, the first light night of spring.

CHAPTER II

THE JOURNEY OUT

WE travelled third class and reached Korsör without mishap. Buffalo was in excellent form, enlivened by the people's enthusiasm at our departure. He entranced his fellow-passengers by a flow of witticisms and funny stories.

Next day we arrived at Kiel and proceeded thence by train to Hamburg. At the station there we bought Danish papers and read accounts of our departure from Copenhagen.

We had our train and boat tickets to Shanghai in our pocket-books and we traversed that route without any other experiences and impressions than those that countless other travellers with tickets in their pockets have been through before us and have recorded in print. But our voyage had the advantage that it was performed in no fashionable tourist steamer, but on one of the East Asiatic Company's cargo boats. We saw nothing perhaps that we ought to have seen on that cruise, but anyhow we saw much that interested us.

At Hamburg we went aboard a little motor-boat which steered out into Rosshafen and brought us to our ship, the *Malaya*. This was a stately four-master with numerous winches, but we observed that it was without funnels. The yellow masts and white superstructure shone in the rays of the afternoon sun and formed a proud contrast with the melancholy surroundings. For times were bad then in Hamburg. Unemployment prevailed everywhere; everywhere one saw ships laid up and the innumerable lading cranes on the wharves stretched out their empty arms to heaven as if praying silently for work.

Then we slipped down the Elbe, glad to leave these

sad impressions far behind us. Calmly and surely the ship ploughed her way through the Channel, passed Cape Finisterre which once upon a time was " the world's end ", rolled in the Bay of Biscay and turned, one starry night, in through the Straits of Gibraltar. Since it was, alas ! dark, all we saw of Gibraltar was the multitude of lights that, climbing straight up into the sky, indicated the shape of the famous rock. But next morning, when we went on deck, we saw the blue waters of the Mediterranean transmuted to white foam before the bows of our steamer.

We were steering into warmer zones. The other passengers on board, a half-dozen of spare and sinewy planters, sat comfortably prostrate in their chairs under the awning, sipping drinks. They were on their way back to their plantations in sun-baked latitudes—capable fellows, but marked by the tropics, which had taken toll of their youthful powers, and by life in the East, which had brought their optimism to an end.

They observed with astonishment the energy we displayed. Krebs had in fact—once we had happily passed through the unruly Bay of Biscay—laid down a programme for the bracing of our physical and moral forces. With the help of the ship's carpenter we had arranged a boxing ring on the upper deck, and here we went for one another every morning. First there was half an hour of physical jerks and then a couple of hard bouts were fought out. Then we went below and washed off the blood, took a bath and were ready for breakfast. From ten to twelve Krebs coached us in Russian, and if we did not know our lessons we had reason to dread our next meeting with him in the ring. Krebs, I should say, was vastly superior to the rest of us as a boxer.

" We'll be in Port Said in the morning," said the mate. Port Said ! Port Said !—that is indeed the port of entry to the East. The name made our hearts throb with expectation.

It was seven bells when we anchored, and we rushed ashore to get a first taste of the glories of the East. The sun was glowing over our heads as we forced our way through the mass of shrieking, gesticulating dragomans, who offered for a mere trifle to show us everything, sell us everything and take us to the most marvellous places. We would have liked to see a Zanzibari dance, but we left Port Said without having experienced that hectic display from "The Light that Failed".

Shining and motionless lay the waters of the Red Sea, and it was so hot that one gasped for breath. The Captain confided in us that here on the Red Sea one

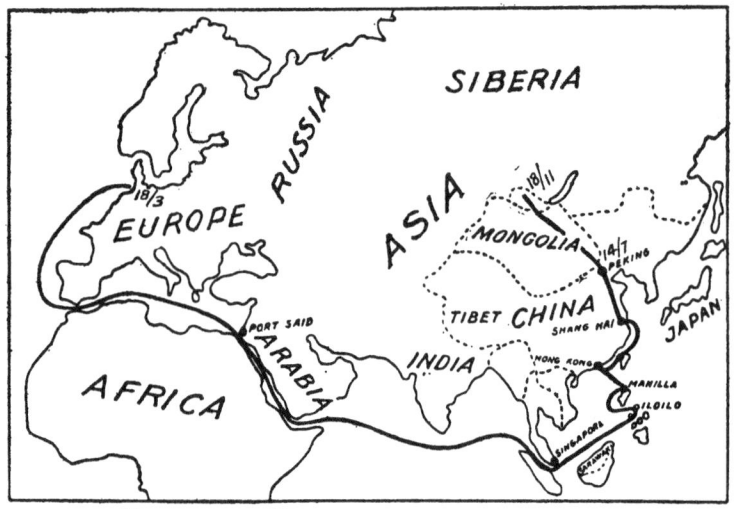

ROUTE OF THE EXPEDITION FROM START TO FINISH.

could experience the highest conceivable form of enjoyment. The recipe sounded odd, but anyhow we tried it. Just before the glowing orb of the sun rose over the Arabian horizon we stood in the forepart of the ship and drank ice-cold "Carlsberg", letting it trickle slowly down our throats—and it was good indeed.

Slender streaks passed over the water. Swift beasts were hovering low over the surface and plunging in again with a rushing sound. They were birds and fish at the same time—the first flying fish we encountered on our voyage.

Now we steered out into the Indian Ocean with a

THE JOURNEY OUT

new pattern in the stars above us. Every night the Pole-star sank nearer to the horizon and the Southern Cross rose up instead like a jewel set with five resplendent diamonds.

The sea was covered with innumerable points of phosphorescence that gleamed like cascades of fire in the wash round the ship's sides. And at night the dolphins took on the aspect of strange fabulous beasts. Always in threes, side by side, they danced forward through the sea sporting with the phosphorescent waves that gilded their gleaming sides from their pointed muzzles to their elegant swinging tail propellers.

For twenty days we ploughed the waters of the Arabian and Indian Oceans and thus reached Singapore. Kreb's youngest sister was a doctor in government service in Java, and had undertaken the long journey thence so as to greet her brother before he plunged into the remote wilderness.

We found ourselves almost on the Equator and in the streets of Singapore experienced the sensation of walking under the scorching midday sun without casting a shadow in any direction.

We danced through the tropic night at Raffles' hotel to the most glorious music of a full-blooded native orchestra from Hawaii. But the westerners around us, haggard with life in the tropics, did not look as if they enjoyed life, and we were glad when the *Malaya* once more headed northward, away from the Equator to zones more suited to a northerner.

Slowly we glided past the inviting coast of Sarawak, while we listened to the strange tales of an elderly plantation owner about the family that has ruled for many generations over that kingdom.

We came out through a narrow channel into the Sulu Sea. It was intensely blue, and on the horizon floated low islands with green plumes of swaying palms. Lovely places, but lazy and happy-go-lucky. On our passage through the Sulu Sea we came to Ilo-Ilo, a wonderful little idyll by the sea. Ilo-Ilo is the capital of the small island of Panay, and lies off the usual route of big ships, which must account for its being so enchantingly unspoiled. Once the place flourished under the dominion of the Spaniards, but now it lies more or less neglected by the dominant Yankees.

The quarantine doctor who examined us before we were allowed to land was a fat half-caste who spoke with a hundred per cent American accent. He was genial and friendly and was enraptured to discover that Krebs was a colleague. We were positively compelled to go with him to the American Club, which proved to be a handsome building in an unkempt park. In the club we met more pretty girls than we had seen for many a long day. They represented every conceivable blend of Spanish and Polynesian blood, and they were all beauties. They were in the highest degree Yankee in dress, but when Birck, who among ourselves went by the name of " Tot ", wanted to invite one of them to dance, he was snubbed with the haughtiest señorita gesture. At last we succeeded in luring Tot away from the American Club, and went into the primeval forest where we amused ourselves with knocking down coconuts from the tall palm trees.

We sailed by way of Manila out into the China Sea with Hong Kong as our immediate goal. We stayed only a few hours in this distant Crown Colony of England, one of the most imposing places I had yet seen, but I managed in the course of those hours to treat myself to a small experience on the quiet.

Chance brought me to the magnificent English Club at a time of day when it was almost deserted. While I was sitting in the library, turning over some English magazines, my glance fell upon a pile of old yellowed newspapers that lay high upon a shelf. That which is old and yellowed often provides something of interest, so I seized the old papers which turned out to contain the " latest news " of long-departed days. I turned them over and came upon a copy of *The Friend of China and Hong-kong Gazette*. The number bore the date July 12th, 1846. The yellowing sheet carried me suddenly seventy-seven years back in time.

There I found a report of an attack by Chinese coolies on the Foreign Settlement. An American, a German and several others had been severely wounded by a crowd of infuriated Chinese, and the situation had been extremely critical. The foreign consuls had sent messages to the various *yamens* (government offices), but the mandarins had turned a deaf ear. " But," continued the newspaper of former days, " the Captain of the Danish frigate *Galathea* immediately sent ashore four officers, twenty sailors and fifty marines, and order was rapidly restored." And the paper concluded its account with the statement that, but for this succour, all the foreigners would probably have lost their lives.

The great windows of the library looked out over the harbour where numerous men-of-war were lying with proudly floating American, English, French and Portuguese flags. Grey and menacing they lay heavily upon the oily waves. My thoughts flew back with pride seventy-seven years, and another vision appeared.

The blue water heaves between the " Flowerscented Bay " and the " Nine Dragons ". A frigate with spread sails rocks upon the waves like a proud swan settling after long flight. Seventy-four seamen, bearded and weather-bitten, come ashore just here. They are wearing the seamen's dress of olden times, and the sun of China is reflected in their broad-brimmed shiny leather hats with long fluttering ribbons. At their sides they wear brass-hilted cutlasses, and in their tanned fists gleam their boarding pikes. A bugle call, which I recognize, sounds from the ship : " *Sticker du mig, sa sticker jag dig*," and with Danish oaths and Danish songs the seventy-four of them go to the assault against thousands of raging Chinese—seventy-seven years ago.

THE same evening we weighed anchor and dipped our flag as we passed the assembled representatives of the great powers. Just as we rounded the Kowloon promontory, a Japanese destroyer in a hurry came up, leaving a long black train of smoke behind her. She was so pressed for time that she forgot to salute—and so did we.

The last days on the *Malaya* we were sailing among Chinese junks. The heat decreased and we felt all the better. On one of the last mornings before we reached Shanghai, Krebs had his nose broken by a blow during a furious boxing bout with one of us. It crashed audibly and the blood streamed, but he sat calmly up on deck, sent Tot for a toothbrush and a mirror, and in cold blood performed an operation on himself. He pushed the handle of the toothbrush far into his nose and straightened up the broken nose-bone, so that the nose came straight again. Of course this took time, the blood spouted, the bone grated, and all the time Krebs was scolding the man who held the mirror because his hand shook.

So at last we landed on the vast continent of Asia with all our crates and multitudinous baggage. From Shanghai to Tientsin the train ran through a chessboard of rice fields and through a country full of turbulent people. We had to wait a whole fortnight in Tientsin to get our Chinese passports, *huchat*, arms licences and other documents furnished with quantities of stamps and Chinese signatures. We lived meanwhile with a couple of extraordinarily friendly compatriots, Sophus Black, the Telegraph Inspector, and his wife. Black was a great help to us at the many tedious visits to the various Chinese *yamens*, and he understood how to handle the tardy officials with a mixture of smiling *chinoiserie* and steely determination. Without his valuable help our fourteen days' delay would certainly have extended to as many weeks. And his amiable wife, who soon became " Aunt Minna " to us all, took care of us in every way and helped to make the time pass.

We really lived a dissipated life in those two weeks, and on most days went from one entertainment to another and to bed late, if at all. Buffalo met a Swedish uncle, who reminded him of several other relatives both living and dead, and the two became inseparable. When at length all our documents were duly signed and stamped, we bade farewell to Tientsin, the gay life there and its friendly Scandinavians.

We were only to stay a few days in Peking to pay a number of formal visits to the authorities. We were quartered at " The Danish Mess ", and G. Mogensen,

THE JOURNEY OUT

who was mess president at this time, had arranged an alluring programme for us, consisting of sightseeing by day and farewell banquets in the evenings. Tot and I lived in the same compound with the friendly chief of " The Great Northern ", Mr. Mynter. The last evening in Peking was especially festive ; we gorged upon oysters imported direct from Japan, and it was late when we returned to our respective quarters—I with frightful pains in the stomach.

AFTER a delicious slumber, consciousness slowly returned. I opened my eyes to get my bearings. It was half dark in the room, but outside it was broad daylight, for a few slender sunbeams filtered in through the drawn curtains, crept across the floor, cut off a pair of slippered feet and soon after turned at a sharp angle vertically upward. I let my glance wander back to the ray's point of ingress between the curtains whose folds appeared wherever I turned in the darkness. What I perceived was divided into small perplexing squares, for which I could not account. I slowly stretched out my hand and discovered that the squares were due to a mosquito net which enclosed me like a cage. Again my gaze wandered round, seeking for the cut-off slippers. They were of velvet, with turned up toes and edged with black leather. And I saw that there rose from them a pair of legs in long oriental leggings. The mystical motionless legs ended at the knee and vanished in the darkness.

I felt vigorous, and as if I had slept my fill as one does on a Sunday morning, and rose quickly to a sitting position, so as more closely to observe the slippered feet. There was a shout of " Ay, Ay ", from the neighbourhood of the legs, and they disappeared through a door which was opened and, in the daylight that flowed in, I caught a glimpse of a fluttering white figure which vanished soundlessly. After a short while voices were heard approaching, and the slippered " Ay, Ay ", who turned out to be a grinning Chinese boy, came hurrying in, emitting a series of ay, ay's, mingled with a stream of incomprehensible sounds.

THE JOURNEY OUT

He tore apart the curtains and exhibited me to the visitors with as proud an air as though he had raised me from the dead. The newcomers were Mr. Mynter and Dr. Wulf, and, as they stood smiling at me, I suddenly understood and remembered everything. They told me that my dysentery had been overcome by strong medicine, and that this had thrown me into a coma from which I had just waked and which had lasted three days and nights. I was starved, but, to my great annoyance, instead of an enormous steak and onions, I got only wretched invalid's food which I washed down with weak tea. After I had eaten and drunk all there was on the tray, I felt as good as new and began asking after Birck and the other members of the expedition. To my consternation I was informed that the others had travelled to Kalgan while I slept, and that the expedition was to leave that frontier town in two days. This was fatal, for if I was not in Kalgan before the caravan started, I should not be able to make my entry into the world of steppes and deserts by my comrades' side. And who knew when and where I should see the expedition again.

My kindly host soon saw the uselessness of his protests, and the next morning my amiable compatriot went with me to the Hsi-chih-men station. When I got out of the car, I was very weak and had to make an effort not to betray it. Mr. Mynter gave me a large basket of invalid food and two big bottles containing a pale red fluid. After he had straitly warned me not to drink anything else but the pale red liquid, I took a cordial farewell of my friends and mounted the high step of my coach. This effort was, however, too much for my feeble powers, and the two bottles fell with a crash on to the platform while I myself landed on my nose among the invalid food. My two compatriots looked as though they would drag me down from the train at once, a fate which I tried to avert by an idiotic grin. But then, fortunately, the engine whistled and the train started, away from the turmoil of Peking and out towards the fascinating unknown. The last Peking saw of me was a strained, grinning countenance and a waving of the arms intended to symbolize a wholly non-existent " Kruschen feeling ", but I hope both had a soothing effect upon my friends' good conscience. Then, dripping with sweat, I sank down on a comfortable leather-covered seat, under a whirring punkah, and ordered a Beck's beer, a big bottle.

The train puffed and groaned its winding way over the Nankow pass and through the Great Wall, and after nine hours' travel I arrived, dusty, burning hot and miserable, at Kalgan, where I was met by Krebs and a Mr. Poulsen in whose house the expedition was quartered. Mr. Poulsen thought I looked a bit feeble, to which I replied that I felt glorious. And by the time we started, three days later, the high pure air, Mrs. Poulsen's careful nursing, the place's gay, careless troup of international pioneers and the adventure upon which we were setting out had made me throw off all thought of illness and really feel like a prize baby.

On Krebs's arm I passed through the noisy crowd on the platform to the waiting rickshaws, which slowly and with much shrieking and ringing from the coolies drawing them, threaded their way through the swarming Chinese town. There was so much that was new and thrilling that I had to keep on twisting my neck and my whole body so as not to miss too much.

It was noticeable that we were now in Hsi-pei, the North-West, close to the open steppes which set their mark on the place and its inhabitants. The men were freer and more upright in carriage and demeanour than the people down among the rice-fields, and their grinning faces were rather sunburned than gauntly yellow.

There was life and activity in the narrow streets and lanes through which we made our way. Heavily laden, lean donkeys pattered through the crowd to cries and blows, but they made way respectfully for the majestically striding camels that had come down from the pass in the north with all the riches of Central Asia loaded about their Bactrian humps. Silent and imposing they strode through the swarming multitude. On their swaying, oscillating necks they carried their proud, unfathomable heads on a level with the surrounding warehouse roofs, high over the clamorous insects. Grim, weatherbeaten drivers in gorgeous-coloured robes sat in their raised saddles, gazing unconcernedly out over the crowd. Their expression was as unfathomable as that of the camels, as if the whole wisdom of the world was contained behind their impenetrable eyes. From the remotest corners of Tartary they had come through the vast wilderness to ride that day, after months of incessant journeying through heat and cold, through storms and marvellous stillness, down from the pass, down among the toiling masses of China. Without once turning their heads, without showing a glimmer of interest, they filed with lofty calm through the narrow streets, their glance fixed on the curling smoke from their jade pipes.

Thus impressive was my first meeting with transient Mongols, and I felt a strong desire to learn to know them and to become their friend. I was happy in the thought that it was among such people that I was going to live, and that I should soon be following their footprints in the sand towards the far alluring goal.

We were soon out of the Chinese town and crossing the open fields dividing it from the cluster of bungalows which was inhabited by the western pioneers in these tracts. A mighty petrol tank in the Standard Oil Company's compound indicated one of the outposts of the all-pervading mechanical civilization. We drove in through a gate in the grey mud-wall enclosing another compound next to the Standard Oil Company's. A large painted sign over the gate made known that it belonged to " F. A. Larson & Co. Inc."

The head of this firm's Mongolian branch was the Swede Larson, and its representative here was our host and compatriot, Nils Poulsen. We were thus in good Scandinavian surroundings, and spent a couple of glorious days with Mr. and Mrs. Poulsen before taking leave of the last vestige of western civilization—days which we enjoyed and long remembered.

Nils Poulsen was born in China of Danish parents. The forty-five years he had lived had never taken him out of China, the land he loved. He was a typical

THE JOURNEY OUT

"China coaster"—westerners born and bred in China and who have thriven there—and he was a well-known person in the country north of the Yangtse river. He had been regarded for many years as the best gentleman-rider in North China, and he possessed a whole fortune in silver trophies that he had won on the racecourses of the East. In spite of his Danish nationality, his Danish vocabulary was limited to some fifty words. He used Chinese and English, of which languages he had a complete mastery. His Chinese was far better than that of most Chinese, and he was conspicuous in speaking "Mandarin" and observing the ancient rules of etiquette with an elegance which made an impression on the Generals and other persons of rank of modern China. Besides discussing philosophy with old and learned Chinese, he was fond of mixing with simple people, whom he understood and knew in a manner that led them to admit him among themselves and to give him their confidence.

He had undertaken long and apparently aimless journeys in the interior of the vast empire, which, however, had resulted in his possessing a knowledge of China and everything Chinese such as few western men of science could boast of. It was seldom that Poulsen showed himself in the clubs of the coast towns, but his name was all the more often mentioned there. It was said that he could disguise himself as a Chinese and mix with the Chinese for long periods without betraying his western origin. Once in his green youth he had done great service to the great politician Li Hung Chang by carrying out confidential missions in Chinese disguise; and that he has now and then been of use to modern China is evident from notices in the papers stating briefly that Nils Poulsen had received "The Order of the Golden Harvest" or something of that kind.

But during our short stay in his house Poulsen only wanted himself to ask questions and to hear us talk about Denmark, the distant fatherland that he had never seen. Like most Scandinavians who have lived long in foreign countries, he was rather Scandinavian than Danish, and his more concentrated patriotism was applied to Fyen, the island that had been his father's native place. During the tennis matches which were arranged during our stay in Kalgan in which Larson, Poulsen and the members of the Expedition played against the rest of the white colony, Larson's and Poulsen's well-disciplined war cry was often heard : " Heja Scandihuvia."

Poulsen's eight-year-old Peter had magnificent red hair which framed his pugnacious physiognomy like flaming fire. These locks caused many worries in the Poulsen home, for the sleek, black-haired Chinese youth of the district could never get used to this proud head decoration, with the result that there were many complaints from irate Chinese parents whose untutored scions had had to pay dearly for their inclination to point at or find nicknames for the nordic boy. But it also happened that Peter came home with bleeding scratches and a nose as red as his brilliant hair. That was when the Chinese youth combined in a daring onslaught, and upon such episodes Papa Poulsen founded his theory that disunited China could, in the hour of danger really hold together, and that was all the consolation Peter got.

In the evenings we sat till late in the Poulsen's hospitable house ; and we never could get to bed until we had gone through our whole repertory of Danish songs. Buffalo played the piano and we others sang with all the force of our lungs and hearts to the two weather-beaten Scandinavians. We had soon found out their taste and varied the programme to please them both, Poulsen with lyrically pitched tunes of Hartman, Lange-Müller and Bellman, and Larson with boisterous revue numbers. We enjoyed ourselves royally.

The three great western firms that have their outposts at Kalgan bear the well-known names of " Standard Oil ", " British American Tobacco Co." and " Ligget & Mayer Tobacco Co." Their representatives were splendid fellows, bachelors for the most part, who accepted us as dear and welcome guests in their little world. At the magnificent western dinners that they arranged in our honour, all the members of the foreign colony were

In the villages through which we passed, the Chinese Cultivators brought their tribute in the form of steaming green tea

Our Chinese caravan boys

The Falconer

A piece of the Great Wall of China

THE JOURNEY OUT

assembled, with the exception of the missionaries whom we never saw, and I reckoned out that among the thirty-two participants not less than twelve nations were represented. They all had personal experiences of adventure to tell, and I observed among these pioneers a solidarity and a resemblance in mentality which united them with so strong a bond that they might have served as a pattern for a League of Nations.

In the daytime we were much occupied with preparations for the expedition's departure for Urga. In order to reach our distant goal as quickly as possible, we had at first thought of covering the stretch to Urga in motor cars, but we were soon obliged to abandon this plan. Of the eighty or so cars which maintained communications between Kalgan and the remote steppe town there were only a few suitable for such heavy loads as our machines, and most of the cars were so engaged beforehand that to make use of them would have involved a long delay in Kalgan, and we were far too impatient for that.

The man who could provide us with the most suitable wagons for the journey was a little mechanic, five feet high, from Monaco. He liked talking about his native place and tried to surround his meagre little figure with all possible romance. His feeble chest heaved, his accent and gesticulations became more and more French when he described the gambler's paradise, or when, for the sake of variety, he dilated on the enchanting scenery of Mongolia, or the excellence of his motor caravan. In spite of everything his offer was not accepted, for it was too dear for our gradually diminishing funds. Nor did it strike us favourably that he was unwilling to take a personal part in the transport.

It came to our knowledge later that he was one of the people who are forbidden on pain of death to set foot on Mongolian soil—a prohibition that he had twice infringed, and each time he had escaped only a few hours before the death sentence was to be executed. I was told that the man had belonged to a band of brigands which in the bloody days of the " mad baron " Ungern-Sternberg, had been active in Western Mongolia, where they robbed, plundered and murdered " red " and " white " indifferently.

The helpful Poulsen succeeded, however, in getting together a horse-caravan with wagons large enough for our biggest packing cases, and on the thirteenth of July we packed ready for the start.

CHAPTER III

OUTSIDE THE WALL

WE now left China, where a "white" cannot live without half a dozen boys to wait upon him and cannot walk in the street, but must have himself drawn by a sweating coolie. We had done with dancing on roof gardens and with cocktails at clubs. We packed our dinner jackets at the very bottom of our trunks, exchanged the daily, fresh-ironed, spotless linen for shorts and khaki shirts and threw the other rubbish into the wagons.

We turned in late on the last evening and slept extremely little in our tense anticipation of the morrow. Next morning forty-five sinewy steppe horses were harnessed to the fifteen heavily laden wagons of the caravan, and to the cries and whip-crackings of the eighteen Chinese drivers the long file of wagons moved off.

The Kalgan colony's little international troop accompanied us in a body to the boundary of its settlement, where they gave us a hearty cheer and wished us a fortunate journey. A bit along the road I turned and saw the backs of our newly acquired friends as they drove away in their glittering rickshaws. Their white topees shone in the fierce sunshine. The little group of wiry men would again be swallowed up by their stuffy offices whence, day after day and year after year, the clack-clack-clack-ping of their typewriters kept the head offices informed of fresh progress in their far off market. Uninterruptedly their drily business-like reports went off to New York, London, Leipzig and other distant places. And the few women returned to their grey bungalows, where they struggled daily to keep up, out here in exile, the white man's standard of living. In the midst of the colony lay the American consulate. High from its flag-staff floated the Stars and Stripes, gaily and proudly proclaiming that here the white man's law and justice prevailed.

But we on the other hand were pushing out into the wilderness, away from the last protective outpost of the West. Soon we would be out on the steppe where only the unknown laws of the nomads and the hunters were in force. That free, natural life called to all that was primitive in our human instincts—that life stripped of all anti-natural convention. We felt that the test to which we were now to be subjected demanded strength, tenacity and courage, and that we should soon get the answer to a question which we often put to ourselves, the question what we were fit for.

It was the fourteenth of July, 1923. The day was scorching hot, for the rainy season was late. During the last days in Kalgan we had heard a lot of disquieting reports of the exploits of robbers on the other side of the pass, and we were armed to the teeth. But so as not to arouse too much attention in the Chinese town we had concealed our revolvers by winding our scarves round our waists so that the weapon and the cartridge pouches were covered. Krebs rode at the head of the expedition on the only available horse, Buffalo marched, huge and perspiring, in the middle of the procession, and Birck and I formed the rearguard.

The streets in the Chinese quarter were so narrow that we brought all traffic to a standstill. They were even so narrow that the long " chimney-sweeps' parade " of Chinese of all ages that attached itself to us had no room at the sides of the wagons, but was obliged to follow with the rearguard. We marched in a single cloud of dust that settled upon everything and everyone ; the caravan drivers yelled and smote, one could just see their short breeches and muscles glistening with sweat, and for the rest nothing but grey dust. The town's naked children and masterless dogs rolled in the sand and the dust till they acquired the same hue. The wagons bumped out of one deep rut into another ; the horses stumbled, got entangled in the harness and fell. The bells on the animals and the big bells fixed to the wagons jingled or were silent according as the column forced itself forward in short stretches or stopped. A camel caravan came to meet us and, since it was impossible for us to turn the wagons, the camels had each to turn right round where they stood and retire with the last first. The camels grumbled and screamed at this unaccustomed manœuvre, so that one might have supposed that the heavy wagons had driven over them. Through the dense dust cloud that we raised the glowing sun looked like a tired, sallow moon. Then we drove through a black, echoing tunnel, and when we came out again into the light the sun was shining from a blue heaven and we found ourselves in a large open place. When I looked back, it appeared that the tunnel had been a gate or " opening ", as the Mongols call it, in a projecting part of the Great Wall of China.

The leading wagon had stopped for the horses to drink from a purling brook, and during the time it took for all of them in turn to quench their thirst, our enraptured gaze drank in the new surroundings. And they were completely new to us.

A wild river gorge came from the northern side and continued along the wall until both disappeared in the east; first the river behind a weathered, grey-brown rock terrace, then the wall behind a height which it proudly crowned with a heavy watch-tower of massive flame-coloured brick.

Just where we were standing, outside the opening in the wall, the gorge widened out on either side of the narrow channel with its clear mountain stream, and on that spot there was a characteristic market-place where the Chinese merchants from the east met trading nomads and traders from the fair kingdoms of the west, far outside the wall. It was a noteworthy place with venerable traditions.

Along the foot of the encircling hills stood booth after booth, where eternally smiling Dzungars and Chinese exposed their tempting wares under their miniature awnings, brick-tea, clothing, tobacco, gunpowder, lead and much besides, before the critical gaze of the caravan men.

The wise Chinese know the needs of the nomads and are guided by them. Tea is the commodity most in demand, and it is carried in colossal quantities along the caravan routes which stretch out fanwise hence in all directions over Central Asia. It is brick-tea (caravan tea) that the nomads insist on having, for this is the most suitable for long transport, since it retains its aroma. Brick-tea occurs in various forms and packings, the size and weight of which varies with the method of transport. The different kinds are called " 27 ", " 36 ", " 45 " and " 72 " and the figures indicate the number of cakes in the bale which constitutes a half-load for an animal. The " 72 " are small, very hard-pressed cakes which are suitable for transport on ponies in the wild mountains of the Buriats. The " 45 " are intended for long camel transport to the remote Kirghiz steppes beyond Kobdo. The " 27 " and " 36 " are used in their respective districts of Kalka Mongolia.

Most of the brick-tea is produced and pressed in the Hankow district. It is an ancient industry, and it must require peculiar skill to treat it rightly so that it retains its aroma, for the great tea firm of Lipton's have tried in vain to imitate the art of the Hankow Chinese. In the end the Lipton firm bought tea from Hankow and selected a place, Darjiling, on the borders of Tibet, for the manufacture, because the climatic conditions there were considered favourable. But there, too, it failed, and Lipton's have now given up the project and have practically abandoned the vast Central Asian market to the Chinese.

Dunsa (from the Chinese Tung-sheng), the tobacco used on all the steppes and in the long pipes of the desert dwellers, is produced in Shantung and is always packed in the same way—in the form of a truncated pyramid which is very handy for pushing in under the Mongol's wide sashes.

Dalimba (from the Chinese Ta-lien-pu) is a piece of cotton stuff about sixteen inches wide and of a length exactly seven times the width, which is just the amount

Poverty-stricken Mongols

Rest in Chahar, the lost land of the Mongols

needed to make a Mongol's *däle*, a long mantle reaching to about eight inches below the knee. Dalimbas are sold in red and yellow for lamas and in other brilliant, pure colours for laymen and women. Grey and black are never used by the colour-loving dwellers on the steppes.

Tolegon (lead) and *deri* (powder) are sold in bars, and packed in the proportion of one to two which constitutes the appropriate charge for the Mongol's primitive muzzle-loaders.

On the big open place in front of us and along both banks of the river a motley and gorgeous band was encamped. They lay in groups around the countless camp fires from which the odour of exotic foods arose mingled with the smoke. Long rows of ruminating camels filled the sandy gorge on either side, and whole mountains of merchandise towered everywhere, diffusing all the crude and glorious scents of Central Asia. Mighty bales from Sining, Kuku Nor and Uliassutai smelling of wool, leather bales of the Buriats exhaling from afar the strong, concentrated perfume of musk pouches. Scents of furs, hides, animals, the desert and the steppe swept over the place.

High-heeled Kirghiz with eagles' feathers in their pointed fur caps, and gaily dressed Mongols with long silver-mounted knives stuck in their belts swung carelessly in their richly ornamented saddles. Little bow-legged Buriats in handsome home-made deerskin hunting dress ran among the bales, and dignified, long-bearded Muhammedans sat turbaned upon small quadrangular mats sucking at their gurgling water pipes. Wonderful jade from Khotan and rugs from far Kashgar were examined and criticized by the buyers and praised to the skies by the sellers. Growling dogs showed their patriotic feelings against the long-haired guardians of neighbouring caravans. It was a marvellous picture.

Our caravan now moved farther up the valley which wound forward between savage mountain slopes rising at times so sheer into the air as to hide the very sun, at times gave way to show a panorama of brown mountain ridges and pointed summits. A great many red watch-towers, now weathered and in ruins, erected on apparently unapproachable mountain crests, bear witness to the time when there was constant danger in travelling in these parts. It was indeed by this road that Jenghiz and other invincible nomad chiefs brought their war-seasoned armies from the highlands down over the cultivated plains, where they governed and held sway so long that hard living and primitive skill in war were forgotten and they were swallowed up among the millions of Chinese. It is not only the strong wall and watch-towers of the Chinese that recall those vanished times. The passing Mongols never neglect proudly to contemplate a gigantic natural phenomenon by the road, a mighty cave which pierces through a perpendicular mountain precipice. It is bored by the lance which the angry Jenghiz Bogdo Khan cast and with which he crushed the power of the terror-stricken Chinese—so the Mongols say.

Our progress grew slower and slower as the gradient grew steeper, and we searched the jagged mountainous horizon before us to discern the pass through which we were to enter the high plateau of Central Asia.

Early in the afternoon we pitched our first camp in a lovely spot by the river. Not far off we found a smooth-polished mountain precipice out of which fell a crystal-clear cascade, and nature thus provided us with a fresh, ice-cold douche which removed the day's abundant dust and sweat. Then we rolled ourselves in our blankets and slept for the first time on Asiatic ground and under the clear sky of Asia. I fell asleep during an idle attempt to count a myriad of glittering stars.

Next morning we were abruptly woken by gentle kicks and a gruff, " Top of the morning, boys." Krebs was the early bird who then used for the first time what became the expedition's morning greeting. The Chinese had already fed and watered the horses and were now busy harnessing them. An old Chinaman, the leader of the eighteen, stood on a rock at one side and, with his hands to his mouth, twice repeated the cry ; " YABONAH, yabonah ! " and " Yabonah ! " was

Yabonah.

echoed from the hills and from the seventeen other Chinese. Whips cracked, the horses snorted, and the caravan rolled off on a new day's march.

It was the first time I heard that cry, the first of countless times—the summons to start upon a new day's journey.

We had to work hard at once, for the caravan mounted that day from 2,400 to 6,400 feet. We all helped, we pulled and lashed, we yelled and shoved. We were often obliged to take one wagon at a time and sometimes to unload a wagon so as to take the heavy load in several shifts.

Near the top of the pass, at the edge of an abyss, stood a ruined temple, and here we made a halt for all the Chinese to worship before its open front. The old leader went up and threw a handful of copper coins on the topmost step of the temple stairs, after which he came down again to fall on his knees with his companions. An old Chinaman with a crafty face and humorous eyes came out of the obscurity of the temple and with great dexterity gathered the money in his sinewy hand. Then he pulled a cord which produced two strokes on a melodious gong.

With renewed strength and gladdened by the blessing of the smiling priest, we climbed the remaining three hundred feet, which brought us breathless but exultant to the top of the pass. We stood on the threshold of the wide plateau at the entrance of the land of the nomads.

Before us now stretched Mongolia with deserts trembling in the mirages, with endless steppes covered with emerald-green grass and multitudes of wild flowers, with nameless snow peaks, limitless forests, thundering rivers and swift mountain streams. The way that we had travelled with such toil had disappeared behind us among gorges and ravines. We could not have dreamed of a more captivating entrance to a new country, and when the sun sank upon that day, we felt as though born into a new life—a life which had the strength of the hills, the depth of the heavens and the beauty of the sunrise.

OUTSIDE THE WALL

DAY by day the caravan journeyed slowly forward through Mongolia with many pauses and with daylong halts at places where the grazing was good, for our caravan leader knew, as we knew ourselves, that before us lay the Gobi Desert and that Gobi means great scarcity of grass, very little water and death to man or beast who enters it with nothing to fall back on. We were in Inner Mongolia, the part of the realm of the Mongols which stretches along the Great Wall, the far flung rampart of the Chinese against the savage domain of the Tatars.

Inner Mongolia lies in a long curve from east to west, divided into a series of small principalities which are mainly bound together by their common relation to the exalted Tashi Lama or Panchen Bogdo, as the Mongols reverently name this divinity on earth. The princes are nominally autonomous, but actually dependent, owing to China's great military resources. Not many years ago, in 1912, the Mongols of Inner Mongolia tried to shake off this hateful yoke; it was at the time when China exchanged the Empire and its splendour for a turbulent Republic without traditions. The Mongols had acquiesced in the government of the Manchus, for their lamas declared that He, who occupied the dragon throne, was the elect of Tengger (heaven) and, what signified more, the Ch'ieng dynasty and its Manchus were of a riding, nomad race like the Mongols themselves, lords who held a warrior to be a person of rank, valued a fiery steed as a man's noblest possession, spent much time over the training of hunting falcons and knew how to enjoy ease with dignity.

But when the last Emperor was replaced by a President about whom they knew nothing except that he had been elected by the Chinese, and was himself a member of the same race of donkey-riding pedlars, the Mongols rose in indignant protest. They fought bravely for their cause, but a host of Chinese with modern weapons swarmed in over their country, and when they presently retired, they left behind them depopulated steppes and smouldering heaps of ruins where, before, temples had glittered in the sun.

OUTSIDE THE WALL

Northward the people of Inner Mongolia could not penetrate with their tents and their cattle, for between them and the rich grasslands of the fierce Kalka Mongols, barren and menacing, lay the Gobi Desert. And perhaps times would improve in the grazing grounds to which they were attached by the tradition of centuries. Things had not, they knew, always been so good in the Kalka Kingdom, and it was rumoured that the golden days of Outer Mongolia were drawing to a close.

The part of Inner Mongolia which we chiefly traversed belonged to the Chahar Mongols. But although we had spent several days in journeying through their country, we had not yet encountered any of their camps or their great herds of cattle. Daily we witnessed the melancholy spectacle of a nomad population impoverished, oppressed and finally exterminated by the penetration of an agricultural people.

The period when the Great Wall formed a bulwark against the warlike people of the steppes has vanished. Its watch towers are no longer manned by watchful outposts, for the Chinese have now themselves overstepped the wall, and it is they who are the aggressors. Each year the Chinese advance their front some miles farther to the north, and the Mongols are forced farther out into the desert, become impoverished and disappear. As I crossed the country from south to north, I had occasion to see how this war is carried on, slowly, but with certain defeat for the Mongols and victory for the Chinese usurpers from the south.

The Chinese traders who descend upon a Mongolian monastery or a rich Mongol's encampment are the pioneers. They bring with them Chiu, the Chinese spirit. In his wily way the Chinaman understands how to induce the Mongols to get into his debt, and since the Mongol finds that he gets his money without difficulty, all goes merrily for a time.

When the Chinaman considers that the Mongol owes him more than he can pay, he suddenly becomes an exacting Shylock who holds out threats of the merciless Chinese law and the wrath of the mandarins. And the result is that the Chinaman seizes the Mongol's good

The poor Mongolian Shepherd

Hunter on horseback (from an old Mongolian painting)

grazing-grounds, which he soon leases to other immigrants summoned from Shantung. But the Mongol is driven out into the desert where there is not enough grazing for his many cattle. Such of the animals as do not die are bought, especially in dry years, at low prices by the Chinese, and soon the Mongol has not sheep enough to produce the wool for the new layer of felt which must be laid yearly on his tent, and for the winter coats of his family. Nor has he any cattle to provide meat for the winter and milk and cheese for the summer or horses to sell for tea, tobacco and other necessaries. The young daughters of the Mongols are sold to the Chinese immigrants who gladly take them for wives, since they stand the severe climate and the hard labour better than their own women. In the end the old Mongol drifts back to his former grazing-grounds where, to gain a wretched livelihood, he is employed by the new proprietor to watch the sheep and cattle of which, perhaps, he himself was not long since the owner.

A new generation succeeds the Chinese immigrants and their Mongolian wives, and this is the despised *balder*, or half-caste, who often combines the worst characteristics of both races. It is these who form the greater part of the many bands of *t'u-fei* (bandits) who now ravage and plunder the caravans and settlements on the old grazing-grounds of the Mongols.

Fortunately we were moving northward, and with each day the country grew more Mongolian.

CHAPTER IV

THE LAND OF MEMORIES

AFTER seven days of march and rest we came to Sheng-Wat-Sin, which proved to be a piece of Chinese civilization within a brownish grey brick wall. The strong watch-towers and many loopholes indicated that the Chinese administration of the village did not feel too secure against the *t'u-fei* of the region, or else they were a survival of the yellow man's inherited fear of the Mongols.

We caused a great sensation when we filed along the little community's one street, which was flanked by two rows of open booths and was full of Chinese shopkeepers, trading peasants, slippered soldiers and clouds of dust. We saw no Mongols. At the northern gate in the village wall some soldiers tried to stop the caravan, but we looked fierce and drove on unconcernedly along a narrow road which led through fields of peas and rye; and when these came to an end we pitched camp on an open steppe near a grass-grown ruin. On the highest point of the ruin lay a miniature temple.

Soon the sun went down, and we went to examine the ruin and the little temple above it. When we had worked our way up to the top where the sanctuary lay, an aged monk came rushing out like an angry crow. He was dressed in a long grey gown and wore a black skull-cap on his head. His long white chin-beard wagged up and down as he croaked a flood of incomprehensible words. He looked irresistibly comical standing in front of his temple nest, which looked not much bigger than a sentry-box. But as he did not, apparently, welcome us, we left him in peace and returned to the camp.

We had turned the horses loose and they were moving like dark shadows out on the steppe. The caravan men

THE LAND OF MEMORIES

lay gathered round four blazing camp-fires, and the firelight and shadow played across their impenetrable faces. I threw myself on the ground to sleep, but it was not easy with such stars overhead. They were big and brilliantly clear, and seemed nearer than ever before. From time to time gong strokes sounded from the little temple, velvet-soft strokes sent out into the darkness of the steppe. Presumably it was the old monk trying to protect himself and his sanctuary against the foreign devils.

I lay long awake. The fires burned down and the men fell silent. The temple stood out clearly in the light of the half moon. Far out on the steppe was heard a long drawn whistling and solitary cries from the Chinese guarding the horses. The dimensions of the temple changed; it grew larger and larger and the gong beats farther and more faint, till I fell asleep.

Next morning, or, more accurately, the same night, for it was only three hours after midnight, we started out again upon the steppe. When we pitched camp at nine o'clock, we had passed a number of ruined villages but only few and small cultivated fields. We had also seen solitary Mongolian riders, men with weather-bitten, melancholy faces, staring out over the desolate steppe. They belonged to the remnant of the Chahar Mongols, a people who only some few hundred years ago passed through a period of genuine greatness of which they are still conscious but which they hardly understand, a time of greatness which still lives in their traditions and their songs.

This was the time when Lekdan Khan reigned over Chahar, plundering the surrounding countries and bringing the ascendency of the Emperor of China himself into dispute. Lekdan Khan is known by the whole Mongolian world as having improved the written language of the Mongols and had the holy *Ganjur*, written by Gautama Buddha in a hundred and eight large volumes, translated into their tongue. He became so powerful that the Emperor of China feared him, and a protracted war flared up between them, which continued for many years and extended far beyond the territory of Chahar.

THE LAND OF MEMORIES

In the end Lekdan was killed with many of his people, and the wise Emperor understood not only how to crush opposition but also how to bind the survivors to him. All princes and hereditary dignitaries in Chahar were exterminated, and *Dsasak Darog* (the law of the succession of the princes) was abolished.

Since that time Chahar, in contrast with the surrounding Mongol Kingdoms, has had neither princes nor nobles, but has been administered directly under Peking by Mongolian officials appointed for a certain period, partly by the Chinese and partly by the Mongols themselves. Chahar was divided into districts: Adochin, Temechin, Ugherchin and Honichin, names which indicated respectively the herds of horses (*ado*), camels (*teme*), cattle (*ugher*) and sheep (*honi*), which these districts managed and tended on the Emperor's behalf.

Those of the people capable of bearing arms were divided into eight mounted regiments, named after the colours of their standards, and the loyalty of this effective cavalry was fortified by their being made a part of the Emperor's guard, on which he lavished much favour and honour. The Manchu Emperor employed Chahar's eight mounted regiments wherever fighting was toward, and the battle-loving Mongols approved this arrangement, which gave them occasion for protracted expeditions and opportunities for plunder. When the advance of the Russians in Siberia grew threatening, the Chahar Mongols were twice sent off to guard the distant frontier. And there they married women whom they had captured in war, and their descendants founded a new people that still inhabits the pasture lands by the distant Ili River.

In 1928 and 1929 I lived among these people whose forefathers had left Chahar generations ago and whose ancestresses had all been of foreign race. They call themselves Chahars and dress like Chahars. They came to the Ili valley in two contingents, and are thus divided into *shini* (new) and *hochin* (old) Chahars. The administrative and military systems are the same in this border territory as in the original Chahar, mountains and rivers have the same names as there, and they have called the

THE LAND OF MEMORIES

temples which they built in the new land after those that they left behind them in the old.

The soldiers in old Chahar remained the Manchu Emperor's faithful legionaries to the last. When, during the Boxer rising, the international troops pressed forward on Peking, the Chinese fled, but later in the march the foreigners met with serious resistance, and there was stiff fighting before the way lay open to Peking. This firm resistance materially delayed the international force, cost much blood and necessitated waiting for reinforcements. The Asiatics who offered so firm a resistance, and who were afterwards mentioned in the occidental reports, were a nomad General and his cavalry of the Chahar Guards.

With the fall of the Manchu dynasty in 1912 came the close of these riders' time of greatness. They sank into penury, their arms were taken from them and they were cheated of their land. Year by year they are being squeezed some miles farther to the northward, out into the desert.

The name " Kalgan " still stands upon the map, and this corresponds with the old Mongol name Khalaghan (The Gate), but the town now bears the Chinese name Chang-chia-K'ou, which signifies " the mouth or entry to the court of the Lord Chang " ; and Kuku Khoto (The Blue Town) which was the ancient capital and seat of culture of the Tumut Mongols, has become the Kwei-hua-ch'eng (Return to civilization) of the Chinese.

Riding by, taciturn Mongols gaze out over the lonely steppes. Perhaps they are seeking for the ruined towns that bear witness how on earlier occasions the Chinese had tried to penetrate northward, but had always been thrust back by the rightful inhabitants of the steppe.

The twenty-second of July was a Sunday. This we agreed on after a hot discussion, with the result that an egg-nog was added to the day's ration.

I will here briefly describe our victualling and rationing during our desert journey, not in order that it may serve as a model for other expeditions, but rather to show upon how little one can live, though subjecting one's body to considerable strain, and yet keep very fit. I have never before or since taken part in or heard tell of an expedition so spartanly provisioned as was ours during the journey from Kalgan by Urga to Bulgun Tal, and I suspect that the supplies with which, in spite of the advice and misgivings of all experienced people, we started out essentially contributed to the many rumours of our destruction and death that repeatedly arose during the following years in the civilized part of the world.

On the journey to Shanghai Krebs had been able to keep us in discipline and the admonition of the Lord with the help of daily boxing lessons, for we knew what was coming to us during " training " if we did not behave ourselves as worthy members of the expedition. But in China it had been more difficult for him to keep us Spartan, and the expedition had enjoyed to the full the overflowing friendliness that all Scandinavians there had shown us. When we were a little too forgetful of all the regulations drawn up for the preservation of our health and condition, Krebs had threatened us with all that was going to happen to us once we were " outside the wall ", but—well, it is a long way from the Shanghai Club to the Gobi Desert, and we had drunk and danced and sunned ourselves in the glow of popularity.

Buffalo is always and everywhere popular, but in China the thing passed all bounds. He was something new to our fellow-countrymen there, and during the two months of his visit he had completely made up to them for the Chinese city's lack of theatres, music-halls, concerts and other amusements. He had been dragged from place to place, and had always been ready to sing and play and above all to pour out an inexhaustible flow of funny stories. Everything " reminded him " of a story, and though I have known Buffalo for eighteen years, four of them in the wilderness where he had no chance to renew his repertoire, I do not remember ever being with him without his breaking in with his : " Wait a moment, that reminds me . . ." followed by a new story.

All this popularity resulted in Buffalo's quickly regaining all the flesh that he had starved, sweated and trained off him under Krebs's treatment. When the expedition started from Kalgan he was in full bloom and weighed his full twenty stone or, as Krebs put it, round about a fifth of a ton. Buffalo considered that it was mostly due to his well-developed muscles and powerful bony structure. And when Krebs, with an expression of loathing on his face and with a cane in his hand touched a spot where the bone was particularly well covered with something all too soft to be called muscle, Buffalo protested that it was his nobler organs that were so uncommonly well developed

Krebs consoled Buffalo and delighted himself with the prospect of the giant proving too heavy to mount any of the little Mongol ponies, and Buffalo swore that he would walk the whole way to Urga on his own feet or else stay lying where he fell in the sand.

But our propensity for good living had resulted in Krebs providing very small rations for the desert journey, for he did not wish to arrive at Urga in the company of a pack of guzzlers. With the exception of three packets of home-baked rye bread, which Buffalo and I had got from friendly ladies in Tientsin, and these were intended for our birthdays, which we were to celebrate in the desert, no food was allowed that could be a temptation to luxurious living. The rations were worked out by Krebs, and the stores ordered accordingly, for we were pretty sure that what he could live on we too could put up with.

The daily ration per head was as follows :

Two aluminium cups of cooked rice.

Two single handfuls of dry bread ("single" underlined), and on Sundays two double handfuls.

Two level teaspoonfuls of powdered sugar, on Sundays heaped instead of level.

When it appeared later that Buffalo was helping himself with an indecently large teaspoon, Krebs's teaspoon, which was the smallest of the four we had brought, was always used in serving out the rations. Tea and salt we got as required, though in moderation. Milk, cheese and meat could be bought on the way. As a reserve we took a hundredweight of wheaten flour.

The journey was estimated to take forty-five days, but actually took fifty-four.

With the exception of the eggs and ground-nuts we

bought and ate during the days when we were travelling through the cultivated districts outside Kalgan, we got through on that diet to Urga. No one fell sick ; I certainly got a return of my dysentery, but when we reached Urga I, too, was perfectly fit.

From the time we left Kalgan on July 14th until the fifth of August we ate no meat, but during the latter thirty-five days of the march we consumed two sheep, one lamb and one leg of mutton, which cost us respectively six, five, three and one dollar.

We took no tents, but a square tarpaulin was stretched between two wagons during the hours of the midday rest, so that as a rule we got a certain amount of shelter from the burning rays of the sun.

Each of us had his short sheepskin on which he slept. The rest of our bedding consisted of a single blanket and a saddle as pillow. And we slept magnificently.

The marches were very slow by reason of the heavily laden wagons. The distance we covered in the fifty-four days was calculated as seven hundred and fifteen miles, and since ten of the fifty-four days were days of rest for the horses, we did on the average a day's march of sixteen miles.

Of the ten rest-days eight were in the cultivated neighbourhood of Kalgan and only two in the desert itself.

During the time of our journey the temperature fell as the following readings show.

August 13. 6 a.m., 53° F. 2 p.m., 90° F.
,, 20. 6 a.m., 50° F. 2 p.m., 79° F.
September 5. 6 a.m., 37° F. 2 p.m., 50° F.

Free Mongolian soldiers, fully conscious of their descent from Jenghiz Khan's warriors

Irregular soldiers—or honest bandits?

Dambin Janzang, Mongolia's most notorious and dreaded bandit leader. He was executed in 1926

[face p. 45

Mongolian Princess

CHAPTER V

THE ROBBER PRINCESS

"The Red Princess" (Sart Dance Song)

WE were now out upon the real steppes which undulated endlessly around us as far as the eye could reach, right up to the horizon trembling in the heat. We were outside the cultivated and settled territory, but sought in vain for Mongol tents and the herds of horses and cattle which here should have had the best chance of subsistence.

We gathered from our caravan leader that the deserted state of this favoured tract was due to the fact that here the dreaded *t'u-fei* were wont to ravage and plunder passing caravans, and that the Mongols had abandoned the district to preserve their women from the attacks of the bandits.

The Chinese were nervous, and we reassured them by keeping constant armed guard over the caravan. By night we took turns in standing guard for two hours, and by day and on the march two of us were always in the immediate neighbourhood of the caravan.

During the march Krebs made an accurate map of the route with the aid of hypsometer, compass and other instruments, with the idea of the eventual possibility of constructing a railway between Kalgan and Urga. It had appeared that there was much interest taken in China in such a project, and we had been asked to furnish reports on the route so that the plan might take more definite shape.

A plan of battle was drawn up in case of attack whether

on the march or in camp. Our two hundredweight of ammunition was distributed in wagons at various parts of the column so that it was always easy of access, and when we camped the fifteen wagons were always driven in a pre-arranged order so that they formed a compact barricade round the water-hole. And after we had several times rehearsed sham attacks and found that all worked well, we looked out longingly for the *t'u-fei* of the steppes. We often saw in the distance bands of riders who brought the Chinese around us in a gesticulating bunch, but no attack was made.

Sometimes such a troop would ride for hours on a line parallel with that of the caravan, halt when the caravan stopped, and ride on when we resumed our march. Once such a band accompanied us for three whole days, during which we were so well prepared for defence that we agreed in being sorry for the poor fellows if they should attack.

On the morning of the fourth day the supposed bandits were not to be seen, but the day provided a little interlude, welcome in the monotony of our journey. We started out over the dew-drenched steppe at half-past three in the morning. The sun came up and dispelled the night chill, and by eight o'clock it was too hot for man or beast to go on. We pitched camp in an undulating, grassy spot beside a deep stoned well, round the ice-cold waters of which we gathered eagerly. We lay under the little awning between two of the wagons of the stronghold and gulped the cool water out of a bucket. Birck, whose turn it was to be cook, sat out in the burning sunshine and blew till he was red in the face in the attempt to make a smoking heap of camel droppings take fire. We lay in the shade watching him grow redder and redder while we shouted good advice to him. The sweat poured from the rim of his sun helmet and his face was streaked with black and grew filthier still as he wiped off the sweat with his dung-smeared hands. He looked so ludicrous that it was difficult for us to take our siesta with proper dignity. It occurred to me that it would be my turn to be cook next day, and the thought brought sleep to my sun-tormented eyes.

THE ROBBER PRINCESS

Suddenly the caravan dogs gave tongue, and Birck bellowed: " Cavalry, fall in!" We rolled over one another and tumbled out into the heat of the sun with rifles ready. The Chinese disappeared noisily in the direction of the horses. Down a long slope to the eastward a billowing cloud of dust was rolling towards us. Krebs gave the order: " Range 300." The cloud came nearer and thundering hoof-beats approached. " Range 200." One, two, three, four, five riders galloped out of the dust and—we were completely disarmed.

A sunburnt girl with a smile as fresh as a steppe morning reined in her fiery steed before our shamefacedly lowered rifle barrels. Her teeth were pearly white, her eyes as clear as day, her smile disarming, her grip on the reins strong and her movements in the saddle full of grace. She was a daughter of Mongolia, she was herself the free, wild, captivating steppe.

She was dressed in bright-coloured silks, and when she moved there was a ringing of silver and a rattling of precious stones. She shone with the joy of living, and her demeanour bore witness to pride and noble birth. Over her forehead she wore a wide, massive silver band in which were set five large pale red corals. From this diadem half a dozen small chains of coral hung down to the boldly curved and sharply drawn black eyebrows that marked her race. From the sides of the diadem and from her ears hung chains of silver ornaments and strings of corals, pearls and turquoises which fell jingling over her strong shoulders. Her hair was kept in check by a coral-studded black veil, fastened behind by a jewelled silver diadem.

Her long robe was of pale blue silk, and over it she wore a short, sleeveless waistcoat of crimson brocade in which were inwoven dim symbols of fortune and long life. The waistcoat was fastened in front with golden laces attached to buttons of chased silver.

Her cloak reached to her knees where it met her long black velvet riding boots. Her small, neat feet were shod in boots whose elegance was enhanced by the sharply turned up toes. Her hands were strong, but small and shapely. Her fingers were studded with coral ornaments and heavy silver rings, and thick bracelets clashed upon her wrists.

The girl's horse snorted with nervousness and exertion after the hard ride; it cocked its ears and rolled its eyes, but she held it steady with a compelling grip until she threw down the reins and, with a lithe spring, landed in the middle of us. A picture of wild barbaric beauty.

We hastily concealed our unfriendly rifles and invited " Miss Mongolia " to take the shadiest place under the awning, while Krebs shouted to Birck for tea. But Birck had hastened to the well to wash himself and watercomb his hair, and when at long last he presented himself with a clean-scoured aluminium cup full of steaming tea, he was more beautiful to behold than we had seen him since Kalgan. Our guest burned her fingers, as one always does on cups of this practical kind, whereupon she called to one of her suite who brought a leather case out of which he took a flat cup of birchwood, plated on the inside with silver and poured the contents of the aluminium cup into it.

The only one of us who knew any Mongolian was Krebs, and even his knowledge of the language was limited to a northern dialect widely different from that in use in the country to the south of Gobi. In any case he showed his good will by counting up to ten in Buriat, that we others assisted her comprehension by illustrating that number by the same number of fingers in the air. Whether she understood or not we were not really sure, since no one understood a word she said, but she smiled and laughed when she was not drinking tea, and we had great fun.

As the laughter beneath the awning became general and grew more and more hearty, two of her followers also crept into the shade. These were well-dressed young Mongols, one in a Chinese uniform tunic decked with white buttons and a semi-European straw hat, the other in a more dignified blue Mongolian cloak. The other two of her suite were apparently servants, for they stood by the well and guarded the five horses of the company. Our caravan drivers had meanwhile ventured out from

THE ROBBER PRINCESS

the neighbourhood of the wagons and now stood behind our guests, making all sorts of remarkable faces while they pointed to the backs of the Mongols with evident signs of fear and trembling.

We did not understand what this meant, but went on entertaining the Mongols by showing them our rifles, field-glasses and other instruments, and ourselves by a closer inspection of their long silver-mounted knives, tinder-boxes and jade ornamented pipes. Over and over again the company tried to make us understand something that clearly lay close to their hearts. They spoke more and more slowly, pointed across the hills to the eastward, showed us time after time three fingers, saying at the same time the Chinese word for a certain distance. Three *li*, that was about a mile, and so not very far. Then they took a couple of us up to their magnificent horses and pointed to their backs and made us understand by signs that there were masses of splendid food there. It was obvious that they wished to invite us to their camp where they would prepare a banquet in our honour, and this was mighty tempting. But when we spoke of going with them, our caravan men became completely woebegone and protested that we must start at once in order to reach the next water-hole, and advanced a whole lot of other arguments against our visit to the Mongols.

So we took leave of the young Mongol girl and her suite, and, like a roll of drums dying away in the distance, they all disappeared among the hills. Our caravan leader was still upset and anxious, and we made a hurried start. We were hungry and recollected that we had not had our usual meal of rice, and accordingly swore at Birck for the rest of the day because he had performed none of the duties of cook beyond serving tea to the smiling beauty.

We went on till nine o'clock that evening, and all the time the Chinese were peering anxiously round, as if they were afraid of some danger. They told a lot of tales to the effect that the young horsewoman was the daughter of the prince of Jun Sunit and that the princess's beloved had fallen into disfavour with the prince and had been driven from his country. But the princess fled to follow him into exile, and they had gathered a band of the feared *t'u-fei* with which they plundered passing caravans. The horsemen who had followed us were assuredly a division of these *t'u-fei* who had not dared to attack us for fear of our European weapons. The visit to our camp and the invitation to accompany them to their tent was, without doubt, only a stratagem. Besides this our scared Chinese related a multitude of instances of the robbers' cruelty.

But no attack upon the caravan ever came, and we long preserved the " robber princess's " visit to our camp in tender memory, for she came into our life as something outside our experience and unique ; she came as a sweet manifestation of the steppe itself, a galloping daughter of the steppe.

The same evening we encamped by a little lake, bordered by meadows of lush grass over which was drawn a blue veil of irises. It was now two days before full moon and the night was clear and cool. We had a double ration of rice, but only the usual flat teaspoonful of sugar. The horses grazed out on the steppe, rolled in the grass and irises and whinnied with enjoyment. Puffs of air passed whispering over our heads at short intervals. A splashing could be heard from the little lake—of horses drinking or perhaps of ducks alighting on its smooth surface. Krebs and I took our guns and went down to the lake shore. It was fringed with tall bullrushes, but from a little mound we could see the polished mirror of the water and follow the moon-path, stretched like a swaying bridge from shore to shore.

We found a couple of elevated positions and separated. All was silent, and in the camp they were presumably asleep. I sat long with the moon behind me and my eyes on the moon-path across which my prey must pass if I was to be able to take aim. Suddenly the stillness was broken by a soft whistling, followed by the sound of the fluttering short wing-stroke which announces that a large bird is checking itself in flight. For a brief moment a flock of long-necked silhouettes passed over that part of the lake which reflected the moonbeams. I fired one shot, the silhouettes vanished, and I could hear by the beat of their wings that the birds had resumed their flight. But a sharp thud told me that a bird had fallen, that its flight had been checked, and after some searching with the help of Krebs I found a long-legged victim. We went back to the camp, and I saw by the light of the fire that it was alas, not a goose or a duck but a long-legged crane. I was tolerably consoled next day by finding that its head was adorned by a magnificent crest. That was my first shot in Mongolia.

We ate the crane after boiling it for hours. Not that it was tender then, but we lost patience, and our mouths watered at the thought of meat—in whatever form, since we had seen none for eleven days. I swallowed the heart, for " hunter's luck " in Mongolia, and I sent the plume by the first messenger to a blue-eyed girl in Denmark.

Next morning we drove out into a sea of blue iris. It shimmered blue as far as one could see, and the dewdrops twinkled on flower and leaf, as the horses pushed their way through it. The flowers were so splendid and so blue that one wanted to avoid stepping on them, but as far as eye could reach there was nothing but blue iris, all equally erect and all equally blue. So we rode straight forward, but it hurt us when the flowers were snapped and murdered under our horses' heavy hooves.

We soon left all this splendour of flowers and fertility behind ; the following days we rode over yellow and dried-up steppe. For two days we mounted a slowly rising slope enclosed at the sides by blue hills of gentle outline. These were Bogdo Ola—the hills of the Gods, the Chinese told us. This poetic name is an often recurring designation of beautiful hills in Mongolia. The Mongol is always alive to the beauties of nature, thus differing from many other peoples who are born, live and earn their livelihood in natural surroundings. They have an admirable instinct for laying out and building their sanctuaries in such a way that an entrancing harmony arises between the work of man and God's free nature. Especially lovely hills are preserved and receive names worthy of their beauty. Such names as Bogdo

Ola and Noyan Bogdo (Divine Prince) are frequently met with.

On July 26th we saw the first of the swift-footed antelopes of the steppe. A herd of about fifty head crossed our path in light and graceful bounds. Now and then, for no apparent reason, they would jump yards into the air time after time, bouncing like an india-rubber ball. They were far out of range, but, in pure mischief, we sent a shot after them with the result that they vanished with the speed of an arrow like a yellowish-white streak over the steppe which engulfed them.

Antelopes occur of two species, which the Mongols call *Sultei gurus* (The Tailed Antelope, *Gazella subgutterosa*) and *Share gurus* (The Yellow Antelope, *Gazella gutterosa*). The former kind have long black horns and a twelve-inch tail, while the latter have short, yellowish-brown horns and hardly any tail. The former is not so difficult to approach, but it is almost impossible to get within range of the latter on the steppe where there is no cover. By chasing these antelopes in motor-cars it has been established that they can run for a stretch of over ten miles at the colossal speed of a mile a minute. How long they could keep up such a speed is unknown, for, says Mr. Andrews who made this experiment, after ten miles' pursuit the car sustained a puncture—but not the antelope.

Sometimes we passed large herds of apparently untended camels, among which the antelopes were grazing. In the daytime we seldom saw the latter in herds of more than fifty, and they were oftenest in groups of from six to ten, but in the mornings before sunrise and in the evenings we often found them in thousands, an army assembled for the march to distant unknown waterholes in the untrodden loneliness of the desert.

In the scattered wells along the old caravan routes and in the settlements of the Mongols the surface of the water always lies too far down for the antelopes to reach it. Deep within the sand-dunes there is doubtless open, accessible water in places so remote that only the swift-footed antelopes can make their way through the sterile belt surrounding them. In the very early morning they come out from the desert to split up into innumerable small herds that spread, grazing, over the steppe, and in the evening they again assembled to disappear at sunset. Towards what goal ? Often, looking after them, I wished I could follow them to see what the desert concealed. But I could not, for what to the antelopes is a few hours' gallop would mean for me a journey of days without water, through drifting sand, in an uncertain direction and to an unknown goal.

The country through which we were passing now was purely Mongolian, dry, inhospitable and endless. Its inhabitants had no need to fear the encroachment of Chinese cultivators, for their land was too infertile to permit any form of agriculture. Their camps lay scattered, and hardy goats and easily contented camels formed the preponderating part of their livestock.

These Mongols belong to a race called Barun Sunit and are nearly related to the Jun Sunit. *Barun* and *Jun* signify " right " and " left ", but in Mongolia correspond with our " west " and " east ", since the Mongol always conceives himself in a position facing towards Lhasa, the holy city.

According to their own tradition they have the name Sunit because they are descended from a party of Mongols from the Sain Noyan Khanate in Kalka that once fled from Kalka to settle where they now dwell. The flight was led by the Khan's youngest son, and since the start took place under cover of night, they took the name of Sunit from *suni* (night).

ON the primitive map of the route from Kalgan to Urga that we had with us very few names were marked, but P'ang-chiang was stressed with heavy type. We had often heard in China talk of " the city of P'ang-chiang " and imagined the place as a little Chinese town with the usual obligatory bazaar street. Our boots needed repair, and we had moreover drawn up a list of miscellaneous articles which we supposed ourselves to require for the march through Gobi and counted on being able to obtain in the desert city.

We came to P'ang-chiang on the fifth of August, but

found no trace of either city or bazaar street. The telegraph line led us to a little roughcast house surrounded by a few ruined and uninhabited mud hovels and some poverty-stricken Mongol tents. A Chinese telegraphist was living in the house, and we found him deeply sunk in opium intoxication. We shook him, but did not succeed in getting any further information out of him than that we had now covered a hundred and twenty of the telegraph line's six hundred and sixty miles to Urga.

To the north of P'ang-chiang we saw a large Mongolian monastery not far from the road. We at once steered our course thither, glad of the chance to encounter living beings. But within the whitewashed walls with their gay red edgings all lay desolate and abandoned. On the steppe in front we had seen numerous Chinese uniforms, felt boots and sheepskins lying widely scattered around, and within the cloister lay the many-coloured remnants of lamaistic robes, red togas and rusty yellow hats, and many of the red cloaks contained bleached fragments of skeletons.

Less than two years ago there had been an active monastic life in this now so dismal spot ; it had been a pilgrims' resort for the nomads of the surrounding steppes. But a last remnant of General Hsü's ten thousand soldiers had halted there in their flight from the avenging Mongols, and all this silence and death was the last achievement of the Chinese soldiery in the " Grass Country ". But in that very place the Chinese troops had been overtaken by a dreaded Kalka General with his mounted Mongols, and not one of the ten thousand invaders had found his way home to China. With the natural exception of the Chinese Generals who, after the first defeat of the Chinese at Urga, had left Mongolia in fast motor-cars.

The wild dogs of the steppe now nosing round among the ruined buildings indicated the fate that had overtaken both lamas and soldiers after death.

CHAPTER VI

THE DESERT

"The Western Sea—the desert"   (Mongolian Song)

THE way through the desert between the monastery of P'ang-chiang and the large monastic village of Turin near Urga was strewn for a certain distance with the skeletons of Chinese soldiers. We passed the place that had evidently been the camp, and there the skeletons lay in heaps. The stretches between the camping-grounds were strewn with felt boots and skin coats which the fugitives had thrown off so as to get away the faster from the terrors of the night and the pursuing death. It was as though a reflection of that terror stared at us from the many grinning skulls in the desert sand.

Another week's march brought us to the next telegraph station, bearing the Chinese name of Erh-lien. The Mongols call the place Iren Dabusu. We camped there in the dreariest and most desolate surroundings that can be imagined. The ground exudes salt, and the burning sun has dried out the surface to a powdery white crust. The only relief for the eye is in the small heaps of sand that have piled up in the lee of isolated thorny shrubs and clumps of Gobi sage.

This was the place where the well-known Andrews expedition had made, the year before, its memorable find of Dinosaurus, the first of its kind in Asia north of the Himalayas. Science conjectures that, six million years ago, this country had a tropical climate and that the district was dotted with lakes surrounded by luxuriant vegetation. The animal life was abundant and included tortoises and crocodiles as well as those fantastic giant lizards, the dinosaurs. Of all the strange things I came across in Mongolia this theory seemed to me the most astounding.

On later occasions I myself found similar fossils in Central Asia, and I sometimes tried to expound to my Mongolian travelling companions the scientific theories about the find. They were royally amused by what I told them and looked at me with a sort of tolerant indulgence. They did not say I was lying, but deprecated my excessive taste for romance and mystery. " Nay, look you," said a grey-haired philosopher, " this is nothing new to us in this country. It is only for you white people with your new learning that it is anything new. We call these *Tenggerin losang yasa* (the bones of the Dragons of Heaven,) and we have used these bones for many years as a cure for certain diseases. For these are the bones of the Dragons of Heaven that fell in ancient wars, and the spirits of nature have given them a worthy burial-place in the bosom of Mongolia."

We continued our journey through the desert in two stages each day.

The stages were so arranged that we usually reached a well at the end of the morning's march. There we rested during the heat of the day and thoroughly watered the thirsty horses before starting out again at four in the afternoon. The place for the evening camp was chosen where there was good grazing for the animals. At sunrise the herbage was moistened with dew, and the horses had to get along on that scanty liquid until we came to the next well, which happened as a rule towards nine in the morning. Several times, however, we had to struggle through two whole days without meeting with any water. Before entering on a sterile tract of this kind we filled all the water casks so that there was enough for the scanty tea ration for the men, but the horses commonly had to go thirsty to the next watering-place. The caravan crawled ever in the same

Mongolia's swift-footed Antelope (*Gazella subgutterosa*)

The Desert

"The western sea—the desert" (Mongolian song)

THE DESERT

direction, to the north-west, and our left arms and knees became more severely burnt by the grilling sun than our right.

We passed through a district where the strangest animal life prevailed. In the early morning inquisitive sand rats (Meriones), gluttonous hamsters (Cricetulus) and playful Kangaroo rats (Dipus) peeped out of small holes in the sand, and the strangest four-footed animals bathed all day long in the sun's hot rays. Ravens and kites sat on the telegraph poles on the watch for dying caravan beasts. At abandoned wells and water-holes we had to drive away the wild dogs of the desert. They looked miserable and famished and left the water-place reluctantly, with much growling and barking. When we broke camp the birds of prey competed for the poor fragments of our meal.

Late one evening we came to an almost dried up water-hole in the sand. The water looked brown and slimy, and an offensive stench met us from afar off. In the middle of the little water-hole we found a dead camel, but we boiled the water and put in an extra dose of tea and saccharine and at least it served to quench our thirst. We thought of the wretched caravan to which the dead camel belonged. After a long march in the heat of the sun they had come, burning with thirst, to the water-hole, only to find it dried up—and man and beast had to start out again into the desert in the hope of finding another watering-place.

Buffalo began to speak with increasing frequency of the many bottles of " Old Carlsberg " and " Hofbrau " he had drunk in the Red Sea and swore over all the " cold Pilsener " he had neglected to drink in the course of his life.

We kept in the shade of the heavily laden wagons, but the rate of progress was irritatingly slow. We knew in the mornings that if the water casks had not been filled up on the previous day there would be a well within the compass of the morning march. On such days Tot and I used to trot briskly on in advance so as to get on as far as possible while it was still cool. We followed the tracks of the caravans that had gone before us. If we had not reached water by eight o'clock we lay down on a high sand-dune to await the caravan. There were no shady places. We lay flat on our backs in the soft sand, pulled our sun helmets over our faces and waited. The sun rose in the sky and the heat made us drowsy. Once we must both have slept, for we were roused by a violent rushing close above our heads that made us sit up in a hurry. Our hasty movement warded off the attack of an eagle. For a brief moment we had his keen eyes right over us, but then he swept on on outspread wings and described a wide circle above us. Suddenly he swooped down on to the sand some twenty yards away. Now fully awake, we lay down on our backs again to observe his further tactics. Two more eagles came and settled in the neighbourhood of the first. If we lay quite still they came flapping heavily forward towards us, but at our slightest movement they checked and observed us narrowly before venturing to advance farther. Finally we sprang up, alive and kicking, to continue our journey, much to the surprise and annoyance of the eagles.

When, later, I saw skeletons in the sand I could not help thinking that the poor beasts and men, who lay dying and felt life ebbing by degrees, perhaps observed the rapacious brutes around them, coming ever closer, and knew that the last spark of life would be snuffed out by birds of prey.

THE caravan route from Kalgan to Urga, which is continued by the road from Urga to Kiachta, constitutes one of the oldest and until lately most used overland connections between the Far East and Europe. Until quite recently the greater part of the tea consumed in Europe travelled by that route. And up to 1920 most of the wealth of Mongolia was transported along this line to Kalgan whence it was carried on by rail to the seaport town of Tientsin which was the trading centre of the great western firms.

But Baron Ungern-Sternberg's reign of terror, succeeded in its turn by that of the Bolsheviks, coupled with the bloody guerilla warfare between Mongols and

THE DESERT

Chinese along the whole line from Turin to Pankiang had resulted in the Mongols who lived along the caravan route transferring their camping-places to more peaceful districts. Since, moreover, trading relations between China and Mongolia were now almost entirely broken off, our line of march, formerly so crowded with traffic, lay more deserted than it had perhaps been for many hundred years.

From their youth up our caravan drivers had been travelling this route twice yearly, but this was their first journey since 1919. The many skeletons of Chinese soldiers made a strong impression on them, and they looked forward to the journey through Outer Mongolia with even greater dread than they had felt for the *t'u-fei* bands of Chahar.

One day we passed by two colossal heaps of stones, which the caravan men called *obos*. They lay one on either side of the track in the sand, and on the top of one was a little altar of sacrifice. The caravan made a halt of several hours to permit the Chinese to perform a ceremony whose great importance could be read in the tense expression of their yellow faces.

The Chinese had for some days been leading with them a bleating goat which they had bought from a passing shepherd. This goat was now to bleat for the last time, but first it was to give the expectant yellow men an oracular answer as to whether they would escape with a whole skin from their journey among the savage Kalka Mongols. The two *obo* were in fact erected at the point where the caravan route crosses the boundary between Inner and Outer Mongolia.

The old caravan leader dragged the resisting goat up to the place of sacrifice on the top of the *obo*. All the Chinamen knelt a little lower down and looked on while the old man sprinkled the goat with precious drops of water, brought for the purpose from the last well. The goat did not worry about the water, but caught sight of a tuft of grass which it made an effort to reach. At length it got to the grass, but this did not interest the Chinese. They stared fixedly at the poor beast and mumbled a flood of words which were presumably prayers. The goat gradually became so wet that she noticed it herself and began with a contented air to lick her damp pelt. The prayers of the Chinamen rose higher and higher and they began to look disconsolate. It took two hours of praying and a quantity of water to make the goat behave as she should. Then, however, she shook herself till the water rose like a cloud and bleated noisily. And this was clearly what she ought to do, for now all the Chinese sprang up and positively danced with joy. But the poor goat had to lay down her life, and her blood soon spurted over the place of sacrifice. She was eaten the same evening by happy Chinamen at our first camping-place in Outer Mongolia.

The days' marches in the desert grew longer and we came into a region where we overtook or met caravans almost every day.

During the period from November to April the transport through the desert is carried on by hardy Bactrian camels. Now was the time when the camels were led to good grazing-grounds to recuperate after the exertions of the winter and to accumulate new nourishment in their flabby humps so that these should grow firm and upstanding against next winter's toils. We often passed herds of thousands of grazing camels spread over a desert tract that looked so poor and sterile that it was inconceivable that any living thing could exist, still less gather new powers on a herbage so sparse and dry. But the camel's taste is peculiar like everything else about that strange beast.

Horse caravans of the kind that we were employing can only undertake one journey a year to and fro between Kalgan and Urga. One cannot start before the rainy season is over which generally happens in the beginning of July, and then the horses must be back in the cultivated tracts outside Kalgan before the snow covers the grasslands of Inner Mongolia, which occurs in October. With good horses and not excessive loads, the horse caravans reckon forty-five days each way, with some weeks' stay in Urga to let the horses recover their strength.

Ox Caravans crawl forward through the country

Camel Caravans winding between the sand dunes on the way to distant goals

Summer . . .

and Winter

THE DESERT

Traffic with ox caravans can be maintained all the year round, but is most profitable between April and November when the camel traffic is suspended. Travelling with oxen is a very tedious business; one has to allow at least three months for the distance between Kalgan and Urga. The oxen are quite dependent on water and do not endure the burning sun. Accordingly such caravans move by night over the long stretches between the watering-places and then rest for several days before starting on the long march to the next well.

During the short hours of the night we rested between the wells at places where the grazing was fit for horses and not eaten up by the oxen, which devour everything eatable in the neighbourhood of the wells. Then we lay under the stars which sparkled and glowed as they only can do over the land of the Mongols and listened to all the unaccustomed and fascinating sounds of the desert night. From the far distance came the enchanting ringing of the deep-toned camel bells. It was some caravan of unladen camels moving by night to fresh grazing-grounds. They did not come near to the caravan route but struck soundlessly across between distant sand-dunes. It was only the bells that betrayed their existence and indicated the direction of their movement.

And we heard the more rapid tinkling of the ox caravans. One first became aware of the sound of a single bell moving slowly through the night, then the more distant bells chimed in as a faint accompaniment to the nearest. Such a caravan might consist of a hundred carts. For hours one heard the sound of the many bells like a composition on three notes, from bells approaching, passing and receding. It was like the desert's own hymn to the deep night-sky. Then the last wagon passed, the sound quite softly faded and vanished into the far unknown.

The glowing midday hours were a daily discomfort through which we tried to sleep. But we were never safe from the Mongolian storms which often arose just at the time of the midday rest and caught us as unwelcome surprises. A dull, distant roar heralds their approach and in a moment one is in the midst of a raging cyclone. The air becomes rust-coloured; eyes, ears and nose are filled with fine sand, and all movable objects whirl off through the air.

Then there is nothing to do but to pull down the tarpaulin and throw oneself flat on the ground, each under his corner of the canvas, which one tries to hold tight to the earth with elbows, knees, teeth and anything else one can grip with. Fortunately it passes over as quickly as it comes, and fortunately the whirlwind leaves the other fellows in the same absurd predicament as oneself, so that everyone gets a good laugh. After it one has to go out into the surrounding country to collect tin plates, cups, pans, lids and other things that have accompanied the storm in its wild dance. Then one puts the awning up again and enjoys the coolness that lingers for a while after the storm.

On August the eighteenth we arrived at Ude which forms the official entrance to the country of the Kalka Mongols. Ude may, like the Mongolian name for Kalgan, *Khalaghan*, be translated as " gate ", " passage " or " door ". But there is an important shade of difference between the names, as a Mongol once explained to me in the following way.

The felt-hung entrance to a Mongol's tent is called *ude*. It is the entrance, in the strictest sense, to the Mongol's home, within which the laws of hospitality are sacred. Therefore the entrance to the Kalka Mongols' own grasslands, the great hospitable Kalka Mongolia, is called Ude. Khalaghan or Kalgan is the opening in the Chinese wall through which the Mongols have so often galloped over the cultivated tracts of the Chinese, " the gate " to the world outside their homeland, in which they can never settle or thrive, but which lures them by the chance of fighting and loot which the country out there offers.

I have heard people call Ude the Timbuktoo of the Gobi Desert, but I have certainly never been able to find anything that made the place worthy of the name " Queen of the Desert " like the fabled town of the

THE DESERT

Sahara. Here are none of the virtues one ascribes to women.

The centre of Ude consists of a few small mud houses, the largest of which is occupied by the Russian telegraphist, Mr. Vallov and his stalwart lady. Mr. Vallov's house consists of a telegraph room and a bedroom, and meals were served under the naked sky on a couple of old petrol cans. The mud-house was surrounded by some forty Mongol tents which housed the garrison of eighty soldiers. The General and a couple of customs officers in long pigtails lived in three large tents near the telegraph station.

The fat Mrs. Vallov was the only woman in the place. We sought in vain for somewhere to buy cigarettes. The place was thus destitute alike of charm and of facilities for amusement.

Our caravan had to be examined by the customs, and this kept us in Ude for twenty-four hours, during which the grim Mongol soldiers amused themselves by striking terror into our Chinese caravan drivers. Next day we got our papers from the customs, and though the sun was already high, we yielded to the wish of our Chinese to depart immediately from that place of many terrifying soldiers. " Yabonah, yabonah ! " was the cry, and again the caravan turned out into the sun and the sand.

To the north of Ude the caravan route coincides with that followed by motor-cars, and we were overtaken next day by Mr. Larson who had left Kalgan in his Dodge four days earlier. He gave us two big water melons, and we blessed him and his offspring.

We were approaching blue hills, and one day we halted by a gravel-filled furrow in the sand. It had been cut by water from the hills in rainy summers, but there was nothing now but the driest sand and gravel.

They talk of " the three trees of Gobi ", and Larson had told us that one of these marvels was to be found beside this rain channel. After a long ride we found it. We sat down in its shade—we felt it—smelled its leaves—and photographed it. It was a peculiar sensation, which I would not have supposed a lonely little poplar capable of producing. Although we had for so long been cursing the sun-dried camel and cattle droppings that constituted our only fuel, we had not the heart to rob the tree of any of its branches.

The Gobi Desert's almost complete lack of trees is, from a purely practical standpoint, a great defect. At least so long as one is a greenhorn. All fires have to be maintained with the droppings one can collect on the march, and this fuel demands uninterrupted blowing and is unpleasant for cooking, since the food acquires an odour which takes some getting used to. When the first whiff of the smoke or taste of the food meets one's organs of sense and one sees around nothing but the treeless desert, one has a melancholy recollection of the lovely scent of blue wood-smoke from the stoves of home or from nightly camp-fires. And when the grilling sun torments one's scorched head day after day for fourteen hours out of the twenty-four, one remembers walks in " Charlotte's " shady beechwoods.

And yet, standing at sunset on a sandhill thrust up above the desert, when the shadows fill the inequalities in the landscape, or, after the sun has sunk, when the wind has laid itself to rest and the vast horizon closes in at the meeting with the shades of night, then one feels that Gobi too has its unique character and its charm.

At one water-place we adopted an abandoned puppy which, in spite of all our friendly advances, showed in many ways that he had temperament. He was a lively fellow and a suitable dog for us. We christened him *Hudcha*, " the tiger ".

" Yabonah, yabonah ! " sounded over the steppe, and we continued our march—always to the north-west, always with the sun roasting the same side of us.

Gobi now lay behind us and we were travelling across the grass country. On either side of the road, quite close, inquisitive *tarbagan* (marmots) sat watching us with many squeals and chirpings. The dogs rushed after them, but at the last moment the marmots would vanish into some of their earths to pop up again at once from others and resume their squeaking, to the great annoyance of the dogs.

One of the Gobi Desert's " three trees "

Censer of hammered copper—on the front side of the censer are seen "the eight glorious symbols" (in Tibetan, tashi dazai'a) which are regarded in the Lamaistic world as propitious emblems. From left to right these are : 1. The white baldaquin—unrestricted dominion. 2. The two auspicious golden fishes. 3. The vase containing the holy water that confers Eternal Life. 4. The Lotos flower—purity and heavenly birth. 5. The spiral trumpet that announces victory. 6. The auspicious diagram representing Buddha's bowels. This symbolizes the endless series of rebirths in a sinful world. 7. The invincible banner. 8. The victorious wheel—a kingdom where the sun never sets. (The wheel of life or the sun)

[*face p.* 65

THE DESERT

We were now passing through the magnificent Mongolian steppes, and everywhere we saw the camping-places of the nomads and vast herds of cattle. Long before we came to the monastery town of Turin we could see the cleft hill-tops in whose shelter several thousand lamas have their refuge. Like a legendary castle this granite mass stands up a thousand feet above the surrounding steppe. Once in the morning of time the hill formed the base of a heaven-aspiring mountain which wind and weather has transformed to this wild chaos of granite.

As we pushed on through the rocks we saw in several places traces of recent encounters. Quantities of cartridge cases and accoutrements lay scattered among bleached remnants of bones.

During the " terrible winter " a detachment of several thousands of General Hsü's soldiers had encamped here. Baron Ungern sent Cossacks to attack them, but a Mongol General had scented the prey and got ahead of them. At the head of three hundred battle-hungry Mongols, he galloped to Turin and arrived there at night. Without waiting to rest either his men or his horses he attacked at once. With a wild yell the cavalry galloped full tilt across the Chinese camp, cutting down all who came in their way. The Chinese ran like frightened sheep and the Mongols killed them in hundreds.

This is a method of warfare that the Mongols love; days of hard riding without thought of food or sleep and then a sudden tumultuous, yelling onslaught followed by relentless slaughter. It is performances like this that have made the Mongols feared throughout the ages from Peking to Poland.

CHAPTER VII

THE CLOISTER OF GOD

"Pilgrims" (Mongolian Song)

ON September 8th Urga lay at our feet, traversed by the abundant waters of the Tola river and encircled by Bogdo Ola's wooded steeps. The rays of the sun, which for weeks we had been cursing, now threw an enchanting light over thousands of birch and larch trees clothed in autumn foliage. The innumerable gilded roofs and minarets of the monastic city, the goal of our desert journey, lay before our enraptured eyes.

Before making our entry into the city of the Mongols, we washed ourselves and bathed in the river, put on our last change of clean khaki and fixed a fine Danish flag high upon the foremost wagon of the caravan. We aroused considerable attention when we passed through the city gates on our way to Larson's. "Well done, Scandihuvia!" shouted Larson, and the same evening he gave a great feast in our honour at which we met all the members of Urga's little occidental colony.

But before the feast began, Krebs gave orders that we should all record the effect of the desert journey upon our physique. It appeared that Buffalo, who had performed the whole march on foot, had lost eighty-two pounds, Birck seventeen and a half, Krebs ten, and I—yes, I had gained one pound.

At that evening's unforgettable feast we all four achieved the title of bear's-meat eaters, and that night we slept like logs.

IN a corner of the room which I occupied at Larson's, stood a big Danish flag on a white-painted staff. Curious, I asked where it came from, and Larson pointed to a photograph on the table, of a young man of gallant bearing with a keen, frank glance. It was a wedding photograph, and by the young man's side stood a black-eyed beauty in bridal dress with flowers at her breast. "That is Olufsen," said Larson. "The flag belonged to him. He was a lad of the right sort—and I liked him." I had heard of Olufsen and his tragic fate, but very much wanted to know the reason for his having been killed. "You see," said old Mongol Larson, "he was one of those people who, if they think a fellow is a cad, positively have to go straight up to him and tell him so to his face with due emphasis. Several times during the 'mad baron's' rule in Urga he found himself obliged to rout round the town till he got hold of Ungern and could hiss the truth in his face. He did it once too often."

E. V. Olufsen was born in Copenhagen and, like so many other young Danish dairy-farmers, had gone to Siberia, in the days of the Tsar, to seek his fortune. The revolution came and his dairy-farm, like all the others eastward of the Urals, became the property of the Soviet. Since there was no longer any outlet there for a young man's energy and ambition, he went to China, where he got an appointment in the Danish-American firm of Andersen and Meyer. He was drafted to that firm's Urga branch, which was managed by Larson, and worked under the latter's direction. When, in 1920, Larson went across to the United States, Olufsen was sole manager of the branch during the difficult and trying days of the revolution.

His open and straightforward character caused him to become good friends with the Mongol princes and the officials of the old regime. Then he met a pretty Russian Jewess, fell in love with her, and took her to

Peking, where they were married at the Danish Legation by Ove Krebs, who at that time was Chargé d'Affaires.

Conditions in Urga became so unsafe in the "mad baron's" time that the members of the white colony started in May, 1921, to make their way to the coast, but Olufsen, who had a lot of horses and cattle afoot outside the town, delayed his departure for a couple of days so as to sell them and a lot of other property belonging to his firm. I later obtained an account of Olufsen's death from Wilson, a former American flying officer.

Colonel Sepailov, who was commandant at Urga, informed Olufsen that he wanted to buy the cattle, and they agreed to go by car to the place where the *tabun* (herd) was, in order to have the beasts valued. With Sepailov, the latter's executioner Tiestiakov and a couple of others, Olufsen left Urga for the last time. Sepailov imagined that Olufsen had a treasure buried somewhere and began questioning him about it. Olufsen denied the existence of the treasure. When they were well outside Urga, the chauffeur announced that there was something wrong with the back wheel. He got out and called to Olufsen to come and help him. Olufsen got out and was standing forward when the car, driven by Tiestiakov, suddenly began to move forward at the same time that the chauffeur threw a running noose, fastened to the car, round Olufsen's neck. While he was slowly dragged along the ground Olufsen was interrogated about the hiding-place of the treasure, and since he had no information to give, he was dragged to death in this barbarous manner by these white bandits. In 1925 I read in a Chinese newspaper that Sepailov lay dying in a Chinese prison in Manchuria, where he was serving his sentence for this crime.

No town in the world is like Urga. Upon us newcomers it made an extremely strange impression. The most conservative eastern life and customs and western innovations like the telegraph, the telephone and the motor-car exist side by side in motley combination. The houses of the Russians cluster around the church with Byzantine cupolas; colossal Buddhist temples rise high over thousands of felt-covered Mongol tents.

Ungern-Sternberg, "the mad baron", who proclaimed himself a reincarnation of the Mongols' god of war and who held sway in Kalka-Mongolia in the beginning of "The iron bird's year", 1921

Woman of the Durbet-Khukhet Tribe

THE CLOISTER OF GOD

Mounted Mongols, slippered Chinese, long-bearded Russians and smiling Tibetans swarm between pallisaded compounds whose walls are hung with gaily fluttering prayer-flags. At the most eastern end lies the *mai-mai-ch'eng* of the Chinese, a complete fragment of China in whose innumerable shops the sons of Han offer their wares to the Mongols riding by.

On the dusty, filthy market-place, yellow and red lamas in pointed headgear with wreaths of roses, and swinging prayer-mills in their hands, hurry about among mounted nomads clad in the splendid, parti-coloured robes of the many different tribes. Caravans of camels rock forward through the narrow winding lanes. Dogs everywhere prowl, everywhere there is filth, heaps of garbage and an unbelievable stench.

Among all the strange costumes we saw, that of the married Kalka women aroused our greatest astonishment. Their dress was costlier and quainter, if not more beautiful, than that of all the others. The cloaks are furnished with great wadded protuberances which rise about six inches from their shoulders, and their hair is so saturated with congealed fat that it can be shaped into a sort of long horn that stands out as much as sixteen inches from the head.

I could not wonder enough how the otherwise so practical steppe-dwellers came to devise so idiotic and unpractical a dress for their hard-working women. I asked many Mongols for an explanation but they knew no more than that their women were dressed and decked in the same fashion that they had learned from former generations. My wonder continued until long afterwards I met a Mongolian prince who was versed in the ancient books and who told me the following legend.

The Kalka Mongols derive their origin from a union between one of the nature spirits and a cow. The cow that gave suck to the first Kalka Mongol infused into him the love of cattle-rearing and nomadic life and, that the coming race should not forget their origin, the Kalka women were charged to wear a coiffeur reminiscent of a cow's horn, and their dresses were furnished with pro-

THE CLOISTER OF GOD

jections on the shoulders which called to mind the prominent shoulder-blades of the cow.

In 1923 the Kalka women still wore this costume without in general knowing why, but after the usual way of women they had succeeded in making use of the peculiarities of the dress to show off their jewels and ornaments. Their long coiffeurs were richly embellished with gold and silver ornaments and studded with whole fortunes in pearls and precious stones.

The westerners' Urga, Bogdo Kure (God's Cloister) to the Mongols and Da Kulen (Great Cloister) to the Chinese, was founded in about the year 1650. At first it was only a place for the principal monastery of Mongolia, the seat of the Mongols' first *hutuktu* or reincarnation of a Buddhist divinity, who at that point was summoned from Tibet. At this time it was only a mobile, travelling cloister, and its temples were installed in large felt tents. The first permanent temple was only built in 1779 on the northern bank of the Tola River where this takes in the waters of the Selba. By degrees the monastery was extended by more temples and more lamas, and lamaistic schools of philosophy, astronomy and divinity were established under the guidance of imported Tibetan teachers. Thus the place gradually became the chief seat of the Chinese and Russian administration as well as the pilgrim resort of the faithful.

When in 1912 Kalka Mongolia declared its independence of China and proclaimed Hutuktu Gegen, the primate of the Mongolian Church, Emperor of the four Kalka Khanates, Urga became the seat of government of the new kingdom.

Several times we rode over the long bridge to the south bank of the Tola river, where Bogdo Hutuktu Gegen's two palaces lie in the midst of the loveliest surroundings at the foot of Bogdo Ola (The Mountain of the Gods). The woods on the mountain side swarmed with wild life, for Bogdo Ola is sacred and one may not dig in its soil, fell its trees nor hunt in its forests.

Along the outermost enclosure of the palace moved an endless host of lamas and pilgrims assembled here in thousands from the remotest corners of Central Asia.

Unmarried and married woman from Kalka-Mongolia. The married woman's head-dress symbolizes cows' horns, and the wadded ornaments the cow's prominent shoulder blades

For many years, the Kalka-Mongols were under the guardianship of the Tsar's Cossacks and the Mandarins of the Dragon Throne

THE CLOISTER OF GOD

It was an eternally flowing human stream, men and women of all ages with heavy loads of sacred books on their bent backs. Some were walking, others crawling, many fell upon their faces at every step. Numerous pilgrims had sacrificed years of their lives to drag themselves in some laborious fashion over the endless miles to the holy place. But before them loomed the fortune and felicity of touching the red silk cord that hangs down upon the outside of the temple wall and whose other end they believe to be held by the living Buddha.

Since the year 1912 this living divinity had also been in possession of the highest worldly power in Outer Mongolia. He governed the country in council with four Great khans and a number of lesser princes, each of whom had almost unlimited power within his hereditary domain. The supreme power, the right alone to pronounce sentence of death on evil doers, was vested only in Bogdo Gegen himself and the four Khans. The lesser princes could only pronounce sentence in concert with a *Khuruldei* (council) summoned from among the principal Mongols of the district.

The Mongols relate the following legend concerning the rise of the four Khans and the summoning of the first Hutuktu Bogdo Gegen from Tibet.

When the new (Manchu) dynasty had ascended the dragon throne, the whole of the hereditary princes of the Mongolian tribes were summoned to Peking to swear allegiance to Bogdo Khan (the divine Khan, the Emperor) the elect of heaven on earth. Bogdo Khan intimated that Kalka Mongolia was to be divided into four new *aimaks* (administrative provinces) and that the four ablest and best of the assembled princes would be proclaimed as rulers over them.

Among the assembled Mongol princes Erebugher Wang made himself the most conspicuous, for he was wise and cunning of speech. Bogdo Khan arranged a series of feasts for the princes in which he himself took part, so that he might more closely observe the guests. At one such feast Bogdo Khan had all the princes put to the proof that he might judge which of them were worthy to reign over the newly established Khanates.

Before the guests was placed a horse made of dough, rice and flesh, the eyes, saddle and bridle being decked with the most delicious sweetmeats. The Mongols helped themselves eagerly to the viands, each according to his taste. Some filled their mouths with rice and flesh, while others stuffed themselves with the sweetmeats. But Erebugher Wang lifted the saddle from the beast, saying : " One judges the worth of a horse by the condition of its back, for it is the back that must bear the heaviest burden." And behold, under the saddle was a round hole leading to the hollow interior of the horse, and when he thrust his hand through the opening he found there the most splendid jewels. And Bogdo Khan was well content with Erebugher's conduct.

After the banquet Bogdo Khan handed to each of the princes a sort of rosary of costly pearls threaded on hempen cord, the ends of which hung far down from the pearl wreaths. The lamaistic princes placed the palms of their hands together in token of worship and gratitude and then hung the chaplets round their necks. But Erebugher cut off the loose ends of the cord with his knife, returned thanks for the gift with a secular salutation and thrust it into the leg of his riding boot. The cut-off ends of the cord he handed to one of the servants. Bogdo Khan now demanded an explanation of his conduct which differed from that of all the other Mongol princes and involved a breach of etiquette, which required that the rosary should be hung round the neck when it was not being used for prayer. And Erebugher answered: " I have in no wise deserved that any man should place a cord round my neck as one does in executing criminals. The pearl rosary was a precious gift which I, that I may not lose it, keep safe in my boot-leg, but only after it has been blessed and consecrated by a lama can it serve me in my prayers, and only when I use it for counting my prayers will it be worthy to hang about my neck."

Bogdo Khan was well pleased with this reply of Erebugher's also, and, as a reward, relieved him of the tribute which all other Mongol princes had to pay to the Dragon Throne. Then the Mongols were served with great silver goblets full of scalding hot wine. The

The principal entrance to the Living Buddha's Palace at Urga

Mongolian pilgrims on their toilsome way to Bogdo Kure (the Cloister of God)

Pilgrims on the way to Bogdo Kure

Having reached their goal, the pilgrims collapse exhausted outside the outer enclosure surrounding Bogdo Hutuktu Gegen's Palace. Here they remain in prayer for days and weeks

rounded base of the goblets made it impossible to put them down on the table, and the silver vessels which grew hot from the wine could not be held in the hand for more than a moment. One of the princes set the goblet on the table so close to the edge that it rested, without upsetting, against his breast. Bogdo Khan made this prince Khan over one of the four *aimaks* and gave him the title of Tushetu Khan (to prop against, to support is, in Mongolian, *tushalkhu*). Another of the princes took three articles on the table and placed them in a triangle within which he set his goblet. He too was made Khan of an *aimak* with the title of Tsasaktu Khan (from *tsasakhu*, to contrive, to arrange). A third prince declined the wine by bowing towards Bogdo Khan and saying " Sain-sain " (*sain*, good : used also when one wishes politely to decline an invitation). This prince was likewise appointed Khan with the title of Naamogon Khan (*naamogon*, meek, submissive, peaceable), and his khanate obtained the name of Sain Noyan Aimak (the *aimak* of the good prince).

But Erebugher took his pearl rosary out of his boot, rolled it into a ring on the table and put his goblet into this. The Chinese dignitaries asked him how he could use a gift from the Emperor as support for a wine cup, to which the Mongol replied that an Emperor's gift, like the wine, was a cause for rejoicing, but that once he had the pearls blessed by a lama they would help him with his prayers against wine and all else that was unworthy of a good Buddhist. And thereupon he delivered an impassioned speech in glorification of the lamaistic faith. Bogdo Khan was so enraptured that he acceded to Erebugher's request that he would send a mission to Lhasa to persuade the Dalai Lama to send a *hutuktu* to Urga. Erebugher was made ruler over the largest Khanate, which embraced twenty *hoshun* (districts) and received the title of Tsetsen Khan (the wise, the able).

The four Khans appointed were, as a special favour, invested with the right to execute death sentences in their Khanates, but Tsetsen Khan obtained the largest powers and was the only one to be excused from paying tribute to Peking.

THE CLOISTER OF GOD

At the request of Bogdo Khan the Dalai Lama sent a *hutuktu* to preach lamaism among the Mongols, and this *hutuktu* was the first Bogdo Gegen, who settled by the Tola river and there began the erection of *Bogdo Kure*, the Cloister of God.

We had frequent dealings with the Mongolian ministers, the majority of whom were friends of Larson's, and the kindly Mongols were much interested in our plans. They would have preferred that we should settle in the neighbourhood of Urga, but Krebs, like the rest of us, was determined on the Sable Plateau.

One of the strongest men in Mongolia was the war minister, Danzan, who was Larson's particular friend. We often saw him in his Mongolian riding dress driving through the streets of Urga in a rattling " Harley Davidson ", which set camels and ponies off at a gallop, and we often met him in Larson's house.

We also came into friendly relations with the sympathetic leaders of the newly arisen " young Mongolian party ". One of these was Badmasiapov, an intelligent young Mongol, whose father was Minister of Justice in the Government of the day. Badmasiapov had studied in Japan and spoke English and German fluently. He was a supporter of Mongolia's independence of both Russia and China, and was friendly disposed to all foreigners other than those belonging to these two nations.

Another leader in this movement was Michail Siasting. His father was Urga's Russian doctor, but the son had lived so long in Mongolia and among the Mongols that he himself had become Mongol in his habit of thought, and he worked only for what he thought to be best for the Mongols without regard to his own nationality.

Some days after our arrival, a notice appeared in Urga's only newspaper, the contents of which gave us all occasion for satisfaction. The *Urga Dawn* was a little sheet that came out " not less than six times in the month ", and in the issue of September 20th on the front page under the headline " Welcome ", the following appeared :

" A Danish agricultural expedition has arrived in Mongolia with machinery, seeds and necessary implements with a view

Khans and Chiefs of Kalka-Mongolia in past times

Mongolian hutuktu (reincarnation of a divinity)

to establishing modern agriculture west of Van Kure. The programme includes the cultivation of sugar beet, dairy-farming, etc.

"The head of the expedition is a physician, Krebs. He was in Mongolia three years ago and afterwards worked for the Danish Red Cross in Poland and in Russia by the Volga during the famine. He then assembled his fellow-workers and has come here to us for the purpose of organizing this work, which may bring about great cultural progress and material gain to Mongolia and therefore deserves recognition and support."

The expedition's treasury was almost empty, and it was therefore necessary to look about us for the ready money requisite to carry us through to the still distant goal. It was not difficult. Almost all the western firms sought alliance with us in order to secure a contingent market in the unknown country in the north-west. We were thus able to choose the alliance that offered us the best terms. After many negotiations we decided to work during the first season for a large Russian-American firm that was willing to advance us capital and goods on easy terms upon our agreement to let them have our first winter's takings of furs delivered in Urga at a price ten per cent below the price current in Urga on the day of delivery. To assist us in the selection of furs during the coming season we engaged a Chinese expert by the name of Ping.

Before this we had "sold Joseph to the Egyptians". That is to say, after drawing lots between Tot and me, we had lent the former to Larson & Co. for a period of six months for a payment to the expedition of three hundred dollars a month and his keep. This gave the expedition an extra eighteen hundred dollars and on conclusion of the bargain Larson threw in a fine horse and a noble hunting dog. So, once more we had our heads above water.

Larson & Co. had a great wool campaign in progress in the country west of Uliassutai, and the intention was that Tot should try to transport two carloads of silver for purchases in the various districts.

CHAPTER VIII

ON TO THE NORTH-WEST

AT last we had all necessary contracts and documents drawn up and signed. Forty ox-carts and two horse-wagons stood ready packed with all our goods, besides all the wares we were bringing from Urga in order to carry on trade on the Sable Plateau. We were ready to set off.

September 26th was the day fixed for the start. Early in the morning, at the house of Söderbom the Swede, we met the little foreign colony. They said good-bye, drank to our next merry meeting, wished us a lucky journey and many other good things. A single glass of vodka was Krebs's order for the members of the expedition, and so we left our newly acquired friends amid incessant cheering. The caravan had started earlier in the morning, and now we galloped after them on fresh horses in the clear autumn sunshine, the joy in our hearts beating in emulation of the horses' thundering hooves.

On this day flags were floating everywhere at home in Denmark, and Danish festivities were being held in all the clubs in the East, for it was King Christian's birthday.

We swam our horses across the river and then rode till, long after dusk had fallen, we saw the camp-fire of the caravan. Then once more we sat by the fire, surrounded by the wide steppe and all the sounds of the night, again we were on the way to our goal—it was an enchanting feeling.

We had now left the telegraph line and the motor road in proximity to which we had travelled from Kalgan to Urga. That highway of civilization continued due north from Urga, while we were going north-west, out on the untouched, unexplored steppes.

ON TO THE NORTH-WEST

For the most part we travelled through the long nights and pitched camp in broad daylight. They were tedious, slow night marches, and the monotonous repetition of the same sounds and the same visual impressions profoundly affected our spirits.

The caravan was divided into four sections, and at the head of each of them went a wise and well-trained leader ox. The oxen in each section were attached by a nose-rope to the cart in front.

The last cart in each group carried a cylindrical bell about twelve inches long. These bells were made of thin iron plates edged at the bottom by a band of copper an inch and a half wide. The clapper was a block of wood almost as long as the whole cylinder and so cut that there was only an interval of about a quarter of an inch between clapper and bell. Strips of red paper and silk, painted with Tibetan prayers were pasted to the bells. At the bottom of the clappers were long red horsehair tassels. On the leading wagon of each section was erected a tall lance with a yak's tail fluttering below the metal head.

By day the carts stood drawn up beside the wells in long, orderly rows, with their loads of boxes and bales; when dusk fell the train moved off again. The caravan wound like a snake across the steppe, and the clank of the nearest bells was accompanied by the sound from the more distant. Always the same notes, always the same time, always the same melody in the darkness.

We often rode ahead to await the slow caravan at some point farther on. Then we watched it crawling by—a succession of queer silhouettes, the long diversely shaped horns of the oxen moving far off along the horizon and the yak-tail-decked lances standing out sharply against the starry sky—it was like a vision from the days of Jenghiz Khan.

The mounted Mongols kept station about a hundred yards to the side of the caravan. Two of the leading ones whistled between their teeth, and when they ceased there were answering whistles from others farther off —quiet, soft notes that were heard far through the night. In this way they kept a check on one another that no one had fallen asleep. There was something queer about this whistling that sounded so low and could yet be heard so far. It was often difficult to determine whether the notes came from close by or far away.

The caravan leader rode in front of the foremost oxen. If we met with an obstacle he gave warning of it by sharp cries that made the other Mongols close up with the caravan. At the tail of the procession rode two Mongols. Now and then sparks were seen when they struck fire from their primitive tinder boxes to light their long pipes.

Thus, travelling by night and sleeping by day, noting the levels, the temperature and the water courses, we gradually drew near to the monastic town of Van Kure.

After fourteen days' travel we came to the great river Orchon, which we crossed on a picturesque ferry boat consisting of three hollowed-out tree-trunks adorned with carven dragon heads. The ferry was poled across by two Mongols, and since they could not take more than two wagons at a time it was two whole days and nights before we got the whole caravan across.

We did not, however, complain of this delay, for the Orchon Valley was a sportsman's paradise. We gorged upon game, and we shot far more than we could eat, so that when we went on we took with us two large sacks of the finest duck, ptarmigan, black game and other birds.

The thermometer now fell rapidly, and at night there were as many as twelve degrees of frost. We came to a tract where we met with the first example of that strange bird, the bustard, a gigantic fowl, whose neck and legs and spread of wing were considerably larger than those of a goose. They sat in groups of three or more out in the middle of the great hollows of the steppe.

WE reached Van Kure on October 16th. None of Krebs's Russian friends of the time of his earlier visit were still there, but a couple of other Russians, immigrants from the country to the northward, were living in their houses, and by them we were hospitably received.

Our caravan drivers were unwilling to go beyond this

place, not caring to travel farther from their homes in the neighbourhood of Urga. Krebs had in his time covered the stretch from Sable Plateau to Van Kure in five days, but though the distance between the places was no longer, we found no one here who knew of Bulgun Tal, the Mongol name of Sable Plateau. We chaffered with several caravan leaders, but none was willing to venture with his animals into the mountains out north. At last we succeeded in getting some wealthy lamas to drive for us, and after five days' delay trundled out again on to the steppes.

We had reckoned on ten days for the journey to Bulgun Tal, but it took considerably longer. We had small reason to praise the bunch of lamas who conducted our caravan. They had been unblushing in their demands and we had been foolish enough to accede to their request to have the greater part of the price before starting.

In five days our new caravan drivers took us to the Selenga river, and Krebs recognized the crossing as the same he had used four years earlier. The rushing water of the river had begun to bring down drift-ice, but the primitive raft was still able to make the crossing, and in three days we got the whole caravan across to the northern bank of the river. In his time Krebs had ridden the distance between here and Sable Plateau in three days.

But after we had crossed the river the lamas turned the caravan on to a different road from that which he had followed on his journey, and we came into narrow paths among wild rocks. Krebs protested that they were taking a far too northerly direction and that our destination lay more to the westward, but they held to the way they had chosen, explaining that the mountains farther west were of course accessible on horseback, but not with heavy ox-carts. We let ourselves be pacified by their assurances that they would soon bring us to Bulgun Tal.

But the days passed, the road grew worse and worse, the country wilder and wilder, and it was obvious that the caravan drivers were uncertain by which way to proceed. We often halted at places where there was a choice of several different valleys, and debated long before going on again. Twice we got on to wrong roads which led us into impassable country, and had to go back the way we came and then try another direction.

We worked out a map based upon our notes of bearings from the Selenga and came to the conclusion that our march on this stretch had been completely without plan. We had covered a mileage several times greater than the distance by which we had come nearer to our goal.

The temperature fell considerably and we recorded as much as − 25° at night. Our outfit was not calculated for such cold, so we froze unbelievably. We had no fur caps and were marching in ordinary leather boots. The nights were a trial since, in spite of our weariness, we could not sleep and suffered desperately from the cold. We were now up among snow-clad mountains and we dreaded the times when we were obliged to spend the night in the snow. But the very fact that we were so cold led to our constantly having to turn out of our snug sleeping sacks to attend to our affairs outside the tent.

Among his many treasures, Buffalo had brought a handsome pair of slippers. They were hand-made and worked in a pattern of the most beautiful roses and tulips. We had often scoffed at those slippers and Buffalo had had to listen to many witticisms about them. But he was fond of his botanically bedizened footwear, which, into the bargain, were an inheritance from an easy-going uncle, burgomaster in his time of one of the easy-going towns of the neighbouring country of Scania. "My uncle's slippers", as Buffalo always with dignity called them, now became "*our* uncle's slippers". They were in fact beautifully warm, and when we crept at night into our sleeping sacks they were carefully put out at the entrance to the tent for general use on our nightly excursions. They were very serviceable to us all.

Now came a snowstorm that held us up for three days, and the oxen grew thin and exhausted. The

Interior of Temple

Three high Lamas with their shabis

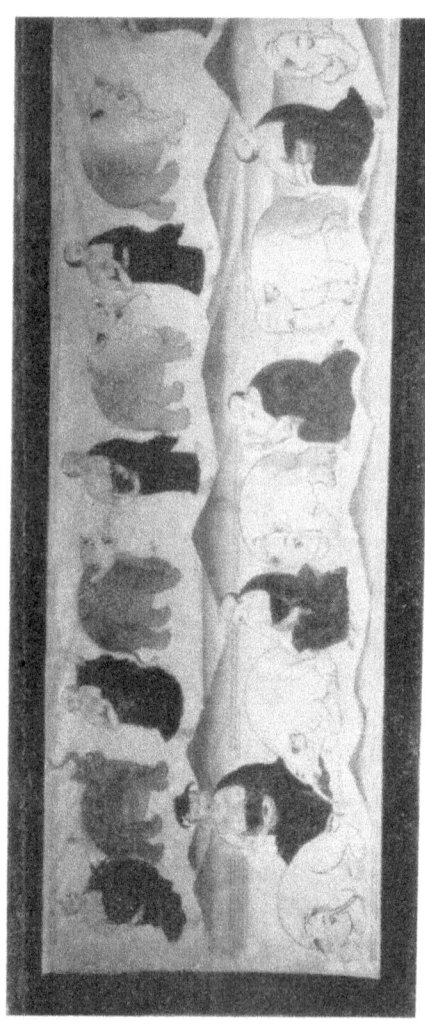

Temple painting illustrating the purifying and saving influence of Lamaism upon the unclean and intractable people. (The inscription reads: "A people without religion is like a horse without reins")

ON TO THE NORTH-WEST

Chinese whom we had brought from Urga often wept, while we just froze. One night our caravan people wanted to desert us with oxen, wagons and all, so we had to keep constant armed watch on them.

Then we moved on again at a snail's pace through the deep snow with exhausted oxen and unwilling drivers. We went up a valley leading to the westward, and at the end of it rose a pass higher than any we had yet seen. All day long beasts and men struggled to surmount the pass, which was steep and in parts completely sheathed with ice. When we sank that night into our sleeping sacks we were dead tired and both Krebs and Buffalo had frozen toes.

Next day we went on down the other side of the pass, and there we got a little recompense in the shape of certain exhilarating experiences. The snow by the side of the road was covered with the tracks of roe deer and wolves, and at noon, while we were resting and drinking tea, we heard the wolves singing their indescribable song around us in the sunlit valleys. And it is really not given to many to hear the song of the wolves at noon in dazzling sunlight.

In the evening we came to a large lake not marked on any map. There were a few Mongols living there and we learned from them that it was called Aichen Nor. Moreover, we obtained confirmation of our surmise that we were not far from a monastery that Krebs knew, Borildje Kure.

By this time the whole caravan was a deplorable sight. The oxen were almost at the end of their tether, the caravan men on the verge of mutiny, and Krebs and Buffalo limping and hardly able to walk for the pain in their frozen feet. The Chinaman, Ping, lay in a kind of lethargy on the top of his wagon when he was not groaning in his sleeping sack. And it was still a long way to Bulgun Tal.

We now promised the caravan drivers that if they brought our goods to Borildje Kure we would release them from their contract and that they would get an extra payment into the bargain. We took along a Mongol from Aicha Nor as guide, and after three more

ON TO THE NORTH-WEST

painful days we at last arrived at the friendly monastery. It was high time.

WE hired a fenced yard with two warm felt tents from the friendly lamas and got a whole Mongol family to attend on us. Warm fires burned in the tent day and night, we slaughtered sheep, and Krebs operated on his own and Buffalo's toes. They both lay " in bed " in their sleeping sacks, and I, who was fit, employed the days of rest in examining the mysterious interior of the temple.

The monastery was built on a slope with its front towards a large steppe to the south. As background it had the wooded hill-sides intersected by wild ravines. It consisted of nine *dugun* (temple buildings) and around them, concealed behind high palings, lay innumerable small mud huts and felt tents which were the dwellings of the six hundred lamas attached to the monastery. Divine service was conducted in one or more of the temples during almost every hour of the twenty-four.

I ventured up to the open doors of the temple to observe the unfamiliar and fascinating scene. The huge room lay in mysterious twilight, illuminated only by the flickering, uncertain light from lotus-shaped candelabra upon the altar at the back. From the altar and the walls hung multitudes of painted temple banners and artfully embroidered draperies whose clear colours shifted in the flickering candle-light. Far off one could dimly perceive the contours of a gigantic gilded image of Buddha and of other more fantastic gods, and images of lamaistic saints. The central aisle of the Hall of the Gods was flanked on either side by chanting lamas, who sat cross-legged on yellow cushions. Next the entrance sat small *shabi* (disciples) who accompanied the lamas' chant upon drums, trumpets and cymbals.

In the vestibules to the temple halls the walls were decked with fantastic mural paintings, symbolizing all the saints and spirits worshipped by the Mongols, whether in gratitude for benefits received or from fear of future misfortunes. There are also paintings in which some lama artist has used his brush to illustrate moral maxims.

On a sunlit wall I found a " wheel of life " painted in flaming colours, and recognized it from the description of the old lama in Kipling. And there was the lamaistic version of the original Buddhistic legend that exhorts to concord. A large bird is plucking the most delicious fruits from a tall tree. He is sitting on the head of a hare, and the hare in his turn is sitting on his hind legs upon the upstretched hands of an ape, while the ape strains upward from the back of an elephant. Separately the four animals would not be able to reach the tempting fruit, but by mutual aid they all get what they desire.

The friendly lamas succeeded in getting together a caravan for our continued journey to Bulgun Tal, and we got them to make us caps, mittens and boots of warm lamb-skin, and long, soft, light antelope-skin coats.

When we had stayed a week at the monastery we could delay no longer. We must go forward to our steppe, forward to Shishkin's warm stove and lovely Russian food, forward to our goal. So we started on the last stage of our journey and were swallowed up by a canyon leading into a river valley, and this in its turn debouched into Egin Gol, the river that flows through Bulgun Tal.

The landscape was the most beautiful we had hitherto seen, with stately forests on all sides and innumerable tracks of every kind of game in the snow. It was cold, but the sun shone and the forest gave shelter from the wind.

For four days we made long marches. By the huge evening camp fires we enjoyed the natural surroundings, the stars over our heads, the smell of wood-smoke from the fire, but above all we rejoiced in the thought of all the hardships and anxieties we had now left behind us, and the consciousness that we were now on the threshold of our goal. " We're almost there now," said Krebs. And we sat long by the fire, preparing ourselves for the meeting with our new home.

BOOK II

CHAPTER I

THE ARRIVAL AT BULGUN TAL

NEXT morning we were awakened very early by the impatient Krebs, and at daybreak we were on our way towards the north. We left the tardy caravan behind us at the camping-place.

Buffalo and Ping drove our two horse wagons, while Krebs and I trotted ahead tracing and clearing a way through the deep snow and the fallen giants of the forest. The northward slope of the ground became more and more pronounced the farther we travelled, the valley opened out and the frozen surface of the Tichang River grew wider and wider. Here and there the undercurrent of the river had pushed up through the ice, forming cascades of water that steamed in the cold air. The water " boils ", the Mongols say. It is, of course, ice cold, but relatively to the air it is warm and it steams like boiling water. The spray had congealed on the surrounding bushes in long icicles, and the mighty rime-covered trees at the foot of savage, rugged precipices were a splendid sight in the blinding sunlight.

The forest became less wild and the distance between the trees greater. We came to an opening, sloping down to a narrow belt of forest that stretched from east to west. Krebs stopped the wagons and peered round him. His eyes were shining with the joy of recognition and we, Buffalo and I, were full of expectation. Ping thrust his nose out of the depths of his furs and asked if we were there at last. He read the answer in our glance and breathed more freely.

Then we drove almost at a gallop down to the belt of wood and pushed through it. There we saw a snow-covered sheet of ice some sixty feet wide, winding away between high banks in both directions, to be afterwards concealed by projecting points to east and west. It was Egin Gol, our river, and on the other side of it lay Bulgun Tal, the goal of our journey and our longing. We laughed and shrieked and thumped each other on the back and generally behaved as boyishly as one tends to do when one is really happy. Our enthusiasm infected the phlegmatic Ping and the exhausted horses.

Bulgun Tal was hidden by the belt of trees on the other side of the river, and one last little obstacle still lay in our path, for a six-foot torrent rushed roaring down the middle of the river. But we unloaded the wagons and threw bridges across the channel and soon were happily over the river with our horses, carts and goods, and through the belt of trees, at the edge of which we stopped to survey the steppe in front of us.

It was " wide and fair " like the plateau on which the castle of Utgård Loki stood.

Krebs spied earnestly in a particular direction and passed the glasses to us. Far out to the eastward, at a point where the butter-yellow steppe reached right up to Egin Gol, some dark spots were visible which must be Shishkin's place. But peer as we would we could not see the inviting pillar of smoke of which we had dreamt so long and which should have assured us that a warm fireside awaited us at the end of our long, laborious journey.

Once more the steppe resounded with the thunder of our galloping horses and the rattle of our jolting wagons —a silent steppe upon which no tent sent up friendly smoke and no cattle were grazing. We galloped through long grass that bore witness to the fact that no cattle nor any herds of horses had grazed there during the summer. We rode past stone-paved grave mounds that told of a long extinct and forgotten people who had lived and worked on the plateau. And we ended our ride at a farmstead whose dismantled house and blackened timbers told of the destruction of a scarcely founded Russian colony. Begrimed and smashed objects of western origin lay scattered among the ruins. Dead

ARRIVAL AT BULGUN TAL

remains of cattle testified to violence. Half-burnt sheets of written paper were a reminder of the life which had been. And we called to mind Krebs's account of the family that had expected and prepared for our arrival at Bulgun Tal—the hard-working old colonist, the capable, kindly housewife and the two plucky young Cossack sons.

But the whole undulating steppe lay awaiting us within its setting of dark, wooded hills, still reddened by the glow of the setting sun. And distant, snow-clad peaks shone rosy red, bestowing fortitude and confidence. Krebs sprang up on to the highest point of the ruin and planted there our sun-bleached, wind-torn Danish flag, and nine measured shots from our three heavy calibre pistols sounded over the steppe, proclaiming that the place was now ours. And we gave our new property the name of Igagården.

The horses started and danced, and Ping turned pale, so far as was possible through the dirt on his yellow face. He was ready to faint with terror, and let go his horse which disappeared at a wild gallop out on to the steppe.

We shall never forget that day. It was November 18th, 1923, and eight months to a day after our departure from Denmark.

THE caravan arrived next day, and as soon as the carts were unloaded, the friendly lamas turned back to their monastery and left us in solitude at Bulgun Tal. These were splendid days. The blows of axe and hammer and the rasping sound of saws, like a song of rejoicing, awakened the place to new life. During the work of clearance it appeared that two of the houses could be restored without overmuch labour. Our black oxen hauled such of the beams and planks as had not been destroyed out of the ruins, and we piled them according to size and length. All that could not be used were carted out to the river by Ping, and we soon had a room made habitable with the help of Chinese mats and felts. It was a great advance on living in the draughty tent.

Next we made a large *ambar* (storehouse) under cover, into which all our goods were dragged into safety from snow storms. So soon as we had got the most necessary

ARRIVAL AT BULGUN TAL

arrangements made, Krebs and I began to explore the district, while Buffalo was left as " commandant " of the homestead and " chief " of the meteorological station which we had established.

The farm lay down by the river on its northern bank. This was now covered with thick ice, but in summer, Krebs explained, it forms a sixty-foot channel with about six feet of crystal-clear water from the mountains. To the north and east the steppe sloped evenly up to the wooded hills, and due south there was an island covered with trees and scrub between the Egin River itself and a branch which was kept open all winter by hot springs. In the brushwood on the island, red and black currants were growing, and since there had been no one to pick them in the summer, they were still hanging frozen on the boughs. On the other side of the " warm " branch stream the real forest began and stretched for miles to the south, east and west.

We took samples of the soil in various places with spade and pick and made grandiose plans. We made a sketch-map showing ploughed fields and meadows, and marked the place where the plough should first be set in the earth, where the irrigation channels could be laid and where dams would be necessary. Much and heavy labour lay before us, but labour that promised good results.

After a week's stay on the farm, Krebs set off on the expedition's best horse, " Mads ". It was necessary for him to get into touch with the members of the expedition still at home, and then there was the post awaiting us at Irkutsk, where it had been taken charge of by the Danish telegraphist of " The Great Northern."

CHAPTER II
PIONEER LIFE, EXORCISM AND RUSSIAN BATHS

WHEN Krebs had left us, Buffalo and I came to a tacit agreement that he should find the place a pleasant surprise on his return, and the consciousness that Christmas was at hand was a further inducement to us to work at making the place as soon as possible worthy of the name of home.

One day we received a visit from some Buriats in hunting dress, who asserted that they were skilful in the art of building, and we availed ourselves of their help. They vanished into the north on their little horses to return next day with large primitive axes in their belts. They were Tunka Buriats, Baldan, Boldon and the latter's foster son Yalserai. They had fled from their own district during the revolution and had settled a couple of years back in a peaceful spot on the fringe of the forest at the northern corner of the steppe.

With wondering eyes they watched us unpacking crates of modern American implements, which we demonstrated to them, but never succeeded in teaching them, with the exception of Yalserai, to use. They could do everything with their own big axes in a masterly fashion.

Buffalo and I had now assumed the rôle of unskilled labourers, and spent the days in hauling windfallen treetrunks from the forest to the Buriats' working place by the houses, which were ceasing to look like ruins. As the work went on we unpacked from our many crates such things as we needed. Yalserai, who was the most efficient joiner, specialized in making doors and windows, which the handy Buffalo glazed from our stock of window glass and putty.

When Buffalo and I had got out a large enough supply

of logs from the forest we set to work on the preparations for re-erecting the palisading that had been burnt down. It was a difficult and tedious job, for the temperature now fell as low as $-35°$ C., and the ground was consequently frozen to a great depth. Every evening before sunset we lighted a row of fires on the spots where the posts were to be driven into the ground, and at sunrise we were out working at the thawed earth crust. Since the posts had to be sunk far into the ground, and we only managed to go down a foot or so in the twenty-four hours, the work proceeded very slowly.

But in order to be able to work hard ourselves and to fill many stomachs, we had to have food, and our scanty provisions soon came to an end. Early one morning I rode out with Yalserai, who led me to a little river gorge among the mountains north of the steppe where we found a large Mongol camp. We bought two big oxen from the Mongols and slaughtered them next day at the farm, cutting them up before the meat froze. We lived for a long time like fighting cocks on beef and broth, and tea sweetened with saccharin. We throve splendidly on this unvaried diet, but it had the oddest effect on our digestion.

One day in the course of the clearance work I found some blackened photographs. In the evening I showed them to Yalserai, and he was able to tell us about the tragic fate that had overtaken the persons whose faces smiled at me from the portraits in my hand.

Old Shishkin had toiled and built, looking forward to and preparing for our coming to Bulgun Tal. But one day General Kasagrenin had arrived there with a detachment of Baron Ungern-Sternberg's guerillas and had been agreeably surprised suddenly to find, after a long expedition in the Mongolian wilderness, a substantial house with provisions and warm hearths. After a stay of a few days the freebooters had left Bulgun Tal, taking with them all Shishkin's cattle, as well as his two young sons, whom they impressed as soldiers. But Kasagrenin and his people had scarcely set out for Van Kure before the first party of Red Guards appeared. Shishkin and his wife, however, had succeeded in escaping from them, but the Reds, in their rage at finding all the cattle and provisions taken by the enemy, had sacked the farm and left the place a smoking heap of ruins. Nothing had been heard at Bulgun Tal of the fate of Shishkin and his wife, but one of the sons had been captured by a Red guerilla band and dragged to death behind a galloping horse.

Another colonist, Spiegel, had been robbed of his cattle by the Bolsheviks, on which ground the exasperated White Guards later hanged him. We had never met these colonists, but in the course of the years Krebs had told us so much about the friends who awaited us at Bulgun Tal, that we felt as though we were hearing of the tragic fate of old comrades.

Yalserai, Boldon's foster son, was a tall young trapper of twenty-two. He had himself been pressed into the ranks of the White Guards and had taken part in many battles under Baron Ungern, but after the latter's capture by the Bolsheviks near Kiachta, he had succeeded in escaping back to Bulgun Tal. He spoke Russian fluently, but felt nothing but loathing and contempt for all that bore the name of Russian, White as well as Red.

He soon became good friends with us, and since he was not only a handy worker but also intelligent and willing to learn, he became very useful to us. Every evening we "kept school", Buffalo, Yalserai and I. With the aid of a Russian dictionary, pencils, paper and multifarious gesticulations we all three made good progress and daily increased our vocabulary by about five-and-twenty words. Yalserai was soon able to count in Danish and when he came and asked us for a tool or something of the kind he almost always did so in pure Danish. And Buffalo and I made out small Danish-Mongolian lists of words which we kept always in our pockets, and with the help of these we got along in our daily intercourse with the Mongols. This, of course, was part of the surprise we were preparing against the return of Krebs.

ONE day Buffalo and I agreed that it must be Sunday, and we celebrated the day by searching the neighbourhood for a worthy flagstaff. It was not easy, for we had to have the tallest and straightest available. At last we found a majestic fir to our liking and hewed at it with our American field axes till it fell with a crash in a cloud of fine snow.

Ping, who relished a place by the fire, acted as cook. He put his whole Chinese soul into the work and asked every day whether the meat was cooked to our complete satisfaction, for he was in deadly fear of being transferred to some work outside the ice-covered windows of the house.

But then one day the first trappers came to the farm with their splendid catch of furs, and Ping had to go out in the snow to look them over. His otherwise so stony and unfathomable mask lighted up at the sight of ermine and silver fox, his mercenary eyes gleamed, and he caressingly stroked the glossy pelts with slender, long-nailed fingers.

Ping bought the trappers' whole catch and it was as if life from that day acquired a certain interest for him too. A two-roomed house was built and provided with felt-lined doors and double windows, and here Ping was appointed ruler. With the carpenter's assistance he soon got a warm stove set up, the walls covered with shelves and a long shop-counter erected which divided the front room into two parts. In the inner room sleeping places were contrived for Ping and our carpenters.

For several days Ping now boldly defied the cold and stood on his head in the boxes and bales of the *ambar* from which he extracted *dalimba*, *suyemba* and *siandaba* [1] (cotton cloths of different qualities), fragrant brick tea and *dunsa* tobacco, powder, lead and many other things attractive to the Mongols.

We had sometimes to go and look at Ping in his wonderful shop, the like of which was not to be found within hundreds of miles, and he beamed against the background of his well-furnished shelves. Chinese paper pictures hung on the walls and many coloured advertisements of multifarious goods which Mongolia knew not of and which we had not on sale. These Ping had brought with him from China and had put

[1] From the Chinese *Shantung-ta-pu*.

in his wagon to strike Bulgun Tal with wonder and amazement. And he succeeded admirably, for new trappers came to us every day and there were crowds for days on end in Ping's picturesque *p'u-tse* (shop).

ONE day two old Mongols arrived at the farm. They were lamas and wore dignified red robes under their long yellow sheepskin coats. The elder looked friendly, though nervous, while the younger was a vociferous person whose appearance inspired less confidence. Because of his attributes, Buffalo conferred upon the latter the title of " The Trumpet ", and he bore the name for long. But the two lamas came in the cause of friendship, and in God's name, to inform us that we must at once move our dwelling to another place, because the spot where we now dwelt was accursed and infested by the most malevolent demons. Many ill deeds had been done here, blood had flowed and fire laid waste, until the whole steppe had been abandoned by man and beast, and a frightful fate awaited us if we sought to defy the dominant and destructive spirits of the steppe. They said a great deal about the things that might happen to us if we did not move—gruesome things. But we were hard to persuade, and they felt obliged to stay for several days, during which we entertained them royally with tea and beef.

We continued building work at full speed, but we observed that our people had been upset by the lamas' talk. Something clearly had to be done. And we did it.

Three days after the coming of the lamas the palisade was finished, a three foot edifice of massive logs, surrounding our dwelling-place on all sides. In the middle of the enclosure stood the tall pine-trunk, reaching half-way to heaven, with a long halyard passed through a block at its top.

In his collection of " objects of value "—Krebs called them toys—Buffalo had a watch which was a marvel. It was in the form of a pocket watch, but demanded a pocket of considerable size, since it measured three inches in diameter and three quarters of an inch in thickness. But then from this watch one could not only tell the hour, minute and second, but its round and richly decorated face showed also the month, the day of the week and the date. And, further, there was in the face a little star-decked hole through which one saw the moon, and it was so marvellously constructed that the moon on the clock face rotated exactly like the real moon and one could see through the hole whether the real moon was new or old, waning or waxing. It was a wonderful watch which, in Buffalo's eyes, was superior to all Krebs's intricate and bulky scientific instruments, and we others, with the exception of Krebs, had several times delighted Buffalo with remarks to the effect that perhaps it was worth the trouble of dragging about if only it went properly. But it did not, for the combined effect of the fine sand of Gobi and the severe cold between Van Kure and Bulgun Tal had been that its complicated mechanism had ceased to function.

Now, however, Buffalo found a long desired occasion to exhibit his " watch " to a more appreciative public than we had been, and he sat up the greater part of the night thawing it out and cleaning it. And in the morning the watch was going. Since we did not know either the hour, the day or the date, we could not set it with certainty, but we got the moon right, and the hands all went round, and the whole bag of tricks ticked and ticked, and that, for the moment, was the main thing.

In the morning we drank tea with our lama guests in Ping's picture-hung pavilion, and there we found opportunity to exhibit some small proofs of our own power. The Mongols knew sugar only in the form in which they bought it from the scattered Chinese traders, crystals of very little sweetening power, of which one has to use big pieces to overcome the bitter flavour of the brick tea. We now demonstrated how, by putting an infinitely little bit of *our* sugar into the cup, we could change the bitter taste to the sweetest imaginable. It made a deep impression on the lamas, and we foresaw big business in saccharine in the future.

Then Buffalo performed some of his best conjuring tricks and card tricks, which, both to his own and the spectators' astonishment, all came off. Buffalo, carried away by his success, would have gone on for ever, and I had to kick his shins at an opportune moment to induce him to stop while still in his glory.

The appropriate moment had now come for the demonstration of the watch, and it made a deep impression on the high lamas. They saw for the first time a sort of living horoscope by which anyone could read for himself all that they must employ long and laborious hours to gather from fat books. And then Buffalo pressed a catch, and the watch struggled painfully through half of a bygone popular melody. But the priests, who did not know it, thought they were getting the whole tune in correct time, so all went off splendidly.

Afterwards we all went out into the yard where Yalserai was standing ready by the flagstaff. There was a shout that made everyone turn towards us, axe and hammer ceased work and a cloth slowly unfolded as it rose and rose towards the sky, a sort of strange prayer-flag divided by a white band into four quarters, and the quarters were of the sacred red colour. A cold gust made the Dannebrog flap merrily in the frosty air.

Then we employed our whole Mongolian vocabulary and Yalserai's assistance to explain to the two priests that beneath the cloth floating up there one need not fear the demons and their wrath.

After a few more cups of tea the priests departed pondering deeply, but that joy and satisfaction might be mutual, we agreed that some lamas should come from the neighbouring monastery of Odagna Kure to ward off the wrath of the demons by their own method of several days' *nom* (prayer reading). And that this *nom* should be really effective we offered a good price for it by promising ten large cakes of brick-tea to the monastery.

A couple of days later several lamas came from the monastery and at once began their weighty work. All over the yard and its vicinity there was a ringing of bells, a drumming and a chanting, and in the end we had to put the hungry lamas on reduced rations to induce them to go back to their monastery.

One day Buffalo discovered a mirror at the bottom of one of his trunks and found to his great astonishment that his appearance was just as comical as mine. And the contemplation of my own reflection brought me to a similar conclusion. Up till then each of us had wondered how the other could go about looking like a golliwog, but, finding now that we ourselves were equally dirty, bearded, frost-bitten and unkempt, we agreed that something must be done about it in the hygienic interest of the community.

Down by the river there lay the broken-down remnant of a Russian bath, and upon this we now concentrated our efforts. It took us three days to get the stones of the furnace into place, to lay the roof and replace the burnt beams with new ones, and Yalserai needed a week to make a new door and window frames and to glaze the windows.

Then came the historic day on which we took our first steam bath at Bulgun Tal. From early in the morning and all through the forenoon the furnace, in whose opening big boulders had been laid, was kept stoked. The furnace was about four feet six high and above it was built in a Chinese pan some three feet in diameter. As the water in this boiled, it was poured into buckets which were placed in the hot room. Soap and other almost forgotten toilet requisites had been dug out of the boxes, and the most splendid wood-wool pulled out of the cases in which delicate articles were packed.

At midday the fire was drawn from the furnace, and Buffalo and I stepped out of twenty degrees of frost into the hot room. Water was thrown on the red-hot stones in the furnace which at once emitted a gush of steam that made us gasp for breath. The sweat beaded and poured off us and we saw clear proof that we were not clean. Half of the bath-house was taken up by a *k'ang* (platform) two feet high, and on this we lay panting and watched with mingled alarm and gratification the quantity of dirt of which the steam relieved our pores. When we had swilled down, soaped ourselves, scraped ourselves and swilled down again for several hours we were thoroughly clean and enjoyed putting on clean clothes, and the new furs that our Buriats' womenfolk had made for us.

The dress was practical and light, and greatly to be preferred to the heavy sheepskins and felt boots. We now put on, besides woollen underclothing and stockings, breeches and short coats of antelope skin with the hair inside, *unti*, a sort of long stockings of the same material also with the hair inside, and soled with a piece of thick oxhide, and big dogskin caps. On our hands we wore long-cuffed lambskin gloves. In this light and supple costume we could get along all winter while working, but if we went for a ride we had to wear our colossal sheepskins over these clothes—and still froze.

The steam bath aroused our ambition to smarten up both ourselves and our surroundings. We plunged again into boxes and trunks and there discovered articles which we or our friends had packed there nine months earlier—so long ago and in so different a world. We cut each other's hair and trimmed our long, full beards. Mine looked absurd and was bleached like a west-coast fisherman's, Buffalo's was coal black and dignified, like that of a Russian Grand Duke.

All day long we were collecting supplies from the forest ; logs for fuel and timber, moss to thatch the house, and frozen berries to use for Christmas sweets. In the mornings before sunrise we went with Yalserai up into the chill valleys among the mountains in quest of roe deer ; we sat with Ping by the hour learning to value furs, and in the evenings we " kept school " with Yalserai. When three houses had been roofed in and provided with doors and windows, we set our carpenters to boarding the floors. We learned also from these forest people much that was necessary for our new life in the wilds. They taught us to fell trees with a minimum of axe work, to take aim with the axe and to hit the spot aimed at, as well as to drop the tree in the desired direction. And we were soon able to cut them into building logs with the axe and to dovetail the corners.

Then Buffalo and I set to work on our own house. Our axe strokes sang " home ", and our little log-house was shaped in gladness, and as the work went forward our love for this pioneer home of ours grew. We took stones from the ruins of the former house, and built with them the noblest feature of a house, a great open hearth. The roof timbers were covered with a foot of earth from what we had dug out for the fence posts. We rammed moss between the logs of the wall, and the door was lined with felt. Along one wall we built a long bunk three planks in width, and there we had our sleeping places, end on. At our bedheads we hung the two photographs that had accompanied us through the whole journey. With Yalserai's help we made a long table and a bench. We hung the walls with the skins of the deer we shot and curtained the window with gaily coloured stuff " bought " in Ping's shop, bought because the stock belonged to our little company and Ping had to account for it. Then Buffalo and I dragged our private trunks into our new home. In their limited space lay what we were fondest of and the memories to which we clung most firmly, and from now on the log-house became even more dear and homelike to us.

Buffalo's concertina was there and my banjo, the books we could read over and over again and never tire of, and there were things that we kept in little locked boxes. In the evenings we sat with our wheezing pipes by the flickering firelight and transported ourselves to far off places and to times vanished but not forgotten. Or we renewed memories of merry times and called in music to bring back happy festivals. Or again we listened to the creaking and booming of the river ice, to the melancholy singing of the Buriats and the howling of the wolves among the hills, now close, now far away, but always on the same ringing, uniform and long-drawn note. And we joyed in the work we had done during the day and made plans for the morrow and for many days to come.

But we never felt homesick and never repented the step we had taken.

It was the Christmas month, and now we longed for Krebs. By our reckoning he ought to have been back by now. The thought that he was bringing seven months' mail with him made us the more impatient, and

PIONEER LIFE

the knowledge that he had ridden into the country of the Bolsheviks made us uneasy as the days went on beyond the calculated time.

Our largest log-house, which was fifty-two feet by twenty-two, was christened " The Mess ". The house was divided into two rooms by a massive log wall. The smaller of these was reserved for Krebs, and the larger, which was a regular banqueting hall, was fitted up as the " holy of holies " of the community. In the log wall that divided the two rooms our Buriats had built a big open grate of granite. It occupied half the wall and was built with sides sloping to the top like a Norwegian " *peis* ". The room had five windows. These made it very cold in spite of double sashes. For this reason, besides the *peis*, we set up in the middle of the room a sheet iron stove that we had brought with us. In front of the hearth lay a large bearskin that the trappers had brought us from the mountains.

In the middle of one wall stood a Chinese chest, six feet long, with massive brass mountings, a gift from our friends in China, and upon it stood two brass flagstaffs which, with the hand-sewn Danish flags, were a present from Scandinavian ladies in China. Above the chest hung a large flag with the royal cypher in gold. This had accompanied Krebs in the last Russo-Polish war and waved over his ambulance. In each of the four corners of the room hung Chinese lanterns carved from black wood and with artistically painted panels.

Our carpenters had made a long dining-table, two long benches and a " gramophone table ", which was placed in the warmest corner of the room. Our gramophone would not, in fact, endure cold. When we had unpacked it and wound it up as far as the spring would go, it refused to work, and it took several days to thaw it out by the fire before it became usable. It now stood, fully efficient, in the " musical corner " of the room, and only two of the records had been broken on the long and trying journey. In the " literary corner " the walls were covered with bookshelves, and here the expedition's archives and library were disposed. The table and benches occupied the fourth corner which constituted the eating recess, and to the right of the entrance door were hooks for coats.

The fire in the grate was kept up day and night to warm the room in view of Christmas and the arrival of Krebs—it did in fact warm both the dining-hall and his room. And Buffalo and I went about enjoying the pleasant change that had come over this demon-haunted place and the thought of the astonishment of Krebs on his return.

But Krebs did not come.

THE trappers went on bringing us more and more furs and we had now so many that we had to begin packing them in bales of fifty skins, ready for transport to Urga. Time after time Ping sold out the contents of his shelves and fresh goods had to be fetched from the *ambar*. The number of trading trappers grew with every day, and when they returned to the wilderness they carried with them the news of our arrival.

The smoke rose daily from the three chimneys vertically to the sky, the flag floated over the yard and every day the thermometer sank lower.

The noble hunting dog we had got from Larson could not stand the severe cold and had to be kept indoors, but " Hudcha ", the " tiger " from Gobi, grew a tremendous coat and became twice as big and terrible to behold.

CHAPTER III
CHRISTMAS AT BULGUN TAL

THE night before Christmas Eve, Buffalo and I were sitting alone in our log-house, deep in thought. We had decided that if Krebs did not come within three days, one of us would try to ride to Irkutsk to make enquiries about him. Neither of us was very strong on Russian or Mongolian, and Krebs had taken with him the expedition's only map of the district to the northward. We knew that it meant crossing snow-clad mountains and icy passes, and Krebs had told us that he had recorded temperatures as low as $-54°$ C. in those parts. We could not take any of our Buriats with us, since they were refugees from Russian jurisdiction and dared not enter Soviet territory. Buffalo was still lame from his frozen foot and new flakes of skin came off his toes daily, so it was I who had to prepare for the journey. I packed up the light outfit recommended by Yalserai, and he made from memory a sketch of the way I had to follow.

But first we were to keep Christmas. Buffalo had dug up a cardboard box containing a Christmas tree eight inches high, adorned with miniature Christmas candles and Christmas ornaments. We put this on the table in the great hall at the Mess, and it was to form the centre of the morrow's festivities. Then we turned in, and the whole place slept.

We were suddenly awakened by the violent barking of the dogs, and immediately afterwards the voices of the Buriats could be heard from the yard. We wriggled out of our snug sleeping sacks, slipped quickly into our leather clothing and ran out into the darkness. It was bitterly cold and the snow crackled and crunched under our feet. Hudcha barked and rushed along the palisade out towards the steppe. We succeeded in catching him and for a brief moment there was silence while we held a coat over his muzzle. The night was dead silent, but soon we heard a far-off shout—a signal that we recognized.

At once there was general rejoicing, for the shout signified that Krebs had come back from Irkutsk, back from the unknown. A lantern was run up to the top of the flagstaff, the Buriats hurried to light fires in the grates, and Ping squashed his flat nose even flatter against the frosted window of the *p'u-tse*. The shouts came nearer; soon we heard the trampling of many horses in the snow, and Hudcha's rage gave way to tail-wagging, as Krebs and his cavalcade rode in through the gates in the palisade opened wide to receive them. Five horses, two of which carried riders, pulled up in the yard, steaming and covered with rime.

"Hullo, boys!" came cheerily from the bearded Krebs, and we stared at the other rider, whom we did not know. "Good day," said the latter in broad, rough Jylland dialect. And we shook hands cordially with Isager, the Jyllander member of the expedition who on this night before Christmas Eve was made heartily welcome to our party. The two newcomers looked like veritable Father Christmases in their long fur coats with ice hanging in bunches from their beards. Krebs was holding a snowy cedar tree [1] to his breast, a greeting from the northern pass, designed to serve as a Christmas tree. The three packhorses carried bulging saddlebags which we brought into the Mess, in which Krebs and Isager were to be quartered for the night. Krebs had the mail with him, but despite all our prayers we did not get it. It was to be kept for Christmas Eve.

Next morning we were all up early, and Buffalo and

[1] Our Russians called this tree *kedr* which is the name of a kind of cedar occurring in Siberia. In 1925 I met a Balti employed by the new Mongolian Government as forestry expert. From my description of this tree he expressed the opinion that it must be a species of cedar which he knew was to be found in the district round Hubso Gol. Professor Carl Scottsberg is, however, of the opinion that it cannot possibly be a cedar, but is *pinus siberia*.

CHRISTMAS AT BULGUN TAL

I exhibited the place with pride; the flag on its tall mast, Ping's well-stocked shop, the valuable furs in the *ambar*, and the Russian bath which was giving forth its heat and would be in condition to receive the new guests before dinner. Krebs was delighted with the results attained and impressed by the apparent ease with which we conversed with the Mongols. Isager said in reply to our questions that he found the place quite nice. We soon realized that this was the highest degree of approval that one could extract from the dour Jyllander.

But when the exhibition was over Buffalo and I found ourselves homeless in our own place. Krebs and Ping ran to and fro between the *p'u-tse* and the Mess, but we were refused admission to either place.

But even this short day, that seemed so long, came to an end, and the time for the Christmas dinner, to which Krebs and Isager had invited us in the Mess, approached. The bath-house had been in use all day, and we were clean and spruce. Hair and beards had been clipped and water-combed unendingly, and then we plunged once more into our trunks, at the bottom of which our best clothes lay buried.

An hour before dinner we were ready and imbued with the holiday spirit. I sat silent, overcome with admiration of Buffalo. He was in " long and white " and from his broad chest gleamed the insignia of the " Defence Brotherhood ", and on the lapel of his coat tinkled orders sparkling in emulation of the brilliants in his shirt front. His hands were gloved in white, and his crush hat was tilted at a gallant angle. He looked more than ever like a very great Grand Duke, and Mongolia had certainly never seen his like. With a fatherly air he set right my black tie and simple dinner-jacket. And, whistling a pot-pourri of the Copenhagen successes of the last ten years, he glided across the floor in an easy waltz step while he related over his shoulder a little adventure from the last occasion of his wearing those glad rags. And many other adventures and experiences were brought to life in his memory by that costume.

CHRISTMAS AT BULGUN TAL

On the stroke of six Ping stuck his nose in and asked if we would give the Mess the honour of our company at Christmas dinner. " Hurrah ! " yelled Buffalo, and in our thin clothes we ran over to the Mess. Our patent leather shoes crunched and crackled in the cold snow.

The Mess was a miracle. Christmas presents for the expedition had come on the three packhorses as well as candles and other pretty things that Krebs had got from kindly compatriots at the Irkutsk telegraph station. The hall was resplendent with candles, wreaths and other finery. The bare places on the walls had been draped with fabrics in gay oriental colours. In the middle of the floor the dark cedar was majestically enthroned as a Christmas tree, blazing with candles and tinsel. In the " literary corner " of the hall stood a table weighed down with presents and letters from friends, and our longing gaze was at once directed to it.

But first we were to dine. The table looked unfamiliar and inapproachable in its gleaming white damask. It was decked with candles and gnomes. Our dinner service was the finest " Bing and Gröndhal ", a gift from the factory in Copenhagen to the expedition and was now taken into use for the first time. Spoons, knives and forks were of heavy solid silver which Krebs had acquired at a bargain at the Jewish market in Irkutsk. Monograms and armorial bearings indicated that they were a part of the revolution's loot from the abolished aristocracy. Ping waited at table and acted as boy. The Buriats stood in the open doorway to the side room surveying with wonder the four festally clad *noyan* sitting on benches round a table more brilliantly lighted and more richly spread with sacrificial gifts than the altar in front of the highest god in their little temple. A wonderful picture in the midst of darkest Asia.

Of course we had a rice porridge, and since we had neither goose nor turkey with which to eat the apples and prunes that we nevertheless had, we used those fruits instead of the cinnamon that our porridge lacked. Splendid, rich, cold Mongolian milk replaced the sugared

CHRISTMAS AT BULGUN TAL

Christmas ale. The other dish was roast ox tongue with melted butter. As a substitute for potatoes we used fried bread. After the meal we drank coffee from Irkutsk with which excellent pancakes, the work of Ping, were served. Then we wished one another a happy Christmas in excellent punch compounded by Buffalo of arrack, saccharine, frozen berries and raisins. It skinned our throats, but warmed us and did us good.

We sang two Christmas hymns beside the lighted Christmas tree. Isager passed round some " Plantadores " he had brought, and each was then left to himself with his mass of greetings and gifts from home and friends.

It was silent in the room, and our thoughts went home to Denmark. I lay for a long time on the bearskin going through my seven months' mail. There were many precious letters, so it took time. But from two of my nearest, the two who last took farewell of me and who had most cordially wished me au revoir, there was no letter—from them I should receive letters never any more.

It was late at night when I walked back under the glittering stars to my home, and round about me the wolves of forest and mountain were tuning up their songs of love.

We celebrated Christmas with three days' holiday.

CHAPTER IV

THE STEPPE BECOMES OUR HOME

THE delicacies that Krebs had brought from Irkutsk lasted over the New Year, after which we returned to our two daily meals of meat, though we improved it by a daily variation. In the mornings we ate boiled meat and soup, and in the evenings we roasted the meat and omitted the soup.

WHILE Buffalo watched over the farm, we others tramped round the surrounding country to determine where we ought first to set the plough in the virgin soil, and where it would be necessary to fence in the crops against the cattle. And many other questions arose.

Isager had come as a new message from the outer world and we made him tell us about it in the evenings. He had to whistle the last summer's tunes for Buffalo, and soon the Mess resounded with Buffalo's concertina playing the languishing strains of " The Nautch Girl ".

Of course we celebrated New Year's Eve also, though in other fashion than Christmas. Lest we should acquire " genteel habits ", Krebs had decreed that evening dress was to be worn only once a year, at Christmas, and on very special occasions. Such would be those on which the expedition's Bible came into use, namely marriage, baptism and burial. The expedition did, in fact, possess a Bible, a large and imposing one, which was kept in the big Chinese chest among the objects which formed the foundation of the new community.

On New Year's Eve we drank the remainder of Buffalo's " punch ". We drank to three things that are higher than all else, we shook hands as men and comrades, and when the clock struck twelve we went out and fired a triple salvo from four rifles.

THE STEPPE BECOMES OUR HOME

THE New Year came in with cold, and Buffalo's temperature curve fell daily. Soon it was down at —40° C. But the woods were full of fuel, and when there was no sun in the sky we crept in to the fire. We went early to bed. Some slept under sheets and blankets, others in Spartan goatskin bags. Buffalo's bed was magnificent, a regular bed of paradise, and he was constantly hitting upon new improvements. He was obliged to be an early riser, for he had to go to his meteorological station and read the instruments and enter the figures and observations in the journal. The Mongols took a great interest in Buffalo's reading of the apparatus, and his attempts to explain them to the natives were often funny, but always practical. It was the thermometer that interested them most, for they could understand its significance.

The Mongols at Bulgun Tal had learnt from the Buriats to use the Russian weights, according to which a *pud* (36 lb.) is divided into forty *funt*. For lack of a better, Buffalo used this method of reckoning when he wanted to explain to the Mongols how cold it had been at night. And some of the Mongols soon learned to read the thermometer themselves and announced to the others that the night had been thirty-five *funt* cold. One day it was said on the farm that the night before had been a whole *pud* cold (" *Nighen pud hütün beina* "), and from that day all the Mongols described the complicated system as " *Halun hütün tsak* "—the hot-cold clock.

The first meal of the day was eaten in Buffalo's and my house, and when the sun lighted up the tree tops we went out to our work. The most popular job in very cold weather was felling trees. The hewing warmed one up, and it developed into a regular sport among us. When a mighty larch tree crashed over, Isager regarded it with the satisfied air of a connoisseur. " That's worth all of three hundred crowns ", he would say to the bystanders, dreaming himself back to his native place, Gudenaa, where he would soon have become a millionaire by the sale of all our forest giants at three hundred crowns apiece. When the trees had been felled the branches were trimmed off, and then the oxen hauled them home.

In the evenings we explained to the carpenters our drawings for contemplated new construction, and they carried out skilfully all that we required of them. If it was a complicated thing that had to be made, we made small wooden models, and if they had not understood the drawings they could always work to the models on the required scale. Big water-wheels about five feet six in diameter were got ready and placed by the river to await the time when it should be clear of ice. Horse mills were set up in connection with circular saws and threshing machines. The ice cellar was cleaned out, deepened and insulated with hay, branches and soil, ready to receive the last ice from the river, and logs were barked and trimmed for two new houses.

AT the end of January it was decided that two different expeditions should be undertaken. Krebs planned a tour to the northward to buy sables, and Ping was to go with him to help in valuing the skins. I was to travel to Van Kure to deliver our first batch of purchases to the Russian, Boldikov, and get goods in exchange for our further trading on the farm. All I knew about the way to my destination was that I was not going to follow the one by which we had come with the caravan.

I set off on " Sophus ", taking with me a piece of frozen meat, a lump of brick-tea and my sleeping sack. I rode over hill and dale, and the gods were propitious to me. After two days' riding I came to the Selenga, which lay under a firm covering of ice, and after two more days the monastic town's colourful and gilded spires appeared over a hill-top. I thought myself lucky to have got there, for " Sophus " was in poor condition and so thin that his bones rattled. But no goods had come from Urga, so I arranged that when they came they should be brought on to Bulgun Tal by a Russian with pack-horses. In Van Kure I met with two Russian Cossacks, Misha and Sava. Misha was small and strong with sea blue eyes and fiery red

My comrade on the Steppe

Mother-love on the Steppe. (A few minutes before this picture was taken a herd of several hundred half wild horses was grazing on the spot, but they vanished at a gallop when we approached with the camera. A new-born foal caused the anxious mother to remain)

Bukha Barildena

To the right, under the awning, sit the Chiefs and Noyans (nobles and officials). To the left the men of the people. In the background women of the people.

THE STEPPE BECOMES OUR HOME

hair. He stood stiffly to attention with his hand to his high Cossack cap if one so much as looked at him. Sava was younger, about twenty-eight, with brown eyes and black hair. He seemed low-spirited and melancholy. Both had engaged in innumerable encounters with the Bolsheviks and both had been obliged to abandon their home north of the boundary. Now they had no country, no leader and no home. All they had left were their Cossack horses for which they showed a touching affection, and I had a feeling that it was of a home and care for their horses that they were chiefly thinking when they came to me to ask for work. Boldikov recommended them warmly, and I took them into my service. With their last coppers they bought fodder to feed their horses on the way. After five days' ride I got back to Igagården with the two newly recruited members of our colony. The Cossacks at once showed themselves to be very industrious workers, and since they were capable woodmen, carpenters and farmers, they became very useful to us.

Buffalo on my departure had given me an important commission, namely to buy cigarettes, for without cigarettes or good pipe tobacco it is often hard to live. But neither cigarettes nor western pipe tobacco was to be had in Van Kure, and our own scanty supply now came to an end. We then searched in our earlier working places and found cast-off cigarette ends in the snow. These we dried in the sun, and smoked the tobacco in our pipes.

When the last cigarette end in the place had gone up in smoke, we would sit in the evenings trying to remember places where we had been for any length of time tree-felling in the woods, and go off next day on a hunting expedition, which had for its real aim not the wild beasts of the forest but our old cigarette stumps. We began now to blend these with the mosslike *dunsa* tobacco which Ping sold to the Mongols. The flavour was not agreeable, but it made smoke. Finally we went quite over to *dunsa* tobacco, but since it could not be smoked in our own well-seasoned briars, we put them carefully away till better times and took to Mongolian *dangse*.[1] They are about eighteen inches long, with a small brass bowl and a jade mouthpiece.

The business of Ping's *p'u-tse* was now tended by whichever of us happened to be at home to guard the farm. The two Cossacks were a great help to us in valuing the furs. They had both been born and brought up in the richest fur-bearing tracts of Siberia and they themselves had been hunters from the time they could handle a gun, which for a Cossack boy means the time they were ten years old.

We now began, too, to think about beginning to stock the farm with cattle. We made long excursions on horseback with Yalsarai to the rich Mongols of the district and inspected their herds, for it was important to get first-rate beasts from the start, such as might form a good basis for our future herd. Horse-breeding and cattle-raising are the chief industries of Mongolia and were also to become our chief source of income. In the course of the winter and early spring we acquired a yak bull, five cows with their calves, seventeen ewes with lambs, ten horses and five draught oxen.

At the cattle census in 1918–19 there were found to be in Mongolia three hundred thousand camels, a million and a half of horses, fourteen hundred thousand cattle and nine and a half million sheep and goats. The population of Kalka (Outer Mongolia) was estimated at the same time to be six hundred thousand.

Most Mongolian horses are finely built, but the animals from the mountain districts often remind one of the Ardennes horses on a smaller scale. The average Mongol horse stands barely fourteen hands, but what it can do on long journeys is unparalleled. Like the rest of the Mongols' domestic animals he has to find his own keep out in the open, both summer and winter, and he gets along on incredibly little. Our little desert horse " Hao " drank only once a day in the hottest weather, and only once every third day in winter, and when there was snow on the steppe he did not drink at all.

A horse is called in Mongolian *mori*, but a herd of them is collectively named *ado* or in Northern Kalka

[1] From the Chinese *Kan-tse*.

tabun. In summer the horses run free, grazing, and a couple of mounted herdsmen keep them together in a herd. In winter, if the number is small, they are driven at evening into the fold. If the herd is very large it is guarded at night in a sheltered valley. In the course of my travels I have come upon herds of horses so large that they covered the steppe as far as eye could reach. The richest Mongol I met owned fourteen thousand horses.

In the winter all the horses run together in the herd, but when the spring comes the geldings are separated to prevent the stallions' violent attack on them. To each stallion one reckons thirty full-grown mares. From about the first of July the mares are milked, and the milk is used by the Mongols for the preparation of *arik* [1] (koumiss) and *arihi* [1] (arrack).

It is a pleasure to see the Mongols in association with their horses, and to see them on horseback is a joy. If one of the wild or half-wild horses of the herd is to be caught, the Mongol rides on a specially trained catching-horse, holding in his hands an *urga*, a very long pole with a noose at the end. The catching-horse soon understands which horse his rider wants to get hold of, and follows it until it is cut out of the herd. Then the pursuit goes at a flying gallop over the steppe, until the Mongol gets his lasso over the pursued horse's neck, when the catching-horse slowly but surely holds back till the wild horse is tired out, and the Mongols hurry up to saddle it. The wild horse is not let go until it has a rider in the saddle, and then it gallops, buckjumps and throws itself on the ground in the attempt to get rid of its rider. But the Mongol sits fast and the horse is soon broken.

Such a horse-breaking is admirable, and the strength, swiftness and elegance of the Mongol surpass those of any ballet dancer. I once saw a Mongol ungirth and throw off the saddle from under him and continue to ride the horse bareback, bucking wildly all the time, till it was broken.

Horses are the Mongol's chief investment. He knows

[1] See Note at end of book.

nothing of banks, and silver does not interest him beyond the quantity that he and his women can use for ornament. But if he has many horses on the steppe, then he is a well-to-do man. Then he sits on a hillock looking out over his wealth, and counts up the many-coloured multitude of splendid animals grazing on the steppe with slim necks and flowing manes, just as a man in the west counts his notes, and when the neighing of the stallions rings bell-like over the grass lands, his eyes shine with greater pride than the ring of minted silver can call forth in us.

But now and then he may want a little silver in his tent to facilitate the purchase of tea, tobacco and other necessaries, and then he obtains it by the sale of horses to China. A number of useful geldings and occasionally specially fast horses are bought by the westerners in the great coast towns of China. Young mares of from three to five years are bought by the Chinese for use in mule breeding. The price of such a mare varies between fifteen and eighteen Mexican dollars (16s. 6d. to 20s.). The price of geldings is very variable. An ordinary good gelding is worth forty Mexican dollars, but the best, which are very hard to come by, cost a hundred or more. On one occasion a Mongolian racehorse reached in China the colossal price of twenty-four thousand dollars.

The Mongols themselves are great lovers of horse-racing, and at the annual festival in honour of the *obo*, " *Obo takhilna* ", contests are held in the various districts. The best horses from the whole of Mongolia are sent to a race-meeting at Urga, and the winning horse in this race is handed over as a gift to the ruler of Mongolia, Hutuktu Gegen. Of forty-two Mongolian songs which I noted down during my years in Mongolia no less than seventeen are about horses. They have titles like : " The little black with velvet back," " The dun with lively ears," and they are all full of touching evidences of the Mongol's love for his horses. I do not remember ever having seen a Mongol illtreat a horse, and it is a crime to hit one's horse with the whip anywhere forward of the stirrups. Mongols who have

Bukha Barildena, the Mongolian wrestling match, is a favourite sport, and at the festivals arranged for the amusement of the Chiefs and people the bator (strong men) of the tribes meet to compete for victory and honour

Our Mongolian house girl, Surong

THE STEPPE BECOMES OUR HOME

been on trading or pilgrim journeys to China usually come back filled with righteous wrath and indignation over the heavy loads and cruel treatment that human beings there deal out to their animals.

The Mongolian cattle are small, but shapely and very easily satisfied and hardy, as they must needs be in the conditions in which they live. They are not first-class milkers, but are pretty good beef cattle. The oxen are excellent as draught cattle. The biggest and best cows may weigh up to eight hundred and twenty-seven pounds, and the butter yield during a milking period, which always occurs in the summer, reaches thirty-three pounds. The oxen may weigh a hundredweight more than the cows. There are as well, in the mountain districts of Northern and Western Mongolia, the long-haired yak cattle. These are distinguished for their hardiness and capacity for feeding themselves even in very severe winters. Yaks weigh about the same as the Mongolian cattle, but their meat is less good and their yield of milk smaller, though with a greater fat content, so that the butter yield is about the same. It is difficult to get yak bulls to cross with Mongolian cows, but, when this succeeds, the product, which is called *khainak*, is an excellent beast. The *khainak* surpasses both the other breeds in quantity and quality of milk and meat. A big *khainak* ox can weigh up to ten hundredweight.

The Mongols derive most of their food from cattle. Meat is their main diet, and those who can afford it easily get through an ox between two persons in the course of a winter.

The dairy-farming methods of the Mongols are peculiar to themselves, but in the circumstances quite practical. The milk is boiled immediately after milking and then allowed to stand for twenty-four hours, when the cream is skimmed off in a thick, leathery layer which is called *urum*. The *urum* is collected for a long time and finally forms a porridge-like substance, *tsaghan tos*. This *tsaghan tos* is heated in a pan, so that the butter fat melts and the milk refuse can be skimmed off. The melted *tsaghan tos* is poured into ox bladders and stored for winter use. With the skimmed milk *baslik* and *arol* are made, two kinds of cheese which are excellent food on a journey. If they have plenty of milk, the skimmed milk is thrown in with the mares' milk to be used in making *koumiss*. The skins of the cattle are employed for making boots, saddles and hide ropes.

Sheep are indispensable to the Mongols. From their wool he gets material for *oimus* (felt stockings) and for his *ger* (tent), and their meat is a delicacy to the Mongol. The sheep is easily satisfied, and its tail is so contrived that, like the camel's hump, it enlarges in good times and stores up fat which the animal draws upon in the rigorous winter. In the autumn such a tail may weigh six or seven pounds. The wool of this sheep is abundant, but is regarded in the markets of the world as being of poor quality. Fat sheeps' tails are the best provision one can have on a winter journey. The milk is very rich and it takes only seven pounds of it to make a pound of butter.

To tend our growing droves of horses and sheep we installed a Mongol family consisting of four members, three of whom took service with us. The fourth member threw lustre on the family, for he was a lama in Urga itself, but he was also the cause of the family's poverty which now compelled it to enter our service. It was expensive to have a son who had to be maintained in the distant " Cloister of God ". The family otherwise consisted of the old mother, a son of thirty who also was a lama but of the lowest grade, and a daughter of eighteen. The mother, Puntsuk, loved foals, calves, lambs and all small things. An exception to this was Buffalo, whom she surrounded with a mixture of admiration and love. She tended our livestock splendidly.

Bater, the son, was lazy but good-humoured and full of tales and legends. The daughter, Surong, served as our maid of all work indoors. We tried long to get her clean, but she remained filthy. Definitely, and with an air as if we had uttered a blasphemy, she declined to make the acquaintance of our bath house. She knew all too well that " she who washes off the dirt washes off the luck ". And we knew better than to take that on our conscience. And Jenghiz Khan had indeed ordained that clear fresh water should serve only for the *drinking* of man and beast.

AT the end of February Krebs and Ping came home with a cargo of fine furs. It was the last gleaning of the season, for the skins were now beginning to be of inferior quality, and so we stopped buying.

Krebs had on several occasions given medicine to sick Mongols and treated them with good results. Usually the medicine had worked swiftly and surely, and the natives were acquiring a growing respect for him.

One day his carbolic-smelling room was cleaned and scrubbed for hours, for an operation was to take place. Isager, who was a doctor's son, acted as assistant and the rest of us as nurses. Outside the window the whole population of the district stood staring at the miracle. They saw Isager press something against the nose of the sick man who thereupon promptly expired. Then Krebs took sharp knives and marvellous instruments and cut open the corpse. But the marvel was that after a short time the dead man came to life and a few days later was much better than for many years. It was clear that Krebs was a miracle-working doctor, and the rumour of his power spread far and wide. The sick came from near and far, and his room was filled with *hadaks*[1] from grateful Mongols who had been cured. But, lest we should get on the wrong side of the Mongolian lama-doctor from Odogna Kure, Krebs held a consultation with him and agreed that there should be co-operation for the future. All the poor patients came to Krebs, while the monastery took the rich ones. But the lama-doctor nevertheless undertook to send all the more serious cases to the farm, taking half the fee. This arrangement worked to everyone's satisfaction.

---

[1] *Hadak*, a long piece of silk material, usually sky blue or white, which is given to the gods or highly esteemed persons as a sign of veneration. A *hadak* is regarded partly as something very sacred and pleasing to the gods, partly as containing a secret power and partly as symbolizing the rainbow.

CHAPTER V

FUR TRANSPORT UNDER DIFFICULTIES

"Cloud Memories" (Mongolian Song)

ON the thirteenth of March Ping and I left the farm for Urga with a tightly packed wagon-load of several thousand fine skins. The cold had been greatly decreasing of late, and the sun shone day after day from an azure sky, across which small white clouds drifted now and then like light swansdown blown over the vault of heaven. When we rode through the deep gorges, they appeared high up, like fantastic images and formations, to vanish again behind the mountain crest on the other side of the valley. But when we rode over the steppe they thrust up far, far away on the horizon, like proud frigates majestically ploughing forward over the blue vault of heaven. Thus the cloud shapes changed eternally, and the great silence of nature gave us a sense of purity and beauty—as always when a human being is alone in magnificent scenery.

The first part of the journey went quickly and easily, for we were following the trail by which I had already ridden twice that winter. On these earlier occasions I had passed the night with an old Mongol by the name of Bayard, who had his camp on the southern bank of the Selenga at the point where my way crossed the river. I had counted on reaching my Mongolian friend's warm tent on the third day of the journey. The whole of that day, too, passed without mishap, and we rode at a good speed over the steppe to follow later a narrow ravine that plunged abruptly southward down to the river.

FUR TRANSPORT UNDER DIFFICULTIES

But the days were still short and the wagon delayed us. Twilight overtook us while we were still in the gorge between the rocks, and by the time we reached the river it was dark and ice-cold night. The ice on the river was lying under a foot of water and all looked different from when I had last passed the place. The bank where we now halted was cold and desolate, without grass for the horses and without fuel for the fire. Bayard's tent and his warm hearth haunted my brain, and I explored the river to see if there was any possibility of accomplishing the last quarter-mile of our long day's march.

The river was probably frozen to the bottom at some point higher up, and this had produced a barrier against the flood running below the ice. The increasing pressure of water at this barrier had caused the water to be forced up through the ice to the surface and to form there a new stream on top of the ice. On this new river a new ice crust had formed in its turn, but owing to the warmth of the last days this ice was covered by a foot of thaw water. On this thaw water again the sharp cold following the loss of the sun's heat had formed a crust of ice an inch or so thick.

When I rode out on the river the horse's hooves at once went through the uppermost thin ice but it trod safely on the middle layer and the water nowhere reached more than a foot up its legs. In the middle of the river a sort of little island had built itself round some fast-frozen tree-trunks that stuck up through the ice and the water. The river was about two hundred yards wide at this point. On the other side I saw in the distance a point of light which certainly came from the smoke-vent in Bayard's tent.

I decided to make the attempt and gave Ping a last admonition not to stop before we were on the other side and to drive at full speed if the ice began to crack. I rode in front of the wagon, and high above it Ping was enthroned. He and the horses were full of terror. The animals snorted when their hooves cut through the thin ice, but on we went. When I myself reached the frozen-in tree-trunks I stopped and watched the vehicle

FUR TRANSPORT UNDER DIFFICULTIES

which was slowly approaching. Suddenly there was a creaking in the ice, the horses pulled up in alarm and began rearing, and Ping gave a heartrending scream. I shouted to him to whip up the horses, but the wretched fellow instead jumped off the wagon and waded back through the icy water to the northern bank. With a few heavy blows with my whip I succeeded in getting my horse down into the water and worked myself forward towards the wagon. The wagon horses had now contrived to turn the wagon down-stream, and one of the wheels had sunk through the middle layer of ice, bringing the wagon into a dangerously tipped-up position. In imagination I could already see the whole of our capital and the results of a whole winter's labours going to the bottom. And I also saw the mortification of my comrades when they came to know the outcome of the first commission entrusted to me.

It was impossible to turn the horses. They were kicking wildly and belabouring the ice in a very disquieting fashion. The wagon now sank slowly down by the back wheels, and the ice crashed round about and beneath us. I neither heard nor saw anything of Ping. It was essential that I should get the horses unharnessed as quickly as possible, and since this job could not be carried out from horseback, I had to slip down into the water and ice slush. It came up to my waist. All the reins and ropes were frozen stiff and covered with ice, so that I had to cut the horses loose with my knife. I tied the two horses to the tree-trunks in the middle of the river and waded back on my saddle horse to the wagon. There I cut the rope binding the load, took a big package of furs in front of me on the saddle and transported it to firm ground in the neighbourhood of the trees. Eleven times I made the same journey before I had all the furs in safety. The wheels of the wagon had sunk through the ice, but its broad bottom prevented it from sinking deeper. Its upper part lay about a foot under water. The two shafts with the severed harness stuck up almost vertically into the air. I could see them almost all night, and I could hear the ice piling itself round them and taking them into its grip.

FUR TRANSPORT UNDER DIFFICULTIES

I was thankful to be in safety myself with the horses and the load. Then I began to wonder what could have become of Ping. When I shouted into the darkness, his whimpering answer came back. He was safe from the river, he said, but near freezing to death. I promised to warm him with my whip when once I got hold of him, for I was furious. If he had whipped up the horses and driven on when the ice began to crack, we would have got across and might now have been sitting by Bayard's warm fire. But instead of obeying my orders he had jumped off the wagon and thought only of his own safety.

My *unti* and my long riding coat were wet through, but the wet quickly froze into ice so that did not matter so much. But I soon began to feel the cold in my feet. I made a feeble attempt to go on to Bayard's tent, but I could not leave the horses alone there, and they were too exhausted and terrified to let themselves be driven out again into the water.

There was no fuel except that part of the driftwood which stuck up out of the ice, and it needed many pieces before I succeeded in lighting a small fire. At last I contrived a little pyre of chips under the lee of the largest tree-trunk, where it slowly took fire and smouldered, though it gave out more smoke than heat. My feet had finally become numbed, and I was afraid they were going to freeze. I took off my *unti* and woollen stockings and began to rub my feet vigorously with ice, after which I thrust them as far into the glow as possible. I wrapped them up in a corner of my fur coat and held my stockings to the fire to dry them.

The time passed slowly, and unintentionally I fell asleep, and only at dawn woke out of a heavy slumber. I was shaking with cold and my stockings lay charred in the smouldering remains of the fire.

The night frost had strengthened the ice and it was now important to make the best use of the time before the heat of the sun had the opposite effect. I crawled into my stiff-frozen *unti*, led the horses over the ice and reached Bayard's tent at full gallop. A salvage party of four Mongols, equipped with axes, planks and ropes started out with me. Before the heat of the sun had grown too strong we had cut the wagon free from the ice and, by laying planks successively in line under the wheels, we got it up on to the southern bank. The load was dragged up with the help of the boards, and we also used them as a bridge for the scared horses when the ice began to crack. Ping came trudging behind, but kept himself at a respectful distance from me for the rest of the day.

I took a full twenty-four hours rest with the hospitable Mongols. The horses were galloped till they warmed up and were then rubbed dry with old felts. The harness was repaired for me, and one of the women in the camp made me a pair of Mongolian felt boots. Before we set off next morning I swung the whip over the trembling Ping, but he looked so miserable and promised so vehemently to improve, that I let him off the punishment that I had designed for him during the night on the ice.

In two days we reached Van Kure, and here I rested two days to let the horses feed up on liberal rations of oats. The Russians in the monastery town showed me a way to Urga, shorter and better than that which we had followed with the ox caravan five months earlier, and this would bring us to our destination in five days.

We were now driving through desolate steppes. The Mongols had moved up into the hills to seek better grazing and shelter for the cattle. The snow was now thin on the steppe, but everywhere there were signs that the winter had been hard and had taken great toll of cattle and horses. The caravan road was strewn with frozen carcases, stretching like a string of beads from Van Kure to Urga. Where they had fallen, beside the wells for the most part, carcases and half-devoured remains of skeletons lay side by side, so that it was impossible to water my terrified horses. Later we came up on to a high plateau which I recognized, and hit upon the telegraph line that runs from Urga to Kiachta. Here we pitched camp and, since the sunset that evening was threateningly pale, I was glad to know we should be in Urga the next day.

FUR TRANSPORT UNDER DIFFICULTIES

But next morning it was snowing, and before an hour had passed we were having to push our way through a blizzard of hurricane force. The field of vision about us narrowed, and soon I could only see a yard or two either way. The storm was so violent that it came near blowing my horse over with me on its back. Then I began to drag my horse after me, walking backwards myself, so as to protect my smarting face from the wind and the snow it whipped up. All indications of the road had been obliterated, and the feeble light that might have indicated the position of the sun was hidden behind the dense masses of the whirling snow.

If one halted for a moment, the horses immediately swung round with their tails to the wind, and the snow began to pile itself up rapidly against the lee side of the wagon. We had to push on again lest the wheels should be altogether buried and we ourselves snowed under. I had lost the compass in the crossing of the Selenga and I had now no notion of my bearings.

Ping lay rolled up in his fur coat somewhere on the load and was no more use than the toothache. The horses were worn out and dispirited. They stopped more and more frequently, and it became increasingly difficult to get them moving again.

Suddenly I saw on one side something dark that fluttered in the wind. I ran to it and found a snowdrift with a post sticking out of it. From this fluttered a last remnant of a Mongolian travelling tent, and it was this blue rag that had attracted my attention. I dug with my riding whip along the tent pole and came upon a Mongolian saddle and, farther down, two small bags of provisions.

The thought that the owner of the saddle and the food perhaps was lying buried beneath the snow made me run back for our travelling spade which was made fast behind the wagon, and I shouted to Ping to come and help me dig. But he only whimpered, so that I had to drag him down off the load and kick him soundly to get any life and speed into him. Then I shovelled the snow away with the spade, and Ping dug with the whip till the tent pole fell over with its ill-omened flag.

FUR TRANSPORT UNDER DIFFICULTIES

We dug out two Mongols. They lay wrapped up in their fur coats, stiff and cold. I felt their hearts and pulses, but they were both dead.

We left them lying on the top of the snowdrift and set the tent pole up again so that their friends might find them the more easily. The blue fragment of the tent fluttered over them like a funeral banner. We found our wagon half snowed under and the horses indifferent alike to encouragement and lashing. In the end we got the wagon dug out and the animals in slow movement. Finally we turned and drove with the wind, regardless of the arbitrary direction we had hitherto been following. The horses kept on stopping, and I myself could hardly drag my legs after me through the heavy snow, but every time I saw the snow piling up against the side of the wagon I foresaw for myself the fate that had overtaken the two unfortunate Mongols and once more lashed life into the poor animals. I felt myself growing apathetic and longed unutterably to lie down and sleep.

And I must actually have done so, for I was wakened by Ping, and when I opened my eyes it was the morning of a new day.

THE snow lay white upon the steppe, and the sun was shining from a clear sky. I felt that I had tumbled down into a completely new landscape, for everywhere I could see the shapes of objects that I had never seen before. Not very far to the southward appeared bluish mountains, and in several places to the north dark hogs'-backs dimly emerged from the snow where the storm had swept them clean. But except for Ping, who seemed to have had his sleep out and to be thoroughly rested, the immediate surroundings were pretty hopeless. On the windward side of the wagon the snow had piled itself up level with the top of the load, and the horses had thrown themselves down in their harness and were lying half covered with snow, with their necks stretched out in front of them.

I myself awoke by the side of the wagon, where I was lying half sheltered from the storm. The snow must have stopped soon after I had lain down for I

FUR TRANSPORT UNDER DIFFICULTIES

found the depressions of my own tracks in the snow half filled up. We rubbed the horses hard and harried them till we got them to rise on stiff legs, that is to say two of them. The wheel horse of the wagon had died during the night and was almost completely stiff.

The sun now rendered it possible to recover our bearings, and I gazed out towards the mountains, trying to discover a place that might suggest a way through into the Tola valley. My usually so unmanageable saddle horse now willingly let himself be harnessed to the wagon, and we made our way slowly forward, towards the southeast. Suddenly I perceived striped shadows on the snow. They denoted the telegraph line, and I was overjoyed, for it was like grasping a hand outstretched from Urga. I had only to follow the line southward, and it must lead me to the goal.

Before sunset we reached the Tola valley, and in front of me rose the well-known spires and dragon roofs of Urga's cloister city. I was glad beyond description.

OUR worn-out horses carried us slowly over the last short stage of the journey, and it was half-past nine at night when we stopped outside Larson's compound. I left the conveyance to a couple of Larson's Mongols and went on to a window from which light was shining. It looked inviting when I peered in. In a corner a fire was burning in a big open hearth, and at a table four Europeans, all of whom I knew, sat playing cards. The two facing me were Larson and Tot.

I pounded on the glass, hurried forward to the door and screamed that it was I who had come, but it seemed an eternity before the door was opened and we could shake hands, thump one another on the back and exchange greetings face to face.

Then I went straight to the open fire and gave myself up to the pleasure of being once more warmed through by the heat of it. I took off my fur coat—for the first time for many days—nor was that all I stripped off. Larson shouted to his fat Russian housekeeper and told her to bring food, lots of food. And soon I had great plates of steaming soup, meat and potatoes before me, and was eating for dear life, while trying to answer at least some of the many questions that hailed down on me. Where had I been during the severe snowstorm that had kept people in Urga within doors ? Well, out there on the high plateau, where I had trudged about until sleep and exhaustion had overcome me. That plateau, Larson said, was called Jirem and was one of the worst places one could be in during a snowstorm. I told of the crossing of the ice on the Selenga and of the night I spent there, and of the other days when the journey had gone splendidly. And finally I mentioned the big load of furs that we had brought and which had now arrived in good condition at the first station on its way to all the great cities of the world. But Larson was the one who asked the fewest questions. He strode about the room on his great feet and observed me in a peculiar way from various positions, as I have seen him do when he was judging one of his race-horses. At last he stopped in front of me and said: " Well done, my boy. You take to Mongolia like a fish to the water." And I was very proud of those words from old Larson.

Then Larson said I was to turn in, but, since I was sure to have plenty of lice and fleas, he thought I had better spend one more night in my sleeping sack. He promised me a Russian bath next morning and held out prospects of a bed for the remainder of my stay in Urga.

I was to sleep on the floor in Tot's room. The latter would have gone with me, but was prevented by Larson who thought they had better go on playing cards for an hour. Then the tactful Mongolian traveller himself took me to my room and left me in solitude with a thick bundle of letters that he had received on my account since we parted on the first of September in the previous year.

An hour later Tot came creeping in, but I was not yet asleep. We did not sleep the whole of that night, there was so much to talk about. Tot's work for Larson was now finished. He had started off by car with a load of silver which was to be taken to Uliassutai. Half-way the car had gone to pieces, and Tot had been obliged to go on by ox-caravan. But he had taken the silver to the appointed place and had been back in Urga for three

FUR TRANSPORT UNDER DIFFICULTIES

weeks, eagerly awaiting my arrival, so that he might join us as soon as possible and take part in the work at Igagården. He had done well for Larson with the silver dollars, and since he was actually the property of the expedition, which had let him out to Larson, the money was thus the expedition's.

Our agreement with the Russian-American firm that financed our first fur campaign stipulated that we should hand over our purchases to them at a price ten per cent below the market price at Urga on the day we brought in the furs. When I asked Tot about the current price of the different furs, I heard to my surprise that there was no official quotation for such goods in Urga, but that the price of the day between man and man was calculated upon what one could get from the various firms, and that this price was practically dictated by the Russian-American firm with which we had the contract and to which I was to deliver my load next morning. Seeing that I was obliged to deliver my furs to them, it meant that they could make such terms with me as they pleased, and I did not much like it.

Next morning at dawn I took a bundle of skins, of twenty-five pieces, down to the Chinese town where I sold them within an hour to the highest bidder. Besides the money for the skins I brought back with me a priced memorandum from the firm. Ermine was priced at $1.40.

I got back to Larson's compound in time for breakfast and sent Ping to the head of the Russian-American firm with notice of our arrival and whereabouts. We had not yet finished our meal when two representatives of our Urga associates presented themselves to take over the goods, and, soon after, I drove with them to the firm's headquarters. It was evening before I came back, for we had to sort the skins, and it was as well to be present at this proceeding for, as I had been told, fur dealers are fur dealers. The collection I had brought in was the first that had come to Urga from our territory, so that people were interested to see what the forests up there in the north-west could produce. Everyone admired my fine specimens, and it was impossible for the two experts who sorted the skins to adjudge the whole batch as anything but " first class ". It was late when I left the place, and the office was closed for the day, so that I could not get our accounts made up, but I took a receipt for the number of furs of various kinds that I had delivered, as well as a certificate that all had been valued as first class. The paper ended with the signatures of the two experts, the date and nothing else.

Next morning I went down to the office with Tot to settle up. All went well until we came to the determination of prices for the various kinds of fur. First-class ermines, for instance, the firm wanted to assess at $1.24, and to prove that this was the price of the day they took me out into the shop where purchases at that price were just being made. I, of course, protested and demanded $1.40. They produced the contract which provided that we should supply at the price of the day when I made delivery. My contention was that the price of the day in Urga was the price obtainable by sale in the open market, and, as evidence that this price on the previous day had been $1.40, I brought out the receipt for the twenty-five skins I had sold to the Chinese firm.

I got my price, and Tot and I drove back to our quarters with many leather bags full of good silver dollars. We had bought the skins at the farm at an average price of seventy cents, so we did pretty well by our first winter's work.

The foreign colony in Urga enjoyed my little " victory " over the powerful firm's agents, and I observed that these people were not particularly popular among the white pioneers of the cloister city. A couple of these, who before had treated us a trifle superciliously, called on me to shake hands and to assure me that I was no longer a " greenhorn ". They asked me what the country was like up there. Judging by the skins I had brought with me it must be a rich country with great possibilities. Many of these weather-bitten rovers had lived a whole lifetime in Mongolia, but none of them had gone out so far into the unknown as we, and none had seen the country where we had settled. And, as I told them of all my interesting experiences and of all the

FUR TRANSPORT UNDER DIFFICULTIES

hidden wonders up there in the north-west, I felt as if, in my nine months in Mongolia, I had gained a good bit in the race with them, for all their thirty years' experience.

AFTER a week's stay in Urga, Tot and I got ready to start, for we had to return to the farm to take part in the spring work. My two horses had been well fed up during the stay in Urga, but in order to get quickly to Bulgun Tal we bought two more. The wagon that I had brought from the farm had been roughly used at the crossing of the Selenga, so I changed it for a new one. We loaded this with articles of necessity and of luxury. Sixty thousand Virginia cigarettes were decidedly reckoned in the former category.

Several representatives came to me and expressed their willingness to conclude contracts with us for the next fur season, but I had strict instructions that no new contract was to be entered into before the autumn.

One sunny April morning we trotted out of Urga. Tot was impatient to see the country where he was to live, and I—I was downright homesick for Igagården. For the first day or two the new horses were wild and troublesome in harness, but presently we learned how to handle them and found out which places in the team best suited them. We camped early on the third day, for one of the new horses had gone lame. Next morning it was even worse and could hardly move, so we left it at the first Mongol camp we passed.

Next morning, as we were driving through the hills leading down to the Orchon river, the iron tyre of one of the wheels came off. We repaired the wheel by binding on a rawhide thong, first softening it with water. Next day another of the horses got colic, and before night it was dead. The load was too heavy for the two remaining animals, and they soon became exhausted. Whenever we passed a watercourse we had to drive out into it so that the rickety wheel should not come to grief. On the seventh day the wheel did fall to pieces, and there was our wagon on three wheels. We were in the middle of the steppe and had not seen a dwelling for days.

Our provisions ran out, and we cast longing glances

at a packet we were bringing from Urga. It was addressed to Krebs and bore an American postmark. The weight was six pounds according to the endorsement. But what above all hypnotized us was a note on the outside which aroused in us veritable Tantalus sensations : " Contents—Chocolate." Sometimes we surprised one another in the act of looking fixedly at the parcel, and to be on the safe side we decided to hide it in an inaccessible place under the load. We lived for two days on a mandarin duck that we succeeded in shooting. We took turns in going on long excursions to try to find Mongols, but with the sole result of intensifying our hunger. We shot a marmot, but could not bring ourselves to eat it. The fodder for the horses was also finished, and their condition grew more and more pitiable.

When we had waited three days in vain for a passing caravan, I decided to go to Van Kure to get help. It took me four days to cover the distance on foot and two more to get back to the scene of the accident with a horse and a two-wheeled cart I succeeded in borrowing from a Russian at Van Kure. By dint of laying the broken wagon's fore part on the little cart and harnessing all three horses to that we succeeded in hauling the whole bag of tricks into Van Kure, where it took us two more days to get the wagon repaired. We left our worn-out horses behind and bought new, and these brought us to the farm in five days.

One lovely May morning we swung in to Igagården, and my most lasting memory of our arrival is the way in which the boys received the sixty thousand cigarettes. They were so welcome that for some days I went in fear that all the members of the community would succumb to nicotine poisoning.

Jetom, our Mongolian first hand

Mongolian Yak Oxen, in home-made harness and yokes, drew our American ploughs through the virgin soil

Waterwheels brought the river water to our fields day and night

CHAPTER VI
SPRING

IT was spring at Bulgun Tal. There was much lime in the soil, so the grass had a copious admixture of leguminous plants, vetches, clovers and peas. Last year's dry grass had been burnt off a wide area round Igagården, and the most succulent herbage was now putting forth there. Yellow and blue pasque-flowers threw a veil of colour over the ground just like our anemones and crocuses at home. The hills looked inviting in their carpet of fine soft grass. The larch buds had just burst, and filmy pale-green clouds lay about the stately stems. The skylark rose before the horses' hooves and wheeled on fluttering wings towards the blue heavens. His blithe song sounded like a jubilant shout of welcome that made one's heart light and gay—like his own. And one imagined that a cuckoo was sitting in every one of the tall trees of the forest. In the cool morning and evening hours there was a calling that never ceased, and we quite gave up asking them for counsel, for we could not decide where the cry of one ended and that of another began. And masses of small birds twittered and sang of the spring and the approaching summer, as quickly and eagerly they built their nests and laid plans for the future.

And so did we.

When Tot and I reached Bulgun Tal, we found the others in full swing with the ploughing, sowing and fencing of the land down by the river, on either side of our enclosed yard. It was the earliest kind of seed, *arbai*, that they began with, a hardy Siberian barley. W found this job almost finished, so Tot and I were set to work on new areas.

But new ploughs and tackle had first to be got out

SPRING

of the big crates in the *ambar*, and the parts assembled, adjusted and greased. Then harness had to be made from big ox-hides, and yokes carved for the oxen. When all these preparations were completed, Tot and I, with our two Cossacks, went off with the whole outfit loaded on two wagons. We had with us six horses and four oxen that were to be broken in for the plough. We crossed one arm of Egin Gol and pitched our camp in the shade of larches on the bank of the " warm " branch of the river.

The first day was taken up in unpacking, preparing swingle-trees and making a little enclosure into which we could drive the horses and oxen in the morning so that we could catch them more easily. The day began very early with various morning chores ; the morning meal was prepared and eaten, and, as a rule, some of us were out before sunrise with a gun, or to empty the salmon net. We sent our surplus game home to Buffalo and received from him in exchange tea, tobacco, salt, butter and milk.

At sunrise we set our American Oliver ploughs in the ground. It was heavy work, for the virgin soil had lain undisturbed since the creation. Shouts and blows were necessary as, in the sweat of our brows, we drove one long furrow after another through the steppe. And by degrees the furrows formed a wider and wider belt and grew into a field. The field was fenced, and sown with wheat, barley, rye and oats.

Between ten and three it was impossible for either man or beast to carry on this hard work. We loosed the draught animals, and ourselves lay down in the cool shade of the tent, where the temperature seldom rose above $25°$ C. In spite of this long midday rest, our hours of labour greatly exceeded the statutory eight of civilization. We began at eight in the morning and the working day was not over before nine. It was a hard life—and without beer !

There were, moreover, many other things to attend to, since we were mainly dependent on the food we could get for ourselves. Roe deer were to be brought down before sunrise on the southern slopes of the

SPRING

mountains; fish-nets and fykes were set both morning and midday, and harness and other gear sometimes needed to be looked to and repaired. There was no chance of doing anything in the evenings, for as soon as the sun went down behind the mountains it was dark night. As soon as we had drunk our tea and devoured our meal of salmon and milk, silence fell upon the camp. Then it was time for cigarettes and joy in the day's achieved results. The only sound that broke the stillness of the night was the peculiar whirring and whistling noise of the woodcock flying round their nests, and now and then the cry of an owl or a crane.

When we had ploughed and sowed one field, we moved our camp to another open place where the soil and situation promised a good crop. And thus we went on till we had no more seed. In a specially favourable place close to the farm we fenced in a piece of land for experimental cultivation. Here we sowed various kinds of wheat which we had obtained from Canada, and an effective system of irrigation was installed. Water was brought from the river by large wheels furnished with cups of birch-bark, which tipped over when they reached their highest point, and emptied an unending stream of water into hollowed-out tree-trunks, through which the water was distributed to the whole experimental field. The wheels were about sixteen feet high and were supported on pontoons in the river. They had paddles and were driven by the current.

On this experimental field we intended to try out which kind of wheat was best suited to the soil and climate and which gave the most abundant crop under " intensive " cultivation. We had obtained the seed from research stations in Canada and the United States, and the Agricultural Departments of those countries were interested in the results, since they considered that a variety of wheat which we might eventually produce from their seed might perhaps prove suitable for growing in Alaska and other cold parts of North America. Our meteorological station, too, was in relation with stations in Canada, the United States and Denmark, to which we also sent specimens of soil for closer investigation.

SPRING

When all this work was done we set to work on a scheme in which we were much interested and from which we expected great results. All the smiling population of Central Asia loves sweetmeats. The nearest place from which they can obtain them is remote Japan, whence they come to the steppes in small quantities and as a very expensive luxury.

There is a kind of Chinese candy procurable in Mongolia, but its sweetness is very slight in proportion to its bulk. The cost of transport is consequently high, and the Mongols prefer the white, refined Japanese sugar. Nowhere in Central Asia or Siberia had the manufacture of sugar been tried, so no evidence could be advanced that it would not succeed, and thus it was worth attempting.

We had brought from Denmark three bags of sugar-beet seed of the well-known " Trifolium " variety. This was now to be sown, and we had reserved the most suitable piece of ground in the district for the purpose.

In the corner north-east of the point where the Titiang river flows into Egin Gol, lay a triangular steppe which was exposed to the more gentle morning and evening sun, but shaded from the burning heat of midday. Wooded hills lay to the southward, and the slope of the steppe facilitated irrigation with the water of the Titiang. We dammed the river at the southernmost end of the steppe, and a deep irrigation canal was ploughed and dug along the edge of the woods. From this canal an irrigation system was constructed in such a way that the whole area could be put under water at any time. The ground was ploughed and carefully harrowed, and the field fenced by the Cossacks; then Krebs, Tot and I sowed it.

ON the ninth of June the sowing was finished, and we went home again to the farm. There Buffalo had meanwhile sown the area between the farm and the river with all sorts of green vegetables, and many of them had already begun to grow. Buffalo proudly exhibited the different patches, each with its variety—radishes,

SPRING

tomatoes, peas, lettuces, cabbages and many other good things that we had not tasted for a whole year.

During his journey to Irkutsk seven months earlier, Krebs had arranged with a Siberian Buriat to deliver six yak-loads of potatoes. We should have had them in March, but they did not come. April came, and May and June, but not the damned Buriat with our potatoes. We were so incredibly hungry for potatoes that the defaulting Buriat's name became a term of abuse at Igagården. In the end we forgot that such things existed. Suddenly, one day at the end of June, the Buriat arrived with six ox-loads of the most magnificent potatoes. He had had a long and difficult trek over mountains and river, through steppes and forests, so that by the time they arrived a lot of the potatoes had been frosted, others had long yellow " sprouts ", and here and there one had grown so that leaves were pushing out of holes in the sacks. But at least they were potatoes, and we were enraptured.

Lest we should commit an assault on them, Krebs issued an edict which he declared was worthy of fullgrown and reasonable beings. Eleven and a half sacks were to be set in the ground to provide for the future of the community, but half a sack was to be distributed to us as a Sunday treat to revive a taste which we had almost completely forgotten. True, Krebs was mean enough to pour into our sack all the worst damaged specimens and few that were fit either for human food or for setting. Still, they were potatoes and we were glad when Sunday came round. The contents of the remaining eleven and a half sacks were ploughed in with our warm wishes that they would speedily grow and multiply.

Then we took in hand the digging of a deep cellar, in which we put a fireplace, and there potatoes and vegetables were to be stored in winter, protected from the cold. On Sunday we ate venison steaks with mashed potatoes, and in the mash there were skins, sprouts and other things. But it was excellent and made us wish there was more of it.

The same day we rode all round the fields, which

SPRING

promised well for the future. The barley and the oats were coming up vigorously, but the wheat and the rye were still to seek. The irrigation wheel creaked and turned and pumped the river water up over the fields. The canal system worked satisfactorily, and the first small beet plants were coming up and would soon need thinning. Everything pointed to a good harvest and more seed for next year.

On the following day Krebs started for Urga, to go on from there by car and rail to Shanghai, where he was to meet his wife who had left Denmark on April 24th.

Now that the spring work was all finished and the seed lay growing and sprouting in the ground, we felt that both we and the horses could do with a little leisure. But there was never any real leisure, for there were always a thousand and one things that had to be done, and we were constantly finding new things that would be pleasant surprises for Krebs on his return.

We increased our stock of animals by purchase and by trading. Our herd of horses had grown with time to eighteen horses and foals, and we succeeded in getting a handsome thoroughbred stallion smuggled in from Russia. Our cattle had increased to a hundred and fifteen head and of sheep we had over three hundred. We had Mongols for the care of all these, but one of us always had to supervise them, to see that the horses were taken to the best pasture and that the cows were regularly milked.

Then there were the audacious wolves, the Mongols' hereditary foes, whose acquaintance we were forced to make. Every night we heard their song up in the mountains, and sometimes they came much nearer. One day they took a big heifer only six hundred yards from the tent where the cowherds lived. Another time the wolves attacked our flock of sheep in broad daylight. The boy and girl who herded the sheep howled and yelled, and the sheep scattered in every direction, but in a few minutes five sheep were bitten to death and three badly torn. Such of the boys as were at home

SPRING

of course hastened at once to the spot and drove off the brutes with a volley from their rifles. But since they were out of breath from their hurried run the wolves got away. On one occasion, also, several horses perished through being driven into the river by pursuing wolves.

The milk production increased with the growth of the herd. In one of the new houses a dairy was established and here separators and churns were set up. Isager made a cheese every day and every third day he churned butter. The surplus butter and cheese was stored in the ice-house for winter use.

In the mornings there were the nets to drag out of the river. As soon as the blackgame and capercailzie began calling in the woods we started on the salmon fishery. Isager was the keenest fisherman and pulled out the greatest number of salmon and salmon trout. The biggest we got was a whopper of thirty-three pounds. A good night's catch in the nets would give us five-and-twenty fish of an average weight of eleven to thirteen pounds.

CHAPTER VII

A RIDE TO THE POST

"Dear little golden horse"   (Mongolian Song)

ON his visit to Irkutsk Krebs had arranged for us to have better postal connections with home than we had previously enjoyed. Mails were now sent from Denmark to the " Great Northern " offices at Irkutsk, whence the kindly Danish telegraph officials undertook to have them sent on to Khathyl, a little colony of half a dozen Russian houses on the southern point of the lake of Hubso Gol. The distance from Bulgun Tal to Khathyl was about eighty-two miles (124 versts) and thus far less than from Bulgun Tal to Urga which was all of three hundred and seventy miles.

Hitherto we had not had much time to worry about mail, nor had we had a man to spare as post-rider, but now that all the spring jobs were done and all the crops in the ground and growing, we agreed that the time had come to send off and receive letters. The horses were all completely done up after their work on the soil, all except one called " Hao " (Good). This was a wild little desert horse that had enjoyed complete freedom ever since our arrival at the farm. He was, in fact, so difficult to catch and to break to double harness that we had not had time to school him during that busy time. We knew he was somewhere on Bulgun Tal for we had often seen him out on the steppe and he had many a time come down to the farm in the evening to drink with the other horses.

Across the Sable Plateau at a gallop

"Buckjumping"

A RIDE TO THE POST

It was decided that I should undertake the journey with our mail on " Hao ". Misha, the Cossack, who was our horse-breaker, was sent out to catch him, while I got saddle and saddlebags ready and the others brought their correspondence with their friends and relatives up to date. But the hours went by without either Misha or the horse putting in an appearance, and when I had completed my preparations I sent Sava to find out what had become of our man and horse. Time went on but neither of the Cossacks came back. It was not till late in the afternoon that Sava galloped in on his sweating horse, dusty and furious. He shouted for a lasso and said " Hao " was so wild that he and Misha had been fruitlessly chasing him for hours and that it was impossible for the two of them to catch him. Two Europeans and five Mongols now went with Sava to capture " Hao ". On Sava's advice we took with us lasso and *urga* and also a mare that had her foal in the corral.

We rode ten miles towards the north-east corner of the steppe, and there was " Hao ", looking magnificent. Well-fed and muscular, he was standing on a slope watching the approach of our cavalcade. We slowly formed a half-circle on the side of him away from the farm and at the same time let go the mare we had brought with us. The mare galloped off at once in the direction of the farm, driven by her maternal affection.

We now approached cautiously, the innermost rider whistling between his teeth, while the men on the wings cracked their long whips. " Hao " perceived the danger approaching in the shape of saddled horses controlled by people with treacherous lassoes and cracking whips in their hands, and so followed the unsaddled mare. With arched neck, twitching ears and flowing mane he set off across the undulating plain. The sun shone upon his golden quarters. Suspiciously he avoided bushes and large stones. A raven that flew up made him quickly throw himself to one side in a leap of several yards, followed by violent snortings through his dilated nostrils. He was like the very incarnation of freedom, flying on light, swift hooves over the open spaces. Our own " domestic animals " forgot both their weariness and the summer's discipline and thraldom. They took unexpected leaps with their hind-quarters, and soon the beat of the many galloping hooves sounded like an accompaniment to the neighing of the horses, which rang like silver bells across the grass-lands.

" Give a man a horse he can ride. . . . Give a man a girl he can love. . . ." It was Tot who in these words gave vent to his feelings. It was a mad gallop; hats were swept into the air, and the echo of the cracking whips came back to us from the edge of the forest. The Mongol, Yetom, set up a song about Jenghiz Khan's brave warriors slain in battle, whose freed spirits had risen from the field to be transformed into proud steeds, prancing through all eternity over the untrodden steppes of Mongolia.

The fascination of this free, wild ride aroused in me a doubt, hitherto unknown, whether it was really right to come here and set the plough in this primeval prairie, to subdue this multitude of wild blossoms to a forced uniformity of cultivated crops, to subjugate the horses on the steppe and the cattle on the hills—to rob nature of its freedom and stifle the joy that is the life of the steppes.

We flew over the ground, and the compact *hashanda* [1] of the farm came nearer and nearer. The great gates stood wide open, and behind the gates were people ready to shut them again so soon as the wild horse was inside. Now the mare flew in through the opening, closely followed by the hunted horse. " Hao " stopped short in front of the corral, with his forelegs spread out stiffly towards the ground. He wheeled round, his glance took in a new situation and the threatening danger. We closed in on him, shouted to induce him to take the remaining decisive step. Then all at once " Hao " took a leap, as though he heard a call from the wild, and shot like an arrow along the eastern side of the farm. Sava galloped to meet him with swinging

---

[1] *Hashanda*, a Mongolian word signifying an enclosed dwelling-place.

A RIDE TO THE POST

lasso, but the speed on either side was so great that neither thought of avoiding the other. A crash sounded out of the dust cloud as they met, and Sava with his horse and his lasso was lying on the ground, pouring out mighty oaths. " Hao " flew on in a cloud of dust, which rapidly disappeared along with the diminishing sound of thundering hoof-beats. There was no chance of our catching " Hao " on our tame horses, for he possessed all the strength and swiftness of the wild.

But next day we succeeded in getting him into a corral by laying the most delicious bait of salt, and soon he was munching in the inner enclosure, while the other horses remained at a respectful distance. In order to get the saddle on to him we had to hoist the whole horse up to a beam, hobble his legs with stout leather ropes, gag his mouth and blindfold his eyes. Again and again he kicked himself loose. Once he kicked through the wall of the inner corral, but we succeeded in catching him while he was hanging over the upmost plank in his attempt to jump over the barrier of the outer enclosure which was six feet high.

At length " Hao " stood saddled and with all four feet on the ground. His forelegs were still bound together, his eyes were blindfolded, and the two Cossacks stood one on each side of him, holding him with long ropes which were made fast to either side of the bit. " Hao " quivered all over and struck out with his hindlegs when I fastened on the saddlebags.

Then the Cossacks mounted their horses and laid the ropes that held " Hao " under their thighs on the side nearest the horse and then fastened them to the projections provided for that purpose on their Cossack saddles. I walked round the trembling beast a couple of times. " Hao " looked tired and used up after his two days' exertions, so perhaps it was not so dangerous.

I pulled on a pair of thick gloves, fastened the riding-whip to my wrist, put a handkerchief between my teeth and leaped into the saddle. " Hao " made a grunting noise and tried to throw himself down, but I kept him on his legs with the aid of the whip. A lad crept forward and loosed the rope from the forelegs, and I bent forward and removed the bandage from the horse's eyes. " Hao " only stood trembling. The Cossacks were ready, and I gave the horse a cut over the quarters. And then things began to happen.

" Hao " gave a mad scream and began a series of buckjumps into the air, each time landing on the ground with stiffly spread legs, curved back and nose far down between his forelegs. Each time he came down I felt as if I had been hit on the head with a club; things began to swim before my eyes and I lost one stirrup.

At that moment an alert friend gave the bucking horse a mighty swipe over the hind-quarters which set him off across the steppe at a wild gallop. The Cossacks made their horses follow " Hao's " movements, but in such a way as to hold back all the time, thus tiring the beast out and moderating his wildness. We coursed over the steppe in wild career, and when " Hao's " movements became more regular, I cut the ropes that bound us to the Cossacks.

" It's half-past seven," they shouted after me. The sun was sinking below the horizon, we travelled forward in the twilight and soon were galloping in the shades of night. We rode under clear stars, through forests, over meadows, and we swam across a little river. I tried to reduce the gallop to a trot, but every time I pulled him in " Hao " snorted and set off at increased speed. It grew so dark in the forest that I had trouble in keeping to the track that led to my goal. I wanted desperately to camp for the night, but perceived very well that if I dismounted I should never succeed in getting back into the saddle. I came to the place where the track divided into two or more, and I could only hope that the one we took was the right one. Dawn came, but still " Hao " did not slacken his gallop. The sun rose and its rays fell on the pounding, sweat-dripping horse. The sweat was running off me, and when I pushed my hat to the back of my head, it flew off, but I dared not stop to pick it up. But what the exertions of the wild journey had not been able to bring about the sun accomplished as it rose higher and higher in the sky. " Hao " several times slowed down to a canter, and at length I succeeded in pulling him up at a shady spot where there was rich grass. The exhausted animal gorged contentedly on this fodder, but I myself dared not get out of the saddle.

Two lamas passed on horseback, and I called to them to stop, for I was near falling out of the saddle from exhaustion, and the grass looked so inviting. We began with the customary greetings, and then I obtained the information that I was on the right road and that it was only four miles more to *Oros posta* (the Russian post-office). It was only half-past seven, and I had been riding for exactly twelve hours at a stretch since leaving the farm. And then my longing to sink down on the lush grass vanished at the thought of being able to reach Khathyl in record time, for it would be long before such a chance presented itself again. So I dug my heels into " Hao ", and we went on at a steady canter, enlivened during the last miles by the gleam of wide blue water.

Sweating and dusty, " Hao " and I arrived at the little log-house at the southern point of Hubso Gol, the extreme point of the Russian postal service in this direction. The first thing I asked the young Russian postmaster to do was to stamp a blank sheet of paper with the station postmark and the date and hour of my arrival. With this paper as evidence that I had ridden the eighty-two miles in fourteen hours, I could take things easily with a certain satisfaction.

Nikolai the postmaster was a sympathetic young Siberian with flaxen hair and sea-blue eyes. His job involved far too hard work, but it was the intention that Khathyl should very shortly become the central point of a great Russian push forward on this front, in respect both of trade and of propaganda. It was intended to connect Khathyl with Hanga, the terminus of the caravan road to Kultuk, by boat communication across Hubso Gol.

There was a big consignment of mail at the post-office for all of us at Bulgun Tal, and I went down to the lake shore to read my share. It was splendid to get such fresh news, scarcely seven weeks old, and I turned " Hao " loose in the green grass by the shore

A RIDE TO THE POST

so that I might enjoy in solitude yet another reading of my letters. All the mail had been through the censorship, and I understood that several letters were missing, but in any case I was glad of those I had. Before I crawled into my sleeping-sack " Hao " and I had a splendid swim in the waves of Hubso Gol.

Next morning I bought a fowl and set off for home in comfortable ease. I rode home by the way I came, but everything around me looked quite different now in the daylight.

In the evening of the next day I made a halt in a lovely river gorge north of the pass leading to Bulgun Tal. The surrounding rocks were not high, but worn into fantastic shapes by wind and weather. In one place a proud spire of gleaming white marble towered above the weathered limestone rocks. The grass along the river was lit up by the setting sun and changed colour like emerald. Just at the foot of the pass lay a Mongol encampment consisting of four snow-white felt tents. Blue smoke rose invitingly from the smoke vent in the largest. A herd of grazing horses whinnied by the river bank. " Hao " neighed longingly in reply. It was all too inviting to pass. I dismounted and turned " Hao " loose, and he at once galloped off to the herd by the river. Then I went up to the camp at the foot of the pass, little thinking that fate had decided that here I was to become a father !

Silver Khurudu (prayer-mill)

[face p. 143

CHAPTER VIII

I BECOME A FATHER

A ROW of prayer-flags hung above the tent I entered. The flags were white bordered with red and inscribed all over with Tibetan prayers. White prayer-flags with red borders, that meant that the prayers concerned someone born under the same sign of the Zodiac as I, and so I told the young Mongol sitting by the tent fire. He was at most thirty years old, and the little tuft of beard below his underlip indicated that he belonged to the warrior caste. Between his knees he held a prayer-mill which he was turning industriously. We talked of this and that, of horses and the way to Khathyl, but I soon crawled into my sleeping-sack, for I was tired.

Next morning early I got ready to start, for I remembered my friends waiting impatiently for the contents of my saddlebags. But just as I was girthing the saddle on "Hao", my host came up to me and asked me to go with him to one of the other tents. He lifted the felt from the opening for me, but did not follow me in, and I found myself alone with a young woman.

She was prettily dressed in silk, and she smiled at me but not with the usual irresistible Mongol smile. Her smile was languid, her face thin and worn, and her clear eyes large and full of anguish. A sleeping Mongol boy of about four was resting in her arms. The young mother looked at the sleeping child with eyes full of tenderness and tears, then her frightened gaze wandered up towards the almost entirely closed smoke-vent and she begged me with a gesture to come forward to her, really close. Then she told me that her little boy was sick; he was so hot and did nothing but sleep, without taking any food.

She spoke in whispers and continued to let her gaze

I BECOME A FATHER

travel to the smoke vent and the entrance to the tent which was well curtained with felt. Thrice she had given sons to her lord and husband, but each time, when the sons reached the same age as this one—she whispered his name in my ear : Gongerer—the spirits had taken the child from her. She must have committed some great sin in this or in some former life, since the spirits continued to take her sons from her.

Lamas had been called in and had prescribed that she should sit here in the tent in solitude so that no " evil eye " should fall on her and the child. She kept the boy hidden from the spirits—she dared not speak aloud his name, Gongerer, which the spirits knew, for then they would quickly be called hither when they heard it spoken. She loved her son, and she was weak and powerless and would perhaps never more be able to bear a child.

But there was one way by which one might cheat the spirits and rescue her son from them. Would I help her ? Would I accept the child and become its father ? He was so sweet and good, the little one, and he would become such a sturdy boy who would love me and be a great help in my old age. If the boy became mine, received my name and a talisman from me, the spirits would be duped, for they were only concerned to be avenged upon *her* and *her* child. And, moreover, I was of foreign race, was under the protection of powerful foreign gods, so that the spirits would not venture to punish *my* child.

The little Mongol woman's mother-love was as pure and great as any mother's could be, and her appeal and confidence in my power to help was so strong that it was almost impossible to refuse her petition. But what was I going to do with a sick Mongol cub. I explained to her that at Bulgun Tal we were a set of childless bachelors who understood nothing about children, their illnesses and their upbringing. And that, moreover, we were almost constantly out on journeys, and who would look after the child then ? I suggested to her that I should send Krebs there with some medicine which would certainly quickly make her child well. But that

I BECOME A FATHER

did not console her, for she knew all too well that so long as the child was hers the spirits would not leave it in peace until they had succeeded in taking its life.

She continued her prayers, and at length we agreed upon a plan by which I felt able to undertake this new and unexpected fatherhood. Gongerer was to bear my name Arselang (the usual Mongolian corruption of my name Haslund). It was a good name—Arselang, it is the Mongols' name for the lion-like animal often represented in sculpture or painting outside their temples for their protection—and would bring the boy luck. And the spirits would never recognize their desired prey when they heard everyone call him by the new name.

But my son must have a talisman from my hand, and its contents ought to be quite different from the usual contents of talismans among the Mongols and quite strange to the Mongolian spirits. A Danish postage stamp, a revolver cartridge and a lock of my hair, hair which was extremely noticeable in Mongolia, were accordingly sewn up in several layers of silk and hung round Arselang's neck.

For six years the happy woman was to nurse and tend my son and when that time had elapsed, in the year of the Iron Horse, 1930, I should be entitled to come and fetch him. She asked me for exact information as to how I wished my son to be brought up, and I gave definite instructions. He was not to be a lama, he was to be a hunter and a herder of cattle, was to be instructed in music and old legends, and to become a good nomad, with all that this implies deeply imprinted on his mind.

The woman was now as one transfigured by a touching felicity. She thanked me and assured me that I should obtain honour and fortune through Arselang. I fervently hoped that this fortune would be lasting, and folded my hands.

I went out into the sun and the fresh air of morning, threw the felts at the tent's entrance and smoke-vent right to one side and shouted so that it echoed up the valley and was heard by all its spirits: "*Emechun, elip manai Arselang mini hu*" (Woman, come hither with my son, Arselang). And she stepped out into the light

I BECOME A FATHER

and the sun shone into hers and the child's unaccustomed eyes. Arselang wailed at first, then opened his eyes and smiled, and the woman beamed with happiness.

Then the "father" rode upon his way, and before sunset, at a dignified trot, I came to Igagården.

CHAPTER IX

WE FILL OUR BARNS

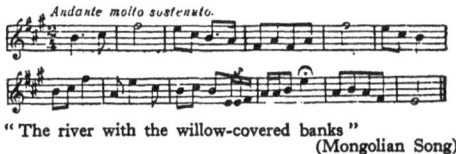

"The river with the willow-covered banks"
(Mongolian Song)

THEN came the hay harvest, and this was to the advantage both of us and of the Mongols of the district. Haymaking was a thing unknown among the Mongols, but we succeeded in convincing them that the many calves and lambs that died on them in the inclement spring might be saved alive if they had a reserve of hay to draw upon.

During the haymaking we drove our machines from daylight till dark, and the Mongols provided horses and supplied the labour. They raked and cocked and we divided the harvest equally with the Mongols who had provided horses and labour. It was the beginning of a time of prosperity for the Mongols of that region, who had been accustomed before to losing many of their young stock in the hard winters.

The green moss in the woods was gathered and dried in the sun to be used for chinking the newly erected log houses. We quarried lime by the river bank and slaked it in a big pit, birchbark was burnt for tar, and blue clay was dug in the forest, to be kneaded and pressed into quadrangular shapes for bricks.

We had agreed that all animal life with the exception of wolves and fish should be preserved within a radius of two miles from Igagården and it consequently throve and was a great pleasure to us. The river teemed with water fowl and waders whose broods were now hatched, and everywhere feathered couples were seen zealously engaged in feeding and bringing up their offspring. There were quacking ducks and cackling geese of many kinds unknown to us. And by the wider reaches of the river, cranes and herons stood on one leg keeping a sharp look out for fish. Black storks flew clattering over the farm and brought us luck. White-breasted ospreys emitted their long vibrant cry, and high up on the heaven-storming mountain battlements sat brown eagles with proud eyes beneath harsh brows.

The Buriat who had brought us the potatoes had, when he left, been promised a very big reward if he could get us two little pigs and six hens with a fine cock. It must have been the big reward that helped him to overcome the great difficulties that the conveyance of the live animals over that long and difficult road must have involved.

It was the first time Bulgun Tal had seen clucking hens and grunting pigs, and they made such an impression on the dogs of the district that we had to keep our new domestic animals on the island between the two branches of the river.

And the hens laid eggs and had chickens, and the latter did not escape the sharp eyes and then the beaks of the eagles, with the result that these birds of prey were also outlawed on the farm.

All through the summer we lived on venison, fish and milk dishes, and simply longed for potatoes. After Krebs went we raided them—twice. The first time we dug up those that had not come up and ate half of each potato. The second time we took up such as had grown slightly and made mashed potatoes of the inside, but put back the rind with an " eye ". By diligent watering, earthing-up and hoeing, we got even the rinds with their " eyes " to grow and the whole potato field flourished. But Krebs never knew anything about this.

As the month of August drew to a close, Bulgun Tal became more glorious than ever. All day long the sun shone from a cloudless blue sky. The green carpet of the steppe lay steaming in the heat, and countless flowers in Asiatic brilliancy of colour fluttered in the cool evening

By a method of my own for calling forth spirits, I drew out voices and tunes from a little box to the great astonishment—and subsequent delight—of the natives

breeze. The clear, deep waters of the Egin river flowed over our domain and brought refreshment to our cattle and growth to our crops which grew taller every day. Rye, barley and wheat for ourselves and oats for our horses and cattle—these meant food and security in the grim winter to come. And green vegetables, a long-forgotten luxury, we could once more enjoy. We kept on going round, after the manner of peasants, rejoicing in all that grew and flourished—the product of our plans and our labours.

At night the horses galloped in a herd along the steppe, with waving manes and flowing tails. In the cool morning and evening hours they grazed on the lush grass, but when the midday heat was at its height they splashed about by the river bank and enjoyed an ideal horse-existence. The cattle dozed at the edge of the forest, chewed the cud and lashed their tails.

Our store of fish and butter increased daily in the underground ice-cellar. Rows of bricks were drying in the sun in the yard, ready to be built into great furnaces against the winter.

At sunrise, out on the steppe, we heard the calling of the lovesick animals—foretelling mischievous foals, licking calves and bleating, helpless lambs in our folds for the coming year.

We ourselves drowsed in our bunks during the hot midday hours, pipe in mouth, happy and thankful. Outside, the crops were growing and the cattle multiplying, and down by the river the water-wheels creaked day and night their hymn of unremitting toil. From its tall staff in the yard the Dannebrog waved, rich in memories, the symbol which on every festival day waved us greetings from something far away that we loved. A girdle of wooded hills encircled all this splendour.

We were now at work getting everything ready for the white woman's arrival in our kingdom. A new dwelling-house was built on an idyllic site by the river bank. The farm's first real bed was made. It was long and wide, and on the bottom we plaited a net of oxhide strips. Buffalo gave it his approval, so it was bound to be all right, for he was, among other things, a judge of beds and of the tastes of womenfolk.

Finally we built, down below the farm, a little, little house, on an out of the way bluff by the murmuring waters of the river. Misha cut out a heart in its door, and the Mongols had strict orders never to come into its neighbourhood. They guessed that it must be a little temple, and we left them in that belief, for if we had told them what the house was to be used for, they would have thought we had gone stark mad.

Then one day a message came that our chief and his wife would reach the Selenga River on the 28th, and Buffalo's watch was consulted as to the day of the month. Misha went off with fresh provisions and driving our best troika with galloping horses, and on the last day of the month, which also happened to be my birthday, the farm was adorned with flags and triumphal arches. The Mongols of the district had poured in to offer their welcome, and when the message came that the troika had crossed the Egin Gol River, we galloped over the steppe to greet the newcomers on their arrival at Bulgun Tal.

And there she sat, our young countrywoman, with the golden-yellow hair fluttering about her fresh red-brown cheeks. Her blue eyes and white teeth smiled a greeting to us from all at home in Denmark. We fired a *feu de joie* as on slim legs she entered our Jomsborg,[1] in which she was so cordially welcome.

While the new arrival was taking possession of her home in the wilderness, and removing the dust of travel, we made arrangements for a banquet in the mess. For the second time in the farm's history a cloth was spread on the long table, our fine dinner service was brought out, fantastic floral decorations and candles were put in all imaginable places, and we got together an appropriate programme of music from our gramophone records.

Then we had to dress in style, and this occasioned much trouble and worry. We had to use much river water to control our refractory hair, and many times to call in the help of our friends before we were ready. Each of us thought the others looked very much like

[1] A Viking stronghold.

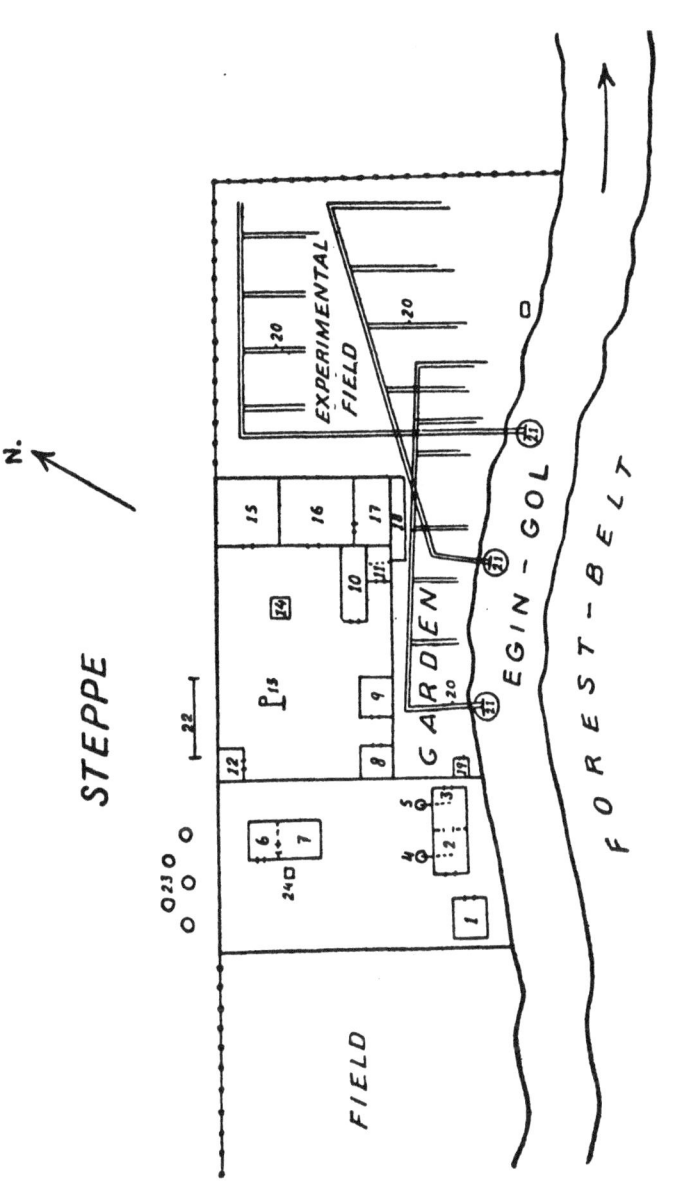

PLAN OF THE IGA FARM.

1, Krebs's house. 2, Sugar factory. 3, Leather factory. 4, Threshing machine. 5, Circular saw. 6, Dairy. 7, Mess. 8, Birck's and Isager's house. 9, Buffalo's and Kidi's house. 10, Ambar. 11, Ping's shop. 12, Kennel. 13, Flagstaff. 14, Smithy. 15, Enclosure for storage of hay and straw. 16, Pen. 17, Stable for young animals. 18, Greenhouse. 19, Bath-house. 20, Irrigation canals. 21, Water-wheels. 22, Rail for tying up horses. 23, Tents for Mongolian herdsmen and labourers. 24, Meteorological station.

yokels on their way to a dance in the barn. Although we had all grown thinner since our dress clothes were cut for us at home in the civilized world, they seemed to pinch and squeeze us everywhere. Our patent leather shoes were the worst.

Then the guests appeared, bringing with them masses of parcels and letters from our relations and friends. This was a joy, and we suddenly felt ourselves transported so near to civilization and all we had left behind us, that we forgot that the most recent greetings from home were over four months old. Mrs. Krebs had left Copenhagen on April 25th.

Among the many fine things brought from civilization was a number of gramophone records which, after the splendid dinner, washed down by a bottle of Buffalo's " wine ", inspired us menfolk in honourable rivalry to partner the farm's only lady in the dance. It was the first time dancing had taken place on our unplaned board floor. The night was far spent when we returned to the sleeping-sacks in our log-house, and the last thing I heard from my stable-mate was a muttering that sounded like : " The devil of it is one will have to shave in the morning."

But the holiday revels did not last long. We were full of plans for the extension of our activities and the long winter had to be employed in some way that would provide an outlet for our energy. We must obtain a new contract for the supply of furs to some western firm, and sufficient capital to finance such a campaign. The work on the farm was not more than Isager, " the little husbandman ", as the Mongols called him, could deal with alone with the help of the other fellows and our two Cossacks even during the impending harvest. It was therefore decided that Tot and I should undertake a hurried journey to Urga and try to interest some capitalist there.

On September 9th we left the farm on good horses and with no more baggage than we could carry on horseback. Three days out we encountered a wintry snowstorm that held us up for forty-eight hours. It did not freeze by day, with the result that both we and the horses tramped round the fire, wet through and shaking with

"The river with the willow-covered banks" (Mongolian song)

The first Mongolian Postage Stamps

Until 1923, in sending letters from Urga, either Chinese or Russian stamps were used according to which of the two powers had at the moment the greater influence in the land of the Mongols. In 1924 the "Young Mongols" issued the stamps depicted above. These were printed by a Western firm in China and were used in Mongolia until the end of 1925, when Soviet Russia introduced new stamps with Mongolian text

Nighen (one) tugherik

The first Mongolian coinage came into use in Urga in 1924. The coins were struck in Moscow. A tugherik, worth 0.78 Mexican dollar, was divided into 100 munggu. Before this time trade was almost exclusively carried on by barter, and standards of value were arranged in different districts in respect of goods from which the district in question obtained its steady income. In Northern Mongolia the unit was nighen (one squirrel skin), and on the steppes a horse or a head of cattle was valued in proportion to how many pud shartos the animal was worth. (One pud shartos = 16.5 kilos of butter.) Officially taxation was assessed with the aid of silver value. A yamba was a lump of silver in the shape of a horse's hoof weighing 1.87 kilos. The yamba was divided into 50 Lahn (Chinese Liang) of ten chan (Chinese ch'ien) of 10 tung (Chinese fen). On the introduction from China of the Mexican dollar this was counted as the equivalent of 0.76 Lahn

cold. The horses, which had not yet got their thick winter coats and had had nothing to eat during the last four days before the storm came on—for such is the custom in these parts when one takes out grass fed horses for the first long ride after the summer's rest—lost flesh enormously and looked dispirited. But fortunately these days were only a little casual reminder from grim King Boreas of his coming rule. On the third day the sun burst forth again, and during all the rest of our journey to Urga, where we arrived on September 25th, the most glorious Indian summer prevailed.

CHAPTER X

THE LONG ARM OF THE SOVIET REVOLUTION

SEVERAL days before we reached Urga we had already heard that Bogdo Kure (God's Cloister) had changed its official name to Ulan Bator Khoto (Stronghold of the Red Power), and this gave us a hint in what direction the political wind had been blowing. When, late one afternoon, we rode through the winding streets of the strange city and its open places crowded with riders, we met, moreover, fewer lamas and more Mongolian soldiers in Soviet uniform than on our earlier visits. We put up at Larson's house where we were made welcome by his English manager, Mr. Attree.

We now received fresh and disquieting reports of what had occurred in the Mongolian capital since our last visit. Larson himself was in Kalgan, as were the majority of the responsible representatives of European and American trading companies. What had happened was, moreover, of the most revolutionary character.

During recent months a series of political occurrences had completely altered the conditions in Kalka Mongolia. The government of the Khans and Princes, which had delivered Mongolia from the yoke of China to place the supreme power in the hands of the spiritual leader of the Mongols, the " exalted " Bogdo Gegen, was now over. Bogdo Gegen himself, the seventh reincarnation of godhead, had died during the summer, and the Soviet had not allowed the lamas to elect any new *hutuktu*. Of the old Khans and other princes some had been driven out to the Mongolian region outside the boundaries of Kalka, others had been killed or were confined in Urga's medieval prisons.

The new Government, which was composed of able

THE SOVIET REVOLUTION

Mongols, had worked for Mongolia's independence of both China and Russia and had depended on the Young Mongol's Party. They had governed with energy and for the good of the Mongols, and had realized that friendship with those foreign nations which merely had commercial interests in the country was preferable to contact with the two neighbouring powers that had always competed for supremacy in Mongolia. The Russians were displeased by the nationalistic and anti-Soviet feeling that spread by degrees within the Government which they themselves had brought into power.

A Russian Buriat named Rintjino had been summoned from Moscow. He was an intelligent man, well versed in the Soviet's propaganda methods, and had a large sum in Soviet roubles behind him. He succeeded in establishing a Communist Party which, however, consisted mainly of imported Buriats from Russian territory.

On August 30th, 1924, the War Minister, Danzan, made a violent speech in the Council, in which he maintained that closer relations with the Soviet would draw Mongolia in under the Russian yoke.

That same night Rintjino with a company of Buriats forced his way into Danzan's house and murdered him and Bavasan, the secretary to the government. And the next day the Soviet's consul in Urga, Comrade Vasilev, issued a proclamation expressing his opinion about this nocturnal murder, that the exploit would powerfully contribute to the uniting of Mongolia to the Union of Soviet Socialist Republics.

Another thing which also concerned us personally was a telegram from Shanghai to the *Vossiche Zeitung* to the effect that Mongolia was ablaze with revolt and that the members of the Krebs expedition had perished or something of the sort. This news had been disseminated over the world and had by now been read by our relatives at home and our friends in various places. It was important, therefore, immediately to show the strongest possible signs of life, and we did so next morning with the help of the telegraph. Thus that trouble was got rid of—as we supposed.

THE carefree little band of white people which we were accustomed to find in the place, and which represented at least half as many nationalities as it had members, was sadly reduced, and the few who were still there only met to discuss the new developments and to estimate their conceivable consequences. These were not at all the times to go round looking for a capitalist willing to invest capital in a district of which no more was known than what we had to tell.

On our arrival Attree had immediately telegraphed to Larson, telling him that we were prepared to organize a fur campaign during the coming season, and now we had nothing to do but to await the answer.

Daily we met the little group of remaining white people, and every single day there were thrilling new stories to hear. Many of the ablest and most adventurous men were away. The United States representative, who used to dominate all the streets of the holy city with his seven-foot athletic figure enveloped in a gigantic bearskin, had now become adviser to the Chinese " Tatar General " at Kalgan and was engaged in propaganda for armed intervention in Urga.

The first time we met Kelley was in the Gobi Desert, when he drove into our camp with his brand-new Dodge car loaded with boxes of shining silver dollars and other treasure. By his side sat a being whose like the desert had never seen. She was Russian, young and fair to look upon, and fresh from Shanghai's Sodom and Gomorrah. In her elegant, airy toilette, reeking of perfumes, she tripped forward over the sand in thin patent leather shoes to our rude camp, and was introduced by Kelley with the words : " Have you met my cow ? "

Kelley was born in Texas of a French mother and an Irish father. He had fiery red hair, blue eyes and smiling white teeth, and the freckles on his youthful face were as numerous as the adventures he had gone through. After a rough upbringing as a cowboy, he was driven out into the world by his adventurous Franco-Irish blood, became a marine on an American man-of-war and on it had sailed the seven seas and taken part in land engagements in Mexico and other unquiet corners of the world. He distinguished himself and became a petty officer on a torpedo boat patrolling the Yangtze-kiang. During this time he earned many silver dollars by smuggling opium, and when he had got together a sufficient capital, he deserted and went to Shanghai and turned himself loose in the town's " gay quarter ". But then, one day, when he had had enough of that life, he happened to catch sight of Mongolia's vacant yellow patch on the map. He bought a car, loaded the remains of his silver on it, kidnapped the fairest flower from the " Del Monte " night-club, placed her at his side, and off they went.

Thus Kelley came to Urga, where he bought himself a house, got together a number of cars and drivers and gave the whole undertaking an imposing name. He took on every kind of job likely to involve adventure and profit, he undertook with his flotilla of cars mysterious cruises in all directions over the desert to distant, unknown goals, but always came back to Urga and his " cow ".

But one time, when he came flying back from a long raiding expedition, he found that his " cow " had been a little too friendly with one of his Russian chauffeurs, and he gave orders that she was to be taken back to her former pleasureless life of pleasure at the " Del Monte " in Shanghai. She, however, loved her big cowboy in her own warm-blooded way, and one night, after emptying a bottle of whisky, she shot herself with Kelley's Colt ·45. So, at least, she protested until her death, after forty-eight hours of frightful suffering, during which time neither doctors nor friends could get near her to console or help, for she drove them away with fluent curses. In spite of her own assurances, evil tongues whispered that it was Kelley who had shot her, and an enquiry was set on foot by the Russian Cheka, which on many grounds had its knife into the American giant. Kelley strode about Urga, looking threatening, with his gigantic fists buried in the pockets of his bearskin coat.

The latest political developments in Urga did not

suit a man of Kelley's dominating nature. Once I came across him sitting on the top of his loaded car in front of the Urga customs house. He was holding his loaded Colt in his big fist and throwing round him the most succulent string of American oaths at the heads of his rowdy audience of Mongolian soldiers and police. I asked what was up, whether they were trying to rob him, and he snarled : " These —— blighters would steal Christ from the cross if they could make money on it." Another time I saw him coming, more than usually flushed, out of a government building where he had had a heated interview with one of the whippersnappers who were gradually coming to occupy more and more of the offices there. When he got outside he shook himself and snorted : " By God, this is the place one had better tie one's goat outside before going in." Then he vanished, snorting and cursing, down the narrow street, where the orientals moved terrorstricken out of the way of the menacing champion.

One day a disloyal chauffeur gave information that Kelley's cars were carrying arms from the Tatar General in Kalgan to the Mongol tribes in the East, and that a counter-revolution against the Soviet rule was in preparation. Two of Kelley's cars were stopped, with the result that the arms, which lay well concealed among innocent goods, came to light. A patrol came at night to arrest Kelley, but the bird had flown. Now he was sitting in Kalgan, hatching plots with the new leaders in Urga.

The young Swede, Söderbom, was also one of those who had disappeared, and with him the jovial cocktail parties. Söderbom the China-coaster, who had been born and brought up in the East, loved Mongolia's open steppes and the free, unconstrained life there. He had felt like a young colt let loose on the emerald carpet of the steppe after a long winter in the stall. He had drunk in the life of nature with all his senses and, like the colt which in autumn is shut in the stable again, he dreamed of coming back later. Söderbom had been transferred by his firm to Harbin, " the Paris of the East ", where he lived a gay life in the evenings to console him after the day's intolerable office work. I met him again in 1926 at the " Pioneers' Inn " in Kalgan on the borders of Mongolia. Over a melancholy *Choda peg* (whisky and soda) he confided in me that he had stayed in Harbin in the constant hope that his firm would send him back to Mongolia. Now, however, the firm had closed its Urga office, and he had left its service, since there was no longer any hope of his getting back in that way to the life he loved. For a time he tried to persuade other firms to send him there, but under the regime then prevailing out there, there was none that cared for the proposal. Then he took his last coppers and travelled alone, not to Kalka but out west where he settled down among the Mongols by Etsin Gol. Here he lived Mongol fashion in the little oasis, surrounded by hundreds of miles of desert and here he died, the sole white man in the tents of a nomad prince and his two hundred subjects, in September, 1930.

AT the time of our arrival in Urga, Wilson, the former American flying officer, was sitting in the medieval prison of the town. His popular young wife was going sadly round the city from one government office to another seeking her husband's release, but without result. Mrs. Wilson, who otherwise was gaiety itself, had always been our friend. To the members of the expedition she had ever shown the greatest kindliness when, famished, frozen and often a pitiable sight, we had arrived from our long sojourn in the wilderness. She had darned and mended our clothes, fed us sumptuously at a hospitable table and in the evenings had danced with us like a goddess to the strains of the gramophone. Now she needed help, and we desired nothing more than to see her as happy as she was by nature.

Bill Wilson was one of the many who had sought an asylum in Mongolia, the country in which there were at that time no inquisitive consuls to dig up one's past. When I first made Bill's acquaintance he was a tanned, slender athlete who looked uncommonly fit. He was ill-dressed and dirty as a mechanic—which, in fact, was what he was. He refused to dress in any Sunday finery, for he had come here to work, to earn a fortune and to show " the old folks at home " what he was worth. The only sign of opulence he carried was a valuable gold chronometer that he had in his pocket. As watch-chain he used a piece of string.

In his Dodge he drove to and fro with valuable loads the six hundred and sixty miles of steppe and desert that separate Kalgan from Urga. Always the same stretch, and always with fine loads. He extended the business, and in 1924 had five cars, manned by Russian chauffeurs.

Lamas gathered at a Temple Festival in Urga

[face p. 161

CHAPTER XI
A DIFFICULT ACT OF FRIENDSHIP

ONE day Tot and I were summoned to Mrs. Wilson's house where we found her alone and very nervous. She informed us that her husband had been imprisoned on suspicion of smuggling strychnine. This was one of the commodities that it was particularly profitable to import, since the poison was in great demand not only by the trappers of Mongolia but also by the nomads, who use it against the wolves, the hereditary foes who constantly attack their cattle. The Soviet has now prohibited its importation with a view to making the trade in strychnine a Russian monopoly, but Wilson, who had considerable quantities lying in Kalgan and knew that there were always buyers in Urga, had sewn his stock into the cover of his car and succeeded in getting through the customs inspection without being caught. One of his Russian chauffeurs had, however, given information about this to the Cheka, and the " green police " had come to examine the cars. Fortunately Mr. and Mrs. Wilson had succeeded in removing the contraband goods and burying them in a place where they thought they would escape discovery. The Cheka, however, had conducted such exhaustive enquiries and made so energetic a search that Mrs. Wilson was now afraid that the cache would come to light, in which case the Soviet would have a welcome pretext for putting a representative of the hated capitalism out of the way. If only the dangerous stock of strychnine could be got out of the town, the release of Wilson was merely a question of time, because in that case no evidence could be brought against him.

This was a serious business with which it was risky to mix oneself up, but now that Mrs. Wilson had given us her confidence and assured us that none but we could help her, we considered it our duty to stand by her. We agreed that, to avert suspicion, we would no longer visit Mrs. Wilson's house, but that when she learned that we were preparing to start she should send us a sketch map showing the place where the strychnine was buried.

Some days later a telegram came from Larson, saying that he was interested in our proposal about furs and that Mr. Attree was to advance us capital. A couple of days now followed in which we were busy buying horses and wagons and getting the latter laden with brick-tea, *dalimba*, tobacco and other goods which the inhabitants of our district needed and which would form a better medium of exchange for our purchases than the silver that Larson's representative had handed to us. The wagons already stood packed and corded in Larson's *hashanda*, the horses were being fed up for the long journey before them, and while we waited for our passports from the *yamen* (chancery), we spent the days in saying good-bye to the little circle of our Urga friends. At the last farewell dinner we received from Mrs. Wilson a small rolled up slip of paper which we hurried home to examine.

On the paper was a rough sketch with a few added explanations. A cross indicated the place where the treasure was buried.

The sketch represented a *hashanda* in the occupation of the Mongolian Minister of Justice, B. We had been on those premises a couple of times, but, the better to find our bearings, we determined to pay the Minister a farewell visit.

The *hashanda*, which lay on the outskirts of the Russian quarter of Urga, Konsulstvo, was surrounded by a palisade about eight feet high and divided into two halves by a six-foot fence in the middle of which was an opening about twelve feet wide and without gates. In one part of the *hashanda* lay the dwelling-house, surrounded by a large garden in which several Mongolian tents had been erected. In the middle of its other part lay an uninhabited Chinese wooden pavilion. In one

A DIFFICULT ACT OF FRIENDSHIP

of the corners farthest from the dwelling-house there was a small building occupied by a few Chinese servants. Some thirty yards from this there was a shed about twenty-five feet long, which was used for milch cows and their calves. This shed was built in such a way that the palisade formed its back wall. It was in a corner of this shed that the cross was placed in the sketch we had.

A large substantial gate led from the road into each of the two parts of the *hashanda*. On our arrival we knocked at the gate leading to the yard in which the cowshed lay, tied up our horses there and walked through the opening into the garden and up to the Minister's house. Here we took a cordial farewell of our Mongolian friend and, in mounting, contrived that our horses should get away from us, so that in trying to catch them we could have a good look round. Then we returned to our quarters.

The explanation of Wilson having succeeded in hiding his stuff in this place probably was that the whole *hashanda*, which had belonged to some missionaries who had been expelled by the new government, had stood empty all the summer, until it was confiscated by the new government and assigned to the Minister of Justice. The difficulties in carrying out our task were firstly that a state of siege prevailed in the town, so that no one might be out after ten o'clock, secondly that savage Mongol dogs prowled about the yard, and lastly that the Chinese servants lived in the little house thirty feet from the cowshed.

We chose the time immediately after the evening meal, which the minister took at nine o'clock, as suitable because then the Chinamen would presumably be busy washing up and eating the leavings of their master's dinner, and the dogs might be expected to be attracted by the smell of cooking and the chance of getting the leavings of the Chinamen.

Luckily for us it was pretty dark when we rode out, taking all our saddlebags. We rode first to the bazaar, where we bought oats, with which we filled the bags. After some wandering hither and thither at random we

A DIFFICULT ACT OF FRIENDSHIP

steered our course for the *hashanda*, keeping to the side which formed the back wall of the cowshed. We had emptied out the oats on the ground a little way off. No dogs, and darkness in the Chinese house.

We tethered the horses some way out in the field. Then we listened for a while. A clop-clop from a Chinaman's wooden shoes across the yard to the house in the corner held up our preparations until we had heard them returning to the great house. We helped each other over the palisade, slipped down on the inside and stole into the shed. We had four of the saddlebags with us. We held our whips in our hands and our big Swedish knives hung from our belts. We groped our way forward along the walls to the corner marked on the sketch.

A rustling behind us made us turn right round with lifted whips. It was only a lone cow beginning to chew the cud again. We began carefully to explore the indicated spot with fingers and knives. A lot of fresh cow droppings had first to be removed before we could begin digging with our knives.

About a foot below the surface we came upon something hard which proved to be a cube of about ten inches sewn up in waterproofed cloth. Before long all eight packets had been dug up. One, however, came to pieces, and this compelled us to light an anxious match and make sure that no betraying traces were left behind. The lone cow silently got up from its place and moved over to the spot where we had been digging, taking up such a position that the result of her digestive processes would cover all traces. We stuffed the packets into the saddlebags and carried them to the palisade, after which we lifted and hauled one another and our booty over to the outside. Then we pulled the small bottles out of the packets and distributed them among all the saddlebags we had brought, filled these to the brim with oats and returned to our quarters.

There we hid the bottles at the bottom of our goatskin sleeping-sacks. At noon next day we took leave, successfully passed the customs with their meddlesome examination and were then taken under military escort

A DIFFICULT ACT OF FRIENDSHIP

to one of the outposts that were set around Urga. Here the necessary outward passes were handed to us, and we were once more out on the open steppe.

Six versts from Urga we pitched camp and awaited with some degree of nervousness the setting in of darkness, for the sleeping-sacks with the strychnine were still lying in our quarters at Urga, and we fervently hoped no inquisitive person would clap eyes on their hiding-place. We carefully weighed the chances for and against the successful issue of our scheme. We had not counted on everyone leaving Urga being so closely inspected. Now, however, there was nothing for it but to do our best to carry out what we had undertaken. Night came and with it the time for action.

The result of our deliberations was that Tot turned his dark brown horse away from the road and rode northward to a plateau lying above the town, intersected by a number of deep ravines that led past that part of Urga in which the temples were situated, down to the Tola river to the west of it. The lamas in the temple city have a habit of going to bed with the sun. Its narrow lanes are consequently silent and deserted until dawn, if one ignores the innumerable dogs that keep up a howling so long as darkness lasts, whether there be any occasion for it or not. One had only to count on a trifle of good luck, to trust to the speed of the horse and to hope that if a patrol came along they would miss in the darkness.

The fire burned low, and I lay down and waited. I moved a bit away from the horses, irritated by their pawing and munching, which prevented me from exactly interpreting all the sounds of the night. I tried to calculate how far Tot could have gone now. If only he would remember the outpost at the corner of Ivanov's house! I stuck my knife into the ground and held the blade in my teeth, the better to catch the sound, if there should be a galloping horse in the distance. And first and last I damned the new government and its many edicts and ordinances, damned Wilson for bringing that wretched stuff into Urga—and waited.

Then all at once two shots sounded from the quarter

to which Tot had ridden. I jumped up, gripped my pistol and ran in the direction from which I had heard the shots, eagerly peering and listening. They had been rifle shots. Tot had only a pistol with him, so there could not have been any interchange of fire between him and a patrol. Tot might indeed have been hit, but then I should still have heard the rapid hoof beats of a riderless horse. The night had regained its profound silence. I dared not make up the fire, since that might give a possible pursuer a line. Back and forth I ranged in zigzags towards the quarter where Tot had disappeared, getting farther and farther every moment from the camp.

The silhouette of a rider emerged from the darkness, I whistled the prearranged signal and the horse pulled up. God be praised, it was really Tot, with the dangerous goods in his pack. He had twice been challenged by passing patrols but had galloped on, sheltered by the darkness. He had heard the shots, but they had not been aimed at him. Perhaps they were connected with the shooting of some prominent Mongol who was too popular for them to dare execute him by daylight.

We now hid the strychnine at the bottom of some big wooden boxes which contained old magazines and Christmas-tree decorations, all presents from our friends at Urga, intended to produce a home-like atmosphere at the farm and pass time during the long, dark winter evenings.

We discussed the situation all night and finally decided that Tot should return yet once more to Urga the next day, quite openly and under the pretext of sending off a telegram. He would then take steps to let Mrs. Wilson know that the strychnine had been successfully removed from Urga, and would find out how the land lay. I, for my part, would go slowly on, and he would catch me up either that day or the next, after which we expected to be back at Bulgun Tal in a fortnight. It was, in fact, necessary to hurry home, for the winter might now be upon us at any time, and we had no winter equipment.

At dawn of day we helped one another to harness up, and while I toiled forward with my caravan over the

A DIFFICULT ACT OF FRIENDSHIP

steppe, Tot rode singing back to Urga—without the strychnine now and with a conscience as clean and light as the clear blue autumn sky. If I had then surmised that I should not see him again for fourteen days, and had I foreseen what those days were going to provide in the way of tribulations, I would perhaps have heaved the whole caravan into the Tola River, turned the horses loose on the highway, while I mounted the swiftest and galloped off.

CHAPTER XII

THE JOURNEY HOME

THE caravan consisted of eight wagons, with the horses harnessed Russian fashion, and far too heavily loaded, as soon appeared. Of living creatures, there were, besides myself, eleven restive horses and a sweet little foal. I was soon to be swearing at that foal from morning till night and a great deal of the night besides. Never before nor since have I lived through a series of days in such constant rage, as during the fortnight that the " picnic " lasted. And never have I possessed so brilliant a virtuosity with oaths in various languages as on the fourteenth day, when I staggered with my whole " circus " into the yard of that decent Russian, Boldikov at Van Kure, and found Tot, who bade me a smiling welcome and expressed his astonishment at the lateness of my arrival. He had been there six days, eagerly expecting me all the time.

My fourteen days had passed thus : at the beginning things had gone pretty well. The first trouble that presented itself was occasioned by the mother of the sweet little foal. Each of the horses was tied to the tail of the wagon in front of it, in a long row. So as to be able to oversee the whole caravan, I went last, singing like a lark and cheerily cracking my whip. The mare, the tender mother of the sweet little foal, ran in the lead, with the task of following the trail across the steppe and the admonition to maintain a proper pace. But, as so often happens in this life, it was the mother that ran after the child and not the child that obediently followed in the mother's footsteps. The result was that if the foal ran out on to the steppe—and that was what it did— the mare followed, taking the whole caravan with her. If the foal fell behind, the mare stopped abruptly, whinnied lamentably and tried to turn and twist so that she could see her beloved offspring, till she had induced as many wagons as possible to get jammed in an inextricable tangle. I then tried tying the mare last in the column, but the result was that, in her eagerness to follow her swift-footed young, she pushed all the wagons into a zigzag across the road. If I tied the mother in the middle, the foal ran, to slake its thirst, hungry and lost, to each of the horses in turn, so that these were annoyed at being disturbed at their work and let out at the unmannerly youngster with their hind-legs. Then the foal squealed, the mother whinnied, and we had to halt while those two each assured themselves that the other was the right one, nosed one another and suckled—and then we got going again. It was all very touching, this affection, but many a time when I was sweating and hoarse enough, I came near shooting both mother and child.

Still, evening came at last and I made a halt in a suitable spot. It was not easy to unhitch single-handed, but I did it. The horses were securely tied up to the wagons while I collected my store of cow-dung, made a fire and ate my dry bread and good mutton and drank steaming hot coffee. I was tired and sleepy, and when the stars began to blink, I found that my spread sleeping sack looked inviting. It was desirable to make an early start next morning, so as to put as great a distance as possible between me and Urga. I wanted to be out of the reach of " the green police ".

In order to facilitate an early start I had to let the horses graze during the night, so I turned them loose as soon as they were sufficiently cooled off after the day's march. I had counted on being able to sit dozing in my sleeping sack, leaning comfortably against a wagon, while keeping a somnolent eye upon the animals' silhouettes in the starlit night. But there was not much time to sit dozing, for although I had placed the wagon-park in a place where there was succulent grass, the best grazing I had seen during the last hour's march, the horses must needs stray out over the steppe, out of my sight, and of course in eleven different directions. I had to spend the

THE JOURNEY HOME

following hours in galloping round in a circle in the endeavour to keep the horses together within a reasonably limited area, to count the black patches in the darkness and decide whether a motionless patch was a horse or only a stone or a bush, and was thus kept hard at work till late, when the night resounded with the melodious howling of the wolves, which brought all eleven shadows back with the speed of arrows to the immediate neighbourhood of the wagons. Nervous and shaking with terror, not daring to touch a blade of grass, the horses spent the rest of the night under the shadow of my wings, until the paling of the stars announced the dawning of a new day.

We have all seen the Russian harness, with its *chomut* and its bow-like *dugá*, which rises above the horse's head, in pretty pictures of troikas flying over Siberian snows, pursued by wolves. It is splendid harness, especially on bad roads, for its elasticity allows the wagon to follow the irregularities of the ground without the shafts breaking, as would often happen with ordinary harness. Moreover the advantage of the elasticity of the *dugá* to which the horse is attached, is that the wagon does not upset so long as the horse keeps its feet. For two practised persons it is an easy business to hitch up. They stand one on each side of the horse, get a purchase with one foot against the *chomut*, and pull with all their might, each on his leather strap, until the stubborn *dugá* is pressed down between the shafts. *Sehr einfach*, when there are two of you.

But when on the other hand you are alone, you are precisely one man too few to manage the harnessing. The point is that unfortunately one's assistant must be on the other side of the horse, in a place which one cannot reach from the position one must take up oneself. And one must pull on both the straps at once. But that the job *can* be done singlehanded I had occasion to demonstrate nearly four hundred times on the journey to Van Kure. One may indeed imagine that, by carrying out this manœuvre so many times in the course of a fortnight, I ought to have acquired a considerable dexterity, but all I attained was a grim determination, a persistent

Three distinguished Lamas on horseback

Bassoon-blowers in a Lamaistic procession

Courageous Lamas from Van Kure venture out on the Orkhon river in a hollowed out tree trunk

THE JOURNEY HOME

rage, and lacerated and frozen fingers. I could never learn to be in two places at once.

The caravan lumbered along across the steppe through a variety of adversities and frequent delays, but Tot, alone on his swift horse, did not appear. I drove on late into the night in the hope that Tot would catch me up so as to help with the unhitching, but all in vain. At last we made a halt, for we were dead tired. I had to have a sleep, so I tied the horses to the wagon, rolled myself up in my sleeping-sack and allowed myself several hours' slumber. When I awoke at daybreak, one of the hungry horses had broke loose and was grazing a good way off in the direction of Urga. I threw myself on to one of the other horses to catch the runaway, but he, in whose equine brain the memory remained of his comfortable stall at Urga and the abundant oat rations of civilization, kept himself out of reach all the time and trotted in the direction of the forbidden city. We were already half-way there before I caught the brute, and by the time we finally got back to our camp and the horses tethered there, the sun had set.

Tot and I had reckoned on six days for the journey to Van Kure, where fresh provisions were to be laid in. We had allowed one kilogram of oats per day for each horse. During my long absence, however, some of the animals, driven by hunger, had contrived to reach both the oat-sacks and had bitten holes in them to get at the good fodder. What they had not eaten lay scattered on the steppe. The result was that some of the horses had their bellies distended with oats, while the rest, who were tied up farther off and had not succeeded in breaking loose, were famished and stood regarding the devastation with Tantalus glances from a distance. And thus it was good-bye to the oat rations which were to have lasted for the rest of the journey to Van Kure.

And now the winter set in with cold and snow. The only semblance of winter outfit I had was a short hunting-jacket of antelope skin which I wore over my khaki shirt. I had no fur cap and the tips of my ears froze. Nor had I any gloves, and I got frost into the scratches and wounds which the daily harnessing caused me. My hands were swollen and inflamed, and hurt me every time I used them to do my work. The worst was when I had to tighten up the many stiff ropes.

Several times during the unending fourteen days I got, however, some relief from my labours. And this was when the solitude was broken by travelling Mongols passing the caravan. I never let such occasions pass without at once engaging the traveller as assistant with the troublesome harnessing to which I daily looked forward with growing anxiety as my hands grew worse. Sometimes a chance of this kind came early in the day after a very short march, but I nevertheless let no occasion pass if the place of meeting was in any way suitable for camping. It happened, too, that I toiled on, long after night had fallen, in the vain hope that a helper would cross my solitary path.

One day I met a poor pilgrim, on his way, scrip on back, to Urga, the "Cloister of God". With extravagant promises I prevailed on him to turn back and accompany my caravan. The fellow was a real experience. He could walk and sleep at the same time—strictly speaking he slept all the time—and his whole stock of words was confined to a melancholy: *Oto yane?* (eh, what?). When a narrow shave or a dangerous passage called for rapid action he would stand gaping at me with his sleepy "*Oto yane*".

We made shorter marches and had more mishaps during the two days when the holy man was my companion than during all the rest of the journey, and when at night I told him to lie against my back for the sake of warmth, I got lice on me. Moreover the man's colossal appetite made such a hole in my scanty stock of food that I soon wished him where the pepper grows. I told him so in courteous terms one morning, when I richly rewarded his valuable services and bade him farewell. He gazed alternately at the pay in his hand and the already departing caravan, repeating the while his philosophic and inspiring "*Oto yane*".

The mountain passes were frequent obstructions in my way. Towards the end of the journey the exhaustion of the horses was an added difficulty in getting over the passes. Steep slopes and abrupt bends made it impossible to direct simultaneously the whole long row of wagons. I had to unhitch at the foot of the pass and set four horses to draw every wagon I took over. Each time it was a matter of unhitching and taking two horses back with me to help with the next wagon. Once a passage like this took two whole days, and when darkness came on I had to spend the night in the middle of the pass with the wagon and horses I was then driving, while all night long my troubled thoughts went back and forth between the two sides of the mountain ridge where horses and laden wagons remained unguarded.

They said I looked frightful when I at last arrived at the monastery town of Van Kure—but a glance at Madame Boldikov's mirror assured me that I still had not a single grey hair in my head—to my very great surprise.

As soon as I caught sight of Tot, I lost all interest in the caravan, once I had explicitly informed him that it *was* the same caravan that he and I, two weeks back, had agreed to conduct from Urga to Van Kure. To my great regret, however, he at once succeeded in getting a couple of Russians to help him when he had to deal with the animals and wagons.

A delicious Russian bath, ointment and bandages on my hands, and I was ready to fall to on the splendid Russian *pelmeni* and *pirozki* to which Madame Boldikov invited me in her warm room.

The horses were now fed and cared for by Boldikov's people and it was wonderful to be released for a time from this worry. And then I at once set some Mongols to work making me a warm fur coat, fur cap and gloves. The resumption of our journey to Bulgun Tal could thus be looked forward to with equanimity.

It is a splendid thing that one so quickly forgets vexations, difficulties and suffering, when they are well over. Once one is clean, fed, warmed through and rested, one has only a sense of relief that one's difficulties have been overcome, and the pleasant feeling of satisfaction that results from a task successfully accomplished. And the

THE JOURNEY HOME

more surmounted difficulties one has behind one, the greater the self-confidence and assurance with which one goes to meet new troubles.

Tot reported that everything was " O.K." at Urga. He had remained there three days and then had ridden swiftly on the return journey, with the idea of overtaking the caravan—a vain hope which he continued to entertain right up to his arrival at Van Kure. He had happened to ride by a quite different way, and to turn back in order to seek tidings of me would have been a very dubious undertaking, for the steppe is endless.

We sat at our ease late into the night, chatting, drinking tea from tall Russian glasses and puffing long Russian cigarettes. The big copper samovar steamed and bubbled at one end of the long table. In a corner of the room an icon hung under the ceiling. The Blessed Virgin's face and the little Christ child that she held to her breast were painted on wood. A little primitive in execution but beautiful in its ancient colouring. The old monk who once—generations back—had executed it had put the pure radiance of maternal love into the Virgin's face, with the lovely eyes tenderly regarding the child in her arms. Later, simple folk in their naïve adoration had covered the aureoles round the two faces with gilded metal, and festooned the picture with coloured beads in which the light from the little oil lamp hanging in front of the picture glittered and gleamed. But the more one looked at the icon, the more dominant became the expression of purity and love in the face of the mother, till this absorbed all one's attention.

Except for the long table and the benches on either side, there was no furniture in the room, and there were no ornaments or pictures on the walls. But it was astonishing how the great stove emitting its bland warmth, the big family samovar bubbling at the end of the table, and the icon gleaming as a luminous point in the dark corner, gave a sense of peace and homeliness to that little room.

After we had consumed many glasses of tea, Boldikov suddenly got up, stroked his long patriarchal beard and said good night. Before he left the room he turned

THE JOURNEY HOME

towards the corner and, with his gaze fixed on the icon, made the sign of the cross from his forehead down over his broad breast while he repeated an earnest prayer, as a man who has been through much.

Tot's saddle-horse was vigorous and well rested, whereas my newly arrived horses were exhausted after the trying journey with the heavy wagons. So that we might get back to the farm as quickly as possible we decided that Tot should ride on ahead to Igagården to fetch fresh horses and the other fellows, who would meet me at the Selenga River to help with the difficult crossing and to take over the transport for the rest of the way to Bulgun Tal.

One of Boldikov's Mongols would go with me as assistant on the road to Selenga.

NEXT morning, however, a new difficulty arose. At the last moment some members of the pro-Russian Young Mongol Party had come from Urga where they had been running propaganda " on behalf of the people ". Most of the inhabitants of Van Kure are lamas who live in peaceful seclusion among the many temples and schools of the cloister town. Their conservative temper was always insusceptible to a doctrine so diametrically opposed to their own religion. The local prince, Daichin Wang, was incarcerated in one of the Soviet's prisons in Urga, and his soldiers and adherents—such as had not been killed—were scattered to the winds and had sought refuge in out of the way mountainous tracts where, with Buddhist fatalism, they watched developments in the hope that the good old times would return.

Daichin Wang's palace, which lay four miles from Van Kure, was desolate and abandoned. Besides the lamas in the cloister town, there were at the time in Van Kure only five distressed Russians of the old school, and a number of Chinese traders who timidly hid behind the palisades surrounding their firm's shops and warehouses. All these Chinese derived from Peking or Tientsin, and represented the trading dynasties that for many generations had worked among the Mongols, where by ability and prudence, they had earned large sums, a fact to which the handsome furnishing, the elaborate woodcarving and the lavish gilding of their houses and pavilions bore witness.

But if the young Soviet prophets found no fit soil for their propaganda among the inhabitants, they had the gratification of establishing all sorts of offices and places to which they appointed themselves.

Van Kure and its peaceful population had lived its dream life on the banks of the Ockhon River for generations without a thought of customs inspections and such like troublesome blessings of civilization. Now they had to learn that it was " for the good of the people " and also in their own interests that all who came and went from their little community should be examined and should pay bright silver dollars to the new authorities.

A number of the Young Mongols from Urga had set up a couple of tents outside the town, and all who came or went had to pass there for examination. They had equipped a handful of the town rabble with rifles, and this troop now constituted the force on which they based their authority. It was an accursed business for us.

We had in our baggage enough poison to put an end to every living creature in Van Kure and its surroundings. We ought to get rid of it before the examination, but how could this be done without frightful consequences? We dared not throw it into the river of whose water so many people and animals drank. If we buried it, our absurd consciences would go in dread of the day when it should be found and occasion disaster in the hands of the ignorant. The risk was great, since the strychnine we were carrying was in the form of powder, whereas the Russian poison which the Mongols were accustomed to use was in crystals.

We did not yet know whether the newly established customs station would examine only passports and other papers from Urga or would also examine goods. Since we had undergone customs inspection in Urga and had our receipt for duty paid on all our goods, it was presumably only a question of an examination of documents. But this doubt ought soon to be cleared up, when Tot went through with his stuffed but innocent saddle bags.

THE JOURNEY HOME

Tot said good-bye and rode off, while I stood on the roof of the house and narrowly watched developments. He rode straight towards the north, but was soon stopped by a couple of galloping Mongols who ordered him to accompany them to the station, which he duly did. He remained sitting in the saddle and handed a bundle of papers to a couple of Young Mongols, who glanced through them, and then Tot rode on without more detailed inspection. So it was not so dangerous. For safety's sake, however, I went out by night and rearranged the packages in the boxes in which the strychnine lay hidden so that they looked as innocent as possible.

CHAPTER XIII

CUSTOMS EXAMINATION AND CHRISTMAS
TREE TINSEL

NEXT morning we started early and, just outside the town, were hailed by a couple of mounted men who took us to the inspection tent. I went at once with the papers in my hand into the principal tent, but found only a Chinese coolie engaged in making a fire. The occupants of the tent, the two controllers of the station, had gone down to one of the Chinese firms to carry out some investigations. If I would take a seat, they would soon return, which they did—after I had been waiting four hours. That is to say, one of them came, who unfortunately was only the second in command, and he could not let me and the caravan proceed until the arrival of the commandant himself. But what he could do was to satisfy his unbelievable curiosity during the two more hours that elasped before his chief arrived. He stuck his flat nose into every part of the loads on my wagons. My Mongol, Dagbar, who suspected nothing about the perilous wares lying hidden at the bottom on the two boxes, was helpfulness itself and assisted the official to shift the goods and open up the packages, so that the latter should be able to see as much as possible. They came appallingly near to the two compromising boxes. To render him harmless I ordered Dagbar to keep the foal at a distance of twenty yards from the wagons, in the hope that this would require all his energy for a good while; and it did—so for once the foal was of some use.

I now took over the exhibition of the goods and tried to direct the inspector's interest to innocuous things. One of the soldiers had meanwhile caught sight of the gaily coloured cover of a number of the *Saturday*

CUSTOMS EXAMINATION

Evening Post, whose copiously illustrated contents soon attracted the attention of all of them. The exciseman's interest in tea and tobacco rapidly vanished when he heard the mirth of the soldiers, and he joined them with eager curiosity. The journal they had got hold of was one of the bundle that concealed the strychnine. The Mongols enjoyed the many brightly coloured illustrations. They found pictures of cows, horses, rifles, pistols and many other things that they were able to understand, and one number after another was pulled out of the box, and all the time we were getting nearer and nearer to the strychnine. Things were getting desperate.

At this critical moment the chief official returned followed by four soldiers and two Chinamen who, with or without reason, had been arrested. I hoped that this interruption would cut short the literary interest of the Mongols, but, instead, it was the chief who, having dismounted, came forward to us. By this time there could not be more than two magazines left in the box, after which it only remained to lift out four cardboard boxes and—the strychnine would be disclosed. And then— goodbye to me! My brain worked feverishly to find a way of escape. When the officer in command himself wanted to open the first cardboard box, I accordingly held him back with every indication of violent alarm. I repeatedly uttered the Mongolian word "*burkhan*" (holy) and laid the palm of my hand on my forehead. The men looked at me, first wonderingly and then doubtfully, but their curiosity soon took the upper hand, and the box must be opened. I did so with vociferous protests and a woebegone air, which certainly was not difficult to me at that moment. The contents of the box looked very "*burkhan*" and they began to be a little hesitant. There were coloured glass globes, gilt stars, Christmas tree tinsel and many other wonderful things which set their fancy in lively movement. With trembling hands I took up one article after another, touched my forehead with it and laid it reverently back in the box. But they were still curious, and I had to open the next box, which I did with much lamentation and complaining. The Mongols had cautiously stepped a little back from

CUSTOMS EXAMINATION

me, but were stretching their necks to get a sight of the new splendours. Slowly I drew a dazzling object out of the box, pressed it against my forehead, lifted it up towards heaven and carried it in upstretched hands round the circle, which grew wider and wider as the natives gave back before my fanatical glance and my mystical deportment. Then I stopped in front of the commanding officer and stretched the object out towards him three times, repeating as many times the first verse of the good old song : " The time I went away ", in a deep, monotonous voice. Then there was a bang which made me fall plump on the ground, howling like an idiot and wriggling like a worm. Out of the object, which was a large glittering cracker, I now drew a Charlie Chaplin mask which I put on, before slowly rising again. By this time all the Mongols were in full flight for the tent opening, into which they vanished, and I stalked after them with long sentry-go steps, singing Hallelujah !

Before I myself went into the commandant's tent, I put Charlie Chaplin in my pocket. I tottered in and sank down exhausted before their wondering and anxious eyes. Then I delivered a long monologue to myself in fluent Danish, rolled my eyes and shook my head, and gave the commandant my papers which he diffidently handed back to me. Not a word was uttered ; there was the silence of death as I left the tent and made use of the psychologically appropriate moment to shout : " Gee up, all my horses ! "

In my hurry I had clean forgotten Dagbar and the foal, but was reminded of them when the latter came galloping up to its mother some way out on the steppe. Dagbar, on the other hand, I never saw again.

The road was quite good, and when we got on to the long slope down towards the valley of the Selenga, progress was rapid. I continued the march till long after dark, and when we camped it was right out in the solitude of the wilderness and beside the first trees I had seen since Urga. I had emitted many a sigh of relief during the day's ride, and when I crawled into my sleeping-sack beside a comforting fire of birchwood, my heart was as light as a bird's.

CUSTOMS EXAMINATION

At noon on the third day I reached the ferry over the Selenga. Many hours before I caught sight of the ferry I heard a violent crashing and groaning which made the horses nervous and forboded a troublesome crossing. When I came up to the three tents in which the ferrymen lived, I found them empty, and the fantastic ferry boats drawn up on land. A foaming mixture of broken ice and water filled the river and produced a deafening din. Small pieces and large leapt and danced in the rushing water. To ferry across in those primitive craft was unthinkable in that maelstrom. In some days all the floating lumps of ice would probably have grown together into a bridge uniting the two banks. But how many days was it likely to be before the ice bridge was firm enough to carry my heavily laden caravan? I had no desire to sit here, so near my journey's end, in this roaring solitude, and just wait. I unhitched, and rode the strongest of the horses along the edge of the bank to look for a place where there was some possibility of getting across.

A little way down, the river widened out to about two hundred yards, with the result that the stream there ran more silently and more calmly. The water ought to be shallower here, since the wider bed allowed the river to extend instead of digging itself in. In the middle of the river was a long sandbank about fifteen feet wide. If an attempt were to be made that was clearly the place. I tried to pick out a spot where the curve of the shore pointed to a gradually increasing depth. An icy wind was blowing along the river. I drove my horse with hard cuts of the whip out into the ice-cold water. I started a hundred yards below the sandbank and rode diagonally against the stream towards the lower end of the island. The water rose slowly, step by step, making my progress more and more difficult. When it reached the horses flanks the current got hold of him, and I had to use reins and whip repeatedly to stop him turning downstream. When the horse turned under the weight of the water and the packed ice floes, I had to turn him right against the stream and with my whip remove the lumps of ice that would pile up against his sides. When

I had a patch of ice-free water in front of me, I swung the horse at as wide an angle as he could manage and rode towards the sandbank, until I was obliged again to go head on against the stream and push the ice away from his sides. The horse snorted anxiously and his hesitating paces grew slower as the water grew deeper. I was kneeling on the saddle, the lower edge of which the water had now reached. We had covered more than half the distance to the bank and I hoped we had reached the deepest place. If the water rose a few more inches, the horse would lose its foothold and we would both be carried away by the ice which was churning and grinding in the swirl of the river. It was dangerous, too, to turn round here, for the moment the horse came broadside on to the current it would probably be thrown over. Numberless accounts of animals and men who had lost their lives in this way passed through my brain.

Twenty yards from the sandbank the horse suddenly lost his footing with his forelegs. For a moment his head and neck disappeared under the water to come up again spluttering and snorting with terror. There was only one thing to do. I loosed my grip on the saddle and slipped down into the water on the upstream side of the horse, but kept hold of the rein with my right hand. The horse, now relieved of the load of my body, got his head and neck clear above the water, which he thrashed with his legs. The water broke over my head, which came in contact with several lumps of ice. Then the tired horse felt firm ground under his hind feet. He got up and struck out in the air with his forelegs, and I observed that my hold on the reins came near pulling him backwards into the stream again. I loosed the reins and caught hold of the stirrup. Then I dropped the stirrup and grasped the horse's tail just as he got ground under all four feet. A moment later I was dragged up on to dry land—on to the desolate sandbank in the middle of the river.

To stay there was, however, to freeze to death. From the sandspit the remaining stretch to the opposite bank looked shorter and easier than the one we had already come through. I drove my horse against the stream

Acclimatized

CUSTOMS EXAMINATION

again and, without the water coming above my knees—I was so wet already that I did not trouble to draw my legs up under me—we reached the opposite bank about four hundred yards higher up the river than the point from which we started. I trotted and galloped the horse up and down on the bank to warm us both up and then began the return journey from a point just opposite that from which I had started from the other side. I had to use the whip freely before I could get the poor beast yet again to throw itself into the icy, foaming water. The greater part of the way I walked in the water, holding the horse by rein and stirrup.

Fortunately, two of the ferrymen had returned and were standing on the bank, amazed to see me step ashore, pounded to a jelly and dripping with water. They helped me to rub down the horse vigorously with old bits of felt, and I myself was soon sitting naked in front of a blazing fire in one of their tents, drinking cup after cup of hot tea.

The ferrymen blamed my foolhardiness, but admitted that the place I had chosen for the crossing was the only one for a very long stretch where one could ride across the river at high water. This was information that they were in the habit of selling to passing travellers for hard cash. Then I told them that I thought of fording the river next day with wagons, horses and all. While their indignant protests hailed upon me, I fell asleep.

One can understand the respect of these Mongols for the rushing water when one knows that no Mongol can swim, not even these ferrymen who have spent many years in ferrying people across the river, and that it usually makes them giddy and seasick to sit in a boat and see the water under and round about them.

Next morning I unloaded two of the wagons and harnessed the best horses to them. These latter were united by a five-foot rod which I fastened to their bits. With the aid of two planks I succeeded in hauling up one of the loaded wagons so that each of its two wheels stood on one of the empty wagons. The loaded wagon was lashed to the two under ones in such a manner that together they formed a pretty solid construction. After

CUSTOMS EXAMINATION

a deal of persuasion the two ferrymen were induced each to take his place on one of the empty wagons, with a good whip in his hand. All the rope that had not been otherwise used was tied together, and with the end of this long line made fast to my saddle, I rode the same way as the previous day, but with less trouble, because the water level in the early morning was somewhat lower than the day before. The sun melts the snow on the mountains during the day and brings considerable extra quantities of water into the Selenga in the course of the afternoon by tributaries and runnels.

This notable equipage was now driven out into the water, and while the two Mongols drove the horses forward with cracking of whips and shouts, I rode slowly up the sandbank, so that the line was kept fairly taut. When the horses were approaching the deep part of the river, I ordered a halt and rode down to the lowest point of the sandspit where I shortened the line. Then we started again, and I now made my horse pull as much as he could. A sudden jerk almost brought him down. The two Mongols bellowed, and the horses' hooves ploughed the waters of the river. The two wagons swayed and then floated in a curve towards the middle of the river where, in the calm water below the bank, I made my horse haul the vessel into safety. We crossed the other part of the river without difficulty, and on the farther shore unloaded the upper wagon without any of the goods having been in contact with the water.

Next time we loaded heavy stones on to the under wagons and so prevented them from floating with the stream in deep water. During the remaining crossings I did not leave the sandbank, but only attended to the work with the line, with the aid of my good horse. With one exception, however, when in the last crossing one of the horses suddenly went down, and I had to go out again into the icy water. The horse refused to get up, so I was obliged to cut it loose from harness, under water, before I succeeded in getting it to land. This manœuvre took me a quarter of an hour, during which I had to stay up to my chest in water and ice.

When at length the last wagons had left the sandbank,

CUSTOMS EXAMINATION

I saw in the distance two troikas driving towards us across the steppe. It was " the little husbandman " and Misha the Cossack, who arrived just at the right moment with full oat sacks, fresh horses and relief for me.

We lighted a huge fire from the plentiful driftwood lying on the bank, and sitting in front of it, among my own people with whom I need not be on my guard, I warmed my frozen fingers, my wet clothes and my miserable soul. Another of those moments that are so glorious that they etch themselves firmly into the memory for ever.

When the blessed warmth and the good news from the farm, where all was well, had put new life into me, I swung myself up on to a fresh horse and rode at any easy and lively trot, with the sun shining in my face, away from the steppe and the river, up towards the adjacent edge of the forest which formed the entrance to the *taiga* that stretches endlessly northward, and within which somewhere far off lay my beloved frontier home. I spent the night by a crackling fire of fragrant cedarwood, inhaled the woodland sweetness and listened to the innumerable living sounds of the forest. At noon next day I passed the last hill behind which lay Bulgun Tal. And luck smiled on me.

So then I sat once more at the long table in the mess, ate and drank, talked and listened to the boys, while Sava got ready the bath in our Russian bath-house. Free from cares and worries, clean and spruce, I crept into my sleeping-sack. Next morning, long after sunrise, I had tea " in bed ", and then turned over on the other side to go on dreaming.

Three days later Isager arrived with the caravan and its quantities of necessaries which made the farm a gathering point for the population of the district. Buffalo took stock of the consignment before it was carried safely into the *ambar* (warehouse). Alluring samples of all the splendid goods were placed on exhibition in the " shop ", where Buffalo soon set to work weighing out sugar, measuring up cloth and counting bricks of tea. The Mongols, eager to buy, brought in the first furs of the

CUSTOMS EXAMINATION

season as currency. There was life and joy on the farm the winter campaign had begun.

The wagons and horses of the caravan looked thoroughly worn out, but they had come through the long and trying journey. The two Cossacks fed and tended the new horses with care and skill, and our Buriat carpenters looked to and repaired the wagons.

In the evenings, when all was quiet, we gathered in the mess before the primitive map we had at our disposal, to arrange for the winter a programme which should bring into play all our powers and all our energy and yield as good and profitable results as possible.

The strychnine was the subject of much discussion. My view was that not a bottle of it ought to be sold from the farm. We agreed to put the whole stock in a safe hiding-place where we could have control of it without arousing remark or suspicion. One late nocturnal hour the poison was buried under the floor of the log-house which was used as a guest-room. This allowed any horrible suspicions to be directed against the many different transient travellers who lodged here for a single night, afterwards to disappear in various directions on the steppe. One of the members of the expedition was to occupy the guest-room at night.

OUR stock of goods was to be divided between the farm and three several expeditions which Krebs, Isager and I were to undertake to distant tracts where furs were abundant. Since I had had the whole trouble of bringing the caravan over the long and difficult way, I demanded the lion's share of the goods.

Krebs and Isager were to travel together to the neighbourhood of the Russian boundary where they would quarter themselves on the Russian widow, Madame Spiegel, who had a large farm and knew the conditions and the people well, having lived long in Mongolia. With her farm as base they intended to make hunting and buying journeys in the district. Among other things, they would visit a large monastery, Darkhat Kure, lying out of the way, west of Hubso Gol.

I myself knew very little of the conditions to the

northward, but had a burning desire to learn to know those tracts. From the mountains round Bulgun Tal I had often gazed out towards the forest-clad mountain slopes and snowy summits in the north. I was drawn to the unknown and longed to penetrate its recesses, where I was sure adventure awaited me.

Dangsurong the widely travelled, one of my closest Mongol friends, said that far up there in the north lay a fertile river valley, Kiäkt, from which four passes led. Over the northernmost pass ran the road to " holy Russia's " wide *taiga*. Westward another pass led to the hunting grounds of the primitive Soyotes. Going eastward one went over a high pass into the land of bears and Sanagen Buriats. Finally, the fourth way was the mountain path that made communication possible between Kiäkt and the wide Mongolian steppes in the south. And this was the one that would interest me.

Travelling this road from Bulgun Tal, one must surmount three passes before reaching the remote valley where hunters of three different religions meet. Thither would I turn my steps.

CHAPTER XIV

WINTER FUR CAMPAIGN

AFTER taking cordial farewell of our friends, whom we should not see again for a long and indefinite time, Sava the Cossack and I started out from the farm early one November morning. We were carefully but lightly equipped. We carried with us a selection of goods which we judged would meet the taste of the unknown mountain population and prove suitable for exchange purposes. In addition we had two thousand shining silver dollars of whose genuine ring we assured ourselves before starting.

The Mongols are very critical in accepting silver in payment, and when the person paying it is unknown in the district, they examine the coins carefully before they accept them at their face value. The most usual method of testing coins is to take the *yenshan* (the Chinese silver dollar) between the nailpoints of the thumb and forefinger. They then blow upon the edge of the coin and carry it quickly up to the ear to hear if the slight ringing and the right note, which the correct silver alloy should give out, is present. Sava and I had submitted the whole of the coins to this test, and the two thousand we selected all rang in a particularly convincing manner, with the ring of genuine silver.

The three horses we took with us were in good condition and were selected from among those that had got on best on the difficult passes between Urga and Van Kure. Behind the wagons we had made fast a spare wagon-wheel and a reserve *dugá*. We had also forged at the farm special shoes for the horses, with sharp frost-nails which would enable them to hold up on slippery ice-slopes, and we took plenty of rope and the tools necessary for carrying out repairs to the wagons. I carried my

8 mm. Mannlicher rifle and Sava a Belgian repeating pistol. Our only article of luxury was a Mongolian tent, whose blue cloth was adorned with sewn-on white figures symbolizing long life, twofold luck and heaps of riches.

Thus equipped we drove over the wide yellow steppe towards the adventure in the north for which our restless blood was longing. Naturally we both sang. One sings so readily and so light-heartedly in the presence of pure, unspoiled nature, where there is so much to lift up and animate one's latent emotions, and no discouraging critic to impose silence. Sava sang an inspiriting melody, the unwritten strains of the steppe, harmonized for the strings of the balalaika by some nameless Cossack—a composer who had never written a note.

The song's Russian words followed the path of the Cossack from the parting with his mother and little Verushka with the long pale plaits, out to the wars against the heathen Turks; it sang of the howling of the wolves at night, of the falcon's flight in the storm, of the horse's light dancing paces across the steppe. All of it called up memories in Sava. When at last he sang of the Cossack's homecoming to the cottage and Verushka, the song changed into the minor key, for behind the mountains in front of us lay the exiled Sava's home—so near for a wistful young Cossack on a swift horse, but —through those mountains were drawn a boundary line, snow-white on one side, but red as blood on the other. A boundary of fanatical hatred and blind desire for vengeance, more dangerous to cross than any obstacle nature can lay in the path of a bold rider.

I had to sing to the strange melody, and since I did not know the Russian words of the song, I sang of all that rejoiced my heart and made my mood so gay, the wild mountains we rode to meet and all that lay behind their pointed crests in the unknown valleys among cedar-clad mountain slopes.

THEN one day we passed the rise that hid our home on the steppe from our gaze. We were following Egin Gol, which seemed to us more and more changed the farther we went from Bulgun Tal. The hills ran sometimes right down to the river which rushed foaming and roaring far below us in its narrow bed with such violence that no ice could form in its centre. In places the slope was so steep that we could not drive the wagons on the bank but had to lower them on to the ice which lay firm and fit to bear along the sides of the river. At sundown we came to the place where the Uri River flows into Egin Gol. Thus increased in volume and now of imposing dimensions, Egin Gol disappears from the eye far away in the east, later to unite with the great Selenga which, with its tributaries, carries the waters of Northern Mongolia to far-off Lake Baikal.

A hundred yards up the Uri we camped on the edge of the forest. Long after we had crawled into our sleeping-sacks I lay listening to the roar of the river, and in dreams I fought my way through the rushing water up to its unknown sources, far up among the mountains—the ultimate goal of our journey. We slept splendidly in our tent with a fire between us and did not begin to freeze until the stars were paling and it was time to get up.

That morning I had a little adventure, for, not far from the camping-place, I found a group of stunted apple trees. I imprinted the place on my memory with the idea of bringing some specimens to the garden at Bulgun Tal. Even if the fruit should not be particularly luscious, it would still be splendid to have blossoming apple trees as an annually recurring delight. These were the first and last apple trees I saw in Mongolia.

After the horses had been fed and watered and the wagons looked to and greased, we started just as the sun touched the surrounding mountain tops. At noon we reached a little monastery built entirely of wood. It consisted of a few *Duguns* (temples within a cloister) of simple architecture, well placed on an idyllic site on the verge of the forest by the river bank. The sweeping lines of towers and roof rose above the undulant contours of the snow-weighted tree-tops. The architect had followed the curve of the boughs, so that from a distance the gilded spires looked like giant larch trees in a fairy tale.

Chinese bells hung at the corners of the temple roof. The profound silence was broken only by the tinkling of the bells before the wind and the cooing of the doves that answered from the darkness of the woods.

As we approached the palisading a couple of dogs rushed at us, barking. Their bark, however, sounded more like a welcome, and had a cadence quite different from that which I was accustomed to hear from savage Mongolian dogs. Half-way to us one of them stopped and, soon after, the other, deprived of the competition of his fellow, saw no reason to go farther in the deep snow. Having now done their duty by barking, they shook themselves in the sun and awaited our coming. When we passed them they sniffed the air inquisitively, nosed our legs, wagged their bushy tails and trotted after us up to the monastery gate. They were the friendliest dogs I encountered in the whole of Central Asia.

We tied up the horses and stepped through the gate of the palisade into the courtyard. There was apparently no living being there. In one corner of the *hashanda* stood three Mongol tents and a slight smoke was rising from the opening of one of them. We went into this one and found before the fire an ancient crone, sitting alone and talking to herself. The upper part of her body was naked, and her hair was clipped short. We threw ourselves down on the opposite side of the fire and greeted her with a: " *Mendu sain beino ?* " (Have you peace in your soul ?) She nodded to us amiably but continued her uninterrupted muttering, while she blew up the fire and prepared to make tea. We observed that she was stone deaf, but her friendliness was unmistakable, and she offered us as much tea as we could drink. But when, later, we left the tent to try to get hold of someone who could answer our questions, she did not once look after us, but only continued her amiable muttering.

The other tents also showed signs of occupation, though vacant for the moment. The monastic building lay silent, with wide open doors. Small lamps were burning before the altar, but the human beings who had lighted them were not to be seen.

We determined to stay in that lovely place to see whether we could not awaken the sleeping cloister. After having unharnessed the horses and fed them, we wandered round, curious and wondering. We could have driven off with the temple's most sacred possessions without anyone appearing to protest. We ate and sunned ourselves till the sun's early setting behind the mountain ridge drove the chill down into the valley and forced us into the tent, where the old woman was sitting as before, nodding amiably and talking to herself.

Suddenly the dogs gave tongue again, and soon after came the echo of a shepherd's yodelling. When we ran out we saw a mighty herd of horses, oxen and sheep slowly approaching the monastery. The herd was driven by an aged lama and his *shabi* (disciple). The old man greeted us in friendly wise and showed not the least surprise or distrust at finding two armed strangers on his lonely lands.

The monastery was called Dain Derchen Kure and was quite wealthy. Besides the old lama and his disciple eight other lamas were attached to it, who at the time were with their respective families in the neighbourhood helping them to move house. The cattle we had seen belonged to the monastery, and the necessary service of the monastery was performed by the old man and his pupil.

The trappers of the district, who otherwise often came in troops on pilgrimage to the sanctuary, were now swallowed up in the great forests in search of furs. Later in the winter a couple of Chinamen would come from Van Kure with silver and trading goods for exchange against the trappers' catch, and then things would grow lively again at the monastery. If the year had been profitable for the trappers, they never neglected to present ample gifts to the divinity who ruled over them, as well as over nature of whose riches they took toll. The old man explained all this to us while he was leading the cattle into their folds.

The little *shabi* was the only person in the place who paid us any further attention. His sharp black eyes followed us uninterruptedly and remained full of wonder.

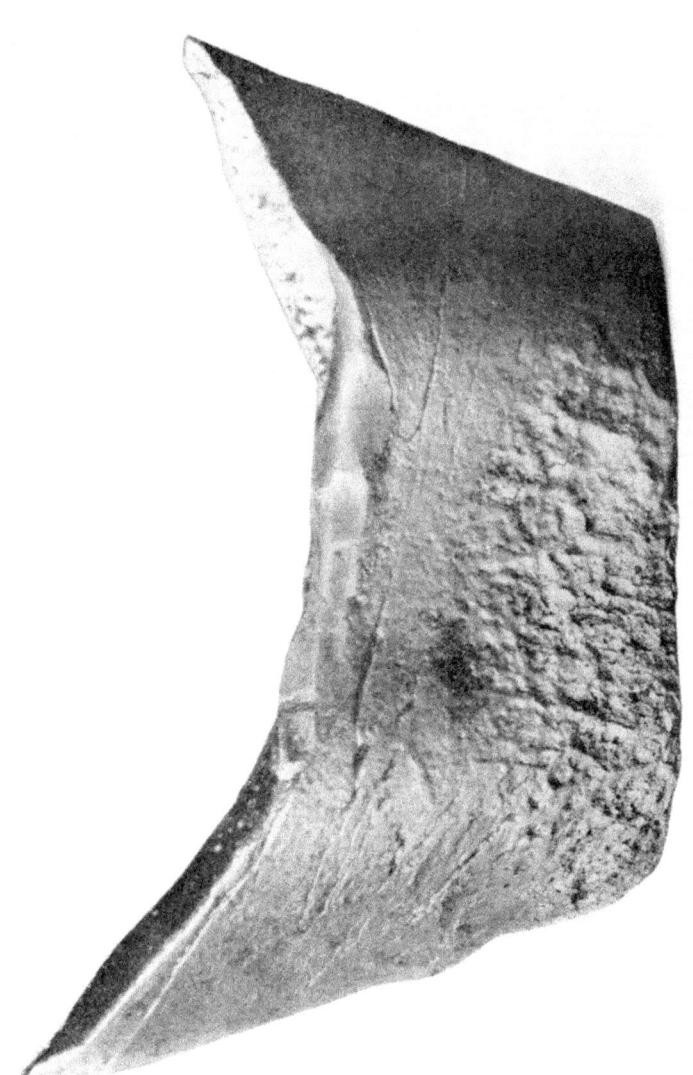

Silver Yamba (Chinese yüan-pao). Natural size

The Gods

At dusk the old lama went into the temple whence he fetched a big conch, after which he climbed up a fifty-foot tower. On his head was a tall, flame-coloured helm, adorned with fringes and shaped like a Roman gladiator's, and over his shoulders hung a cloak of the same colour, reaching to his feet. The keen and changeful light, which in cold, clear mountain air commonly precedes the darkness, formed a fine background to his fantastic silhouette as he raised the conch to his lips. Deep, long-drawn notes floated away along the river's wooded banks when he blew on his queer instrument, and the still evening air resounded with the strange notes. They swelled and dwindled, long and clear; they echoed back and died. The call was several times repeated, and then all grew silent. Some birds fluttered away, disturbed in their nocturnal rest. An evening breeze stole like a caress through the tree tops and made the forest draw a deep breath before it fell asleep.

The first stars were shining when the silhouette vanished from the raised platform, and it was biting cold when we dropped our gaze again from the tower and crept in to the fire in the tent.

We now got from the lama a closer description of Kiäkt. The way thither with our wagons would be difficult enough, but we were firmly determined not to stop without making the attempt. The old lama soon went to sleep, after he had filled with tallow the little bowl burning before the altar in the tent and had covered the glowing embers of the fire with ashes. All the little cloister slept. The flame burned lower and lower in the bowl, whose rim cast its shadow ever higher on the tent's sides. At last I too slept, after making up my mind that this was the place to come back to when, after many labours had been brought to a conclusion, one needed peace and rest. Here solitude would never be oppressive, here where one heard the cooing of the wood pigeons, the whistling of the hawk, the merry chattering of the squirrel and the long drawn hoot of the owl.

Next day we started in good time, accompanied by the inquisitive little *shabi*, who was to show us the ford over the Uri. When we were well across the river we took leave of the little trapper's son, who was dedicated to the cloister. He got a bright silver coin for his help, but his eyes were full of longing when he saw us disappearing up through the narrow canyon that marked our course. We had brought an idea of adventure into his young life. Our visit was an event which upset his conceptions, and he now perceived that there was something else besides his serene dream-life. It was the lust of travel that had been awakened in him, the longing to see what was hidden on the other side of the high mountains—and I understood him so well.

That day the march was difficult. So long as the sun was mounting in the sky we followed the rise in the ground. We had to stop innumerable times to let all the horses help one wagon at a time up the steep inclines. Fallen trees must be dragged aside to make progress possible, and we had to use our axes to fell trees that stood in our way. Twice we met hunters and stopped to ask our way and gather knowledge of the country that lay before us. The hunting was poor that year. During the summer a sickness had killed many of the young squirrels that should have supplied the winter's valuable fur.

In the afternoon we reached the highest point of the pass, and a snow-covered mountain plateau stretched before us. The road was pretty good but the landscape was desolate. We were above the tree belt, but single cedars were growing in occasional sheltered clefts. Close to one of these we halted so as to avail ourselves of its fragrant warmth during the cold night. And it was cold. We were frozen to the marrow, and it was certainly $-35°$ C.

Next morning we had to drive the wagon wheels over the remains of the fire so as to soften the grease on the wooden axles a little. Our toilet was not any too thorough. We filled our mouths with snow and, when it melted, held our hands before our mouths and spat out the water in driblets, which we tried to distribute over as large an area of our faces as possible. The result was certainly to make the dirt of the day more noticeable,

WINTER FUR CAMPAIGN

but we at least got the sleep out of our eyes and became wide awake.

The march went easily at the beginning, when the ground sloped in the direction in which we had to drive. But then the plateau came to an end and we began the descent through a ravine which later widened out into a broad canyon. We came down again to the tree belt and passed through cedar, pine and finally birch woods, after which we were on open steppe again. We had to come down to the Uri River again, but a good bit farther up towards its source. Two tributaries joined the river here, Kuko Gol from the west and Bure Gol from the east.

It had grown late, but bearing in mind the good advice of the old lama at Dain Derchen Kure we went on a little way along Bure Gol, to halt just where a magnificent wild canyon debouches from the eastern side of the mountains. Here it is that the mysterious and mighty Uri Hangrän dwells concealed, the God of Nature most worshipped, honoured and feared by the dwellers in these mountain tracts. Even the priests, who have Gautama Buddha or the yellow Tsong Kapa for their highest divinity, bow before his power.

The old lama had told us that we must not pass Uri Hangrän without bringing him an offering, but must neither stay to camp nor prepare food in the sacred canyon. If one prepared meat in the neighbourhood of the *obo*, the food would bring about the severest sickness, ending in death; and if one lay down to sleep in the sacred canyon, one would wake in a strange place far off.

Early next morning we climbed on foot up through the wild thickets of the canyon and soon came upon a memorable sight. In front of us rose Uri Hangrän, the biggest *obo* I have ever met with in my travels in Asia. Innumerable tall slender trees had been joined together into a gigantic pyramidal tent. This was richly hung with side cloths in various colours, of which sky-blue was the most conspicuous. Some of the coverings were old and faded, while others were new and bright in colour. Whole lengths of white and parti-coloured cotton cloth hung like garlands round the mystical Uri Hangrän.

From the branches of the surrounding trees hung tatters of silk, carried there by the wind from the *obo* itself. At the foot of this strange offering place lay heaps of brick-tea, bread, meat and pelts, as well as masses of gold and silver ingots. Within the *obo* could be dimly seen heaps of coins stamped with the heads of generations of Chinese and Russian rulers. I saw silver coins with the profile of Catherine II and bundles of bleached Russian paper roubles.

Uri Hangrän has certainly stood there from time immemorial and is a relic of the period when the population of the place was purely shamanistic. It lies in a remote, wild corner of the mighty hills, and the scanty population see in it the incarnation of the powers against which they constantly struggle, the invisible forces of nature which throughout their lives make them feel their littleness.

Soyote hunters professing the black doctrine (Shamanism) have here their great sanctuary—Mongolian nomads, Buddhistic lamas and Chinese pedlars never omit to pay their tribute when they travel by. The " White Tsar's " Cossacks, of foreign race and religion, who, in their flight from the discordant realm of Russia, passed the place in small bands—with horrors, fresh in their memory, behind them and the great unknown before—these too have offered their poor copper.

Sava offered his two pieces of brick-tea, and I threw a Danish silver coin into the motley collection in the interior of the *obo*, my tribute to Uri Hangrän and the mystical romance that brooded over the place.

Although but few people pass by yearly and although Uri Hangrän has no place in the literature of lamaism, the rumour of it and its power have spread widely over Central Asia. Among the horses belonging to Bogdo Gegen (the living god) in Urga there are always eleven snow-white, vigorous mountain ponies that have never borne saddle nor tasted bit, and which represent Uri Hangrän, the primitive deity of the children of nature, who even to-day lies nearest to their hearts.

WE continued our way along the narrow gorge, whose

WINTER FUR CAMPAIGN

steep, wooded mountain sides plunge down to the rushing Bure Gol. We passed by spruces, the first I had seen in Mongolia, and it was glorious to see these familiar trees again. We worked our way towards a low pass that was wooded to the top. In some places we passed by Soyote camps. We did not understand the Soyotes' own language, but several of them could understand and make themselves understood in Mongolian. They lived in felt tents like the Mongols, but the tents were smaller and ill made.

After we had crossed the watershed it became considerably colder. We pitched camp by the new river, Aremark Gol. While we were lying there a couple of Mongols passed with yak oxen heavily laden with grain in leather sacks.

Next day we began the march early and went through a low but very difficult pass. We followed a path that had been trampled by ponies and oxen carrying flour and corn from Kiäkt to the cornless steppes to the southward. To get the wagons forward we often had to clear trees out of our way. Once a horse rolled, with a loaded wagon after it, thirty feet down the steep slope, but although the whole concern turned several somersaults before it reached the bottom, we found everything in the best of order when we got down. The day before, I had had a dispute with Sava about the advantages and disadvantages of the Russian harness. Now he pointed proudly to the equipage with the horse standing in the shafts and the load lying undisturbed on the wagon after their perilous journey.

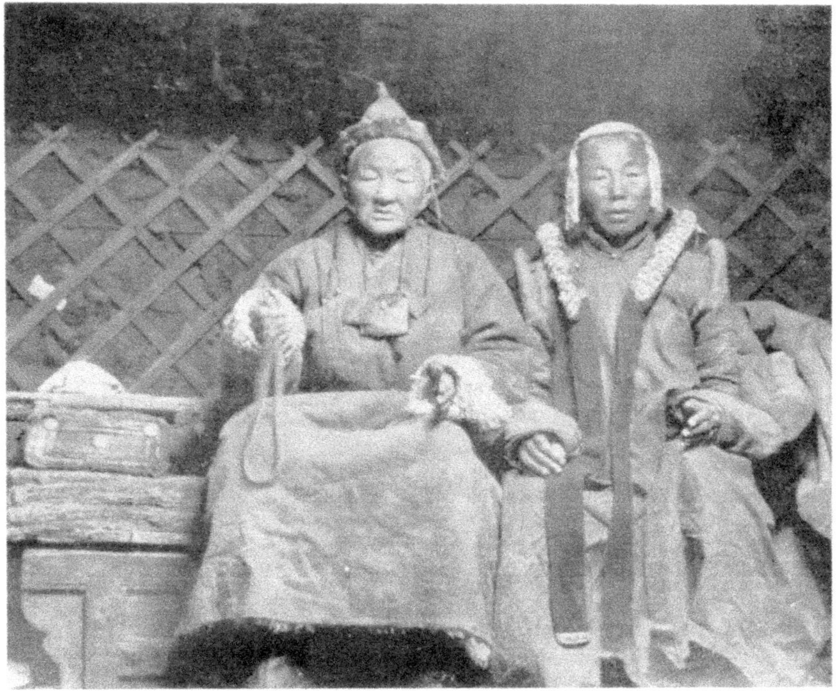

The old Lama and his deaf servant at Dain Derchen Kure

Tsong Kapa (in Mongolian, Bogdo Lama), the reformer of Lamaism and founder of the yellow sect (1356-1418)

BOOK III

CHAPTER I

JOURNEY'S END—KIÄKT

(Mongolian Folk-tune.)

A COUPLE of hundred yards beyond the head of the pass we rounded a projecting spur of rock, and Kiäkt, the goal of our journey, lay at our feet. We called a halt to smoke a pipe while we enjoyed the magnificent view and the consciousness that we had left all obstacles behind us. We saw a big steppe-like plain between snow-covered, wooded hills. At the edge of the steppe, close to the forest verge, were scattered clusters of dark specks, which suggested human settlements. Through the middle of the steppe flowed the Kiäkt River, its course marked by narrow belts of trees along both banks. The river began at the opposite side of the steppe where it had its source in the conjunction of two smaller streams. These were visible at the foot of the mountains far away to the north-east and north-west. The background was formed by wooded hills, and above them rose rows of snow-clad crests, one behind another, higher and higher the farther the eye looked. These were the outposts of the Sayan Mountains, descending in waves towards us from the mighty Altai. Icy pinnacles gleamed in the sunlight like foam on the petrified surf at whose foot we stood.

At last we were at the gateway to Kiäkt, the little realm between the mountains which was the goal of our strenuous journey—and yet our gaze was drawn irresistibly farther to the radiant view beyond—whiter than all white.

Behind it red Russia lay hidden.

It was all so pure and fresh, and one felt so young and vigorous that one had to draw a deep breath—and it was hard to tear oneself away in order to continue the journey.

A winged shadow glided over the snow towards us; high up against the azure sky an eagle floated majestically on powerful outspread wings. Our eyes followed it in its flight until it disappeared as a small speck, swallowed up by the blue ether, accompanied by our dreams and our longing.

Fancy anyone wishing to exchange the exalted symbol of that bird for the sickle and the hammer! As prosaic tools in beneficial work I can conceive them, but not as emblems of the thing one strives for.

As we approached the Kiäkt valley, the road grew wider, and soon we came upon sleigh tracks. In the mouth of the valley we found a dwelling-place, and we pitched our camp as near to it as the aggressive dogs permitted. It was a group of three low log-houses built of rough-hewn tree-trunks. They had neither doors nor windows, but smoke issued through a hole in the roof. This was pyramidal in form and was covered with turves. After we had made camp and unharnessed the horses we went up to the house, eager to make the acquaintance of the first representatives of the people among whom we were to pass the winter.

Two men were sitting by the fire in the middle of the house. They amicably invited us to sit down. The wooden floor, set about three feet above the ground, had an opening in the middle some six feet square. In the middle of this opening stood a wooden frame filled with stones, which formed the substratum on which a fire burned freely somewhat lower than the level of the floor. We sat on embroidered blankets on the floor, with our legs hanging down between the edge of the floor and the hearth. The smoke found its way out through the square opening in the apex of the pyramidal roof, and this also served to let light into the house. The light fell in a circle round the hearth and did not reach the corners of the room, which lay in shadow. To the right of the entrance stood some shelves where kitchen utensils and well-made bowls of birch bark were kept.

In a dark corner a woman lay suckling a boy at least three years old. A couple of young women came and went between their indoor duties and the milking of the cows in the yard. On their breasts they carried large plaques of beautifully worked silver, hanging from their necks by leather thongs. Some of these were set with old Russian gold coins of ten and twenty roubles. They wore their hair in simple braids at the back of the neck. From their ears hung long silver ornaments set with coral and turquoise.

The skin coats were alike for men and women and differed from those of the Mongols in being ornamented with narrow black bands sown on in decorative patterns. The sleeves did not, as with the Mongols, reach down far over the hands, but ended at the wrist, so that they had to wear gloves, which the Mongols do not need even in the severest cold, since their long sleeves serve as muffs.

The Kiäkt Buriats' language is reminiscent of Mongolian. The words have the same roots but other terminations, and great differences of dialect make it difficult at first for the one to understand the other. Thus, for example, the Mongolian word for cloak is *däle*, while the Kiäkt people call it *dägerli*. It is noteworthy that the dialect of the Kiäkt Buriats far more closely resembles the language of the Torguts at Kara Shar, nine hundred miles away, than that of the Kalka Mongols who are their nearest neighbours.

The population of Kiäkt has absorbed into itself a number of elements from various surrounding races. During the revolution, sundry Buriats came there in their flight from Russian territory, with the result that in this out of the way valley one may meet with the most unexpected things and people. I once visited a family at a newly established settlement. To my astonishment I saw on a neighbouring slope a network of irrigation channels which indicated that the field was used in summer for agriculture. The master of the house, a man of sixty, of the hunter type, of marked features and keen eyes, was dressed like the rest of the hunters of the district, but was less smiling and more reserved in his manner to me. Suddenly in the course of the conversation I was startled by hearing him introduce some German words into his speech. He watched me keenly and smiled somewhat ironically when he saw my surprise. Then he took from a chest a portrait of a fine-looking officer in the uniform of a Russian colonel. I looked at the picture, studied it carefully and discovered that the gold-laced officer in the portrait and the primitive hunter squatting opposite me by the fire were the same person.

" Once when I was very young," said the man, " I pined for the civilization and culture that you represent. It was a mistake," he added, after a moment's reflection. He spoke harshly and bitterly, and it seemed as though he saw in me the representative of a civilization that had done him an injury. But I did not let myself be repelled, and we sat together by the fire late into the night. When I rode home next morning we were the best of friends, and I was in possession of his story.

He was the son of wealthy Buriat parents and had lived an easy-going hunter's life in the places to which the nomadic life of the tribe had carried its tent-poles. All fair Transbaikalia was his home, familiar and beloved. At times he attended a Russian school at Irkutsk. Then came the Russo-Japanese war, and the lure of handsome uniforms and military music, and the desire to get hold of a modern rifle led him one day to enlist as a volunteer. He distinguished himself and went, after the war, to an officer's school at Orenburg. At the outbreak of the great war he was an officer of the Orenburg Cossacks and with them fought on the battlefields of Eastern Europe. He had many amusing stories to tell of the time when as a Russian colonel he took part in society life in Warsaw, Lemberg and other cities.

But there were also accounts of the gallant but hope-

JOURNEY'S END

less attacks by the Cossacks upon a front defended by poison gas and machine-guns, a type of warfare that rendered valueless the Cossacks' strength and courage. He told how he had been taken prisoner as he lay poisoned and helpless on the field of battle, he told of life as a captive behind barbed wire fencing in a far off, strange land, of hunger and destitution and of his ever increasing longing to return to the free hunting-grounds of his youth. Then the end of the war had come and with it the release and return of the prisoners to Russia, which he found ablaze with revolution. It had taken two years for the little free company of Baikal Cossacks to make their way through Russia and Siberia, and when they reached the goal of their longing, to which they had struggled through so many perils and privations, they found that the " freedom " which the Jews had dictated and the Bolsheviks proclaimed had reached there too, and had driven out the true freedom that they loved.

Then the old hunter and soldier had abandoned the land of his fathers and gone up among the mountains, until one day he had found Kiäkt and the personal freedom it offered him. Here he now was happy in the life that his forefathers had lived before him. His acquaintance with the West, its civilization and culture were only dark memories that he was trying to forget.

The population of Kiäkt consists of about two hundred souls. There are neither princes nor nobles, but the little community is governed by a number of magistrates of the ecclesiastical order, appointed for a term of years. Like Bulgun Tal, but in contrast with all the surrounding country which is subject to local princes, the Kiäkt valley appertains to and is administered as a *shabi* (dependency) of " the living Buddha ", Bogdo Gegen, at Urga. At the time when I was living at Kiäkt, the conditions of government were a little obscure, since Bogdo Gegen was dead and no new incarnation of the godhead had revealed itself. They hoped that a new Bogdo Gegen would soon appear, and at the same time dreaded the arrival of the Young Mongols, the representatives of the Soviet power. Rumours that such were in the district and were trying to conduct a propaganda for the red doctrine had reached Kiäkt.

It was stated that three Buriats had arrived in a valley by the Uri river inhabited by a little Mongol tribe whose chief was a young and energetic *noyan*.[1] The three Buriats visited the tents and preached revolt against the young ruler. This, however, was quickly reported to him by loyal subjects, and the chief promptly took action in a typically Asiatic manner.

The disturbers of the peace were seized and bound to the tent-poles and, before the eyes of the assembled Mongols, the chief himself tore their clothes off them and gave them several vigorous cuts with his heavy whip. Then the Mongols present came forward in turn and each struck nine blows, three for each of the offenders, at the same time expressing their loyalty to " *Yassa* " the immemorial law which the emissary of the gods, Jenghiz Bogdo Khan—the greatest of all Mongols and Khan of Khans—had laid down for all Mongols for all time. While the stripes were falling on the bleeding backs of the fomenters of revolt, the mouths of the faithful repeated the precept that every subject shall show obedience and respect to the appointed ruler.

When the chastisement had been administered, the chastized were driven out on to the steppe and, so soon as they were able, fled, a warning to their like and a reminder to the Mongols in other parts of the country that there still were people who held sacred the ancient " Yassa ".

But the story had a sequel, the effect of which was that the chief was the last champion in these tracts of a doctrine and a regime that had been founded by Jenghiz Khan and his *Khuruldei* (council of chiefs) six centuries earlier.

When the news of the severe punishment inflicted on the three Buriats reached the Soviet Government at Urga, they sent a strong detachment of soldiers to Uri. These made a night attack and killed the young chief and many of his subjects, and carried off a number as prisoners to Urga. A committee was then set up to see that the

[1] *Noyan*, noble, or high official.

Mongol Chief with his Suite

"The herdsman's call-note among the hills" (Mongolian song)

JOURNEY'S END

remaining old people, women and children lived according to Soviet principles.

For me personally the affair might also have had a sequel, for I came later to know from my friends, when I went to Urga in 1925, that I had been put on the Soviet's black list under suspicion of having been the instigator of the Uri chief's vigorous intervention against Soviet propaganda. I went at once to the Cheka to get the matter cleared up, and it appeared that they had already become aware that the suspicion was unfounded. Later on the three Buriats were cast into prison for some reason unknown to me, and there suffered the fate they had contrived for so many others.

CHAPTER II

ROUND THE CAMP-FIRE

"The herdsman's call-note among the hills"
(Mongolian Song)

I DEVOTED the first weeks in Kiäkt to obtaining a knowledge of the people and conditions of the district. It was an interesting time. Every night I slept in a new camp, and in the evenings I sat by hospitable hearths and listened attentively to the tales of old hunters. These dealt with courageous fighting against the wild beasts of the forest, with proud resignation in bad times and with tough endurance on long journeys. The fire blazed, and the narrators' faces, tanned by alpine sun and furrowed by the wind of the steppes, were alternatively lighted up by the flames and disappeared in the shadow.

But there were also evenings when we sat silent round the fire, passing round the pipe and sipping our tea. The young women of the house crouched respectfully in their corner. Their diligent hands worked skilfully with leather and deer sinews and their clear voices often sounded in strains that rose and fell like the flames upon the hearth. The melodies were simple but very expressive. They reflected strong emotions.

The songs seem usually to consist of short motifs which are repeated until one feels oneself under the influence of the mood that the melody wishes to induce. The shepherd's song in the mountains is full of pure air and high snow peaks. The motif changes according as the glance travels with longing and melancholy to the distant peaks, or rests with gladness on the vivid and fragrant alpine flowers where the frolicsome lambs gambol around the shepherd.

Another song changes with the landscape through which the young *urtoni*-rider flies forward. With bells and three eagle feathers in his hat—sign of the importance of his errand—he sets off from Dzungaria with tidings from his general of a battle won. Across the mountains, deserts and steppes of Central Asia he gallops the many thousand *urtoni* (relays) to Kha Khan's camp at Karakorum. The herdsmen who catch sight of the feather-decked horseman on the horizon or hear the bells in the night hold their swiftest horses ready for him. An invigorating drink, a bit of raw meat, and the horseman continues his long ride on a well-rested horse. He has bound wide silken bands round his waist, ankles

"Bomberja"   (Mongolian Song of Love)

and wrists so as to endure the fatigues until his utmost powers are exhausted. The rider sings of the exultation of victory, of his horse's swift feet and of the honour vouchsafed to him of standing soon face to face with Kha Khan himself. We follow him on his journey through night and day across half a continent.

This song made the old hunter beside me straighten his back and tenderly contemplate his long two-edged knife. Its hilt was adorned with beautifully chased silver and it lay well in his strong hand. It was an heirloom, worn by the use of many generations.

After a brief period of silence, another song followed, treating of a little love tragedy.

Bomberja, the bold, handsome Mongol, comes home from his campaign in foreign lands rich with spoil and seething with longing for the girl he loves. He finds her married to a Mongol who had been too old to go to the war. She does not love the old man, but it was her father's wish that she should marry him and thus an inescapable fate. Bomberja now offers her all his treasure and his burning love if she will agree to fly with him, but in vain. She cannot break the nomad's law and desert the tent to which she has been assigned, for if she should do so she would not fulfil the destiny intended for her, and the mark of the traitress would be branded on her brow. But the song ends cheerfully, for the girl, who loves the bold and impassioned warrior, lets him know that her husband is often away on long journeys and that it is cold and lonely in her childless tent.

The girls seem to be fond of that song, which they sing with much giggling and roguish side glances at the men's place by the fire.

THEN by degrees the young trappers came back from the hunting grounds with their spoil of pelts. There were splendid white-throated wolf, cross and black fox, marten, ermine, sable and squirrel. The last-named kind of fur used to yield the most certain profit, but it was hard to come by this year. We had now to think about getting a place of our own where we could show our trade goods to the trappers and later could store the furs we bought. We came across a house which a young Buriat had built for his approaching marriage. At first it was difficult to persuade him to sell it, but when we offered him thirty-five pieces of brick-tea, the temptation was too great, and the wedding was put off until he could get another house ready. It would take him almost a whole year, since the various building operations had to be carried out at different seasons.

We hired a couple of youths to caulk the chinks between the logs with moss so that our dwelling should be tight and warm for the bitter winter. The house was situated on a sunny slope and could be seen from the whole valley. A lone firtree stripped of its branches became a tall flagstaff from which the flag flew so long as we were at home. This had the advantage that people in the valley could tell when we were not at home and the shop was closed. Trade was good, and we bought at favourable prices. For squirrel we paid goods to the value of $1.10, for good fox $10 and for wolf $14. I put the price of the goods high enough to pay me for the transport from Urga to Kiäkt with a certain percentage of profit as well. Thus the barter

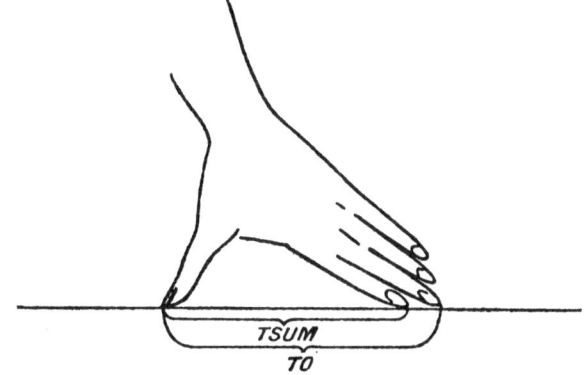

MEASUREMENT USED IN THE MONGOLIAN BAZAARS.

produced double profit and so reduced the risk in case of a fall in prices on the Shanghai market.

It was a full and interesting life, and from the accounts of the hunters we soon obtained an accurate knowledge of the mountains round Kiäkt. The business always

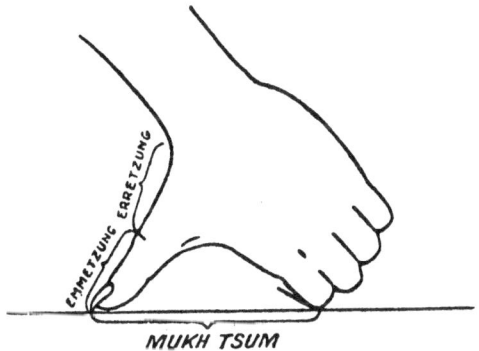

MEASUREMENT USED IN THE MONGOLIAN BAZAARS.

took ample time, for the trappers wanted to look carefully over the whole stock before making up their minds. Sometimes they stayed with us for several days, and it was understood that on such occasions we entertained both them and their horses according to the hospitable custom of the country. We sat talking late into the night before we crawled into our sleeping-sacks, and on each of these evenings I learned much of the country and the people.

ONE day a couple of Chinese traders came to Kiäkt, bringing a large and well-assorted stock of goods, in order to start a similar business. They were evidently annoyed to find competition already in the field, and that we had bought up many of the furs they had counted on for themselves.

The trappers laughed and called them " riders upon asses " or else *Khitat* which means Slav, an epithet which to them indicates the deepest degradation. A man with any respect for himself and his forefathers rides through the desert on a camel and over the steppe on a horse, but the being who puts himself on the back of a braying, long-eared ass, with his legs trailing along the ground, is not worthy of a place among decent people.

And the trappers continued to come to us with their furs and their stories.

One evening an old hunter related how he with a small troop of men had cut to pieces a force of three hundred *gam-min* (Chinese irregular soldiers) that had been sent by General Hsü against the insurgent mountain folk. " There was no war," he said with an ironical smile, " and considered as sport it was too simple to be good." The three hundred *gam-min* marched, freezing and making a great noise through the silent hill country, without seeing a living soul. But watchful eyes followed them the whole time. At sunset the noisy band pitched camp in a hollow. There was shelter, but no safety, for the dell offered an attacker every advantage, and made it impossible for the defenders to draw back, to surround the enemy or ultimately to save themselves by flight. The old hunter laughed scornfully before continuing : " Several huge fires lighted up the troop of weary and sleeping fools. Then began a slow but well-directed firing from the darkness ; now it flashed from a high spur of rock, now from the dim forest in the opposite direction, and each

Bomberja

shot silenced a howling Chinaman. The sleeping camp was soon like a swarming ant-hill, with terror-stricken men firing off volleys at random in all directions. As soon as the Mongols had got the Chinese to start shooting, they themselves ceased firing and stole away to a new position. When the nervous yellow men at last slacked off their meaningless fireworks, the Mongols again sent in a couple of effective bullets which once more raised the firing from the camp to a frenzied pitch. In this manner a handful of Mongols kept three hundred Chinamen awake and intimidated the whole night, and when morning came they were exhausted and without ammunition and were an easy prey to the long knives of the Mongols."

The Mongols are extraordinarily skilful in attack and in planning their onslaught in such a manner and at such a moment that, despite a paucity of numbers and scanty ammunition, they are able to counterbalance the enemy's many times greater strength and modern war material. A Mongol shoots slowly but with precision, and three shots mean as many executed death sentences. He always aims at his quarry's most vulnerable point; if it is a question of a human enemy, the Mongol shoots him in the ear, and the result is a rapid turn on the heel, a jump into the air and—the fellow immediately falls dead.

An old Mongolian song, " Chikherli bodena," extols the hero who in the confusion of battle remains calm and self-possessed and drills his foe's head from ear to ear.

The Mongol tolerates the Chinese traders because they can supply him with goods which he is reluctant to do without. But he profoundly despises them, since he cannot respect a person who is an unskilled hunter, an incompetent rider and a cowardly soldier. But there is no doubt that the Chinese are capable men of business, and we soon found that our two competitors were no exception to the general rule.

It requires much and long experience to become an expert in furs. It is a pleasure to examine and value the raw pelts, still fresh and redolent of the wilderness.

One enjoys their silky soft surface and shifting colours, and one perhaps follows them in thought on their way to the great cities of civilization where they—long before oneself even—will caress the bodies of charming women.

It is easy enough to decide which specimens belong to class one. It is also easy to see which pelts one may at once throw aside as " worthless ". But the difficulty lies in estimating the many intermediate categories and in selecting from among these those which a skilful furrier can work up to pass in the trade as " class one ", and those which will serve for the imitation of better furs—and in that case which and of what class.

During my visits to Urga I had spent many mornings in watching the experts sorting their pelts. Sometimes I would sort a batch myself and afterwards get the

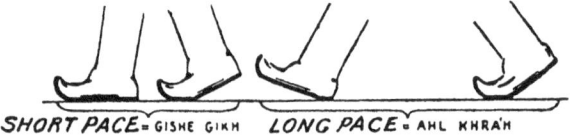

MONGOLIAN BAZAAR MEASUREMENTS.

expert to check the result. Once an expert gave me six sables to judge, one of each class. As they lay side by side on the counter it was easy to tell the difference between class 1 and classes 5 or 6, and on closer examination I could also distinguish class 2 from class 4. But if I only saw one of the pelts at a time, it was impossible for me to place it more exactly than in one of the three middle classes. And yet the value might differ by a couple of hundred dollars.

When I came to Kiäkt, I had so far advanced in my knowledge of furs that I knew which I could not value with certainty, and I left the skins of doubtful value entirely alone. In buying I never accepted any but those of the best quality, and the trappers, for obvious reasons, had nothing against this.

At the time of the Chinamen's arrival in Kiäkt many trappers had furs of inferior or doubtful quality on their hands, and they now went with them to the Chinamen to try their luck.

ROUND THE CAMP-FIRE

My competitors, who had been forced to sit idle since their arrival and who understood that there was one factory too many in the place for them to do good business, now discovered my vulnerable point. They found that they could make use of their more profound knowledge of furs.

They began buying up all the skins that I rejected, and paid well for them. They placed inferior skins in class 1 and accepted worthless ones at a decent price. These tactics did not worry me at first. I was living in the bright hope that the finest skins of the district would be mine and that the Chinamen would get my leavings, a very satisfactory arrangement for the rest of the season. But then one day, when the Chinamen were sufficiently in touch with the natives, they let it be known that they would only buy pelts of inferior

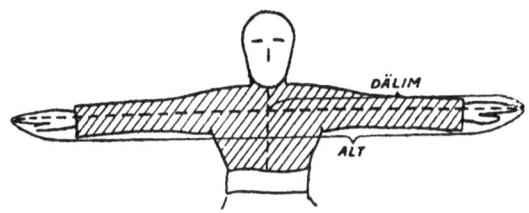

MONGOLIAN BAZAAR MEASUREMENTS.

quality when these formed part of a batch and constituted not more than twenty per cent of the whole. The trappers had now the choice between selling the best skins to me and having those I did not want left on their hands or selling the whole stock to the Chinamen. Since the latter was the more profitable, one could not blame them for choosing it. I had no desire to run any risk and wished moreover to keep up the reputation I had won in Urga the previous year when my furs formed the finest collection that were brought in during the entire season. It is always easy to sell an absolutely first-class consignment of pelts, and, besides, it inspires such confidence that one easily gets capital entrusted to one for further work.

SAVA had lately been growing more and more silent and low spirited. When he did speak it was almost always of the home he had not seen for many years. This indeed was quite near, only three days' journey from Kiäkt, so he heard from a hunter who had been there several times. Sava often went about with this Buriat and gradually gathered detailed information about the way. If he rode through the country of the Sanagen Buriats, a secluded path would lead him over two passes and a high plateau to a point on the border from which he could easily reach his home in a couple of hours. A single night's protective darkness, and he would be able to walk in upon his dear ones in the flesh, to clasp them in his arms and to inhale the atmosphere that would give him renewed forces and fresh memories upon which to live in exile.

On the same day that Cholo Bater, "the stone-strong", one of the herdsmen at the farm, came with mail from Buffalo, Sava asked for a week's leave. I pointed out to him the danger of his enterprise, but when I realized that a few nocturnal hours in his home outweighed all the risks in the world, he obtained my consent. He got a little money to give his old parents, and the same night he rode off over the crackling snow. In the clear moonlight his slender silhouette was visible long after the distance had swallowed up all sound. Then he vanished into the night and its uncertainty, seen only by the silent, twinkling stars.

By now the Chinamen had acquired pretty well the whole trade of Kiäkt, and I had come to the end neither of my goods nor of my dollars. They had been able to cut me out thanks to their superior skill as judges of furs. But it was bad sport to give in to a brace of crafty Chinamen, and I cudgelled my brains to hit upon a method which might give me the upper hand. And I succeeded.

It had naturally got abroad in the district that Bater had arrived with mail for me. Next day it also became known that Sava had disappeared, no one knew where. I hauled down the flag and suspended all buying. During the course of the day I told several talkative Mongols that I was a ruined man, and in the evening

ROUND THE CAMP-FIRE

I took several bundles of furs and went down to the Chinamen's station. The house was hot and barred up, and they were lying on a raised platform by the fire, getting the opium pipes ready for the night's blissful dreams, that would carry them home to densely populated China, where gold and silver awaited them as compensation for their hard life in this barbarous land. In spite of the warmth, they were muffled in furs which only left visible their trembling hands and parchment-like faces. They had made the long journey from hearth and home, driven only by the hope of large profits, without the smallest interest in the country, its natural features and its people, or the life these lived. Ever since their arrival they had not stuck their noses outside the door. They would sit in that stuffy room until the spring sun once more tempted their bloodless limbs out under the blue sky.

When I walked into their den they regarded me, their vanquished competitor, with suspicious eyes. I tried to appear nervous as I threw down the two bundles of pelts in front of them and asked them to satisfy themselves that they were first-class furs. They glowered with big eyes full of fear and suspicion when I invited them to take over my whole winter's purchase at a cheap price. They tried in every way to get me to tell them the contents of yesterday's letters and the reason why I wanted to sell such a magnificent lot of furs on the spot, when I could get much more for it by taking it to Urga. They refused to buy the pelts at once and asked for some days to think it over, and I went, leaving behind me an atmosphere of mystification. I had seen in their faces that the risk of a sudden fall of the market prices or an imminent new revolution had begun to haunt their opium-clouded brains.

More and more Tunka Buriats had lately been arriving in Kiäkt, bringing large parcels of high-class squirrel pelts. The reason why these people undertook the long and toilsome journey was that furs commanded a poor price on the Russian side of the border, and that the Soviet authorities put such heavy taxes on their livestock that they preferred to exchange cattle for squirrel pelts which, on their arrival in Kiäkt, they exchanged in their turn for goods for which there was a strong demand in Siberia. To prevent this traffic the Soviet had established a number of posts and patrols along the boundary, so that it was necessary to cross the frontier by night. On arrival at Kiäkt these wretched people were always in a frightful state of cold and starvation, since they had been obliged to cross a high pass on the boundary under cover of the ice-cold night.

The Mongols indicate time with the aid of the 12 zodical beasts. In the case of a time more remote than 12 years they attach the name of the beast to one of the five elements of the Chinese ; wood, fire, earth, metal and water. Each element in turn is assigned to two of the twelve beasts. The sixty year periods thus arrived at are repeated, but are more closely determined by being numbered. In Northern Mongolia the day is divided into twelve hours, which are likewise named after the twelve beasts : 0-2, the hour of the Mouse ; 2-4, of the Ox ; 4-6, of the Tiger ; 6-8, of the Hare ; 8-10, of the Dragon ; 10-12, of the Serpent ; 12-14, of the Horse ; 14-16, of the Sheep ; 16-18, of the Ape ; 18-20, of the Cock ; 20-22, of the Dog ; 22-24, of the Pig. 1923, the year our expedition arrived in Mongolia was the "Water-pigs'" year, the fifty-seventh year in the Mongols fifteenth period

Old copper Amulet with the twelve signs of the Zodiac

"Chikherli bodena", the skull bored from ear to ear, a typical example of the Mongols' skill in shooting

Dalachi, the sorcerer, who after long meditation and repetition of mystic formulas, can divine

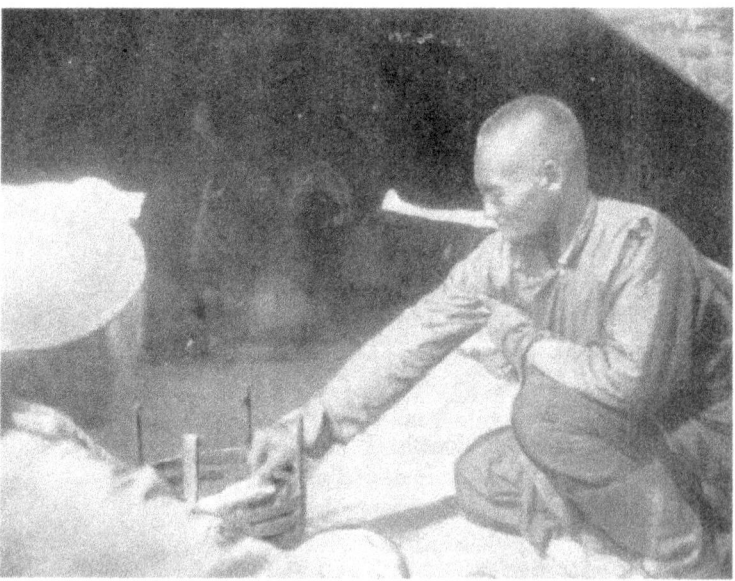

By laying a sheep's shoulder-blade in the fire and then interpreting the cracks made by the heat

CHAPTER III

THE TRADING STATION, "ALPINO SERAI"

NEXT day I bought three sleighs and five sheep, which latter we slaughtered. During the day we packed up our tent, the remainder of our stock of goods and an abundance of provisions. Late at night, while the Kiäkt valley slept, we loaded all this on the three sleighs, carefully locked up our house and set out for the north. At midnight we came to the canyon leading up to the Mus-dawan pass and there pitched camp. Next morning we went on up the canyon and at sunset came to the foot of the pass, where we found an ideal camping-place, sheltered, but so situated that our fire could not fail to be observed by every passing traveller. A noble fire was lighted in front of the tent and within it we put a pan full of embers. A big pot of steaming tea stood ready, and Bater threaded alternate pieces of fat and lean mutton on a skewer, ready to grill over the fire into a splendidly fragrant *shaslik*.

Then I crawled into my sleeping-sack while Bater kept watch by the fire. Towards two in the morning he roused me. He had heard the sound of voices high up on the steep slope of the pass, and it was time for us to make ready for the reception of guests in our little "Alpino Serai".

Bater, with one of the horses, had employed his watch in hauling a lot of fallen cedar trunks up to the fire which now rose like a pillar of flame many yards towards the chill starlit heavens. One could not approach within fifteen feet of it. At a distance of between fifteen and thirty feet the heat was tropical, but if one went outside a circle of forty-five feet one found oneself in a temperature of $-40°$. Over the embers in our washing-basin adapted for use as a brazier Bater grilled his *shaslik*. It sizzled and hissed as the fat dripped along the strung pieces on the skewer, and it smelled alluringly. With a long pole I raked together a heap of embers from the fire within the tropical part of the circle, and there I put the tea to keep hot, while I tossed lively pancakes, which turned fragrant somersaults in the air before coming down again with a smack into the pan. The camp was now so inviting that one could not go twenty yards away from it without longing to be back.

The approaching voices were audible at intervals and each time from a lower point on the mountain-side. Soon we became aware of a crunching in the snow and the snorting of horses, and before long a frozen apparition stepped out of the darkness into our circle of light. Three men and six horses tottered forward to the fire. Four-inch icicles were hanging from the horses' muzzles and they were completely covered with rime. The faces of the men looked like rigid ice masks, for the sweat, which the hard march up the northern side of the pass had extruded, had frozen into ice. Icicles hung from their nostrils, and the edges of their fur caps and their eyebrows were white with the moisture from their breath.

They all began to thaw out in the warmth from the fire, and the travellers helped one another to knock off the ice before it melted and soaked them. They are hardy folk, these trappers, and one can read in their faces what they have gone through.

They took off their coats and turned their bared breasts to the blaze. Then they took off their *unti* and stood alternately with the one naked leg in the snow and the other almost in the fire. Finally they warmed the inside of their coats and *unti* at the fire before they put them on again, and ten minutes after their arrival they stood there transformed, with glowing cheeks and smiling white teeth in their weather-bitten faces.

I plumed myself on my good idea and was overjoyed when I saw the speed with which the bits of meat and fat from Bater's skewers disappeared between the guests' strong teeth. When they had assuaged the worst of their hunger, they began to wonder and ask what all this

THE TRADING STATION

really meant, but we calmed them with the assurance that all was as it should be and that we had masses of food. Then we continued the entertainment with tea and pancakes, and the horses got rations of oats from Bater, and all our " Alpino Serai " was one symphony of contentment.

At last the belchings of the trappers announced that they were really satisfied. They spread out their fur coats on the snow and lay down upon them with their naked backs and footsoles turned towards the fire. Thus a man keeps himself warm and avoids rheumatism, they explained. And there they slept, half naked under the open sky, and a few yards away the night was icy cold.

I got no more sleep that night, for soon came some more trappers who must be received and cared for. Then the stars paled and the light began to steal down along the mountain-sides, announcing a new day, an auspicious day for the young trading station " Alpino Serai ".

The rules of our *serai* (inn) were that all who passed by and their horses must stay there and be entertained for the space of twenty-four hours. If they travelled on to Kiäkt they were to bring on their return journey and deliver to us the same quantity of oats that they had received for their horses on the outward journey. If they sold their furs to me they might stay several days and receive all entertainment for themselves and their horses gratis.

By the time I had stayed sixteen days in the place I had traded the whole of my stock of goods against first-class squirrel, and not a single trapper had continued his journey to Kiäkt. They all dreaded the remaining hundred versts, since they were so well off and were getting good prices. Returning trappers told the others whom they met on the way about " Alpino Serai " and the hospitality there, so that they knew about us long before they arrived. Soon it came about that the distance to various points on the road was described as so many versts from " Alpino Serai ". There was a constant coming and going at that otherwise so silent place, and those were lively and happy days. The trappers, who stayed several days to rest their exhausted horses before the laborious return journey, were easily induced to do odd jobs in the general interest. Corrals were built for the horses and a big sloping roof put up along one side of the fire to collect the heat and serve as a shelter if a snowstorm broke out. In the evenings there were—as all the world over where hunters congregate—plenty of tales and easy mirth.

When I had sold out my stock and had to return to Kiäkt, I was sincerely sorry not to have been able to bring more goods from the farm, but delighted with the times we had had and the good results.

So we packed our furs on the sleighs and drove away, leaving the place once more to the slumber from which we had aroused it. But from my knowledge of the remote corners of Central Asia and their sparse population I assume that the place is still called by the inexplicable name of " Alpino Serai " by passing hunters even now when the snows of many winters have fallen on the charred remnants of the giant fire that was kept burning for sixteen days and nights.

We had on the last occasion left Kiäkt in the darkness of night and, in order to disappear as unperceived as possible, had wrapped up the bells on the *duga*. Now we unbound the bells again and, to their merry ringing, drove our light sleighs into the Kiäkt valley while the sun still stood high in the heavens. As soon as we got home I hoisted the flag as a sign to all in the district that the house was again inhabited.

I HAD expected to find Sava at home, but thought he had very likely moved in to one of the families in the neighbourhood so as to save himself the trouble of cooking and keeping the house warm. We expected that the flag would soon bring him there as well as many inquisitive people anxious to hear about our experiences during our mysterious journey. Bater lighted a fire and made tea, and it was not long before we had visitors to entertain. But Sava did not come, and no one had heard or seen anything of him.

THE TRADING STATION

When the stream of visitors saw our sleigh-loads of pelts they were completely speechless. Did I not know that the price of furs had fallen colossally on the Chinese market? So, at any rate, the two Chinamen said, and they themselves had not bought a single pelt since my departure. And then I had to laugh so much that the assembly believed themselves to have the explanation of my buying so many pelts at such a time in the fact that I was stark mad. During the eventful time at "Alpino Serai" I had completely forgotten my visit to the Chinamen the evening before I left Kiäkt, but now I remembered everything and understood why they had stopped all buying. I told the company how the land lay, and they howled with laughter and delight at the unpopular Chinamen having been led by the nose.

But now it was a question of getting the trade going again in Kiäkt, and since I no longer had anything to trade with, I promised the natives to explain matters to the Chinamen. Bater drove down with an empty sleigh to their station to ask them to come up to me for an important conference. They must have been full of curiosity for they both came—a couple of prodigious bundles of lambskin from which their yellow noses peeped out when they had been placed in front of the fire in my house. I gave them tea and invited them to look at the magnificent collection of prime furs, I had bought on my last little excursion. They were furious and presented a comical appearance. The more fine pelts I spread out in front of them the further they stuck their skinny necks out of the lambskin covering. We all enjoyed ourselves royally with the exception of the Chinese themselves, and even they at last looked quite pleased when they understood that I had no more goods to buy with and that they were thus now relieved of my competition.

Bater began to pack all the pelts for transport to the farm, and I went off on a wild boar hunt with one of the local hunters. It was thrilling sport, and a roast of wild pig can be worth going a long way for.

I puzzled over what could have happened to Sava.

Three times the estimated time had now passed, and I feared the worst. Bater had carefully preserved all the shoulder-blades of the five sheep we had consumed at " Alpino Serai " and now sat through the evenings scrupulously scraping them with his knife. I knew that he too was brooding over Sava's failure to appear and that the preparation of the shoulder-blades was connected with it. I had often seen the Mongols at Bulgun Tal consulting these mystic bones.

Late one evening, when our guests had taken leave, Bater took out one of the smooth polished shoulder-blades and laid it at the edge of the burnt out embers. After a few minutes the bone began to crackle, and Bater took it out with the tongs in order to observe it carefully while he held it up to the firelight. He was clearly dissatisfied with the result, for after having examined the half-charred bone, he threw it carelessly into the middle of the fire. When I asked curiously what he had seen, he only shook his head and went to bed.

On the following day I rode down to one of my friends, an old hunter named Baldan, to hear more of his adventures and in fancy to follow his abundant experiences among silent mountains and dim forests. A horse of Baldan's had, moreover, lately died, and I thought of buying it to use in hunting wolves. When I rode home I had it in tow. On arrival at the house I found Bater ready to start on a journey. He was secretive about the reason and goal of his expedition, but promised to be back within two days. He disappeared in the direction of the Soyote pass.

During the afternoon I dragged the horse carcase up to an open place in the forest about three furlongs from my dwelling. Then I rode back to the fire in my cottage and spent the evening in agreeable solitude with my wheezing pipe. The expected wolf howls failed to appear so long as I was awake, and I fell asleep much earlier than I intended. Next morning there were a number of wolf tracks round the frozen carcase of which only two-thirds remained. I cursed my sluggardliness.

The wolves of late had been particularly insolent and

daring, and it happened almost daily that they came down into the valley and took calves in broad daylight. At six o'clock the same evening several wolves could be heard howling in the direction of my bait. During the day I had chosen a good shooting-place at a distance of about ninety yards from the dead horse and had cleared a way to it, so that I could approach quietly. When the howling had been going on for a while and had increased in volume, I stole out. It was a sight— three big wolves were tearing and biting at the carcase, snarling and growling, and, a little way off, a lone wolf was struggling with one of the horse's legs which it had torn off. From time to time all the wolves would set upon one another, rolling in the snow and making an infernal row. The wild scene was lighted by the moon's pale beams. Farther off in the forest I could hear the howling of other wolves on their way to the feast.

I wished suddenly that I had brought a hunter with me. In the hope that my first shot would drive off those of the brutes that were not killed, I took aim and fired. The lone wolf with the horse's leg gave a leap and the others rushed a few steps in my direction and then trotted round, uncertain from which side the danger threatened. I knew that when one shoots towards the edge of a wood it often happens that the echo misleads the beast and induces it to run towards the hunter. That was not so pleasant, and I was somewhat nervous when I had fired off the whole remainder of the magazine at the scattered shadows of wolves in the middle of the clearing. Luckily, the wolves now observed the flashes from my shots and disappeared like arrows into the forest on the opposite side. I at once lighted a fire and with a burning torch went cautiously forward to the fallen wolf. With my belt tied to one of its forepaws I succeeded in dragging it down to about fifty yards from the house, where I let it lie, so as to escape the rank wild-beast smell during the night.

CHAPTER IV

IS THERE MORE BETWEEN HEAVEN AND EARTH . . . ?

" The twelve years " (Mongolian Song)

NEXT morning Bater returned, not alone, but in the company of a strange being. Bater treated our new guest with a kind of shy reverence and I watched him curiously. He was of indeterminable age, possibly younger than his wrinkled and weatherbitten face suggested, and he was small and very spare, but moved with an assurance and poise such as one seldom finds among the horsemen of Central Asia. He had small black eyes which roved for a moment round the house, suddenly fixing themselves on some particular object, to pass on farther with the speed of lightning until they had taken in everything around him. He was like a wild animal securing itself against danger. Finally he let his eyes rest on me in a long glance, intensely penetrating and searching, to be at last transformed into two wells of friendliness, and his whole face gathered into a network of wrinkles which lay upon his large mouth and friendly eyes in a manner which showed that he lived a great part of his life with a smile upon his lips, yes, with a smile upon his whole flat face. He had white whiskers by his ears, and from his chin hung a long, thin goat's beard. On his head he wore a tall, conical fur cap covered on the outside with yellow silk, faded and tattered. He was wrapped in a great cloak of goatskin with the hair outward. On his feet, outside his long *unti*, he had short boots of the

The wolf, the Mongols' hereditary enemy, alive . . .

and dead

"Ole 'en Lama"

skin of the legs of wolves so made that the hair was turned downward. On his back was fixed a pannier of willow twigs in which he carried a well-filled leather bag.

Bater helped him off with the burden on his back and the great goatskin coat. Under this the stranger wore a short deerskin jacket which made him look even smaller and slenderer than before. Bater laid a blanket in front of the fire, and I invited the guest to take his place there. He smiled a quick, friendly smile at me, but before sitting down he took out of his leather bag a sort of four-sided dirk, carved entirely from wood with a mass of coloured silk ribbons attached to the hilt, and threw it into the air, while he rapidly muttered a rigmarole that I took for a prayer. The wooden dirk turned several times in the air and fell on the blanket, where the stranger narrowly observed it before putting it back in the bag. When he at last took his place by the fire, I observed that he paid no regard to my invitation to sit on the blanket, but placed himself on the spot to which the tip of his queer dagger had pointed. When Bater would have put the pot on the fire, the stranger stretched out a warning hand, and I ordered Bater to go outside and perform his household tasks under the naked sky.

The same morning I had dragged the dead wolf into the house to thaw it out, so that it could be skinned. It was now lying in a corner, stiff and in the same posture as when it was shot, showing the long teeth in its grinning jaws and with its legs gathered up as if to spring. The leg by which I had dragged it home lay stretched out a little in front of its snout—I could not decide whether it pointed towards my guest or myself. The stranger was sitting with his back to the wolf, but as if he could read my thoughts, he said suddenly, with a grin: " They live with me in the mountains." " Who ? " I asked, astonished. " The wolves that you saw and him you killed," he said with a new grin. I considered him through the smoke of the fire on the other side of which he sat. He was sitting on his haunches, not like a Mongol, but with the whole sole of his foot on the ground in the Chinese fashion, and was holding his hands stretched out to the warmth. These were thin and sinewy. His feet in their wolfskin coverings projected from under his coat. His black eyes were two sparkling points in the firelight, and I could not read their expression. His strong white teeth were bared in an unceasing grin.

I called to mind stories which hunters had told me on long tramps through a dark silent forest. By the nightly camp-fire they had spoken, in a low voice and with anxious glances, of people who had disappeared on the same night on which a large and daring wolf began to spread terror over the countryside, of wolves that were transformed into human beings; and of mystical wolves that appeared to announce where a new incarnation of a deceased *hutuktu* would reveal himself. A shiver ran along my spine. What if I were now experiencing something of this romantic nature.

Then Bater opened the door and appeared with the pot full of steaming tea. The daylight streamed in and dispelled the light and shadow round the fire and with them the mystery they evoked.

Bater, who was all attentiveness to our guest, called him only " Lama " when addressing or speaking of him, and I saw to my astonishment that the man actually wore a lamaistic rosary round his wrist.

He spoke fluent Mongolian, but in appearance was more like a Tibetan than any other people I could compare him with. In costume he was almost Soyote except for the strange cap he wore. Really he resembled none of the many races I had met with, and was presumably a mixture of several. At times he would chat quite genially and then suddenly take to staring into the fire without saying a word. A couple of times he ran to the door and peered round the mountains or with tense gaze followed the course of a cloud sailing across the sky. His demeanour was a mixture of tense concentration and nervous vigilance. I hoped he would soon lay aside all reserve and disclose himself to me as to his own people.

For the better understanding of the people of the

district I had made myself familiar with their mystic lore, and I tried now to divest my mind of civilization and its tiresome logic. " The earth is not round, but flat as a pancake, and is divided into four parts by mighty oceans of fire." I tried to attune my mind to the fantastic and, like the Mongols, to find it natural. I mentally recited to myself their marvellous philosophy with the same conviction that one tries to put into one's voice when reading tales of wonder to expectant children.

For some people music is a living thing, immaterial certainly, but something that is perceived and apprehended far more clearly than the reality around them. They are ravished and depressed as the strains find echo in their souls, and they approach music with an open and receptive mind. For others on the contrary music is only a thing of written notes and nimble fingers, and they do not understand those who say that the notes express the fall of leaves from tired autumn trees, the lashing of the storm against the blackening waves or the purity of dewy meadows at dawn. It is something the same, I imagine, with people's capacity to comprehend the mystical.

When I asked the stranger his name, he only answered : " I dwell in the mountains out there," and made a movement with his hand which almost described a circle. It was no use asking Bater, for it would have been contrary to the custom of the country to tell the name of a person or a being to whom one owed reverence. Between ourselves he was called " *Ole'en Lama* " or " the Lama from the mountains ", and he could have had no better name from his own mother.

I asked him about Sava on whose account I supposed Bater had summoned him, but the only reply I could get was : " I believe he is in the mountains, but I cannot yet say so with certainty ". In the evening we sat by the fire without many words being spoken. *Ole'en Lama* had a little box with small pieces of bone which he continually threw on the ground in front of him and again collected with his hand. I was annoyed and disappointed because nothing interesting happened and came near completely losing my belief in anything mystical in connection with the old man.

Late in the evening *Ole'en Lama* suddenly asked Bater to give him one of the sheep's shoulder-blades. Bater jumped up as if he had been sitting waiting for this the whole evening and presented one to him on outstretched hands.

The stranger now let the fire burn down to embers which he broke up with the tongs. Then he threw on the smouldering fire a little dried grass from his pouch, which filled the room with a nauseating smell. With shut eyes and with the shoulder-blade pressed against his forehead he sat a long while muttering rapid unintelligible cantrips. Next he seized it with the tongs and laid it in the hot ashes quite outside the embers and covered it over first with ashes and then with embers. For about five minutes he now sat gabbling formulas, after which he took the bone out carefully with the tongs, shook off the ashes, blew upon it and laid it in the cold ashes by his feet.

I had often seen the whole of this procedure carried out, for many Mongols believe themselves able to read in the fissures which are produced by the heating of the bone the answer to simple questions, but I knew also that very few understand how to interpret completely the complicated meaning of the fine network that spreads over the surface. Those who do are as a rule not lamas. They are generally visited by people from far and near wishing to get answers about something that lies near their hearts. I hoped now that *Ole'en Lama* was one of these skilled ones and was disappointed not to hear him say anything more thrilling and prophetic.

Inasmuch as I had been getting ready my rifle for an early morning hunt, there was nothing remarkable in his announcement that I would go hunting next morning. He went on to say that I would go along a certain canyon where I would see three roe deer that would cross my path at full speed without being hit by the two shots I should send after them. There was nothing remarkable about that. What on the other hand seemed a little less probable was that I should go on up through the thicket where a big buck would be lurking and which I could bring down if I fired. It is regarded in these parts an established rule that if one has fired a shot it is useless to go on, for the first report will have driven off all the deer in that and the neighbouring valleys, not to return for three days.

Next morning I started out on my hunt and took my way along the valley indicated. After half an hour's difficult going, three deer ran across my path, and I missed them with two shots. During my further tramp I discovered a thicket higher up and, against all reason, I went on. And there I now saw the antlers and back of a leaping roe buck. Just as it was going to cross a clearing a few yards wide, I gave a shout which checked it for the few seconds I needed to draw a bead and fire. The buck fell and, since it was heavy and large, I lifted it up across a bough out of reach of the wolves, intending to fetch it later with a horse. As I was going afoot towards the house, I saw Bater riding in my direction. I asked him what he was doing there, and he said he had been standing in the doorway the whole time looking out for me and my bag. When he had seen me coming empty-handed he had mentioned it to *Ole'en Lama*, and the latter had replied that the buck was too heavy for me and that Bater had better bring the horse.

I was annoyed by the fulfilment of this prophecy which I had not reckoned on as being such.

Towards evening it appeared as though something was going to happen. Bater gave the house an extra sweeping, and the old fire with its embers and ashes was laid out in front of the house. Before a new fire was lighted the fireplace was carefully swept and cleaned out. The old man sat for two hours twiddling his rosary and reading Tibetan prayers from a little bundle of parchment leaves. Bater, too, now participated actively, in that at certain intervals he threw incense on the fire and joined in the chanting in the places where the Tibetan words were known to him. At nine o'clock he handed a new shoulder-blade to the old man, who raised it to his forehead and remained for a long time sunk in deep meditation.

When at last the bone was laid in the embers, the old man muttered softly, and every time the heat called forth small crackling sounds, he called out some words in a language incomprehensible to me. His gaze was concentrated on the flames and his expression varied as if he saw or read something in the slowly fading glow. Each time a little bluish flame shot up for a moment, he ceased his patter and observed it with head bent forward and an inquiring glance, as if he were reading an answer in the uncertain movements of the little tongue of flame. Twice the shoulder-blade was taken out of the fire and minutely examined and then put back again. The third time he was obviously pleased, for the bone was carefully cleaned before he laid it in the cold ashes. He closely scrutinized it on both sides, held it up to the firelight and at last threw it on the fire with an exclamation that interrupted the long silence.

The lama now rose and hurried out, leaving the door of the house wide open after him. The cold night air brought in the echo of a wolf's howl from the forest. I went to the door where the old man now came smiling towards me.

The sky was strewn with brilliant stars which made the black mountain peaks stand out against the luminous night sky. The long-drawn howling of the wolves in the forest was accompanied by the angry barking of the dogs in the valley. The " tu whoo " of a mountain owl sounded like a presage of ill, which we shut out when we closed the thick door again. Bater was now sitting in front of the cheerfully blazing fire, making tea. The fresh cold air from outside had driven away the reek of incense and burnt bone. We were once more three people sitting round a warm hearth, waiting for tea and speedy sleep.

I had hoped to witness something of the occult arts I had heard the Mongols tell about, so as to find out how it would affect me. What had just happened was a disappointment to me. " Well, how runs the prediction ? " I asked the Lama, who persistently went on drinking tea when I thought it was time to turn in. He stopped his tea at once and looked at me sharply and searchingly. Then he said slowly and with emphasis on every word : " We shall have a snowstorm before sunrise ". It was not the usual time for snowstorms, which in that region belong to the months of March and November. At other times of year they are extremely rare. Moreover, the sunset had been red, not yellow, and the sky was quite clear without the least little premonitory wisp of cloud. I said so to the old man, but he went on, as if he had not heard my expression of doubt : " A snowstorm will come from the mountains before day dawns ; three days will dawn without the rays of the sun or the moon being able to pierce through the driving snow. In the evening of the third day the storm will cease, and that night, at the dog's hour (8–10), the cloud will pass in divers directions and the moon's beams again pierce through, throwing light and shadow on Kiäkt. In the mouse's hour (12–2) Sava will come from the mountains in the East, and his tracks will be the first in the virgin snow." He looked long at me with an intense and penetrating gaze as though to dispel my doubt.

CHAPTER V

THE SNOWSTORM. SAVA COMES BACK

I WAS awakened at dawn by an infernal din outside the house. It was almost dark, and snow was drifting down through the roof opening. I woke Bater and told him to make up the fire, and myself went to the door. The old Lama had disappeared. The door was wrenched out of my hand and thrown wide open. All old tracks round the house were covered over by a foot of snow. A single track led from the door of the house in the direction of the Soyote pass, a human trail, but the impression in the snow did not form two lines as human trails are wont to do, but only a single long line like the track of a wolf.

The snow was falling from a grey sky, and violent blasts of wind rushed down from the mountains over the steppe, where they blew up the newly fallen snow into tall columns and carried them along with them. Every new gust brought into being new columns that flew past and vanished before one's gaze in a swirling dance of snow. *Duche* (butterflies), the Mongols call these swirling columns which arise, spin by and disappear. The fir trees groaned and creaked in their struggle with the storm. The snow fell thicker and thicker. There were all the signs of a severe and long continued snowstorm.

We made haste to throw long ropes with heavy stones at their ends over our haystacks. Carts and boughs were applied to buttress and screen the horse corral, dry fuel was piled up indoors and two-thirds of the opening in the roof closed up with blankets. Then we shut ourselves in and let the snow rage outside, while Bater cooked pancakes.

THE SNOWSTORM

And the storm raged and the snowfall increased in violence. Then gradually the din against the plank walls of the house sounded more distant and softer as the snow piled up against them. I had to admit to myself that Ole'en Lama was a better weather-prophet than I had taken him for. In the evening we had to go out to attend to the horses, but the door was completely snowed up. We helped one another up through the roof opening and on the roof found ourselves almost on a level with the snow on the ground. The horses were warm and comfortable, for a huge snow wall had piled itself up in front of the entrance and gave them shelter from the blast. We gave them their oat ration and scrambled back through snow and gale, exhausted and blown to bits, to our lair.

We did not suffer from lack of water since we were able with some difficulty to melt the abundance of snow that fell on us through the roof opening. We poured the snow water against the door where it froze at once into ice. When the door was one big block of ice we brought the water to the boil and handed it up to one another on the roof where it was poured over a loose snow embankment which we threw up round the opening a little way from it. In this way we built up a kind of chimney.

Day and night ran into one; and it became more and more difficult to maintain communication with the horses. When the noise around us ceased, we worked our way up through the tall chimney like marmots poking their noses out of spring greenery. But no trace of spring or its verdure was to be seen here. The gale had certainly stopped, but the snow fell incessantly from an invisible sky, silent and thick.

"To-day is the third day," said Bater and, convinced that the snow would soon stop as the lama had predicted, he began to dig a way from the roof down to the door of the house. Bater regarded the fulfilment as a foregone conclusion; indeed, he was so certain of it that I almost hoped the storm would break loose again and with increased violence. But as time went on the snowfall abated and the day grew lighter. Low white clouds detached themselves and rushed over our heads against a background of grey sky. A faint flush spread over the snow-covered mountains, announcing the setting of the sun and the approach of night.

Bater had dug a channel to the entrance and was now busy chopping away the ice from the door. A couple of stars peeped out of the sky. More and more stars became visible. I gave in, and anyhow a way to the horses had to be dug. Bater and I began shovelling, each from one end, and met in the middle. The snow crackled, but we did not notice the cold as we worked in the windless night. We went on to the house where Bater remained standing, peering up at the sky and out over the steppe. The shadow of a big cloud passed over the snow field which otherwise lay in pale moonlight. It passed over us and vanished in the direction of the mountains leaving us and the whole steppe in the full light of the rising moon. " It is now the hour of the mouse," suggested Bater, contemplating the heavens, to which I replied that if Sava came now I should not only be glad but would also become an orthodox pagan.

THE barking of dogs sounded from the valley. It came nearer and nearer, shifted from dwelling to dwelling as though it was provoked by someone passing by. Half unconsciously I went to meet a dark animated point that I fancied I perceived. When I heard crunching steps approaching I shouted with the full strength of my lungs : " Sava ! " and like an echo came his well-known and respectful : " *Da, Mr. Kidi.*" (Yes, Mr. Kidi—Kidi being my nickname at the farm.) We ran and soon fell into each other's arms, and in true Russian fashion he kissed my bearded cheeks.

A glorious evening was now before us in the joy of our reunion. When we came into the house Bater was sitting in front of the fire making tea. He raised his eyes for a moment from the fire to ask : " *Sava amorkhan sain beino?* (How are you, Sava ?) and had already resumed his work when he completed his greeting with : " *Sava sain irrechi beina* " (Glad to see you, Sava.)

THE SNOWSTORM

Sava was glad to have food and drink again, and we gave him the best the house afforded. I refrained from at once beginning my bombardment of questions, but was content to have him back alive and to observe the energy with which he munched and swallowed the prodigious quantities of *shaslik*, fat-tail and pancakes with which we uninterruptedly supplied him. It was late, and we were all lying in our sleeping-sacks before he found leisure to answer our questions and give an account of his travels.

He had followed the prescribed route through the mountains of the Sanagen Buriats, and on the fourth day had reached a point on the boundary where he could get his bearings. On the following night he had crossed the frontier and, by a way known to him from childhood, had reached his village at midnight.

His childhood's home, which he had not seen for six years, was still standing in its place, but everything looked changed in the darkness. Hidden behind some trees, he had bombarded the window of the house with pebbles until a light was struck and people became visible. The people were all strangers and the appearance of the room was changed. He had not gone forward.

When all had grown silent again he had stolen away to the village smithy to see if the old smith was still there. As a child Sava had spent many an hour with the old man, whom he had helped with his work. The smith was a good man, Sava knew, a " White " who was loyal to his Tsar and his religion in his quiet and modest way, but had been too old to take part in war or civil strife, so Sava hoped he had escaped slaughter. He had adopted with the smith the same cautious method of approach as at his old home, and great was his joy when his old friend became visible and received him with emotion.

Sava had then heard of the fate that had befallen his family. His mother had died of grief after all the male members of the family had either been killed or had disappeared leaving no trace, and the only one of his large family remaining in the village was a sister who had married. The old smith advised Sava against going to her, since he was not certain that her husband was to be trusted, as he had accepted an appointment from the Bolsheviks. Sava, however, was unwilling to ride back without having seen this sole surviving member of the family and had therefore gone to his sister's house. She had been glad at first to see her brother, but later had become uneasy, and had bidden him go at once for he was in danger. However someone—he did not know if it was his brother-in-law—had already seen Sava, and the alarm had been given.

Sava had remained in hiding for two weeks, first with the smith and afterwards at a place in the woods that the smith had shown him. At the end of that time the faithful man had brought him his horse. Things had grown quieter by then and the frontier was less sharply watched.

The return journey had gone well until the snowstorm broke out, when Sava had sought refuge and spent the night with a Sanagen hunter a day's journey from Kiäkt. He had stayed with him until the morning of that day. All day he had been leading the horse, since it was too heavy going in the loose snow for the horse to be able to carry him. I got Sava's story in the form of sleepy answers to my questions before he fell into a well-earned slumber.

Next day the sun was shining, and we set to work digging paths to let us move about outside the house. The roof, too, was cleared of snow, and to celebrate the return of Sava, the blue sky and the sun, we ran up the flag. Sava felt himself to be almost a good Danish citizen after his long sojourn with the colony, which indeed was the only asylum he had found in his exile. Accordingly he stood stiffly to attention with his hand to his smart Cossack cap, and watched while the white cross rose towards the sky. It was indeed the white cross for which he had suffered and fought— but I had to explain to him that the red field represented the warmth of love and not the brutal colour of blood.

The white snow was bestrewn with small ice crystals that sparkled in the sunshine. The dark shapes in the

THE SNOWSTORM

distance which earlier had indicated dwelling-places had now been changed into scarcely visible mounds of snow on the surface of the ground, from which the smoke rose vertically towards the sky. But the sunny morning soon transformed this quiet picture. Little dots became everywhere visible, people working to dig their houses out of the snow, and sleighs drove between the various dwellings, making a new network of trails in precisely the same pattern as the old. The tinkle of bells approached, and the first sleigh followed in Sava's trail and swung up in front of our dwelling. The valley began to swarm like an anthill. The various dwellings had lain isolated from one another for three days and nights, and now there was a rush to resume neglected tasks. Herdsmen were sent out in all directions to round up the cattle and horses that had gone off in the storm, and the hunters disappeared into the woods to follow the fresh tracks in the newly fallen snow.

Sava's return was one of the day's sensations in the Kiäkt valley, and more guests than ever came to our fireside to hear about his journey across the frontier.

Again and again I tried to get to know something about the Lama from the mountains, but every time I touched upon that topic the air became as it were charged with a mystery to which I had not the *entrée*. All I could gather was that he kept to the mountains and seldom left them

He was certainly a lama, but belonged to no monastery. He was so mighty that no man dared name his name. None knew his age nor his place of birth. But he was very old, for the oldest among the people of the region could remember a time during their childhood when he did not leave his cave in the mountains for twelve years. During these twelve years the people had daily brought him food from the valley, but no one had ever spoken to him. It was said that the wild beasts of the forest had visited him in his cave and that he had learned their language. There had been times when no one saw him for several years and when none knew where he dwelt.

During the time I spent at "*Alpino Serai*" I had

heard much from visiting hunters of a large town, Tunka, that lay only two days' journey from the place at the foot of the Mus-dawan pass where we held our sixteen days' bazaar and pelt market. Most of the hunters had, before the revolution, visited Tunka, and this advanced outpost of European civilization had made an impression on even if it had not appealed to their primitive instincts.

When the waves of civil war spread to remote Tunka, to roll to and fro for a couple of years through the Tunka valley, according as changing fortune favoured the Red cause or the White, the original inhabitants of the region retreated beyond the mountains into desert tracts incapable of providing sustenance for bodies of soldiers larger than the scattered hunter folk, by joining forces, could eject or destroy.

The hunters' knowledge of Tunka thus derived from a time when the town had been the seat of the White Tsar's representatives in that remote spot. Their tales were of proud Cossacks on fiery steeds, of the thunder of hooves and the rattle of arms as they swept through the valley in a cloud of dust. They told of chiming bells that rang out at evening from gilded, cross-surmounted cupolas over the heathen land. They dealt with flying troikas carrying gold-laced officers, of ecclesiastical processions and impressive buildings—all things which in days gone by had made such an impression upon these primitive people that their descriptions glowed with a legendary and barbaric splendour and formed a maze of sunshine and colour.

All this talk of Tunka sounded temptingly and alluringly in my ears. It would be glorious to enjoy a couple of days of civilization, of proper food and of the company of white people. Even if the place had seen a trifle of revolution and war, there must still be some decent and agreeable people left there. It seemed to me incredible that these should all have been killed.

But what attracted me more than anything else was the prospect of there being a post and telegraph office, so that I should be able to establish more direct communications with home and friends than I had had for

THE SNOWSTORM

long. I had had no possibility of contact with the outer world for several months, and my saddlebags contained a whole bundle of letters which I was eager to send off.

Accordingly I resolved, in spite of Sava's warnings, to undertake a journey to Tunka, confident that my Danish passport would help me over all political obstacles.

I had procured for the journey two native horses which I bought on the spot and which were used to the difficult mountain paths by which we had to travel. Except for a little bag of parched meal, a corner of a cake of brick tea and my many letters for the post, we had no baggage with us at all. To avert misunderstanding at the frontier, I decided to take no weapons, and that I might not be taken for a smuggler my journey money was limited to twenty Russian roubles in gold.

Before starting on the exacting journey I had taken a number of trial trips with my new horse and I was delighted. He was white as snow, small but powerful, and had such control over his legs that he always set them with precision in the right place. If he snorted and refused to go forward, it always turned out that he was standing on the edge of a place where there was a risk of slipping. With spirited energy he pushed up the steepest inclines; his hooves seemed to cling fast to the mountain paths, his ears vibrated with eagerness, his head was stretched forward and dropped so that his muzzle moved along the ground; and all I had to do was to stick tight, bent well forward in the saddle. When the difficulty had been overcome, he would stop and breathe deeply, and with dilated nostrils and bared teeth raise his comely head high towards the sky above the mountain peaks he had climbed and the difficulties he had left behind him. And a clear whinnying rolled out like the sound of bells among the blue mountains. Then he would turn his head upon his slender neck with the air of a conqueror and regard his rider with an expression of : " Well, here we are, old chap." But if I remained too long sunk in contemplation of the beauty of the surroundings he would push my knee impatiently with his ice-clad nose. Several times I regarded a bit of ground in front of us as impossible to pass, but my horse always carried me up to the top. I christened him "*Voilà*", and the name suited him.

On his journey through the Sanagen mountains Sava had seen so many tracks of wolves, foxes and other fur-bearing beasts that the country attracted him. He now borrowed my Mannlicher and, well furnished with ammunition and strychnine, rode back to the mountains.

And then I shut up the house, put hatches over the opening in the roof, and one sunny morning Bater and I set off towards the northern peaks.

The heavily laden horses made their way laboriously up the narrow valleys

CHAPTER VI
PERIL TO NORTHWARD

AGAIN we followed the Kiäkt River until we came to the smaller tributaries of which the more easterly led us into the northern mountains. We were now following a line that led more directly towards Tunka than the way over the Mus-dawan Pass.

The difficulties increased as we penetrated farther in and higher up among the mountains. The bottom of the river gorge narrowed, and the snow lay deeper on the mountain-sides. At last we found a trail following the river gorge although high up on the mountain slope. Here the snow did not lie so deep, because the steep mountain-side, under the influence of the strong sun, every day "calved" small avalanches that rushed booming down into the depths. The trail had been trodden by two hunters on foot, and since they were certainly men well acquainted with the country, we trusted to their having chosen the best places.

We advanced slowly. The horses walked as if on stilts, so much snow collected under their hooves. Sometimes the way led through small thickets of young birch, and in one of these Voilà suddenly began to snort uneasily and finally refused to go forward. I dismounted and led him, after I had satisfied myself that no danger threatened from the nature of the ground. Voilà grew more and more restive, and Bater, who was walking behind, had to urge him on with his whip. Suddenly we rounded a spur and stopped short. A hundred yards in front of us six wolves stood glaring. They kept close together and stood in the middle of the trail, clearly awaiting our arrival.

I had never in broad daylight seen wolves at such close range. And never, either before or since, have I seen wolves calmly observing me at such close range without seeking cover. They just stood glaring at me, while their warm breath rose like steam from their jaws and nostrils in the cold air.

In my experience of wolves it was impossible to get nearer to them than four or five hundred yards. It was a thing I had often sworn over, when I had seen my bullets hit the snow behind their trailing tails. Before one shoots, wolves do not hurry themselves but trot along towards an arbitrary point at an angle of forty-five degrees to one's own line of march. Only when the bullet hits the snow does the wolf give a bound and disappear like an arrow in a direction at an angle of ninety degrees to that which they have been following. It had always been the same when I had encountered wolves by daylight, and I had never even dreamed of meeting the brutes face to face as now.

There were six of them, one for each bullet in the magazine of my Mannlicher rifle. But—the weapon was at Kiäkt. I was unarmed, and the wolves seemed suddenly to grow to colossal proportions. Their red tongues hung far out of their slavering rapacious jaws. The horses snorted with terror and shrank back. I dared not look round, but tried to remember whether there had been any tall and reliable timber in the last few yards. But all I remembered having seen were stunted, scrubby birches. I knew that wolves far oftener attack Chinese than Mongols or Europeans and that this is explained by the fact that the Chinese encourage the wolves by showing their fear. The same applies to the savage Mongolian dogs which can as a rule be kept at a distance by stern looks, sharp words of command and lifted whip, whereas one would be lost if one took to flight and were overtaken by pursuing dogs.

If the six wolves attacked us, it was inconceivable that we could escape on foot or on horseback in the heavy snow. I kept a sharp eye on the wolves while I considered the situation. The wolves were absolute masters of it, but it was important for me not to let them know it. I did not wish to risk challenging them by shouting or throwing branches at them. I quietly told Bater, who was behind me, to light a fire. He had no matches, but I threw him mine. Bater tied his horse to my saddle and I heard a soft crunching in the snow and the snapping of branches as he broke them. An eternity passed during which a couple of white-hackled wolves contrived to come some ten yards closer—slowly, two steps at a time. I remember that I did not dare to stamp my ice-cold feet in the snow and that at the same time the sweat stood in beads on my forehead. At last I heard the familiar sound of green boughs catching fire, and the smell of smoke rose as the most delectable incense to my nostrils.

The two nearest wolves lumbered back to their comrades and the whole pack began trotting to and fro in a bunch while they sniffed eagerly high in the air with their hot muzzles. But they showed no sign of fear nor any disposition to flight. I told Bater to move the fire forward to the corner of the rocky spur alongside of me, so that the flames might be visible to the brutes, but that, too, produced no greater effect than perhaps a slight surprise in the six beasts of prey that blocked our path.

The supply of dry fuel within reach was very inconsiderable and so a plan had to be devised and carried into effect. I threw some bits of burning birch bark in the direction of the wolves, and even if this did not put them to flight, I observed that they had a respect for the element so universally feared by beasts of prey.

From where I stood it looked as if the mountain slope above us could possibly be followed a hundred and fifty feet higher up than the trodden trail on which we and the wolves were standing. Bater and I took turns in collecting dry birch twigs, which we tied into faggots with long strips of birch bark, and when we had furnished ourselves with five such faggots each we began the ascent on foot with our horses' reins in one hand and a burning faggot in the other. The wolf pack now veered round so that the brutes' greedy eyes followed us all the time, but we only twice had occasion to throw a lighted smoking torch at the boldest when they came too near.

The snow concealed invisible obstacles in the terrain over which we had to find a path, and our progress was slow and laborious. Therefore, as soon as we had come a good bit past the place where the danger lurked for us, we turned down again towards the trodden path and rejoined it a hundred yards on the other side of the wolves. These held their ground and watched us from the same spot, which now of course lay behind us, and since the brutes showed no inclination to pursue us and our last torch was on the point of going up in smoke, we mounted our horses which impatiently obeyed our summons to a smart trot. The terrified animals kept up this pace, driven by fear and eager to get far away from the danger as quickly as possible, and when at last we pulled up our winded horses for a rest, the brief moment of danger and the vision of the six monstrous wolves were so far behind us that I was inclined to regard the whole story as a fairy-tale or the fantasy of a brain affected by loneliness.

But by the evening's camp fire, as I listened to Bater developing his purely Mongolian reflections, full of mysticism and exaggerations which grew with the remoteness of the occurrence, I had abundant occasion to exert my soberest criticism and fall back on my own observations.

Bater the shepherd had had plenty of experience of the wolves of the mountains and the steppes. He had spent his whole life in strife with them, defending his flock against the hereditary foe, but never had he seen wolves so large or of such strange behaviour. They could not have been natural beasts of prey, but were rather spirits, well-disposed towards us, who wished to get us to turn back and abandon a path leading surely to unknown perils. In vain I tried to calm him with the assurance that these were certainly Siberian wolves of another race than those found in Mongolia. The cold climate caused the wolves in these high mountains to grow far thicker pelts and of a different colour from those with which he was acquainted, and this was why they looked so unnatural. These wolves in the north were far bolder than their kin that are found among the brave Mongols, and that was why they had not run away. That they had not attacked their defenceless prey had certainly been due to their having fed to satiety and sluggishness on other game.

All my arguments failed to shake Bater's conviction that they had been preternatural wolves desiring to warn us against a danger that waited on the way we were following. In the end I had to be stern and peremptory to prevent him setting out at once on the return journey.

We passed the night by a mighty fire of cedar. With the day's encounter with the wolves fresh in our memory, we found it advisable to take turns in standing guard over the horses and ourselves through the night. But our exertions had been such that exhaustion soon took the upper hand of precaution. After we had seen to the horses we both fell down by the warm fire and, wrapped in our warm coats slept in the snow until we were wakened by a new day.

The horses were standing serenely in the place where we had tied them, and we ourselves were both alive. Filled with wonder we saw the flush of dawn spread across the gleaming silver of the glacier. Untrodden snow and ice as far as eye could see. The sun rose, the colours quickly changed and that grim landscape silently awoke.

Northward the snow rose high against the heavens. To our eyes it looked like a vertical snow wall. There was no known mark in the boundless waste of snow to enable us to estimate its extent and contours. At the summit we caught a glimpse of what seemed a saddle of dazzling white, surrounded by patches of clear ice. The warming sun aroused an icy wind which was drawn down from the heights over our heads into the depths behind us. It was the Shivert Pass, the eternally ice-covered, that lay in our way, one of Nature's giant obstacles to overcome.

The people down in Kiäkt knew little of this pass, and few of them had crossed it, but it was said that freezing winds and driving snow prevailed constantly at the summit. It was only possible without risking certain death to cross the highest glacier surface during two hours of the twenty-four, and those were the two immediately before sunrise.

Bater had found out about this and other things during the days when I was making my preparations for the journey—and now, full of doubt and fear, he must go up against the white giant of the north.

A pair of screaming ravens sailed over our heads towards the valley in the south, and this had an encouraging effect on Bater, since the black *khiltei shobo*, or " talking birds ", as the Mongols call them, conducted themselves in a manner which satisfied him.

The ravens play for the Mongols a like important rôle as they did in the ancient North of Odin. The black widely-travelled birds are equipped with keen intelligence and are able to understand human speech. It is vouchsafed to certain favoured human beings to understand the ravens' language, for ravens have a language, and these favoured human beings can acquire unbelievable wisdom and learning by listening to the communications of the sagacious birds.

We loaded a lot of fuel on our two horses and set out on the day's march. It turned out not to be long, for at noon we reached the steep ascent of the pass itself, and there we made a halt. The wind whistled from the pass whose contours were now hidden behind a veil of whirling snow. Every time we held in our winded horses for a moment, they turned round with their hindquarters to the blast. To go on was not to be thought of, for, higher up, the storm was so wild that we should have had to make the perilous ascent in complete blindness and would almost certainly have lost our bearings and very likely our lives.

We dug out a cave in the snow which to some extent sheltered us and the horses from the weather and the storm over our heads. Part of our fuel was devoted to maintaining a gently smouldering fire. The sun's rays grew pale and disappeared, but the tempest behind us continued. And the light was smothered by the darkness without Bater having seen any of the ravens he peered after at the top of the pass. So we rolled ourselves again in our fur coats, shutting out the cold and the noise, and slept until a new day.

When we stuck our noses out again it was ice-cold

dawn. It was silent as the grave, and Bater at once began peering with an anxious air after his damned dusky ravens, which came not. I was shivering with cold so that I could hardly speak, and used a considerable quantity of our scanty fuel before I recovered feeling in my limbs. The horses stood spangled with hoar frost with hanging heads and slack bellies.

It was clear that this could not go on much longer; we must soon look for a less grim camping-place, forward or back, and preferably forward. But before I had sufficiently collected my energies to come to an optimistic conclusion, the din and hurricane began again and dispelled the short-lived morning calm.

All that day we lay in our lair, and when, late in the afternoon, things began to look a little brighter, it was only thanks to a prediction from a pair of Bater's winged prophets that flew screeching over our heads.

Bater interpreted the prophecy, and to my great relief it indicated that fortune would follow our passage that night. We took turns to watch, so as to be ready to start so soon as the spirits of the pass should be more favourably disposed. It was a long night, without fire, and most of it was spent in stamping round in the snow, vainly seeking to keep some kind of warmth in us.

Just when the last stars of Charles's Wain disappeared behind the mountain horizon, the pass itself became visible. It's saddle-shaped silhouette was sharply defined against myriads of frostily twinkling stars. The Pole star lay right in the hollow at the summit of the pass, like the bead in a rifle sight, providing a fixed and confidence-inspiring direction point in the midst of the darkness and uncertainty.

The horses were in bad shape from want of fodder and we ourselves were chilled beyond description. We listened tensely to the whine of the wind through the pass. Several times we believed that the tempest up there had abated, but always a new outburst came and dispirited us. But we agreed that the lulls between the hurricane outbursts were growing longer and longer and the outbursts less violent.

We got the horses ready for the start, a labour which

had constantly to be interrupted while we warmed our stiff fingers between the saddle and the horse's back. The stars were paling and all was silent, so silent that we hardly dared to speak. And then we began the ascent. It was carried out in short and violent spurts, interrupted by many and long pauses to get our breath and calm our respiration. Thus we reached the glacier ice and the horses stumbled and fell time after time. In difficult places the saddle blankets were laid under the horses' hooves. Heart and lungs were so strained in the thin air that every word hurt.

Now only single tardy stars were seen in the new day's pale heaven, we made shorter halts and pressed on our climbing. Then we took the last upward step and stood on the summit of the glacier, surrounded by ice and snow so far as our eyes reached. We sat down to quiet our palpitating hearts. Round about us fantastic formations of snow and ice crystals were reddening.

FOR a little while it was vouchsafed to us to stand on the boundary between two ancient empires. Southward ran the long caravan routes that led to the thousand-year-old centres of civilization in the " Middle Kingdom " down among the toiling masses of the " Sons of Heaven ". And to the north and west lay the wide snow field through which the dreaded Cossacks of the " White Tsar " had through centuries driven wretched chained troops of homeless exiles. It was this boundary that had divided six hundred millions of mankind between the earth's two mightiest dynasties. No painted boundary pillar, no armed guard kept watch over this frontier which nature had placed in the most desolate " no man's land ".

A slight breeze brought the surface snow dancing over the ice and reminded us where we were. The descent went swiftly, even if it was not always easy. We slid and glided down in zigzags till we came to the snow. Then we slithered on till we were arrested by a view. We stood a little way above the tree belt and peered out over a forest of snowclad tree-tops that fell away towards a large open valley in whose centre the town of Tunka lay like a great dark patch in all the whiteness.

PERIL TO NORTHWARD

Behind was seen the mountain whose ice-clad ragged crest stretched protectively along the northern side of the valley. This was Tunkinski gleaming in the sunshine, the Gold Mountain, in whose bosom precious metal lies concealed.

We went on till we reached the forest, where we halted to warm ourselves and the horses at the flames of a big fire. It was so delightful that we went no farther that day. We happened on a place where tall grass, of which the horses were much in need, stuck up through the snow.

Next morning we started early in dazzling sunshine, and travelled down through deep snow under snow-laden branches. Tunka was now out of sight, but we could see the Tunkinski range all the time, and we knew that our goal lay on the hither side of its gleaming summits. In the afternoon we came to a canyon which we followed, and towards sunset met with the tracks of domestic animals, which led us to the first dwelling-place in Russian territory.

The house was inhabited by Tunkinski Buriats, and was built after the same plan as those of the Buriats of Kiäkt; but it was considerably larger and the roof was supported on the inside by four massive posts which had been patinated by the smoke from the hearth during many generations.

We were received with the immemorial hospitality of the people of the wild, but it soon became evident that the " Red " atmosphere had begun to penetrate even this out-of-the-way home. The old married couple of the house had held to the old traditions in dress and way of living. The altar stood in its place with the seven offering bowls, symbolizing the Pleiades, before the image of the god. Rice, butter and water were placed in the bowl and, before the meal began, a selected piece of flesh was laid upon the altar. But the two daughters of the house, pretty girls of eighteen and twenty, had not assumed the traditional coiffure and dress to which their age entitled them. They were vivacious and friendly, but less respectful to their elders than the ancient laws prescribed.

In the corner where the cooking utensils were kept, a

crude and impious picture was nailed to the wall, printed in red and black, and of Russian origin. It depicted a table loaded with dishes and wine round which was sitting a party of ecclesiastics in full canonicals, gold-laced generals, princes and finely dressed bejewelled ladies. They were all drawn as fat as pigs, with bestial, greedy eyes, and at the end of the table appeared a caricature of Russia's last Romanov. Through the door of the princely hall could be seen a great troop of famished and emaciated beings stretching out their skeleton hands in entreaty and holding up their hungry children to the exalted ones in hope of an alms. The poor wretches were on their knees and many of them carried crucifixes which they pressed beseechingly to their lips. But the fat swine were not worrying about all this want in their neighbourhood, for in the doorway stood a malevolent and sneering Christ, holding back the crowd with outstretched cross. Under the picture was the inscription : " Jesus of Nazareth, the protector of the rich and powerful ".

It may well be that the manner of life among the former ruling class in Russia, in contrast with the destitution among the great mass of the people, justified dissatisfaction and inspired such thoughts as that picture expressed ; but it seemed so uncalled for to try to sow discontent among the primitive, contented children of nature, who have nothing to trust in but their own powers and who have never known any constraint other than nature's unconquerable might.

In the course of conversation with the young girls, I gathered that all they had acquired and comprehended of the new doctrine was that all elder people were useless, and that everything ancient was humbug and superstition, and must be exterminated. Duties and all unpleasant things were to go, and the new way of salvation lay in pleasure and amusement. But their inborn good character forbade them to show to their own parents anything worse than condescension and pitying tolerance. And the old people regarded the new conditions with true Buddhistic fatalism, convinced that they were the last generation of something outworn, and that the dear children would be blessed in the new doctrines whose first devotees they were born to be.

The four human beings in that solitary dwelling lived through a time of crisis which saw the last aging generation of *Burkhani nome* (the teaching of Buddha) give way before the two fresh and blooming representatives of the emergent *Aratin nome* (Cause of the people doctrine) that had been forged in dirty, grimy and over-populated industrial centres far from the lonely and clean wilderness.

But the two young people had not altogether forgotten what they had learnt as children, and at my invitation they sang the melancholy songs and moved gracefully in the ancient dances of their race. They took it for granted that I, as a white man, was of the new doctrine, which indeed came from the West, and this was probably the reason why I was treated with such favour by the

(Mongolian Dance)

young girls. In the course of the evening the elder of them repaired my badly worn coat and put new felt in my *unti*.

Later in the evening we heard the sound of approaching hooves, and a young Buriat stepped into the cottage. He put down his weapon, a modern Russian rifle, inside the door and sat down by the fire between the girls and me. His demeanour was offhand and uncivil, as is often the case when coloured races try to ape the western peoples. He was altogether too modern to care to employ his people's dignified greeting, but treated me instead to a Russian "*Zdravstvuite, tovarish*" ("Good day, comrade") as he offered me his dirty paw. His dress was an imitation of what he supposed to be western costume, and the lankness of his hair was emphasized by his attempt to effect a parting in the middle. He was a by no means attractive specimen of the new generation. He had discarded the traditions of his own race and in exchange had acquired only the worst of what the west provided.

It was obvious that he was a frequent visitor to the family, and he tried in a not very agreeable manner to make an impression on the young girls. When later on in the evening they once more yielded to my request to perform the ancient songs, and dances, he tried to prevent them. He reproached me for my conservative taste, and I in my turn expostulated with him for his foolish and uncritical aping of everything modern. At last I urged upon him that he was a Buriat and ought to be proud to wear the beautiful dress of his forefathers, instead of going about " like a cedar tree dressed in birch leaves ". This common Mongolian expression for anything which is not what it pretends to be appealed to the young girls, and they burst out laughing and said he looked comical and that they greatly preferred him in his old dress. The boy was furious and tried to insult me, whereupon I gave him a friendly dig in the ribs and told him to keep his mouth shut.

Then we went to bed, and I slept deliciously, after the girls had tucked me in warmly with wolfskins which they held in place by lying down one on either side of me. It was glorious again to be sleeping in a warm room with the consciousness that the horses were in shelter with a good feed of oats.

NEXT morning I was awakened not by icy cold, but by the crackling flames of the fire. The young Buriat was not there, and I was told he had gone the night before, after I was asleep. Bater and I drank tea, ate meat and then took leave of our first hosts in Russian territory.

All day long our way led us through deep forest in which the fir and spruce boughs were weighted down to the ground with snow. We followed a trodden path through the snow which lay three feet deep in the narrow gorge through which it ran. The sun disappeared early behind the trees and mountain tops, no trace of civilization appeared and we made a halt when the cold became intense. We had brought with us food for ourselves and hay for the horses, and dead trees lay ready to provide warmth during the night. And our second night on Russian soil was spent in comfort.

Next morning we crawled early out of our sleeping-sacks, so as to reach our goal, Tunka, before nightfall, and I dreamed of once more lying in a proper bed between white sheets, a thing that I had not experienced for the last nineteen months.

But it turned out otherwise—I was to live through yet another hundred days before such a felicity was vouchsafed to me.

CHAPTER VII

IN CAPTIVITY

JUST as we were ready to start, and were standing astride over the embers of the fire so as to absorb its last warmth under our big coats, we suddenly heard a crunching sound in the snow and a snapping of twigs, and the jingle of bells and harsh cries rapidly approached. A moment later two sleighs manned by soldiers in Soviet uniform drove up to the fire. The sleighs were pulled up abruptly, and six hostile rifles were levelled at us, while words incomprehensible to me resounded through the forest. I stood as if struck with paralysis by this unexpected appearance, while Bater fell on his knees in the snow with his hands raised towards heaven.

The six strangers were all Buriats. They were clad in long, grey military capes, and wore helmet-shaped felt caps on their heads, leaving only their eyes and noses visible. A hammer and a sickle, crosswise, in red, formed the badge on their caps, symbolizing the cause which the men and their menacing rifle barrels represented.

This encounter and the impression of it constituted my first personal acquaintance with the red Soviet, whose chief centre lies only forty-eight hours' journey from my native place.

Bater knelt in an attitude of supplication in the snow, and I stood as if petrified, staring at their rifles. The fellows in their grey uniforms looked mysterious and threatening. I heard the click of triggers as they were cocked, and a sharp word of command angrily repeated. " *Ruki v verch* ! " they shouted furiously, while a couple of soldiers ran towards me with outstretched weapons. I stood motionless, and the two men threw down their

IN CAPTIVITY

rifles and seized me violently by the shoulders. It was not until later that I learned that the Russian " *Ruki v verch* " means " Hands up." I was not, however, shot on this occasion, although I never obeyed the order. And when I later grasped the connection, I was able to take the following days' furious shouts and threatening gestures with some degree of equanimity.

The rest of the soldiers now tumbled out of the sleighs, and Bater and I were searched and pinioned. The six held a palaver by the fire which resulted in my being made fast to a substantial fir tree, and a Buriat sneeringly explained to me in Mongolian that I was to be left there to solitude and the wolves, which would come by sundown at latest. And he pointed out the tracks of wild beasts only a few yards from the tree. Some abusive language and a mocking laugh followed from the men, who then got back into the sleighs, taking Bater with them.

The sound of bells soon died away. I heard a whip crack twice and then all was once more silent. Only the sleigh tracks and a couple of discarded cigarette ends remained to recall the brief scene that had been played a few minutes earlier. Near the fire lay Bater's pipe from which a faint ribbon of smoke was still rising. I could hear our horses pawing the snow behind me where they still stood by the tree to which I had tied them just before ; and I wondered whether they would succeed in breaking loose.

A pair of ravens circled croaking over the camping ground. Finally they settled and began looking for remains of food, till they started quarrelling over a bone they both wanted. I remembered that ravens generally scent a quarry sooner than eagles, vultures, wolves and other undertakers of the wilderness. They assure themselves of the choicest parts of the dead—or half-dead—body, by pecking out the eyes.

I was beginning to freeze, and the rope cut into my wrists. My hands smarted and pricked as though needles and knives were being driven into them. A shaft of sunlight was moving slowly over the snow, growing longer and extending towards me. I followed

IN CAPTIVITY

it with my eyes. Its movement was infinitely slow, but at last it reached the foot of my tree. Then it climbed up my legs, and I enjoyed the warmth it brought me. With difficulty I succeeded in twisting myself round the tree so that my frozen hands came into the sun. It warmed them but the rope cut in all the more and increased the throbbing in my arms, and the pain grew worse with every attempt to free myself.

I thought that if one of the horses broke loose it would perhaps run back to the Buriat dwelling, where it had got such good fodder and, by its empty saddle, give the alarm to my friendly hosts. I raised a yell to frighten the horses, but it did not succeed. After a moment's silence I could hear them resume their gnawing at the bark of the tree to which they were tethered. They recognized my voice and had become used to hearing me raise it during the crossing of the pass.

The sunbeam had now passed my tree, and it quickly grew cold. Thoughts flew through my brain—would the night cold or the wolves fall upon me first? I hoped the icy wind of night would stop the beating of my heart before the wolves ventured to approach me. . . .

THEN all at once hope awoke, for the woods resounded with the distant cracking of whips. My hopes increased as the sound of bells came nearer. Then I heard human voices and I began at once to shout as loud as I could. I soon regretted having done so, for when the sleigh drove up to the camping-place I saw that it contained four of the six who had taken me prisoner that morning. They laughed scornfully at my evident eagerness to obtain help. After jeering at me for a while, they did, however, cut the rope that held me to the tree, and I was thrown into the sleigh with my hands still bound behind me. Both my horses were tied behind the sleigh and it went off through the forest at a flying gallop. But my worn-out cattle could not keep up this pace for long, so one of the soldiers got out to ride them after us.

I had supposed that I had spent the greater part of

IN CAPTIVITY

a long day tied to the tree, but when we came out into a big clearing in the forest I saw that the sun was still high in the heavens. The pace was rapid, the open places grew larger and more frequent, and a little before sunset we swung out into the Tunka valley and saw in the distance the smoke of the many dwellings of the town. The town was extensive, but I saw no gilded spires or cupolas and, as I got no farther than its outskirts, I never knew for certain whether any such existed.

It was night when we reached our goal, which was a two-storied wooden building situated in an open yard surrounded by a high palisade. At several entrances sentries in Soviet uniform were standing, but they all left their posts to join the inquisitive crowd staring at the prisoner and his gallant captors. I was shown up an outer stairway leading to a large office-like room. On a long bench against the wall Bater was sitting among a lot of squatting Buriats and a couple of long-bearded Russians. They were clearly prisoners, for several of them were in fetters. At the far end of the room stood several desks at which sat a number of young Buriats in smart uniforms and elegant Russian riding boots reaching above the knee. They wore English Sam Browne belts round their slim waists, and big Nagan revolvers flapped against their thighs. They wore Lenin's portrait on sundry enamelled badges on their breasts, arms and all other conceivable places.

Bater had jumped up when I came into the room, but one of the soldiers at once knocked him brutally back on to the bench. I was led forward to a fellow who, to judge from the number of his enamelled emblems, must have been a great admirer of Lenin's. He was a charming youngster of at most twenty-five, with regular features, wise eyes and a sympathetic appearance. He spoke fluent Mongolian with a slight Buriat accent and at once began to put a number of questions to me. I refused to answer until my aching hands were set free. He himself loosed the rope after he had examined my hands. They were blue-black and the release from the rope only increased the pain in them. A soldier was ordered to bring snow, and my hands were rubbed with it for a long while, which caused me torments. After a time they became burning hot when the blood began to circulate again.

It was already late, and the interrogation was not resumed. The prisoners had been taken away and all except two officers had left the room. I was now led down a long passage with a row of massive doors on either side before one of which my escort halted. The door was opened and I saw a cell lighted by a faint starlight that came in through a grated opening high in the wall. I thought of the soldiers' strict command to me in the forest, which I had refused to obey and yet had not been shot, and I refused to go in. I had committed no crime that justified their casting me into prison, and I predicted severe punishment for them all when their blunder became known in higher quarters.

It worked. I was taken back to the big office where I was allotted a sleeping-place on a bench. The sympathetic young officer kept watch by the door and himself slept on two tables joined together. Outside the door leading to the yard stood a sentry who fired shots into the air at short intervals, evidently to show me that he was at his post and that escape would involve danger to my life. I asked the officer what this shooting signified, and he explained somewhat shamefacedly that it was to keep off the wolves. I could not help laughing and expressed my astonishment that a troop of brave young Buriat soldiers should be so frightened of wolves and so ignorant as to suppose that they would venture into a place guarded by so many dead shots, all sons of hunters who had lived their lives in the mountains in constant warfare with wild beasts. And then I told the story of my meeting with the six wolves—and afterwards slept till daylight without hearing another shot fired.

In the morning my horses arrived, and I recovered the saddlebags containing my passport from the Foreign Minister. They were impressed by the gilt lion and crown on the blue cover but later discovered that the photograph did not resemble me. They fetched a mirror and I understood their point of view. I had not seen myself in a mirror for many months, and washing with snow melted in the mouth had not extended beyond the eyes and nose. A long unkempt beard framed nose and cheeks which were tanned with alpine sun, cold and wind. My hair was a single matted mass that lay in tangles on my head with isolated tufts pushing out coquettishly at the top and at the sides. My forehead and ears, which throughout a long winter had been covered by my heavy bearskin cap, were the only clean parts and showed up white against the leathery, furrowed mask of my face. I looked like my own grandfather, though without the family resemblance. I did not recognize myself. I explained to the officers that the picture was a youthful portrait, and the interrogation continued. I explained to them how it was that I could speak Mongolian, why I lived in Mongolia, and the occasion for my having crossed the frontier to come to Tunka.

A long report was drawn up and I came to know that I was accused of being a Russian officer who had fought against the Soviet under Baron Ungern-Sternberg. I gathered that the young Buriat whom I met on my first evening in Soviet territory had recognized and denounced me. He himself had fought in the Soviet's ranks against Ungern-Sternberg, and had been a prisoner at Urga where he had seen me in the White Guard's uniform. I tried in vain to explain to them that Ungern-Sternberg had died while I was still in Copenhagen and that his guardsmen had been exterminated and dispersed long before I came to Mongolia.

The rest of that day I sat in front of the stove picking off the lice that swarmed in my coat and deerskin breeches and now became more than usually insistent under the stimulating influence of the heat. At dinner-time I got one of the soldier's portions, mutton in broth, which tasted marvellous. In the evening I was given tea and a handful of millet. I got so much tea that I could put my beard in to soak, which I did. And then I began cutting and slashing at my beard with my razor. When after arduous labour I had got rid of all superfluous hair, I was profoundly changed, but in another way comical to behold, for the parts of my face that had been protected by the beard were now as pale as my forehead, so that it looked as if I was wearing a brown half-mask. The change was astonishing, and on closer examination a faint resemblance to the portrait could be detected. They began to believe my assertion that I was a member of a foreign nation so distant that it did not belong to the Red Soviet.

That evening I sat long in talk with the young Buriat officer and two of his comrades. I belonged to one of the detestable capitalistic communities about which, thanks to Soviet propaganda, they had very decided views and " profound " knowledge. They asked me if I was one of the oppressed or one of the oppressors, those who believe in a god and other sorcery, who grind the faces of the poor and want to make all coloured races the white man's slaves. I told them then about the Northern Kingdoms, about kings who ruled *with* their people and for their people's good ; about Eskimos and Lapps who were helped by the northern peoples to advance towards better conditions and about freedom of speech and writing and personal opinions. About countries that had not been at war for generations and in which no death sentence had been executed within the memory of man. And at last I told them about Bulgun Tal and our task there.

We desired friendship with the Mongols, we wanted to establish modern farms where the Mongols could go to school and learn to improve their condition, to live in peace and industry and to become useful and efficient citizens of the world. We wanted peace and understanding between nations and races, and not hatred and blind fanaticism.

They asked many questions and wondered why such things had not been explained to them in the new literature, and before we turned in we were the best of friends. The sympathetic young officer let me know that he would willingly let me go free but that he must await the reply to the report that he had unfortunately already sent off.

The answer to the report came next day with orders that I was to be brought under escort to Shinkish. The

IN CAPTIVITY

Buriats told me that I would now be taken to a Russian station where all would go well with me if only I defended myself in the same way as I had done to them. The young officer promised to send a new explanatory report to Shinkish which would certainly remove all suspicions. Bater had been sent to Shinkish the day before, and I would meet him there.

After a cordial farewell I rode off on my own " Voilá " accompanied by a single trooper. The Russian looked as grim and unapproachable as the rifle muzzle he kept the whole time pointed in my direction, and we rode the whole thirty versts without trying to exchange a word.

Shinkish was a considerably smaller town than Tunka, but with buildings far larger and more imposing than the few I had seen in Tunka. Shinkish is a customs station of " Tunkinski Trakt ", the valley through which the road goes from Kultuk on the Trans-Siberian railway to Hanga on Hubso Gol in Mongolia. The boundary passes through Mundi, but the customs inspection takes place at Shinkish, which consequently has a number of official buildings.

The road is continued within the town by a wide street. At the entrance to the town I saw a crucifix behind a window. The pane was smashed and the crucifix damaged. Later I passed a Russian church. It was closed, the windows knocked out and the cross torn down. At the top of the gilded cupola fluttered a red rag. The whole place bore witness to the devastation which the fanatical adherents of a new religion leave in their trail.

We dismounted in front of a large and imposing but dilapidated building. The marks on the door told a tale of recently torn down imperial emblems.

The horses were taken from us in the yard, and I was led upstairs and through long corridors with numerous doors on either side, from which issued the sound of clattering typewriters. Two other Russian soldiers guarded me while my escort went into a room to announce our arrival. For a little while I stood waiting and studied the great closed door where the

IN CAPTIVITY

defaced painted and finely carved emblems bore witness to departed greatness.

The noise of the busy typewriters grew louder as the door slowly opened. The soldiers bade me step in, and I crossed the threshold. All the machines were at once silenced, and all eyes were turned upon me. The room was filled with Russians sitting at long worktables. Despite their clerical employment they were all wearing the grey uniform of the Soviet with the peaked felt caps. It was long since I had seen so many men of my own race, and I smiled at them, prepared for friendliness. But the bearded faces were grim and my wandering glances met only rows of hostile eyes. The whole assembly looked like a bunch of convicts.

But to the extreme right a simply dressed person was sitting, a young woman in a full Russian blouse and short grey skirt. Her legs were visible under the table, and she had small neat feet clad in long Russian riding boots. Her well-kept hands rested on the typewriter, and her kindly eyes looked at me with friendliness. This was such a relief in that chilling atmosphere that I turned towards her in hope of sympathy. But I got no further than saying " Mademoiselle " before the soldiers seized me by the shoulders and hurried me through the room towards another door. By the time I had been violently pushed through it I was furious.

At a large table sat a uniformed person with fiery red hair. He was holding his felt cap rolled up in one hand on the table. I fumed at him, swore in five languages, thumped the table and once more soldiers hastened forward to seize and hold me tight. No one in the whole assemblage understood any language but Russian, and of that tongue I could remember nothing but three strings of foul language that I had heard our Cossacks use whenever they were particularly incensed. I did not know what the words signified, but had a feeling that they were appropriate to the present situation and so made diligent use of them. This cleared the air, and soon I was in a position to put a lot of questions to the Russian-speaking Buriat who was summoned. I demanded an explanation why I was regarded and

IN CAPTIVITY

treated as a prisoner. And of much else besides. I was now informed by the chief of the group, through the Buriat, that everything would soon be arranged. I had entered Russian territory by a forbidden route, and the fact must be reported to Irkutsk. This had now been done, and in a few days I would receive permission to return to Mongolia, when the *propusk*, as they called the permit to travel, arrived.

I asked where and upon what I was to live, since I did not know a soul in the place and had no money, and was told there would be no trouble about that. I could live with the Buriat's family during the time of waiting, and he would take care of me and my horses. Bater was there already, they said.

I followed the young Buriat to the door, but when the soldiers closed up on either side of me I became suspicious and asked at the threshold whether it was the intention to take me to prison, to which they soothingly replied by asking whether I supposed they put people in prison who had done no ill.

Later I rode out of the town with the young Buriat. A troop of armed soldiers who, according to the Buriat's story, happened to be going the same way, followed at a little distance. As we were swinging up a narrow lane that ran between high palisades and scattered houses a sleigh came towards us at a rapid pace. Round the equipage rode a troop of noisy, laughing soldiers with drawn cavalry sabres. I caught a glimpse of two pale, frightened women's faces and a number of children clinging to two black-clad figures. In answer to my questions, the Buriat told me that the two women were malefactresses, wives of highly placed representatives of the old régime and enemies of the new time. They were presumably going to be executed since so many armed soldiers were escorting them out of the town.

I wished at that moment that I had a squadron of free peasants and artisans from my own country at my disposal, for I was convinced that their Nordic sense of justice would at once have disposed them to intervene.

We stopped in front of a large building of public character and stepped into a big office which also was

IN CAPTIVITY

full of clerically engaged people in grey uniforms with revolvers in their belts. I was taken to a long desk where a man put a number of gruff questions to me in Russian. Since I did not understand him, he tried to awe me with his glance and then directed his questions to my Buriat companion. I was given to understand that I was shamming ignorance of the Russian language. I was in fact Russian and was only trying to conceal my crimes against the people's cause under a false name, passport and nationality. However we got no farther with the matter than that the man presented me with a printed questionnaire to fill in. When I told the Buriat to translate the printed questions for me, he did so, while the uniformed Russian listened, smiling scornfully. There was a long row of questions to be answered, and most of them seemed to me quite irrelevant. Among other things I was to give an account of my father's life, the amount of his income, whether he lived in his own house, whether he was an adherent of the cause of the people, whether he had defended it or had fought against it. Further I was to give an account of all my places of abode since 1916, especially if I had at any time been in India or Egypt. That I had visited both these countries was counted as a minus mark in my conduct, and I had to explain the occasion and what I had been doing there. I had replied to the question to what realm I belonged by " The Kingdom of Denmark ", which the Russian felt himself obliged to alter to " The Republic of Denmark ". All these questions were necessary to the issue of my outward *propusk*.

The final formalities having been completed, I was taken to a door at the opposite end of the room and assumed that I should now be at liberty to accompany the Buriat to his house. The door was opened for me, and a stair led into a large open place. I looked round for the Buriat, who had not followed me down the stair. He was still standing in the open doorway, looking gravely after me, and alongside of him I saw armed Russian soldiers, grey-clad and bearded, all watching me with a scornful smile on their lips.

The door still stood open, but a row of long bayonets

IN CAPTIVITY

barred the way. I swung round and observed the surroundings. A large open place lay before me enclosed on two sides by two-storey buildings of wood, whose dismal façades were only interrupted by three rows of small square windows all furnished with thick iron bars. The fourth side of the yard was cut off from freedom by a twelve-foot palisade at the top of which were a further three feet of impassable barbed wire.

I had been lured into this trap by lies and falsehood, and I rushed towards the open door which was the only visible way back to the freedom I had already lost. The mocking laughter of the soldiers met me as I flew up the stair. When I reached the topmost step, the bayonets were plunged towards me, and two of the soldiers drove me down, jeering and laughing, step by step, till I once more stood in the yard. A sharp bang announced that the door had been shut and locked—and I was in prison.

The snow lay deep in the yard, but a well-beaten path along its outer sides indicated that many persons had tramped there, round and round. Against the boardfence to the east was a larger trampled path and the marks of bullets could be seen in the wood. When I stopped at this place the two soldiers immediately came forward to me and, beaming with delight and with graphic gestures, began to explain to me that this was the place where the executions took place. The soldiers opened a door at the end of the building bounding the yard on the south. Within was seen a long corridor with a row of doors on either side. I continued my round, and the door was shut again without the soldiers trying to force me in. After several hours' wandering it was absolutely clear to me that there was no possible escape from this place. The only way back to freedom was through the door in the densely populated building through which I had come.

Late in the afternoon the doors to the two prison buildings were opened, and a number of soldiers came out and formed up along the outer sides of the yard. A dull clanking was heard from the big corridors and a pitiable crowd appeared. They were Russians of all ages and both sexes. Among them walked Bater, my faithful follower in freedom; fate had brought us to the same prison.

A number of the prisoners carried iron fetters on their legs, which clanked as they tramped heavily through the snow. The faces that issued from the two buildings were all pale, some hardened and repulsive, others terrified and unhappy, here and there one dignified and resigned. These last often belonged to tall, upright figures, and it was generally these men who were ironed. The first category of prisoners shouted and swopped jests with the soldiers; the others walked in silence and apparently unmoved through the hail of foul language and abuse that the soldiers poured upon them.

It was revolting and humiliating to think of such usage being ordered by authorities of one's own race.

With tedious monotony the miserable band trudged round the yard on the path trodden by unfortunates before them. After the lapse of half an hour the prisoners formed a queue by a hatchway that opened from the administrative building. After each had received an earthenware jug of hot water and a coarse rye loaf, they disappeared again into the two prison buildings. The yard was soon empty and the last echo of the clanking chains died away in the long corridors. A soldier came up to me and asked me by signs whether I wanted my ration for the day. I was hungry and thirsty, and these torments conquered my pride, so that the day's last prison ration fell to my lot.

CHAPTER VIII

DAILY LIFE IN THE PRISON AT SHINKISH

THE soldiers summoned me to go the same way in as the other prisoners, but I refused. With the darkness came the cold, and when, later in the evening, a soldier appeared, accompanied by Bater, I complied with the latter's invitation to join him in his cell. We went in silence along the corridor until Bater stopped in front of a massive door marked with the figure nine. A turnkey came and opened the door, and I was now one of the four prisoners confined by the Soviet in cell number nine of the Shinkish prison.

THE room had whitewashed walls and was twelve feet square. Half of this area was however taken up by a raised platform like a Chinese *k'ang*. The cell's one window was furnished with iron bars and barbed wire intertwined. A big Russian stove stood in the middle of the room, emitting a warmth that would have been delightful if the air had not been so close and oppressive. In the massive wooden doors, leading to the corridor, was a small round opening, closed on the outside by a metal shutter. On the *k'ang* I could dimly see in the darkness some beings who, on closer inspection, turned out to be two bearded Russians who at once began to bombard me with questions.
I was not in the humour to try to understand what they said, but spent the night in considering all the possible consequences of my desperate position. None of my friends knew where I was. When I failed to return to the farm they would make enquiries, the upshot of which would be that I had disappeared in the deep snow of the mountains, as so many before me.
I could not think of any possible way of getting into

touch with the outside world. All my warders were fanatics, hardened by the brutalizing influence of civil war. All of them had certainly killed people in cold blood—so often that they would not shrink from taking another life if it served their interest. If I succeeded in convincing them of my identity, it would perhaps serve their purpose better to let me disappear than to release me, which might later bring about political complications with a foreign nation and consequently inconvenience to themselves.

The two Russians snored. Bater sat silently twiddling his rosary. Twice the Russians got up and relieved themselves in the room whose nauseating stench was oppressive after life in the open. The consciousness of being confined within strong walls, grated windows and a massive iron studded door made me desperate.

Next morning at seven, heavy steps were heard and a jingling of keys, and the door was opened for a salutary whiff of fresh air. The two Russian gaolbirds knew the rules after months of detention in that room, and Bater and I followed their example. With the empty jugs in our hands we took our places along the wall next the door until the warder ordered us out into the corridor, and we followed the line of prisoners out to the yard. Now that my lungs were filled with the fresh air and the sun was streaming on me from the clear blue sky, the night's gloomy reflections gave way to a more optimistic view of existence and the future. When the tramp round was over we returned to the cell with our jugs full of hot water and the day's scanty ration of bread. One of the Russians also brought an armful of fuel. On our return we tidied up, the latrine was emptied and the stove lighted, while the warder with his jingling bunch of keys was present in the room.

The fellow was a mixture of amiable condescension and offensive malice. He was no Russian, but a German-speaking Czech who, after prolonged sojourn in one of the Siberian prison camps, had forgotten his country, his home and his friends, and attached himself to the Soviet, and had behaved so well during the civil war that he had been entrusted with the whole of the keys of the

IN THE PRISON AT SHINKISH

Shinkish prison. He was short and thick set, with a disagreeable expression.

During his daily visit to our cell he liked to draw his revolver from its leather holster under pretence of examining the magazine full of ball cartridges. He often showed his face in the door shutter to jeer at me. At ten one morning shots were heard from the yard. Immediately the warder appeared in the doorway and turning encouragingly to me, remarked: "*Jetzt haben die dummen Russen wieder drei Personen geschossen. Morgen bist du dabei wahrscheinlich.*"

One of my Russian fellow-prisoners had travelled in Mongolia and had acquired enough Mongolian words for us to understand one another. I got from him his own story and those of several of the other prisoners. He was companionable in his way and immediately took me into his confidence.

The man had been born to the north of Lake Baikal of parents banished to the wilderness on the ground of political opposition to the old Russian regime. At a very early age he had fled from the convict colony to which his parents belonged. And then had followed a long series of years, during which his perambulation of Siberia and Mongolia was only interrupted by regularly recurring stays in various prisons. He called himself an anarchist and his head was full of rancorous plans against all existing institutions. The assumption by the Bolsheviks of the government in Omsk had set him free from the prison of that town, but now he was confined again, since the local peasant council demanded vengeance for a murder he had committed on a family of three.

I asked him his reason for perpetrating this triple murder, and he explained that on his way through a neighbouring forest he had quarrelled with an elderly peasant about a trifle. They had both been under the influence of vodka. After they had separated, the other's utterances had irritated him to such a degree that he had followed to the little house where the peasant lived. There they had continued the exchange of views, and he had suddenly become so enraged that he had seized an axe and killed first the old man and afterwards his son

IN THE PRISON AT SHINKISH

who had hurried to the place, and the son's wife. A small boy had, however, escaped and denounced him to the neighbours, and their indignant accusations before the new authorities had led to his becoming an inmate of cell number nine. He confessed to me fifteen murders, which did not seem to weigh upon his conscience in the very least.

He preferred the new regime to the old, because he was much better off in this prison than he had ever been in his many gaol experiences. To my question with what punishment he was to expiate his latest crime, he said that sentence had not yet been pronounced, but that he expected to get off with two years' detention in that comfortable prison.

The morning before he told me all this, he had shaved me. When he saw me take my razor out of my saddlebag, he had offered his assistance and I had unsuspectingly handed him the razor. Moreover he did the job uncommonly well and ran the razor lightly and swiftly over my cheeks and throat. Afterwards he used the razor to remove his own and his fellow-prisoners' bushy beards.

In the afternoon a Russian officer, attended by a number of armed soldiers, came to inspect the prison. The officer and the Czech warder came into our cell and started at the unwonted sight of newly shaved prisoners. A search was instituted which, despite my protests, resulted in the confiscation of the razor.

My other Russian fellow-prisoner was younger and seemed more weighed down by feelings of remorse. He had been eleven months in the prison under accusation of smuggling cattle out of Siberia into Mongolian territory. No sentence had yet been pronounced on him, and he did not know how long he would still have to stay in prison.

Among the prisoners who, during the daily trudge round the yard, particularly stirred my compassion, was an old woman with an infinitely weary and defeated air. She was advanced in years and worn out, and went through the wearisome tramp through the snow with her eyes fixed on the ground and without paying any attention at all to her surroundings. She looked ill and

IN THE PRISON AT SHINKISH

wretched and could surely not have many outings left, before her harassed soul and body should escape from all earthly bondage and anxiety. Ivan, the wholesale murderer, told me one evening about the crime for which she was suffering.

During the disorder of the civil war, a grandson of the old woman had stolen a cow from a neighbouring village. He was denounced, and a detachment of soldiers was sent to arrest him. He had, however, succeeded in escaping into the mountains and had lain hidden there for over nine months out of reach of the clutches of the law. The soldiers, unable to imprison the thief, had locked up his old grandmother instead, and now held her as a sort of hostage in the Shinkish prison until they could succeed in catching the actual malefactor.

The fare in the prison consisted of two daily portions of black bread, and one got the same number of chances of filling one's jug with boiling water. The bread rations were so small that they came far short of satisfying our hunger. But the prisoners had permission to receive food from friends outside the prison, and the size of the portions was calculated on the assumption that every one would have friends to supply them with their proper fare.

One day great preparations were made for getting the prison to look as clean and tidy as possible, and a rumour went about the *tovarish komandir* (the comrade commandant) himself, was coming to inspect.

Bater and my two Russian fellow-prisoners were sent down to the yard to shovel snow, and the warder came in to me in the cell with a bucket full of whitewash. He asked if I could whitewash walls, to which I answered: "Yes." Then he handed me a large brush and told me to begin the job with the big Russian stove. But before I took the brush I asked him what pay I was to get for my labour. He gaped at me idiotically and asked angrily: "*Was zum Teufel meinst du?*" Then I explained to him that I came from a free country where a labourer is worthy of his hire, and whose citizens, from the king to the peasants and workmen, have duties as well as rights. The King received the appanage fixed by the people and the workman the wage he was worth and to which he is entitled. And I spread myself in a long discourse on the position of the workmen in Scandinavia, on trades-unions and other things that were entirely new to this champion of the workers' and peasants' cause. I pointed out to him that with us the "people's cause" was an actuality with traditions, whereas in the Russian dominions it was a thing unknown, untried and moreover misapprehended, as their treatment of me sufficiently proved. During my brief stay in Russia, I had been unable to discern even the dawn of the noble ideal of liberty, fraternity and equality.

I explained to him that I would be delighted to make the cell resplendently white, but in return for the remuneration that accorded with the minimum that my country's trades-union had laid down for such work, for if I performed work without receiving the sum prescribed for such a task, I should be no better than a blackleg, an instrument in the hands of the sweaters against the hard-won rights of the workers.

The warder did not know what reply to make to my unexpected discourse, but disappeared through the door, to return immediately with an officer. The latter was a big, gross, bull-headed fellow, and the warder's report of my unwillingness to perform my allotted task had completely infuriated him, and his broad soldierly chest was rising and falling violently after coming at the double through the long corridors. The obligatory enamelled portrait of Lenin in the midst of a five-pointed star lay on his breast and heaved up and down in sympathy with his fury. He screamed something at me which the warder translated by a string of German terms of abuse, with the result that I in my turn grew angry.

Strong in the consciousness that the right was on my side, I stretched my hand towards the splendid decoration on his breast and, with the unction of a high priest in my voice, repeated my discourse, glorifying the free man's freedom and pronouncing my condemnation of the coercion and tyranny that pervaded that place. The warder translated for him in such excellent fashion that, just as I was passing on to a new oration, he turned on his heel and vanished, fuming and spluttering, through the door. The warder regarded me for a moment with appreciation, then grinned and followed, bustling and jingling his keys, in the tracks of his master. I was now alone behind the locked door. The pail of whitewash stood on the floor and there I threw the brush which I had been waving in my hand during my lecture.

I had been sitting for a while speculating over the ultimate consequences of my outspokenness, when the rattle of keys once more announced the arrival of visitors. The warder stepped in, followed by a young Russian woman. She was well-made and had fine features, but her eyes were lascivious and brazen. The warder took up a position on the *k'ang* by my side and gave orders to the girl, who bedaubed the stove, ceiling and walls with the brush until they all gleamed gloriously white. Meanwhile, I carried on a friendly conversation with the Czech. He was on a very intimate footing with the young woman, and she seemed to appreciate his advances. " *Ganz hübsch* ", he turned to me, " *aber gefährlich* ". And then he related gleefully how she came, young as she was, to be within the walls of the prison.

A trusted member of the local soldiers' council had honoured her with his favour. But one night a difference of opinion had arisen between them owing to divergent views on that point in the new doctrine which enjoins free love. The result of the dispute was that the defenceless woman grabbed a stone with which she so belaboured the trooper's head that he fell to the ground and rattled his sabre for the last time. He rose no more, and the recollection of it was so funny that the warder and the convict joined in a coarse sneering laugh.

A couple of times the conversation turned on my refusal to work without pay and the subsequent encounter with the superior officer. Then the warder laughed his mirthless laugh and repeated delightedly to himself: " *Morgen wird der Kerl sicher geschossen.*" Then he stared hard at me and, with a grin that contradicted his words, muttered: " *Armer Kerl.*" When the cell was white and fine, I was again left in solitude, and my fellow-prisoners did not return till sunset.

IN THE PRISON AT SHINKISH

The nights were the worst in cell number nine. A foul stench and the bestial snoring of the prisoners made the torment great. The consciousness of being confined between narrow walls under a low roof after life in the open was also frightful. I slept little, and when day dawned I stood waiting to snatch the first breath of fresh air when the door opened.

Next day the expected inspection took place, and I was ready to lay all my complaints before the high authorities. And so I did, when the "comrade commandant" and his suite came to my cell. I had hoped that he would be master of a language known to me, but the conversation again had to be carried on with the Czech as interpreter I complained of the conditions in the prison and the lack of food, and demanded to be told the reason why I had been cast in prison. If they did not believe my statements, they could telegraph to the Great Northern Telegraph Company at Irkutsk or to the Danish Legation in Moscow who were bound to know about the Krebs Expedition and my residence in Northern Mongolia.

The "comrade commandant" appeared to understand and promised to grant my request. He further promised to procure me a bath and to see that my letters, which had been confiscated, were despatched to their destination.

I did not get the bath, nor did my letters ever arrive, but the second day after this visit I was subjected to a brief interrogation which resulted in Bater and me being released from prison and escorted to a military barracks lying outside the town. Here it was carefully explained to me that I was now no longer in captivity.

CHAPTER IX

ON THE WAY TO FREEDOM

IN the barracks to which we had now come we shared a room with the soldiers' cook, a Chinaman named Kao Wen Pu, who went by the name of Nikolai among the Russians. Outside the door of the room stood a double guard whose long bayonets contradicted the freedom we now officially enjoyed. In the evening an officer appeared, who by signs and gesticulations succeeded in explaining to us in a convincing manner that it was not desirable for us to pass through the room's one door. I resided there for two days as Nikolai's guest, and during that time we became good friends.

Nikolai spoke " pidgin English ", so that we could converse without being understood by the others. He had once been valet de chambre to a Russian Countess in Moscow. Those had been good days, and he had put by money so that one day when he returned to his distant home in Manchuria he might have enough capital to open a little shop. But then came the foolish revolution, and at the thought of it Nikolai again became Kao Wen Pu and, in fluent Chinese, cursed the convulsions that had made an end of his fine Countess and his little fortune.

Without capital and with the single thought of getting away from the miserable new conditions, he had passed through numberless vicissitudes. When the Reds came into power he had been pressed into a Chinese machine-gun company with which he went to Siberia to fight against Kolchak. Later he had acted as executioner, cook and much else, but always so contrived that his next job was at a place that lay nearer to his home.

Here at Shinkish, on the borders of Mongolia, he was now making final preparations for flight, and was working to regain a little of the capital of which the revolution had deprived him. Nikolai had succeeded in getting hold of a biggish parcel of opium or, more accurately, he knew where it was and how it could be got away. He questioned me about conditions in Mongolia and the possibilities of profit from selling the poison to the inhabitants. I gave him information about the ways through the mountains and steppes to China, and about the places on the road at which he might encounter his compatriots. By night we conspired in whispers, so as not to interrupt the monotonous tramp of the sentry outside the house.

In exchange for my information and advice I received from Nikolai other things which might be useful to me. Since I was contemplating the possibility of being taken back to the prison in Shinkish, he procured for me two small files which could be used, if necessary, to file through the iron bars. I gave him a written slip of paper and repeated two sentences for him over and over again until he knew them by heart. The one was an account of my situation for my comrades at the farm, if he should succeed in reaching it. The other was a communication to be conveyed to the Danish Legation in Peking. I promised him ample reward for the due delivery of the two messages.

DURING my sojourn in barracks I had good opportunity to observe the Russian soldiers and the conditions in this section of the Soviet army. The soldiers were peasants from distant parts of Siberia, young and powerful men of first-class military bearing. They were well uniformed, well armed and magnificently mounted. The discipline was strict and fear of the " comrade officers " great.

If a superior came into the room where there were soldiers, they all got up at once and shouted in chorus : " Good day, comrade commandant," or whatever his rank was. But they all stood stiffly to attention, and except for the form of greeting there was nothing in the relation between officer and private that suggested comradeship.

At noon on the second day I suddenly received notice

that I was to leave for another place. Nikolai helped me to conceal my prison-breaking tools in my *unti*, and we took a hasty farewell of one another. Two mounted soldiers were waiting outside the house, and a spare horse was placed at my disposal. Except for their long cavalry sabres the soldiers were unarmed, and their attitude towards me was suspiciously friendly.

Some hours' brisk riding brought us to Turansk where we halted outside the little town's most considerable building. I went into the house and was received at the door by an amiably smiling, Soviet-clad Buriat. From him I gathered that I was to be interrogated by the highest *tovarish komandir* in the whole district, who spoke German. I was shown into the largest room where a couple of officers and a few persons in civilian dress were seated round a long table. A cosy samovar—the first I had seen in Russian territory—was steaming on the table.

The Buriat led me to the German-speaking officer who rose courteously and bade me : " *Guten Tag, Kamerad.*" He was friendly, but reserved and taciturn. The whole company regarded me smilingly, and with the true Russian amiability which I knew so well from the emigrants I had met in Urga.

" *Tovarish komandir* ", put a couple of guarded questions to me in shocking German. It appeared that his halting questions had been rehearsed beforehand, for so soon as I entered into detailed explanations he only understood a word here and there, and not the meaning of the sentence. It must have been important for him to keep up his literary reputation as the only German linguist in the district, for he made heroic efforts not to betray his ignorance to the interested audience. Consequently his replies became more fluent as he only repeated those German words that he knew, supported by grimaces and lively gesticulation. And I discovered that his responses were no less ready when I spoke to him in Danish, of which I had a far better command than of my school German, and in this way I could carry on the conversation with the same speed and elegance as my interlocutor.

Our shared secret was perhaps the reason why we apparently became perfectly good friends. I wonder how he afterwards translated to the company my many answers to the prearranged questions. I am certain his version was to my advantage. Later he invited me to take coffee and looked relieved when I began chatting with the Buriat.

I gathered from the latter that " *tovarish komandir* " was a Lett, that he had taken part in the great war and that he had spent some time as a prisoner in Germany. When the talk turned upon the expedition to which I belonged, the Buriat told me that he himself had been a member of the well-known Russian General Koslov's expedition in Mongolia. It was evident that the conversation had now reached a subject of general interest, for the words " expedition " and " Koslov " caused the company to observe me keenly.

The Buriat supposed that I who belonged to a scientific expedition and was also a Scandinavian must surely know Doctor " Sven Gedin " (Sven Hedin). At that time Sven Hedin was only a name to me, but I read in the eyes of those present that their belief in my identity stood or fell with my acquaintance with this universally known person, famous also in Russia. " Sven Hedin," I answered, " of course I know my old friend, Sven Hedin." The Buriat translated, but I saw that all was not yet cleared up. The Buriat vanished quickly, to return with a photograph which he handed me with the enquiry whether I knew any of the persons it represented.

And I did, for, not long before, I had read the Swedish traveller's latest book, *From Peking to Moscow*, from which the picture was taken. Fortunately I remembered the list of names that had accompanied the photograph, for I had studied it with interest. I was thus able at once and without hesitation to point out both Hedin and Koslov. And when, among the group of Russians and natives surrounding those gentlemen in the picture, I was able immediately to point to the little Buriat's smiling face, every doubt of my identity fell to the ground and the whole room became the friends of the

Danish gentleman who was a member of a scientific expedition in Mongolia and who was a friend of gentlemen so well known that their fame had reached even the remote Tunka valley.

Then we drank tea out of long glasses until one of the Russians remembered that vodka tasted better and, since the long glasses from the tea drinking still stood on the table, this size served for the vodka too. The atmosphere became excellent. The mufti-clad Russians called me "*gospodin*" ("Mister"), instead of "*tovarish*", and when at long last I took my leave, they kissed me affectionately on the cheeks, so that their long beards tickled me, and I had to squirm with laughter in spite of the tears of parting that trickled down their cheeks.

"*Tovarish komandir*" pressed my hand, stuttered something to the effect that I should soon be free and repeated many times and in really fluent German "*Auf Wiedersehen*". I replied in equally fluent Danish that I hoped this "*Wiedersehen*" would not happen in a hurry, and leapt upon my waiting horse. There is no doubt that I was in an exalted frame of mind as, whistling and singing, I galloped back to Shinkish, and the two troopers were infected with my good humour and followed me like a guard of honour.

At Shinkish we rode to the administrative block of the prison, where Bater awaited me. The grey-clad armed guards of the place were not infected with my good humour, but gruffly informed me that orders had arrived that I was to be released and to be conveyed across the frontier. In vain they tried to check my mirth by assuring me that they would in future keep a sharp eye on me and my activities.

Bater and I were to spend one last night in cell number nine and were to be taken next day under escort to the boundary. I divided the evening bread ration fraternally with "bloody Ivan" of whom I took a cordial farewell. The Czech came smiling and friendly and enquired about the reason for my release and what it was that had occasioned my happy mood. I declared that I had spent the days in prison in order to investigate the conditions on behalf of the authorities. Now I had held a conference in Turansk with the supreme *tovarish komandir* and other exalted comrades, and had then preferred many grave charges against him. " *Morgen wirst du geschossen, ganz sicher,*" I said, and then laughed heartily to see his terrified look. He left me, wondering and anxious.

Early next morning I was taken to the administrative building where I received a *propusk* for Bater and myself and a bill for the telegrams that had been sent in order to elucidate my mysterious case. The bill was for forty roubles, but I had only the twenty-rouble gold piece concealed in my *unti*. After much explanation and interpreting, however, I got the *propusk* on payment of the twenty roubles in cash, the remaining twenty to be paid to the Soviet as soon as possible.

But the consciousness that on this present day I owe the government of the new Russia twenty shining roubles gives me a little satisfaction when I think of what I had to endure in February, 1925.

COME to that, I got a little modest revenge several years later when I was living in Urumchi, the capital of Chinese Turkestan. The Chinese Governor-General of the province gave a dinner in his palace to distinguished visitors to the capital of his remote realm. Among those were the Soviet's Consul-General as representative of Russia, and I in my capacity of member of " The Chinese Scientific Mission to the North-West ".

It was a warm, sunny day in May, 1929. Dinner was served in the Governor's pavilion which lay in a fairy-tale park with shady trees and babbling brooks. The dinner was magnificent ; troops of yellow servants came and went with dishes piled with viands of European, Russian, Turkish and Chinese origin. From the distance came the melancholy notes of balalaikas from an orchestra of Russian emigrants. The principal mandarins were assembled to entertain us, and the champagne corks popped continually. The few representatives of England, Germany, Sweden, Russia and Denmark were distributed among Chinese, Tatars, Mongols and Manchus. My *vis-à-vis* at the small table was the Soviet's representative, an amiable Jew with long hair and a very " Red " appearance. My partner was the Soviet Consul's wife, a lady of Russo-Turkish extraction with scarlet lips, highly coloured complexion and great feminine charm.

" Madame ", who preferred this form of address to the unromantic " comrade ", often drained her long champagne glass to the bottom, for the evening, she said, was warm, and I did not neglect to fill it again to the brim, eager to show that I had not forgotten my manners in the wilderness. And I spoke Russian far more fluently than ever before, and we got on splendidly. So splendidly that the Consul husband neglected his " lady ", who was a long-bearded mandarin, and leaned across the table to take part in our conversation. Madame took this amiss and displayed towards him a temper ill befitting a good *tovarish*. Then he turned amiably to me and began to express his admiration for science. The distance between us and the general high spirits at the table led to our conversation being carried on in a very loud voice and apparently it was also interesting, for more and more of our neighbours turned towards us. Near us was sitting a Manchu general, commander of a Chinese garrison on the Russian frontier, who was obviously no friend to the new doctrine.

Russian was spoken generally at the table and that language was also employed for the Consul's and my conversation. As I have said, I was speaking uncommonly good Russian that day, so good that the Consul felt obliged to ask where I had obtained my mastery of his mother tongue. I answered—as was true—that the whole east was full of interesting and amiable Russian emigrants with whom I had found it profitable to converse, since they had seen much of life and of things of which I had had only a glimpse or a suspicion.

The atmosphere became more and more tense and there was silence around us.

" But I have been in Russia too," I added. " Where ? " he enquired with interest, and I replied that I had been imprisoned for ten days in Siberia. I grew lyrical at the thought of those days and gave an account of my changing fortunes in Soviet territory, and the whole company became my audience, listening with malicious delight. When I had finished, the Consul muttered feebly and unconvincingly that such things might have happened some years back, but not now under the new, enlightened regime. And then I filled Madame's glass to the brim and we emptied our glasses together, to her "*dragotsennoe zdorovie*"—(" precious health.")

BUT when, in February, 1925, I left the prison at Shinkish, together with the terrified Bater—without money, without provisions, and with an armed escort of four Soviet soldiers, then I certainly brooded upon a weightier revenge, a revenge that was fostered and planned during the two days it took us to reach Mundi on the borders of Mongolia, far away from any place known to me. At Mundi I got back my Danish passport, and Bater and I stood once more on the border-line, on a forlorn and desolate spot, in a district unknown to me and of whose position I had only a dim idea.

CHAPTER X
BACK IN MONGOLIA

AND so, slowly, we rode across the frontier, away from the farthest outposts of the West, back into the wilderness.

My excursion into " civilization ", of which I had expected so much—my sojourn among people of my own colour—did not seem to have been a success this time. I had met a whole lot of white people, but very few of them had regarded me with friendliness. I had seen quantities of modern weapons and a great many typewriters, but nothing of all this had particularly appealed to me.

The splendid Cossack horses that my Red " comrades " rode made my shabby little " Voilà " look very insignificant, but I knew none of them would have got through more than a few days in the wilderness to which I was returning. We now stood and watched them galloping back towards the north-east. The invisible boundary between them and us felt like a Chinese wall. They rode back to the newly delivered land of liberty, Russia ; we stood in free Mongolia. Marvellous !

BATER let his rosary slip through his fingers as he peered southward seeking some *ger* (tent) in which he might meet with Mongols who would invite him to tea and tobacco. " Voilà " at once began pawing the snow for little tufts of grass.

It was so cold that when one spat the spittle crackled in the air, but so absolutely still that, so long as one kept in the sun and was well wrapped up in furs, one did not freeze. To the north the chain of the Sayan Mountains rose on the horizon. Far away to westward Munku Sardyk towered, lifting its glacier-clad peak against the clear blue sky. One's glance was drawn upwards over snowclad birches, firs and cedars, until one was compelled to lower one's eyes before the unprecedented glare of the sun reflected from the mountain's glittering peak.

As the setting sun met its majestic summit, it seemed to me that I was standing on the top of something vast, splendid, holy. . . . The stillness was intense, and in fancy I was drawn up towards the divine above me. This lasted for several moments—and all was transfigured.

Somewhere far off a wolf took up a ringing, constant C that made the frosty air vibrate. I turned towards Bater and again encountered the open, cordial, brilliant smile of this child of nature, which I had missed since the day when we had seen rifle barrels directed towards us by order of people of my own colour. Bater pointed to a temple near by, Hanga Kure, whose gold-plated roof still gleamed in the lingering light of day. At the highest point of its roof-ridge the elegant lines of two sculptured antelopes were dimly visible, kneeling facing one another on either side of a golden wheel.

Bater unfolded to me the legend of this symbol, so often met with in lamaistic sculpture on temple roofs or on the covers of thuribles.

Two children of earth once saw the sight that had just disappeared before our gaze. Their longing to seize upon all this splendour was so great that it transformed them into two antelopes which in swift bounds scaled the mountain battlements inaccessible to human beings. They reached the summit just as the sun touched the peak, casting a golden diadem about its snow-clad sides, and so great was their ravishment in the face of all this splendour of nature, that they fell down and worshipped the sun.

While Bater was hobbling the horses and turning them loose, I prepared our evening meal of boiling hot tea with parched corn and millet. Then we sat by the fire and considered our situation.

We had no money and no tobacco, nor any fat or meat, which are such necessary articles of diet during laborious journeys in that cold climate. The horses were in poor

The two Legendary Antelopes, worshipping the purity and splendour of the sun

BACK IN MONGOLIA

condition and could not endure forced marches. We decided to let them run loose during the night so that they might recover a little before morning. But in that case it was necessary for one of us to remain awake, so as to keep up a fire that would protect the horses from the wolves.

I took the first watch, which I spent in gathering a large stock of fuel in the neighbourhood of the fire. The howling of the wolves could be heard in the depths of the forest. At times it came quite close, and then I made a round of the horses to calm them. At midnight they came right up to the fire and stood trembling with fear and gazing out into the darkness. I woke Bater, and we prepared some torches with which we went shouting noisily in among the trees towards the quarter to which the horses' anguished eyes were directed. A hundred paces from the fire we got a view of the wolves, whose eyes shone like phosphorescent points in the gloom. We threw the torches towards them, with the desired result. A swift crackling in the snow indicated the flight of the wolves, and the horses quickly resumed their grazing.

It must have been very cold that night, for when I awoke I found myself huddled up so close to the fire that one side of my fur coat had been hardened by the heat. Neither Bater nor the horses was in sight, but the saddles were propped up with the under side towards the fire on which the pot was standing. Bater soon came back with the horses, which he had taken to water, and we began to discuss which way we should now proceed.

We calculated that the farm and our friends lay about a hundred and eighty miles to the south-east, Kiäkt, with our depot of provisions and furs, some seventy miles to the east, and thither we intended to go first. But so as not again to come into conflict with the Bolsheviks we determined to ride a bit to the south before turning eastward.

After we had finished our Spartan meal we set out and rode slowly down through the trees, following the lie of the land, which here sloped towards the south-west. We soon reached the edge of the forest, and an unwonted sight met our eyes, which at once clearly indicated our position to Bater. An endless white gleaming surface stretched as far as eye could reach, and large patches of smooth ice glittered in the sunlight. It was the lake of Hubso Gol, which is so large that it is marked even on the imperfect maps which exist of this region.

Hubso Gol is a lake extending from Hanga in the north to Khathyl in the south. It is about ninety miles long, and its width varies from ten to sixteen miles. It gets its water from the mountains in the north and at its southern point discharges into the Egin Gol River. The lake is very deep and is not free from ice until the beginning of June. In spite of the severe cold which comes on as early as the end of August, the ice does not bear until the middle of January.

Even now, at the end of February, it was not entirely without peril to cross it on horseback, for great fissures constantly open with a deafening crash. We encountered a number of these, which were several yards across and towards half a mile in length.

It was dreary and monotonous riding over this vast ice surface, and we made a long march so as to reach an island in the frozen sea, Pub, whose inviting trees could be seen several hours before we arrived there. The island lay about in the middle of Hubso Gol, and it afforded an ideal camping place. Fuel and fodder for the horses were there in abundance. To judge by the numerous tracks of foxes, hares, deer and lynx, the place was a paradise for game. Fox and wolf tracks led over the ice to and from the mainland.

To my surprise we saw no human tracks. In the evening we enjoyed the warmth from the big fire and the sound of the horses munching the long grass that rose above the snow. When I expressed my astonishment at finding so much wild life concentrated in so confined a space, and seeing no human tracks in so ideal a spot, Bater explained that no one dared kill any living thing there, for the place was holy. And he related the legend of the lake.

Kosogol is the Russians' corruption of the Mongols' name for the great lake, Hubso Gol Dalai, " *Ikhe olon jil bolsang* " (" many years ago "), began Bater, and told how a desolate and arid steppe lay where the water now covers the surface of the ground. One blazing day a lone man came wandering from the south. Tired and dusty, and of a woeful appearance, after many days' travel through waterless and sterile tracts, he halted at the place where the island of Pub lies and where we were now spending one of the nights of our vagabond life.

After a while spent in prayer and contemplation, the thirsty man rolled away one of the many stones from its place, and behold, the water gushed forth from the spot where the stone had lain. He drank and bathed, and next morning, revived, he continued his journey towards the north. But the water from the new spring continued to flow. It rose and rose and accompanied him on his way. At the next going down of the sun he turned towards the south, and his old eyes rejoiced to see the abundant waters. But the water continued to rise. Then he took a piece of the mountain and fashioned Munku Sardyk, the highest peak of the Sayan range, which checked the water's progress towards the north, and the water turned southward, where it profited the poor dwellers on the sterile steppes.

Next morning the wanderer ascended Munku Sardyk to contemplate his work. A lake four days' journey in length lay beneath his feet, and from its southern end issued a river along whose banks shady trees and luxuriant grass shot up. Content with his work, the holy man, for such he was, now took and flung a mighty mass of rock, which fell down and closed the spring he had created some days earlier. This mass of rock formed the foundation of the very island upon which we sat, and by reason of its supernatural origin it was held to be holy.

So runs the Mongols' account of the origin of Hubso Gol Dalai.

That so large a lake in Mongolian territory should stir the imagination of the Mongols is quite natural. Water plays a decisive part for all living things, but it is perhaps only when one gets away from civilization, where everything is ordered and arranged for the comfort and amenities of life, and out into the wilderness, that one comes to realize that one's own life and that of the animals fails after a few days, if this important element is not available.

Everytime " *Yabonah* ", the summons to break camp, sounds in steppe or desert, there has first been earnest discussion between the elders of the camp, and the route has been so laid down that the succession of waterless days is never longer than beast and man can endure.

It is with intention that I mention beast before man, for so do the Mongols. If his mount can get through, so can the rider. Torments and suffering for himself do not deter a Mongol from an undertaking. But the nomads know that a rider without a mount is lost. He is delivered over to the barren loneliness of the wilderness, and becomes a prey to the desert wolves and the eagles, who pick his bones clean, to the sun and wind that polish them smooth, until they form new links in the ivory-white chain of skeletons marking the endless caravan roads of Central Asia.

The wells that determine the day's march along the ancient caravan routes have immemorial traditions, and the watering-places conceal memories that from time to time emerge out of the eternally shifting sand, once more to be dedicated to silence by the next storm. I have often found by such wells stone and bronze weapons from neolithic and earlier times, messengers from far-off days, and in fancy have seen pictures of the savage, hardy hordes that once encamped under their yak-decked banners.

The Mongols call these shapely bronze weapons from a vanished and forgotten time of greatness *Tenggerin sumon* (Arrows of heaven), for their fancy leads them to believe that the weapons have fallen from a celestial encounter between the elder gods, nor do they suspect that they themselves are the late descendants of the bearers of those weapons, long since crumbled into dust.

I have sat often by a lone camp-fire in the desert with a day's harvest of such relics of the past before me, and fancy has gone a-travelling with the desert's flying sand, which in the course of time has been stirred by varying winds and has swallowed up the secrets of the waste. Weapons and other objects polished by sand and wind have told their story long after their bearers were

Soyote hunter

The happy child of nature

BACK IN MONGOLIA

vanished and forgotten. A day will come when even these hard objects will have come to nothing—but the race of men endures. . . .

Jenghiz Khan's warriors and Timur's led their sweating horses to the *khuduks* (wells) beside which long-forgotten chieftains before them had halted their mysterious nomad hordes on the march to victory or defeat.

The Mongols have two legendary Khans who are rulers over all waters, and it is partly in reverence for these Osun Lozang Khans that they never permit themselves to whistle or make a noise in the neighbourhood of running or great still waters.

They only know the ocean from holy books and legends deriving from the time when Kublai Khan's Mongols crossed the sea to attack far Japan. Since that remote period the Mongols have not seen the sea, but they have had a conception of its immensity, since they gave the name of " Dalai Lama " to the head of their religion, the reincarnation of Avalokita Buddha, the divinity of mercy.

There are, it is true, lakes in Mongolia, but they are so few that, despite the roving life of the Mongols, there are many who know them only by hearsay. I have never met with a lake in Mongolia to which supernatural legends were not attached. The Mongolian name for lake, *nor*, is not applied to Hubso Gol Dalai, which is so extensive and so deep as to be held worthy of the name of *ocean*, since the unknown *dalai* must surely be something like this. And further to emphasize its greatness they have added the epithet Hubso (the surging), for an expanse of water so vast, in which real waves occur, must indeed be a veritable ocean.

NEXT morning we started very late, for we wanted the horses to make full use of the good grazing on the island. It was ten o'clock when we set out towards the east. When we reached the eastern shore of the lake, we found the ascent from the ice to firm ground quite difficult, since a steep slope thirty feet in width confronted us as far as eye could reach. The ice had been forced up along the shore into a long row of formations which, covered with hoar frost and hung with transparent ice crystals, presented a most fantastic appearance. They stood there like sentinels before the ice queen's palace, protecting the unknown beyond against invaders. The profound silence was only broken by the sound of the horses' hooves echoing among these icy shapes. No living thing was to be seen. Only our shadows followed us—grew longer or shorter, stretched up against an ice giant to broaden out again upon the surface after we had passed. The horses were nervous and sniffed anxiously when we had to pass between two such figures. At times the ice behind us cracked with a prolonged wailing sound.

After much trouble we succeeded in dragging ourselves and our horses up on to firm ground, and a desolate view stretched before us. A level plateau of snow, and yet more snow as far as eye could reach. Far to the north-east appeared the dim blue shapes of mountains, and towards these we directed our course. After some hours we observed the track of a horse crossing our line of march, and after some deliberation we decided to follow the rider, a course which promised greater possibilities of contact with human kind.

The going was heavy and the landscape grim and desolate. Our horses were exhausted, and the tracks we were following were also those of a tired horse ; it had dragged its legs after it, and this made it difficult to determine in which direction it had been going. Several times we stopped to examine the tracks and convince ourselves and one another that we were on the right road. Then we set out again through the same landscape, the same heavy snow. The growing exhaustion of the horses made us despondent, and again we had to dismount to scrutinize the tracks.

We howled like wolves in the hope of provoking a response from angry Mongol dogs. That would have meant tents and human beings, but not once did so much as an echo come in answer.

"Alas," said Bater, "we are riding into a wilderness of snow, away from fire, food and tea. Soon the horses will be finished—and we with them." I thought with downright kindly feelings of the warm stove in our Russian prison, that source of heat which, a couple of days earlier, had been a part of all I had execrated. We considered going back on our own tracks, but the day was so far spent that this would have come to the same thing as spending the night where we were. It was better to go on, hoping for the best, until darkness set in —we could not very well find a worse camping place than our present position—and next day at dawn we could ride back.

We were slowly dragging ourselves along when all at once a new track appeared, coming from the south-west and joining the one we had been following all day. Both tracks continued to the north-east. Water and life lay in the quarter towards which the tracks led, and everything now looked brighter. We were surely on the right road.

But the rejoicing did not last long. The sun went down, and in the dusk we came suddenly to a place where the tracks were swallowed up in the earth. We dismounted and sought an explanation. The double tracks were those of one and the same horse. The rider had come here and had gazed at the same barren wilderness—and had decided to turn round and try another direction. Presumably a rider who, like us, had gone astray. Silently we tied the horses head to tail. We spread the saddle blankets over them, loosed the girths, threw the saddlebags on the ground for pillows and fell asleep.

NEXT morning I awoke at dawn, shivering with cold. Bater was sitting up with a strained expression on his face. He thought he had heard a dog barking, and in a moment we were on our feet. We yodelled, we howled again like wolves—there was no possible doubt now— furious barking sounded like the sweetest music in our ears.

Suddenly three dogs appeared at a distance of five or six hundred yards, followed by three men. We ran to meet them. In front of us lay a river gorge about sixty feet deep coming from the mountains in the north east, and hidden in it was a tent. Blue smoke was rising towards heaven. Bushes and small trees grew on the slopes. This was the kingdom of heaven!

Two Soyote herdsmen hunting for strayed cattle had come there during the night. One of them knew enough Mongolian to give us the necessary information. Our horses were fetched and turned loose for there was good grazing here under the snow. After we ourselves had eaten several skewers of mutton and fat-tail and had drunk a couple of pots of hot tea, we began to ask where we actually were and which way we ought to take. We were also interested to know how far we were from the frontier.

The frontier lay far to the north; they had never been so far. If we followed this gorge towards the north-east we would come in a few hours to a Soyote camp of five tents. There was also a single tent occupied by Mongols from Selenga who would be able to show us the way to Kiäkt.

We now rode at a walk in the direction indicated. We saw tracks of deer, arctic hares, wolves and foxes. Soon too we came upon several of the Soyotes' abandoned summer camping-places with their characteristic tents of boughs and bark, built in the same form as the wigwams of the Indians.

Before sundown we came to the camp which lay upon an open plain surrounded by high mountains. The Soyotes to the east of Hubso Gol live in the winter in yurts, like the Mongols, and in this place we found six of these. We rode up to the one occupied by Mongols and were at once invited to stay with this family. They had come to trade the grain they had brought with them, *arbay*, for the Soyotes' furs.

We did not understand the Soyote language, but I could make out occasional words, since they were strongly reminiscent of Kirghiz. The Soyotes are very primitive and strike one as a dirty people, but they are capable hunters and were very friendly to us.

All the inhabitants of the camp crowded about us, and our Mongolian host was engaged for the rest of the day in questioning us about everything and passing on our answers to the Soyotes who listened eagerly to his certainly exaggerated report. He did good business that day and still better the next, since men from two neighbouring camps came in to hear " news from the great world ". Our host now knew the whole lesson by heart, and each time he repeated it the dramatic gesticulations with which his version of our Odyssey was accompanied increased, and his business transactions grew in the same proportion. We both felt we were making some sort of return for all the good food with which he so hospitably provided us.

Nor did he raise any objection when we supplied our horses with hay and a little corn from his precious store. We came later to know that his chief success had been the account of our stay among the *oros*, the Russians, confined in a little stone room behind a door closed with a big lock. This had made a great impression upon these liberty-loving children of nature:

CHAPTER XI

THE SHAMAN

ON the third day there was great excitement among the Soyotes. A couple of hunters had come in from the east with ill news for the smallest and poorest tent in the camp. We accompanied our host thither and, pressing through the assembled multitude gesticulating around the tent, saw a distressing sight which aroused our sympathy. On a cowhide by the burnt-out fire sat a sweet young Soyote girl, dissolved in tears. She was inconsolable and did not reply to our questions. We returned to the people to hear what tragic tidings the two hunters had carried to the tent.

The eighteen-year-old girl's only relative, her old father Zerang, who was in the service of the rich Soyote Odsha, had been sent two weeks earlier to Uri Gol with three horses, to leave them with Odsha's *tabun* (horse herd) which was grazing there. Uri Gol lay four days' journey from the camp and provided better pasture, since there was less snow in the lower river valley. Zerang had duly delivered the horses and set out upon the return journey on foot. Between Uri Gol and the camp lay two high passes, not entirely free from danger in midwinter, but the Soyotes had raised *obos* in all the more perilous places, where they never neglected to pay an ample tribute to the rightful, if also perverse, rulers of the pass.

The two hunters, who had been wandering for several weeks in the mountains, were on their way down from the hunting grounds to our Mongolian host to sell their furs and fetch provisions. Between the two passes they had come upon Zerang's trail and had followed it to the top of the nearer pass. There they had found him—dying. They did not know whether he had neglected to leave his tribute, nor what the reason might be, but there he lay stricken to the earth, almost dead, unable to utter a word. The hunters had hastily lighted a big fire and placed a big heap of wood between it and the dying man, so that, if he should so far revive, he could make up the fire before it burned down. All this they had done because Zerang was a good man, and to satisfy their own conscience.

Why had they not brought Zerang with them to the camp? Why did not his friends in the camp at once set out to bring him help? He was dying, might die at any moment.

Did I not know that, if one were near to a person at the moment of death, all his released spirits could straightway take up their abode in one's body? To be present when the tent rope of another's life was cut off was the worst that could happen to anyone, next to dying himself. They debated much what could be the reason for his being struck down just there. It was high time to send for the Shaman. They crowded into the largest tent, where the discussion continued, and I went in to our fire to meditate.

I explained to Bater that the pass lay right on our way. We might as well ride up and see how the land lay. If he were dead we had only to continue on our journey. But perhaps the poor man was better now and only needed a little help to get down to the camp where food and warmth would soon make him well again. My God would always assist those who were trying to perform a deed of mercy.

Bater had a multitude of objections to make against so hasty a departure from these comfortable quarters, but when he saw that I was determined, he gave in and went outside the tent to watch the ravens of the air and see what they forboded.

It caused great astonishment in the camp when we packed our saddlebags, made ready for departure and disclosed our purpose. As we were starting the young girl joined us, riding an unsaddled horse and leading a saddled horse which had been hastily loaded with gifts in many forms, to be taken to the *obo* of the pass as tribute from the dwellers in the camp. In so doing the Soyote girl was doing a deed of some little heroism, and it was touching to see the filial love which caused her to defy strong prejudices and inherited beliefs.

We followed the hunters' tracks, which led us up through birch and fir, till we reached the dark cedars sighing in the blast. The wind whined through the pass and icy cold came with it. Bater twirled his rosary and the girl looked anxiously about on all sides. The horses were blowing with the effort. There lay the *obo*, a tall pyramid of piled cedar trunks hung with innumerable ribbons, bleached and whipped to rags by the blast. Figures carved in wood hung everywhere, and at the foot lay caravan tea, corn, frozen butter and other provisions. We deposited our gifts. Bater gabbled long formularies, and the agonized glances of the girl were filled with prayers. The snow around us was reddened for a little while and then paled with the approach of night.

We found Zerang at a short distance from the *obo*. Bater stopped abruptly at the sight, and the girl uttered a little scream. No fire was burning any longer, but the man was not stiff, and I insisted that he was not yet dead. When we lifted him up from the ground we had to tear apart his fur coat, for the part he had been lying on was frozen fast to the ice beneath him. We bound him firmly to the spare horse, and Bater and the girl walked on either side to support him. The Soyote girl pulled out several hairs from the tails of the horses and tied them to the *obo*, and we began the descent. When we got down to the cedars and away from the whining of the wind through the pass, we stopped to look at the sick man. He was talking in delirium, and so was alive.

Now we heard the barking of the dogs far below, soon, too, the camp-fires came into view, but it was starry midnight when we stood once more among our kind.

A messenger was sent for the Shaman. All spare fur robes in the camp were brought to Zerang's tent and after they had undressed him and rubbed him for a long time he was well packed up. The daughter lighted a big fire and made tea, and Bater procured incense and threw

The Obo

Mongolian Gurtum

A gurtum is a Lama who after prolonged prayers and other preparations can put himself into a state of ecstasy, during which he is able to answer questions concerning the future. In practice the gurtum is the same as the Shaman of the "black magic" who has been adopted by Lamaism

THE SHAMAN

it on the fire. I looked through my saddlebags. After I had removed my few belongings, there remained a considerable residue of pulverized sediment, which I shook out into my fur cap. While Bater muttered prayers I sorted out the whitest of this and gave it to the sick man in a cup of piping hot tea. It should have been the well-shaken-up remains of quinine and quadronal tablets with the possible addition of a little tooth-powder.

Then we looked to our horses and went to rest. Everyone in the camp was busy with preparations for the Shaman's arrival.

Shamanism, the " black doctrine ", which in Asia's most isolated and wildest recesses has always such powers of attraction for primitive souls, is still in Urianhai the official faith professed by the whole population. Emperors and Khans, Shahs and Emirs, all regarded as the sons and elect of heaven upon earth, have by decree given the teachings of the prophets the force of law among the hunters and nomads of Central Asia. But where these still live face to face with the rude forces of nature, live without conventions, it is to the Shaman's black magic that they yet turn in the hour of danger and of need.

I had once heard the night air vibrate to the hollow rumble of a Shaman's drum, weird and fascinating. I had now perhaps a unique opportunity to take part at close quarters in the mystic ceremony itself.

I held a brief consultation with Bater, after which we both conferred with our Mongolian host. I explained to him that after intense meditation and with the help of my white god I had saved Zerang from a terrible fate in the solitary pass. But my duty was not fulfilled until I had seen the Shaman drive out the evil spirits that had taken up their abode in Zerang's frail body. It was not my purpose to mix myself up in the Shaman's incantations, in which I was greatly interested, but only, during the expulsion of the spirits, to sit silent in the tent, filled with desire for the purification of the sick man. The Mongol doubted whether I, as a white man, would be allowed to be present at the mystic ceremony, but promised to help me.

THE SHAMAN

Zerang's daughter was fetched, and I have seldom seen such gratitude as she now again evinced towards me. And, lying with her face to the ground, she listened to my desire and promised to pray and implore the Shaman to give his consent.

During the course of the day I heard many stories of the present Shaman, and of his father who had died six years earlier, after having performed many marvellous works as evidence of his powers and his knowledge of the forces of nature.

Once they had put the old Shaman in a cage made of iron bars taken from tea bales. The cage with the Shaman in it had then been placed on a large fire that was kept burning for many hours. When it had burned down the iron bands had been melted, but the Shaman stepped forward before the astonished multitude, shaking with cold and with great icicles hanging from his hair and beard.

On another occasion they had bound the Shaman with strong rope, and thrown him, with big stones fastened to his feet, into a hole in the ice of the river. He had immediately sunk to the bottom with a hissing as when one puts red-hot iron in water. But, after long waiting, the surrounding Soyotes had seen him scramble out of the water on to the ice, bathed in sweat and completely dissolved with heat. Several of those present said that they had personally witnessed the performance of these miracles.

The present Shaman had inherited his father's great qualities and, despite his youth, had already shown himself to be in possession of mystical and supernatural powers. He was considered one of the Soyotes' most eminent drivers-out of spirits.

In the previous summer the Shaman had suddenly appeared in the camp and had called together all its inhabitants in an open place between the tents. After much drumming and incantation he had bared the upper part of his body, and those present had seen two birch trees grow out, one from either shoulder. The trees had shot up several yards in height, leaves had grown from the twigs, till the whole thing had vanished in

THE SHAMAN

smoke, leaving the Shaman lying unconscious and fully clad upon the ground. When the Soyotes afterwards would have carried the Shaman into one of the tents he had hissed at them, foaming at the mouth, and great wild boar's tusks had grown out of his jaws.

This and other mystic things which they had witnessed they described to me with mingled awe and pride. They told me about the powerful Shaman with the same enthusiasm and conviction as a Christian missionary does when he is trying to make a so-called heathen understand that Christ rose from the dead. My Soyote friends had, however, the advantage that they were speaking of what they themselves had experienced. That they actually had seen all they described to me I am certain. And I was now to have a chance to meet this magician!

IN the afternoon the Shaman arrived accompanied by two male kinsmen and the two messengers from the camp. To my great astonishment the Shaman turned out to be —a young woman, slender and with wide-awake vigilant eyes. She was dressed in a yellow lambskin coat with the hair inward and was riding a powerful white horse. Her companions were tall, strong lads, well dressed and well mounted in comparison with the Soyotes. One of them led a packhorse laden with several big bundles, on the top of which lay a large shield-shaped drum.

The company halted within the camping-place, and the Shaman, assisted by one of her male assistants, dismounted with a dignity in full accord with her exalted rank. Silent family groups stood watching the oldest inhabitant of the camp presenting her with a *hadak*, which she nonchalantly accepted and at once handed to one of her servants.

At the entrance to Zerang's tent stood his young daughter, reverently holding aside the flap, while the Shaman strode into the tent.

Dusk fell, but the mystical strife with the spirits was not to begin until night was a little advanced. The people of the camp went to and from Zerang's tent. The dogs had ceased their clamour and lain down in the shelter of their masters' tents. The stars came out and sparkled.

THE SHAMAN

Since no message came to summon me, I went, when I judged it was time, to Zerang's tent, accompanied by Bater and our host.

To the right of the entrance lay the sick man, to whom no one was any longer paying any attention, and in the corner opposite the entrance, turned towards him, sat the Shaman, evidently full-fed and contented after an abundant meal. On a low table in front of her stood quantities of remains of food. She offered me tea. I sat down on her right, while Bater and my host threw themselves down by the entrance. I handed her a *hadak* and two bricks of tea with the same ceremony that the Mongols observe towards a prince. Then I explained to her through my host that I had heard much of her marvellous power, and asked her permission to be present at her contest with the spirits. She looked me straight in the eyes for a moment and then took three vertebræ from a silk handkerchief. She threw on the fire a powder which produced a nauseating smell, muttered a string of formulæ and threw the three bones on the table. After she had observed their position and the manner in which they had fallen, she gathered them up and repeated the manœuvre. The result was satisfactory. I might stay.

It was now "the hour of the dog" (8 to 10 p.m.) and the contest was to begin. All dishes and remains of food were removed, and the assistants invested the woman with the ancient sorcerer's robe inherited from her father. This was made of antelope skin and hung with faded silken rags, each a momento of a victorious struggle against evil spirits, feathers from innumerable birds, bells of iron and brass, pieces of bone, tails of beasts, a couple of long-beaked birds' skulls and much besides. These objects jingled and clattered against each other at the slightest movement. On her head she set a wreath of feathers which continued in a long train down her back. With the drum held like a shield on her left arm, she sat before the fire with her face turned towards the tent opening.

There were now ten of us sitting along the sides of the tent. Only the entrance and the place where the sick man lay were left clear. The fire burned down to embers and its tiny flames cast an uncanny light about the little room. The tense faces of the Soyotes stood out like spectres from the half-darkness. Incense was again thrown upon the dying fire, producing a smoke which made the eyes smart and strangely numbed the senses.

The Shaman now began to rattle off ritual with great fluency, as she swayed her body forward and back from the hips. With the foot of an antelope as drumstick she beat her drum; powerful detached strokes alternated with dull long-drawn rolls. At times she threw herself back and emitted inarticulate gutteral sounds. The tempo was increased and the movements became swifter. The expression of her eyes was transformed. They became wild and bloodshot, her face swelled and assumed a purple hue, her nostrils vibrated rapidly and foam issued from the corners of her mouth. Those present avoided her glance.

Suddenly the antelope foot flew out of her hand and passed in a frantic whirl through the air to alight in front of one of the spectators. He at once reported the direction in which it had flown and the position it had taken up on the ground, and then threw it back on to the drum, which was held horizontally. The feeling in the room grew more and more exalted, and the mystic antelope foot took more and more flights among the watching Soyotes. Each time the drumstick left the Shaman's hand she emitted a snort like a frightened horse accompanied by a whistling between her teeth, which she kept up until she had the antelope foot upon the outstretched drum again.

It was suffocatingly hot in the tent, and the sweat poured from our faces. The heated air throbbed with the dull rumble of the drum, and my ears were pierced by the uncontrolled shrieking of the Soyotes. The atmosphere was filled with ecstasy and unreality. The Shaman and the Soyotes present exchanged long series of short cries. Then was a noise like the rattling of a skeleton as the Shaman suddenly sprang up and began a frenzied dance round the fire. Each time she passed the sick man, who now was surely dying, she passed the drum to and fro over him. Several times she belaboured Zerang vigorously with the antelope foot and, immediately afterwards, violently shook his head and shoulders.

A veritable duel was carried on between the sorceress and her imaginary adversaries. Noisily the wild dance went on round the fire. At last she staggered out through the tent opening with the drum before her. While the assistants held aside the flap a furious drumming was carried on which rolled, like a long-drawn peal of thunder, out into the black night. All those present shrieked and gesticulated. A last furious roll on the drum, and she collapsed on the floor, after the flap had once more been drawn into place before the opening.

It was now " the tiger's hour " (4 to 6 a.m.) and the performance had lasted for more than six hours. I wondered she had not collapsed exhausted earlier.

Wood was put on the fire, and the Shaman's assistants were zealously engaged in sprinkling water on their mistress's face when I fled from the tent, out into the starlit winter night. I stayed long, inhaling the fresh air, before I retired to my sleeping-place. The crackling of the snow underfoot sounded in my ears like the beating of drums, and during the short slumbers of that night, I hunted grisly spirits through space and climbed the sacred birch tree till I reached the ninth heaven of Shamanism, where I called in the aid of the good spirits. I woke on falling back to earth hanging from a parachute that had the form of an oval drum.

NEXT morning I visited Zerang's tent. To my great surprise he not only was alive but was drinking the tea that his daughter brought him. The Shaman was sitting on her dais eating a hearty meal. The sorceress of the night before was again transformed into a smiling young Soyote girl. Her yellow coat was only half drawn on and allowed the bronze coloured skin of her powerful arms and her half-revealed virginal breasts to gleam in the sunlight that fell through the opening in the upper part of the tent. Showing her white teeth in a smile, she invited me to take the place of honour on her right.

"You doubted my power," she said with laughter in her glance, "but see, he is much better already." She regarded Zerang steadily and added: "But it was at the last moment. If I had not come he would be dead now. And you too have done your part, for you tore him from the pass, that had him in its power, and brought him to the camp."

To my question whether he was now out of danger she answered: "No. After four days and three nights he will again be in great danger, and a very hard fight awaits me then."

I expressed my conviction that she would again be victorious, and flattered her by mentioning other examples of her power of which I had heard. I asked her if she could not give me a striking example such as the Soyotes had spoken of, and she replied that she could only give these on particular occasions which came upon her unprepared and unconscious.

When we left the camp that same morning, we left none but friends there, and one brave and grateful little soul gave us her primitive but heartfelt blessing on our journey.

CHAPTER XII

IN NATURE'S BOSOM

OUR horses had renewed their forces in the hospitable Soyote camp and trotted off briskly. The sunlight glittered on the tracks of the previous day's rescue expedition, and we rode with song and gaiety over hill and dale among graceful larches, lofty firs and fragrant cedars.

One cannot possibly live long in the wilderness without taking a great interest in the tracks and signs that the wild animals leave behind them. One may often travel long stages without catching a glimpse of the shy and swift-footed wild creatures, but their tracks cross or follow one's path the whole time. Thus gradually the knowledge of nature and its life grows. Tracks in untrodden regions, tracks in the snow, tracks in the sand, signs in the woods, all tell their story to the observer. And the wilderness has a pulsating life which banishes the sense of loneliness.

The Mongols see and hear a great deal which the greenhorn, fresh from civilization, very likely goes blindly past. During my long wanderings with Mongols I always tried to learn from them the art of seeing and hearing, and they taught me how to interpret nature's silent lessons.

It was a magnificent wild tract through which Bater and I passed after we left the Soyote camp. We had soon left the last traces of man behind us, and if one has saddlebags full of provisions and can be sure of fuel at night, this in itself is delightful. We were independent of water, for snow lay to hand everywhere, and we enjoyed the consciousness of being able to find a pleasant camping-place when and where we would. We rode for three days in this unconstrained mood,

Maytreya (in Mongolian, Maidari), the Messiah of Lamaism

captivated by the vastness of nature and enjoying the life for which mankind is really made.

We were able here to trace a little tragedy. An inexperienced young buck had set out to wander on its own account. Warily, perhaps alarmed, but driven on by the allurements of the danger, he had ventured out upon the ice of a little river to explore what lay hidden beyond the farther bank. With short, hesitating steps he had held a zigzag course. One could almost see how his long, fine ears had twitched, while his beautiful eyes suspiciously investigated the bushes on the high bank. Then, all at once, there was the sharp impression of the points of his hooves where he had taken off for a mighty leap aside. But too late. He never came down again on his swift feet, but fell on his side with the wolf's sharp teeth in his slender throat. His antlers, slight and delicate as befitted his youth, a tuft of hair and some odd bones were all that told of the end of his adventure. And then the heavy foot-marks of a fat and surfeited wolf that had lumbered off to a sunny nook to digest his meal.

Down in the valleys, in open places in the willow scrub, we saw holes left by rooting wild pig and forms where they had lain bathing in the sunshine.

A circle of pawed-out hollows in the snow showed where a small herd of deer had made their nocturnal camp. Before sunrise the roe deer move out into a glade where they graze for some hours, while vigilant sentries on all sides watch the verge of the forest against dangerous surprises. During the day they keep to the dense woods, high up on inaccessible parts of the mountain slopes, and come down again at sunset for a few hours' grazing.

Squirrels, fine in their grey winter coats, peered inquisitively at us from the branches of the trees. White hares scuttled under the low scrub. Wild cat and lynx, ermine and silver fox had trodden the ground before us and watched from their hiding-places the strange beings trespassing in their kingdom.

I felt it as a privilege to live and breathe and have my being in all this unspoilt nature, and wished I could ride on for ever on such paths, in such surroundings and in the same mood.

ONE afternoon, when we halted on the sunny side of a snow-clad mountain, we suddenly heard the unwonted sound of horses' hooves. The rider tethered his horse at a little distance from us and then came forward to our fire and sat down with a nonchalant " *Amorchan sain beino* ". By his dress we could see that he belonged to the newly arisen Young Mongol Party, which had been formed in Urga, but of whose representatives we had encountered none in our remote district. On his head he wore a blue felt cap with sewn-on gold braid, and from the top of it a squirrel tail waved gaily in the wind. His wide *busse* (sash) was carefully wound round him to its full width, giving him an elegant appearance in his full-length coat. In comparison with us and the inhabitants of these parts he was dressed like a dandy.

He took his place by the fire and held out his silver-mounted wooden bowl to Bater to be filled with tea. We drank tea and chatted, and he began, uninvited, to tell us about himself. He had fought under Baron Ungern against the " Reds ". He was a trader by profession and had for many years worked for a Chinese firm in his native district by Uri Gol. But the Bolsheviks had killed such of the Chinese as had not been driven out by the White Guards, and he was now out of a job. He travelled about in the mountains in the hope of finding adventure in one form or another, since life at home in the camp was altogether too monotonous for him. His name was Boyan Hishik, and besides Mongolian he spoke Soyote and Chinese.

He left us, singing a Mongolian battle song whose text, dealing with Chinese Generals riding in *Muhor teleg* (motor-cars), bore witness to its modern origin. Bater looked after him with an expression of mingled scorn and curiosity.

For two days we rode through a fertile valley in which lay scattered Soyote camps, before crossing the Soyote pass which forms the western entrance to Kiäkt. From the summit of the pass we saw the well-known specks that indicated wooden dwellings, and a feeling of homesickness made us hasten the descent.

There lay our little station with smoking chimney, and the Dannebrog waving gaily from the flagstaff. Did it perhaps mean that some of the boys had come to investigate? Our pleasure at the sight of home was so great that we dug our heels into the horses' sides and galloped the last lap of our long journey with yodellings and howls of joy.

Isager came rushing out of the house, closely followed by Dangsurong, and we fell into each other's arms and were all indescribably happy. The house was soon full of our friends from the neighbourhood, who poured in to assure themselves of our arrival and hear the tale of our adventures.

During the time of the revolution the Kiäkt Buriats had suffered much from bands of soldiers, " Red " as well as " White ", from north of the frontier. Like most boundary populations they did not care about the people on the other side, and this perhaps contributed to the extreme indignation they showed on hearing of the Russians' treatment of us.

Isager had come three weeks earlier from Turuk, which he had left because he had found the price of furs there too high, and had come to Kiäkt to see whether the conditions at my station were better. On arrival there he had met with Dangsurong and heard all sorts of tales of our disappearance. He therefore decided to take over charge of the station and await developments until he got some more direct information about us.

T*saghan sar* (the white month), which ushers in the Mongolian New Year, was approaching, and this gave us the idea of a new form of activity. *Tsaghan sar* is celebrated by all Mongols, who then assemble at the monasteries, and it is one of the two annual holidays on which the meat-eating Mongols regard flour as an expensive but necessary commodity.

Butter was scarce and dear in Kiäkt, while there was a superfluity of flour. Two days' journey west of the farm lay a monastery, Murin Kure, rich in herds of cattle, and here butter ought to be cheap, while flour was an article of luxury, imported from far away.

We decided that Isager should ride back to the farm at Bulgun Tal and report that all was well in Kiäkt, and then go on to Murin Kure, taking with him silver and all available ox-carts. He would exchange the silver for butter, which would as quickly as possible be conveyed to Kiäkt in the ox-carts. Meanwhile I would make arrangements here for the immediate barter of the butter for flour, for the idea was to supply the monastery with it in time for the approaching festivities.

If we succeeded in carrying through this transaction before *tsaghan sar* began, it ought to be good business. We went through the details of the plan once more with the result that we became still more enthusiastic and determined that it should be carried out. Isager set out the same afternoon.

BATER and I now discovered we were terribly tired, and we spent the greater part of the following days half asleep by the fire, devouring the food which Dangsurong prepared, and only now and then getting up to rejoice over the horses which were standing deep in hay. Dangsurong understood the depth of our felicity, and he was an incomparable attendant. In the evening he told us legends and tales of adventure which followed me into my nightly dreams.

At this time, 1924-5, I believe Dangsurong was about fifty, but he had the figure of a young athlete. In his youth he had been a monk in a monastery near Kobdo, but for some reason that he never disclosed he had, at the age of twenty-five, left his cloister and his native place to wander on foot out across the steppes. When he had reached the place where the steppes came to an end, he had gone on over mountains and through *taiga* until he came to the town of Irkutsk in Siberia. It was to his sojourn there that he owed his knowledge of the events recorded in the Christian Bible.

On the way home he had crossed the waters of Egin Gol, but had never gone farther. He could tell of

Pilgrims on their way to the temple festival

The Prior of the Monastery

Lamas assembled in the Temple Courtyard to listen to the Prior's reading from the sacred books

many and long journeys, north, south, east and west, but his monastery and his native place he had never seen again. Instead he had always returned to Egin Gol. He must have had an able *baksh* (teacher), for he knew more about his religion than any of the lamas in those parts. He read and wrote both Mongolian and Tibetan. Most of the Tibetan prayer formularies which later helped me through many difficulties on various occasions in Central Asia I learned from Dangsurong.

He now wore the worldly dress of a *Khara-Khun*, but his head was shaved Lama fashion. He no longer belonged to any monastery, but he always had two Tibetan prayer books with him from which he assiduously chanted every morning and evening. He was trustworthy and intelligent, and I was very fond of him.

He was not married, but in spite of his advanced age he was very susceptible to the charms of the opposite sex. Not long before I came to know him, he had been condemned by the local *noyan* (magistrate) to fifteen lashes, and fined a horse, as penalty for having visited a married Mongolian woman in her husband's absence. He had received the lashes but had refused to hand over the horse, explaining that the pain caused by the blows had balanced the pleasure the woman had given him, so they were quits.

He made no secret of his taste for women, but was none the less a favourite in all parts. The men esteemed him because he was a bold rider and an intrepid hunter, and the women were attracted to him, I assume, because he was a proper man.

Once he described to me how he went about his nocturnal amorous excursions. For one approaching a Mongol camp at night the savage Mongolian dogs constitute the greatest danger. The brutes have, however, the peculiarity of regarding human excrement as a delicacy. Therefore, so soon as one spreads out one's coat and crouches down on the ground, the dog forgets all its animosity and remains quietly in one's neighbourhood, eagerly awaiting the moment when one rises after a duty satisfactorily performed.

Of this circumstance Dangsurong availed himself.

Silently he approached the camp from the side on which the sheep-pen lay. As soon as the dogs got wind of him he ran in the direction of the sheep-fold and when the dogs came threateningly near, he immediately adopted the natural crouching attitude. The dogs stopped short and waited. At a favourable moment Dangsurong sprang up and rushed again towards the enclosure. When the brutes had convinced themselves of their mistake and had again nearly caught him up, he once more adopted the same position, further encouraging the dogs by illusory noises. This manœuvre was repeated as often as was necessary to let him, with his last rush, take refuge in the middle of the fenced-in flock of sheep. The sheep now ran bleating hither and thither in the fold, and a great hubbub arose.

When disturbances occur at night it always devolves on the eldest daughter of the tent to investigate the cause, so she silently leaves the tent to fulfil her duty—and lands in Dangsurong's strong arms against his amorous breast. The sheep are quieted by the girl, who also holds up the dogs, when Dangsurong leaves the field of battle. If any remark is made in the tent about her having been away for long, the girl answers that she had to count the sheep several times before she got the number right.

Women, as I have said, are Dangsurong's great weakness, and that perhaps is the reason why at this day he is wandering about in the wild forests of Northern Mongolia instead of sitting as Reverend Prior in a rich and reputable monastery on the steppes by far Kobdo.

ONE morning we found that a fall of snow during the night had covered all old tracks, and Dangsurong at once was on the hunting path. He mounted his horse and started out into the forest. At dinner-time he came back and threw himself down by the fire, full of eagerness. "*Mure ikhe olon beina*" ("quantities of tracks"), he repeated, while he unpacked several pieces of hard resin which he distributed among us. We knew what that signified—hunting with strychnine—and soon we were all sitting munching and chewing the red resin, just like Mexican cowboys with their chewing-gum. It took the whole day and the evening to boot, before the hard material had attained the right consistency, plastic and with the flavour of turpentine chewed away.

Small bits of resin were now squeezed over the ends of pegs which were cut to the size and shape of a finger. Then the pieces of resin on the pegs were cut off at the bottom with a knife, so that they took the form of a bullet and were afterwards put out in the snow to freeze. The strychnine was poured out from its little bottles into a cup in which it was long and carefully pounded to a very fine powder. The pegs with the resin were brought in and the hemispherical pieces taken off. Bater was sent to fetch horsehair from my white horse, the longest that he could get, and we began the remainder of the work with the great caution which is necessary. The right quantity of strychnine was poured into one half of the globule, 0·20 grammes for wolves, 0·15 grammes for foxes.

A long knife was put in the fire till it was red hot, and the edges of the pieces of resin were carefully smoothed with this. When the edges had been sufficiently softened the half globules were joined together with a horsehair in the middle. Then the finished resin globules were put back in the snow to harden.

Two pans were now set over the fire, one with butter and the other with flour, which was incessantly stirred so that it should not burn. When the room was full of the penetrating smell of toasted flour, the pan was taken off the fire and the resin pellets brought in. Held by the free end of the horsehairs, the pellets were dipped one by one alternately in the melted butter and the parched flour until a layer several millimetres in thickness had been formed upon them. Now they were what the Mongols call *chonuni bobo* (wolf cakes), and were ready to be put out. They must not come near anyone or anything, and were therefore carried by the free ends of the horsehairs and at arms'-length, up on to the roof of the house where they were placed in the deep snow.

Next morning I went into the woods with Dangsurong.

We had with us a leather bag full of flour, which we toasted immediately before our departure, and a big piece of frozen meat. When we crossed the river we cut some long willow twigs and stuck them in our belts. Dangsurong carried the strychnine pills, holding them by the horsehairs as far as possible from himself and his horse. When we had gone a long way from the inhabited area the piece of meat was fastened by a long rope to my saddle, so that it trailed after us. Wolf and fox tracks were becoming more and more numerous, and when we came out into a glade in the forest the first pill was thrown, as far to one side of us as possible, on to a place where there were no trees or bushes within ninety yards. This is reckoned as the maximum distance that a wolf will travel after swallowing the poison. To mark the position of the bait one of the willow twigs was stuck in the snow and parched meal was poured out round it. I rode in a circle along the edge of the wood surrounding the glade and made digressions thence to the point to which we wanted to entice our prey. Still dragging the piece of meat after us we went on and repeated the manœuvre in suitable places, twelve times in all.

It was late when, tired and frozen, but content with our day's work, we returned home. Next morning I woke early and, eager to see the result of the previous day's activities, would have gone at once into the forest. But Dangsurong would not hear of it. It was still too early, for the scent of man hung about the places we had visited. Only after several days would the wolves and the still warier foxes venture to approach the bait.

BUT we got variety in another way. One afternoon Bater and I were busy killing a sheep. I stuck it in the throat and cut the beast open, while Bater, who as a lama could not permit himself to kill, skinned and cut it up. Suddenly Dangsurong came rushing up, eagerly gesticulating and shouting that he wanted ropes, many and long ropes. He got hold of several pieces and, without giving himself time to answer our questions, ran back into the woods. He had gone out in the morning to set snares for hares and now came in a hurry for rope strong enough to bind a bear.

So as not to miss anything that might provide a thrill, I ran after him and soon heard the sound of angry voices, which led me to a group of gesticulating Buriats gathered round two sleighs in which sat three terrified Russians. They were smugglers from Tunkinski Trakt, who had transported flour over the mountains in the hope of exchanging it for butter, which in 1925 was not to be had in their part of dairy farming Siberia. They were poor peasants from a pillaged land who perhaps had undertaken a *Terje Vigenfärd* for wife and children at home in their cottages.

But to Dangsurong and the bloodthirsty Buriats the three men represented the power which had been the cause of all the misfortunes that had surged down from the detested frontier over their peaceful land. It was they who had imprisoned me in *Khara baishing* (the black house), the prison at Shinkish where Bater and I had been deprived of our liberty for the space of five days, it was they who had bound me in the forest as food for wild beasts and had threatened their guests with death at the muzzles of their rifles. If I, their guest, could not travel over the pass on a peaceful errand to the *oro's* country, then these *ukhsen honni*, these carrion sheep should indeed not return unpunished to their land. They should be tied up to trees, and their flour heaved out into the snow. The horses should be tethered beside them with their ears cut off so that their plaintive neighing would soon attract the great packs of savage wolves. And they were already going ahead with the preparations for their cruel deed.

The wild hunters were full of the thirst for vengeance, and it was not easy for me, as their guest, to mix myself up in the affair. I turned to Dangsurong as the most intelligent among them, whose character I knew so well that I knew to which of his feelings to appeal. If I succeeded in getting him on my side, we would have no difficulty in controlling the angry crowd.

I repeated a short Tibetan prayer, the same that a

Mongolian *harhung* utters before he extinguishes a life, a prayer for forgiveness for the sin he is on the point of committing. And in an earnest voice I commanded silence for the words I wished to say to Dangsurong before I left the place.

" Dangsurong," I said, " listen to my words which will not be many. But before I begin, think over and answer with a single word my first question, which is this : If it were possible to put the whole spirit of Buddha's teaching in a single word, what word would we choose ? "

A change came upon Dangsurong's face, and his rage-distorted features relaxed. Our glances met, first he looked at me, then past me as though he would seek the answer in far off memories. Finally after a suspense which seemed to me an eternity, came his brief but firm reply : " Righteousness."

And then I announced to the crowd that if the people of this region had any quarrel with the three Russians it was a matter with which I could not meddle, since I was not their chief but only a guest in their hospitable country. But if these Russians were to suffer for the wrong which other men of their race had done me, then I wished most strongly to protest. That an incidental punishment should fall also on their horses I in any circumstances set myself against, for I knew as well as all of those present that the wise law of their forefathers forbade mankind to strike, and so much the more to maltreat the part of a horse in front of the saddle, where reincarnation had its holy seat.

If these three innocent men were put to death in that place I should at once leave Kiäkt, for their released spirits would assuredly haunt this region and its inhabitants for a last and a decisive revenge. I left the place and the crowd of Buriats, who silently made way for me, and went home without turning round.

A little later Dangsurong came into the room and threw himself down by the fire. After a long silence he spoke, saying : " *Dandiade* [1] (master), you are right. The three *oros* shall leave the district unscathed."

[1] In Chinese : *Tang chia-ti.*

Mongolian Hunting Scene

The picture is painted on silk and is ascribed to the end of the fifteenth century. Noble Mongols and Manchus are taking part in the chase. The hunters are armed with bows and arrows, ancient muzzle-loaders and spears. They are employing both hounds and hawks. The original is in Consul Black's Collection at Rungsted

IN NATURE'S BOSOM

But Dangsurong remained silent and depressed the whole evening and read more than usual in his holy books. When I fell asleep he had begun the prayer "*Dunjur Mani*" the submissive invocation which, with a few variations, must be repeated ten thousand times to expiate a heinous offence. He sat cross-legged before the fire, holding in his hands two rosaries with whose help he recorded the count of the prayers recited. Maybe a struggle was being fought out in his soul between his primitive and savage hunting blood and the monastic lessons and ideals of his youth.

Dangsurong's was a strangely compounded character. The same evening on which he had been telling childishly innocent and moving tales and disclosing thoughts so lovely as to do good to one's soul, he was capable of relating how he had drunk a creditor out of his senses and afterwards left him in the snow, an easy prey to the wolves. To me he was a loyal and valued friend, but I should have been very sorry to have him for an enemy. I could, however, forgive him much when I saw his childlike pleasure in a leaping antelope or a lovely morning.

NEXT day we rode out to look to our strychnine. The first resin pill had been pecked open by magpies, and three dead birds bore witness to it. One had been swallowed by a greedy wolf. He had run ninety yards before the cramp, the poisonous effect of strychnine, had seized him. It was a fine specimen with a dog-wolf's black mane running down the back and with white masculine withers. Wary foxes had been to nose at two of the *chononi bobo*, but the pills were untouched. The whole result, accordingly, was one wolf, and with that we had to content ourselves, for much snow fell unexpectedly on the following night covering tracks, strychnine and everything.

Next day we heard that a poor Buriat had come down from the Sanagen mountains with news of a bear's lair that he had tracked down. Driven by hunger, the bear had left its lair for a short excursion and, by following its track, the Buriat had found its winter dwelling. He had now succeeded in selling this discovery of his to a couple of rich Buriats, who gladly paid hard cash for the chance of enjoying their favourite sport.

Six men with two well-trained Siberian hounds set out. Since I myself could not leave the station at this juncture, I was not able to be a spectator of the mighty conflict, but I afterwards saw the shaggy brown beast, ate of his meat from a thigh which the hunters presented to me and enjoyed Dangsurong's description, for of course he was one of the six.

When they had smoked the bear out of its lair and hunted it a good way into open ground, the little Siberian hounds had been slipped against the sleepy colossus. The bear had soon been worked into a rage by the yelping of the hounds, and had drawn itself up to its full height. Then the first of the six men had gone to the attack. With his sash wound about his left arm and the longer of his two Buriat knives in his sinewy right hand, he awaited a favourable moment for the perilous attack. It was not permissible for any of the five others to come to his help, and none of the hunting party might use any but " cold weapons ".

Waiting for a moment when the bear had his attention turned on the irritating hounds the man made his attack, from which he barely escaped with his life. Two succeeding assailants received bloody scratches which would have been worse if they had not nimbly leapt aside in time to escape the bear's deadly embrace.

Now it was the furious bear that went to the attack, ignoring the hounds, and the fourth hunter who was on the defensive. A couple of dexterous countering rushes, in which he shot like an arrow under the bear's right leg, close against his shaggy body, to throw himself again with a leap several yards away from the bellowing giant as he rolled over in the death struggle with the victor's bright knife through his heart. The snow was coloured red when the proud slayer drew out his proven steel and cut off the bear's right forepaw. That mighty paw now adorns the door of his hut, in token of victory won in single combat with one of the wild beasts of the mountains, a courageous fight in which the chances of being struck down are at least as great as those of victory.

I had now begun to make purchases of *avyos* (oats), *krupchatka* (fine wheaten flour) and rye meal against Isager's arrival. The horses were recovering their strength on abundant rations of hay and oats. The one which, despite all my efforts, never learned to eat oats was " Voilà ", but he also recovered quickly and, as appeared later, was to get through the remaining hardships of that winter best of all the horses.

We bought oats for a brick of tea the pood (36 lb.). In a region desolate and difficult of access the price of a commodity is mainly determined by the freightage, since this amounts to far more than the primary value of the goods. And since the transport cost of a pood of oats is the same as that of eight bricks of tea, I made a good bargain, seeing that I myself with my own cattle had attended to the transport of the tea from Urga to Kiäkt.

CHAPTER XIII

A DANGEROUS TRAVELLING COMPANION

ONE day Boyan Hishik turned up at our house, where he seemed to like his quarters, for he stayed with us a long time. One day when Dangsurong rode to the forest to try and find the snow-covered strychnine, Hishik went with him and came back full of plans for all one might do if one had enough of that commodity. He suggested that I should fetch more of the poison from the farm and undertook to find plenty of buyers. When I answered that we had no more strychnine at the farm than we needed ourselves, he confided in me that he had just come from Bulgun Tal and that several of his acquaintances had bought strychnine from the farm.

During the time Hishik was with us I several times gave him business to transact, and he carried out everything to my complete satisfaction, for he understood how to get good stuff at reasonable prices.

One day he returned from one such trip in the company of a distinguished guest. Shara Geling was a rich lama, the principal magistrate of the district and a smart fellow. He lived in a monastery at Uri, whence he took many and long journeys, during which he combined the discharge of his official duties with business on a large scale. Most people in the district owed him money, and now he was out to collect his debts in the form of furs. When the hunters could not pay the whole of their debts in furs, he seized their horses, cattle and sheep instead, and since he took the animals practically at his own valuation, he got everything at a very low price.

Hishik had brought Shara Geling to us as a prospective buyer of strychnine. I repeated that I had no more

A DANGEROUS TRAVELLING COMPANION

than a few bottles for my own use and that this was also the case at the farm. In the evening Hishik came alone to our house to say that unless we did business with Shara Geling we would lose our best chance of getting rid of the strychnine, since Shara Geling, besides being very rich, was the chief magistrate of the district and, as such, could forbid us to sell the poison in Kiäkt, if we refused to sell to him.

Dansurong and I consulted. Was it a trap? We must be cautious. North of the frontier, in Russian territory, hunting with strychnine was not prohibited, but in Urga the young Soviet authorities had forbidden the traffic in it by private persons, under severe penalties. Kiäkt did not belong to any of the four Khanates over which the Soviet had proclaimed its authority, but it might do so at any time. Above all it was important not to give the Red government in Urga a welcome opportunity to injure the expedition as such.

Next day Hishik came, in company with Shara Geling, and I now told the latter that he might have my personal stock of strychnine, six bottles. At the same time I mentioned that I had a fancy for his " brown ", and horse and bottles changed owners. On the following day Dangsurong and I had evidence that the exalted lama had sold five of the bottles and had himself used one.

With Hishik as go-between, we now spent several days in negotiating the price of strychnine in the event of my being able to hunt up any more of the desired commodity. Finally we agreed to fix the price at one sheep per bottle of two grammes.

In the days when the revolution was still fresh in the memory, many rumours went about among the population of Northern Mongolia of great treasure buried by rich emigrants from the country to the north, and I confided in Hishik that I knew a place by Hubso Gol where a lot of strychnine was buried.

The same evening I set off westward, while Dansurong kept Hishik busy, to prevent him from following me. At midnight I turned south and came upon the road that Bater and I had followed, which brought me

A DANGEROUS TRAVELLING COMPANION

to the farm in three days. There I laid my proposal before those of the boys who were at home, and it was accepted. We agreed that it would be a practical method of acquiring a large number of sheep, besides being a relief to get rid at one stroke of the compromising strychnine. After only a few hours rest at the farm I started back with three hundred small bottles in my saddlebags, and arrived one night at Kiäkt, where I immediately buried my load in one of the station's hay-stacks.

Next day the deal was concluded, and three hundred fat sheep, which were all mine, stood bleating in front of the station. Bater and two hired Mongols set out at once for Bulgun Tal with the flock.

THEN the ox-carts arrived with seventy-five poods of butter packed in bladders, and *krupchatka* was bought at the rate of ten poods for one pood of butter. Our own wagons as well as those we hired in Kiäkt went off at once to the farm whence most of the flour was to be sent on immediately to the monastery of Odogna Kure.

Dangsurong was left behind, with enough provisions, to await Sava, who was out on an expedition among the Sanagen mountains to look up traps and strychnine pills he had laid there. When Sava arrived, the station was to be closed and both were to return to the farm.

ONE clear sunny morning I hauled down the flag and took farewell of the place that had been my home during a long and memorable winter. A great part of the population of Kiäkt was there, and I received so many touching farewell greetings and little friendly presents that I promised them to come again next winter. But fate ordained that next winter, when the hunting season began, I should be thousands of versts from Kiäkt, and should never again sit by the camp fire with the Kiäkt hunters or revisit the happy valleys among the Sayan mountains.

WHEN I left Kiäkt, I rode with Hishik. He was to show me a new way that he knew through the mountains, which would bring me to Bulgun Tal in two days and

A DANGEROUS TRAVELLING COMPANION

nights. I had with me the station's most valuable furs, which I had been unwilling to entrust to anyone else, and the remainder of our silver.

"Voilà" was in good fettle and trotted gaily over the sunlit snow, and I sat thinking how good it would be to be back at headquarters with the boys, who by now would certainly all be gathered there. The work of the Kiäkt station was finished for the year, and I was satisfied with the result. Now I was longing to hear how the various members had got through their second winter as pioneers in our new country.

We turned into a narrow canyon whose steep sides were covered with snow-bowed trees, and the sun shone upon the snow hanging like white corals from the boughs. Rejoicing in all around me and in being on the trail again, I sang of warm breezes, of roguish blue eyes and of the unknown girl whom I would like to deck with all my sables. She was young, she was lovely and bewitching!

When the sun stood high in the sky we called a halt. Before us a pass lay in our way. It was not far, and it looked pleasant up there.

Hishik now told me that close by, in a parallel valley, lay his camp. He would like to ride home to greet his family and at the same time fetch a warmer coat. He gave me precise directions as to the way I should follow and enough landmarks to obviate any risk of my going astray. On the other side of the pass lay a gap, and there I was to light a big fire and make camp for the night. He would catch me up before dawn. We swapped horses and went our several ways. Hishik whistled between his teeth, and I heard the cheerful sound until it lost itself high up on the mountain steep to the right of the way by which I rode.

THE region was desolate, without trace of man or beast. The ascent of the pass began, and it was steep. The horse snorted and groaned, and steam rose from his warm body into the cold air. When the sun began its early disappearance behind the high peaks, a warm gleam spread over the frosty surroundings, but the sweat in the horse's long coat froze to ice and my feet grew cold. Higher and higher I worked my way up in zigzags; now it was only a few hundred yards to the summit, and I rejoiced at the thought of a speedy arrival at a camping-place and a warm fire.

Then all at once a sharp flash shot from the summit, followed by a short report whose echo rolled away over the tree tops. The whine of the bullet sounded close to my ear. Report number two followed just as I dropped on my belly in the snow. Pulling the horse after me I crawled in among the trees to the right. There I tied him up and hurriedly buried my saddlebags in the snow a little way off. I loosened the girth enough to let me warm up the action of my Mannlicher between the horse's back and the blanket. After I had assured myself that the lock was working, I stole farther to the right and crept over the ridge about fifty yards from the point from which the shots had come. I continued downwards in a curve till I came upon the tracks of a horse, which I followed upwards back to the top of the pass.

Dusk was quickly giving way to dark night when I suddenly checked myself in front of a white horse tied to a tree. It was "Voilà," my own horse, with my own saddle, the horse that Hashik had borrowed to visit the dear ones in the bosom of his family. This was unthinkable and I was furious, as I crawled on upwards on the war-path. I worked my way forward in a darkness so silent that the crunching of the snow under me was audible a long way. . . .

We both let off our full magazines, but owing to the darkness, the only result was that Hishik disappeared with the horse I had left behind, by the way by which I had come. I heard the slithering and sliding of him and the horse down the steep slope, until the last sound was swallowed up far below in the gloom of the ravine. In his hurry he had not found the saddlebags, so I had all my property in possession. I began the descent of the northern side of the pass and made a halt before daybreak. After some hours' rest I continued my way. I had escaped Boyan Hishik, but it had been what the

A DANGEROUS TRAVELLING COMPANION

Americans call "a close shave". It was not till long afterwards that I came to know more about his life and his ultimate fate.

He was the fruit of a union between a Chinese trader and his poor Mongolian servant-maid. In his youth he had found himself among the outcasts from Mongolian society, otherwise so democratic, with the despised brand of *balder* (half-caste) stamped on his whole countenance. His vagabond life gave occasion for many disreputable and dubious affairs out of which he always succeeded in extricating himself. Then came the revolution in the north, which precipitated the dregs of a gigantic nation over the dreaming plains of the Mongols. It was a time without any other law or right than that which rested upon brute force, and the worst elements prevailed. Fanatical Red and White guerillas perpetrated here their last vindictive deeds of blood, and in their train followed bands of Chinese, Japanese, Kirghiz and demoralized European soldiers from Siberian prison camps.

Those had been golden days for Hishik and people of his sort. That time was now over, but Hishik's restless vagabondage had not ended with it. That same winter of which I speak, and not far from the place where Hishik and I fought our nocturnal duel, he murdered two Mongols and—what is just as bad in the country of the nomads—took their horses and used them on his flight from justice, thereby incurring outlawry under the old law.

On his flight to the south Hishik passed Bulgun Tal, where he stole two horses from our farm. Krebs took command of the pursuers who were on his trail. The man-hunt went southward at furious speed. As occasion offered, Hishik exchanged his exhausted horse for a new one and in two places killed the protesting owner. After five days all trace of the fleeing criminal vanished at the monastery of Van Kure and the chase had to be abandoned.

Hishik was a proclaimed criminal whose sentence of death was made known all over Mongolia, and anyone who encountered him was in duty bound to kill him.

A DANGEROUS TRAVELLING COMPANION

But he fled more swiftly than his reputation, over wide-stretched steppes and endless deserts, until he was received into a band of savage *Chahar* (brigands) who ravaged and murdered in the lawless district along the Great Wall of China. At last their cruel exploits became so many that the Tatar General in Kalgan sent a large body of troops against them. Hishik's head was one of those which, on an August day in 1926, were hung up in a little wooden cage on the wall, just where the caravan road cuts through it on the stretch from Kalgan to Urga.

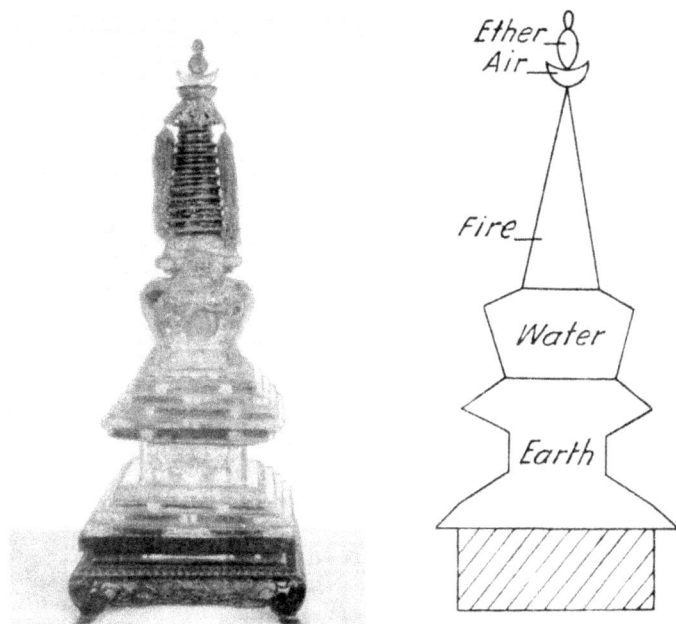

Silver Soborok (in Tibetan Chorten)
The Soborok is a reliquary in which the relics of a deceased hutuktu or high Lama are preserved. Its form symbolizes the five elements into which the body is resolved after death

Lamas from the "Black Hat" community dance in the Temple Courtyard

Gold mining in Northern Mongolia

CHAPTER XIV

A MAN'S WAY IS ONLY ONE—THE WAY PREORDAINED BY FATE
(Mongolian Proverb)

I PRESENTLY emerged from the last canyon that opens out by Bulgun Tal itself. The home steppe lay free from snow, and far away I could see the farm. Three welcoming streaks of smoke rose vertically towards the clearest of all skies.

We now spent a couple of days together at the farm, and the time flew swiftly, while we told one another the tale of our winter's adventures and the results attained, and planned in detail the completion, before the Mongolian New Year (*tsaghan sar*), of the campaign we had initiated.

Krebs had had an adventurous journey in a region lying some way to the north-east of that in which I had been engaged. He had gone up through the wild mountains north of Lake Hubso Gol and on to the place where our old compatriot Herr Riefestahl had said his gold diggings were situated. He found the remote Oka valley and stayed some time among its sparse population, the wild Oka Buriats.

The place where Riefestahl's mine lay was called Sarhöj, and he had told us in Denmark that we should find there the Russian superintendent of mines, Jakob, the latter's Russian servant-girl and a few Chinese labourers. But now it appeared that the Bolsheviks had confiscated our countryman's gold diggings, and when Krebs asked the local Buriats where Jakob and his people had gone, he learned that they had all been killed when they refused to surrender the place voluntarily.

On the way home Krebs had made an excursion into the forests on the Russian side of the boundary, and there he had one day met a single Russian frontier guard riding patrol. The man had wanted to arrest him and take him to a military station in the neighbourhood, but Krebs had dealt with the affair in a way that was very typical of him. He gave the guard to understand that he was amused by the situation and suggested that they should enjoy themselves like " good sports ". They were two lone men in the midst of the deep forest. Each had his good horse and his good rifle. " Fair play ! " They would see which of them would be left on the field. The result was that the duped guard galloped off for reinforcements, and Krebs rode back across the frontier.

Krebs brought home a lot of magnificent sables from his journey, but his account of how conditions had developed in the " gold country " up north was a great disappointment to us.

Our caravans of flour had passed on their way to Odogna Kure, and when the time of the Mongolian New Year approached, Isager and I rode to the monastery to attend to the business. There we were received with enthusiasm by our many Mongolian friends assembled for the festival, and were invited to occupy a tent belonging to the prior himself, the aged Guntse Lama. All the Mongols were dressed in their finest clothes of silk and brocade, and the women had decked themselves with silver and precious stones.

The arrival of our stock of flour was hailed with great satisfaction and contributed to the holiday mood. We sold the flour for the price of a ewe with its lamb for every pood, and before three days were past we had got rid of the whole consignment. The sheep were worth about five dollars each at Bulgun Tal but by means of our various transactions we had succeeded in considerably augmenting our stock of sheep at the moderate price of eighty-two cents per head.

WHEN we returned home from the monastery, Ove Krebs had arrived at the farm. He had travelled in Larson's car from Kalgan to Urga and had then come on with a camel caravan to the monastery of Murin Kure. The rest of the way he had ridden alone. Ove was admitted

THE WAY PREORDAINED BY FATE

with due ceremony as a member of our community, and for many days we were regaled with the latest news from America.

Ove also brought a letter from Larson, in which the latter wrote that he wanted our stock of furs as soon as possible and that he would like to take over the services of a couple of members of the expedition for some time. He wanted two of us for an enterprise he had planned for the spring, and we would receive our full share of the large profit expected.

It was Isager and I who arranged to go, and we started from Bulgun Tal on March 15th in brilliant weather. The horses were fresh and in good fettle, oats and provisions, with a tent and sleeping sacks, lay on the top of the troika, which was otherwise loaded with all the furs we had acquired during the winter. We had Dangsurong with us as handy man and cook, and it promised to be the most comfortable journey it was possible to make in Mongolia. It was Isager's first journey to Urga, but I now knew the road well, since it was the fourth time I had covered that stretch.

On the third day Isager became giddy and out of sorts, and the next morning he lay in his sleeping-sack in high fever and sweating profusely. Dangsurong sat beside him all day muttering Tibetan prayers, but Isager's condition only grew worse. I had heard of a frightful epidemic which had been raging in the neighbourhood of Bulgun Tal a month earlier and was gravely anxious lest it should be this which had struck down my travelling companion.

In the evening the fever was so high that I sent Dangsurong back for Krebs. I could not expect them for four days at the earliest, but to my great surprise Dangsurong walked into the tent the same night, not with Krebs, but accompanied by an old Mongolian lama. Dangsurong explained that the lama was a well-known medicine man from a monastery in the neighbourhood and that he would be able to cure this sickness much better than Krebs. Besides he declared that Isager's sickness was so malignant that it would be all over with him long before Krebs could arrive to help.

THE WAY PREORDAINED BY FATE

The stranger burned a lot of incense and looked long and keenly at the sick man. He did not touch him, but presently took from his medicine bag two kinds of powder, which he handed to Dangsurong. Without waiting for any kind of thanks or reward he thereupon turned to the opening of the tent and disappeared into the darkness of the night.

Dangsurong prepared the medicine in a cup of tea which he administered to Isager. I had in the meanwhile examined the powder. It looked like some sort of powdered bark and appeared to be harmless. The rest of the night Isager slept like a rock, regularly and heavily, and next morning he was free from fever. He felt fit and hearty, but as a measure of precaution he lay for the next two days on the top of the load, on a soft bed of sable, squirrel and fox skins.

Apart from this delay we drove quickly and without stopping till we were within forty miles of Urga. We found ourselves on the grim Jirem plateau where I had encountered the terrible snowstorm in 1924, and once more I had to undergo the same visitation so near our goal.

For three days the snowstorm held us in the same place. Our provisions ran out, and we had to live on a bag of dried cheese which Dangsurong had brought as an offering to one of the temples in Urga. The steppe was treeless, and we could not find any droppings in the deep snow. It was bitterly cold and we shivered in our almost snowed-up tent. We burned up all the woodwork of the wagon that we could remove without its falling to pieces. We whittled the tent-poles and shafts alarmingly thin to keep the fire alive.

The horses became coated with snow and ice, and were on the point of freezing to death. We were obliged to turn them loose, so that they might keep moving. The poor beasts turned tail to the storm and let themselves be carried along by it, and soon they disappeared from our view in the whirling snow flurries. Then we had to take turns in running after them so that they should not stray too far. This revived both us and the horses, but when we wished to return with the animals

Buga (in Tibetan, Sa-ba), the companion of the God of Death, is one of the chief figures in the tsam dance (devil dance). Opposite Buga dances "The Deathshead", who chases away the ravens that attack the sacrifice, "Zor"

The devil dance concludes with the breaking of the sacrifice to pieces. This is a clay figure and is presumably a substitute for the human sacrifice of former times

it was difficult to find our way back to the tent, since it could not be made out at a distance of thirty feet. Accordingly we took embers from the fire and threw them up into the air, and the storm carried them as flying fire balls for half a mile. When the one who had gone out after the horses had been away too long we sent up a fire-ball into the storm every three or four minutes, and with the guidance of these rockets he could always work his way back.

The snowstorm abated during the night, and on the morning of the fourth day the sun was shining. We now discovered that a large camel caravan was encamped about five hundred yards from our tent. It had been there throughout the whole snowstorm without our having a suspicion of its presence. The camels, which had lain during the storm closely packed together and almost buried in the snow, now filed out on the steppe in all directions to assuage their hunger, and they became completely wild when the drivers tried to get them together and drive them up to the loads. They rushed off screaming and looked as absurd as only galloping camels can. Their legs flew out in all directions and they looked as if they had very little control of them.

Majestic as the camel looks when he is slowly pacing through the desert with his load upon his back, he looks no less ridiculous when, screeching like a chicken, he gallops over the steppe on his long wambling legs.

We now made a start and drove over crackling and gleaming snow, passed two ox-caravans that had lost many of their draught animals during the storm, led our scared horses past dead and dying oxen and replied to the questions of mounted Mongols searching for cattle driven away by the storm.

At noon Urga's lofty temples appeared over a low mountain ridge, and they were so lovely that even the impassive Isager said they were " rather pretty ".

WE reached the town at three in the afternoon, but the new government had introduced so many formalities which incoming travellers had to undergo, and we were held up so many hours at the customs house, that it

THE WAY PREORDAINED BY FATE

was not until nine in the evening that we were able to drive to Larson's house. We were famished, and the table in his dining-room was laid. Larson himself was not at home and he had still not arrived when we had washed and tidied ourselves up. His fat housekeeper kept on prancing round the table, and it needed all our self-control to leave the bread and butter alone. At last we got to know where Larson was, and we went to the house indicated. But he was not there, and to our surprise we heard that some hours earlier he had been arrested by the " green police ".

This is what had happened. Larson is very fond of cards, but as an ex-missionary he never plays for money. In spite of this he had been arrested for gambling, and not till very late that night was he released with a serious warning not to gamble for the future. When Larson came home, he did not find much food left on the table.

Conditions in Urga had changed further since I was last there, and it was now a daily occurrence for one or another of the few remaining westerners to be arrested on some trumped-up pretext. On the two following days Larson's Russian housekeeper was missing, and he went again and again to the prison to find out if she had landed there. The police denied that she was incarcerated, but on the third day she came back—straight from gaol.

After we had delivered our furs into Larson's hands, we began to enquire into the business about which he had written to us. His view of things was, however, far less optimistic now than when his letter had been written. Larson had for many years been making money by buying horses in Mongolia and then transporting them to China and selling them there. On his last visit to the east he had contracted with a Chinese firm for the delivery of several thousands of ponies. He had got a good price stipulated in the contract, but the ponies were to be delivered in Kalgan within the year, and it was for this reason that he had called in our help, so as to get together as many as possible in the shortest possible time.

But Larson, who had been on friendly terms with

THE WAY PREORDAINED BY FATE

many Mongols of the old régime and particularly had been the close friend of Danzan, the War Minister murdered by the Bolsheviks, was not in good odour with the new leaders. They put all kinds of difficulties in his way, and the latest was that they had declared the export of horses to be a Government monopoly. It was obvious that no really good trade was to be expected in such circumstances, but Larson still hoped to be able to arrange matters by paying a stiff duty to the Government on each horse exported.

For a whole week we did nothing but run round to the various government offices, but we never arrived at any result. Everywhere we observed the influence of the Bolshevistic higher powers, and in the matter of bureaucracy and vexatious officialism the Mongolian Government had nothing to learn from Soviet Russia. The occupants of the offices were for the most part young Mongols. When they got bored with polishing the office stools—and they had nothing else to do—they hung about in the doorways chattering to one another. They were offensive, these office boys, though they were only callow striplings. Finally we were admitted to a place where sat a Russian. He was annoyed by my defective Russian, so I suggested that we should speak Mongolian. But then he had to employ an interpreter.

After several days had passed, it seemed silly for both of us to wait in Urga, and we decided that Isager should return to the farm. The final arrangement with Larson was that, so soon as the agreement with the Government was fixed up, I should follow with Larson's silver to the farm and buy for cash during the early spring the number of horses Larson required. The horses were to be taken direct across the steppes and the desert to P'ang-chiang, whence Larson himself with his Mongols would take over their transport for the rest of the way to Kalgan.

Conditions in the capital were, however, becoming more impossible every day, and the negotiations were stretching out into infinity. After three weeks of ineffectual work Larson sent me to Tientsin, there to lay the matter before his American partner.

THE WAY PREORDAINED BY FATE

Thus one cold April day I left Urga in the company of three Europeans and an American who were all equally sick of the new conditions in the once so free steppe country. It was hard upon those four Anglo-Saxons. They had spent many happy years among the Mongols, had made fortunes and lost them again, had been alternately gay and melancholy, but always content. One was going to Australia, one to Canada and two to the South Sea Islands, to try again under more tolerable conditions. They had many adventures to relate during our long journey and had certainly experienced more than they told.

We drove fast in our big Dodge car, but often halted in beautiful places. My travelling companions went up on to little heights and sand-dunes to imbibe the atmosphere once more. Silently they gazed out over the country of which they wished to carry away imperishable visual memories. At the last Mongolian camp before the desert began we had again to call a halt, for they absolutely insisted on going once more into a *ger* (Mongolian tent) to drink salted tea in shallow *ayag* (cups). And they sat Mongol fashion by the fire and talked to the elder of the tent about all the things Mongols talk about among themselves. Pipes went round the party and the farewells were long delayed. But the mood was broken by our Chinese chauffeur's impatient tooting on the angry motor horn, and we rushed out into the desert. At frequent intervals we passed some of the watering-places where, two years earlier, I had spent a cool night or a hot midday hour encamped, and the stretch between Kalgan and Urga, which had taken us fifty-four days in 1923, we now covered in four.

It was daily growing warmer, and on the third day I threw my old fur coat out on to the sand. I arrived in Kalgan dressed in a pair of Mongol-tanned leather breeches, a torn khaki shirt, long Russian riding boots and no hat. I discovered to my surprise when I stepped out of the car that I was still carrying my long Mongolian riding whip hanging from my wrist.

My travelling companions were received by friends in Kalgan, and I took the first train on to Peking. When

Scouts of the Desert

Khara-khun (black people) is the term for male Mongols who do not belong to the priesthood. They wear a long pigtail, the longer the better

THE WAY PREORDAINED BY FATE

I got out of the train at Hsi-chih-men, I discovered that I must somehow present an odd appearance. No coolies came running to offer me their rickshaws, and the smart white-clad Europeans regarded me as though I were drunk or dangerous or something of the sort. Me, who had washed and shaved in the train, too!

However, I got hold of a third-class rickshaw and told the coolie to take me to the Danish Telegraph Mess where I looked forward to meeting my friend Mogensen. But at the entrance to the big building, the porter did not want to let me in. I mentioned Mogensen's name to him, but he only shook his head. Then I got angry and swore, with the result that he shut the massive door again in my face.

The dirty rickshaw coolie whispered something to me in Chinese and drew me to the back of the building where a door stood open. I slipped in through the door which led into a yard where several Chinese *ma-fu* (grooms) were grooming Mogensen's horses. A back door to the house itself also stood ajar, and I ran across the yard, then through the kitchen and through a door into the dining-room, before I was overtaken by the cook and two white-clad servants. The Chinamen protested anxiously that *hsien-sheng* (the master) was sleeping, and that something terrible would happen if we woke him. Several more white-clad servants came up, and the fattest of them requested me to apply to the American legation. But then I went wild and roared in a voice of thunder: " Mogensen, come here you devil ! " And Mogensen came, and he got no more sleep that afternoon.

It was an unbelievable mass of questions that Mogensen poured over my head about Urga, about Bulgun Tal and about our friends there. Mogensen sat on the window-sill while I bubbled answers from the depths of the bath-tub. That night, for the first time for twenty months, I lay in a real bed between white sheets.

On the following morning I was waited upon in bed by four Chinamen. The first clipped and arranged my hair, the second took the measure of my feet, the third submitted a book of patterns of Shantung silk for shirts and measured me for clothes. Meanwhile the fourth had spread out a collection of slips, socks, belts and other things which, he declared, were articles of necessity for a gentleman in a civilized country. And when later I travelled first-class by the Blue Express to Tientsin, I looked like a *pukka sahib*.

In Tientsin I delivered Larson's reports to Mr. Davids and we spent many days in conference. One telegram after another came in from Larson. These breathed nothing but pessimism. The Bolsheviks in Urga were confiscating foreign property; many of our old friends among the Mongols had been arrested or executed. Finally Larson gave in and came to China, where I met him in Kalgan.

From Bulgun Tal too I had gloomy reports concerning political developments in the country and what they had brought in their train in the way of taxes, prohibitions, ordinances and other evils. And then it was my turn to be " sold to the Egyptians ". I got a job with an American firm and became a member of the little western colony in Kalgan.

In 1926 Krebs and I had a conference with the Soviet authorities in Urga, but all we could obtain was permission to work at Bulgun Tal for twelve years. And after twelve years? Would they then pay for the result of those twelve years of work? They could not promise that.

Conditions were becoming more and more impossible. The Mongols were by no means pleased with the new laws which came from Russia and were carried through with the help of " Red " Buriats and Soviet propaganda. The worst of them was a prohibition to manufacture felt. The felt tent is indispensable in the nomad life of the Mongol, felt must be used for saddle-covers, for camel saddles and other things. The ordinance was designed to provide more wool for export; it might increase foreign trade and in that way profit the Government's trading. The Government was coming under a constantly more rigid control by its great Soviet neighbour, and the efforts to carry communistic ideas into practice among the nomads were growing more and

THE WAY PREORDAINED BY FATE

more energetic. We had long since had to give up our beautiful dreams of being able to create a new field of activity for our many workless fellow countrymen. The authorities regarded all immigration with aversion and were unwilling that a number of Danes should be collected in one place.

Thus it came about that the members of the expedition were scattered before all the winds. Tot is now ploughing the soil of Canada, Ove is building harbours in Portugal, Isager has bought a farm and is practising intensive cultivation in Jylland, and Buffalo is a genial and respected merchant in Copenhagen. Only Carl Krebs, the father of the expedition, has remained at Bulgun Tal, where the Dannebrog still floats above silent Igagården. I myself have been working in Kalgan on the frontier of Mongolia, by the gate to the whole expanse of Central Asia. And in Kalgan the caravans have continued to come and go. When the way was closed to Kalka they took other ways. At night I heard the caravan bells passing away towards the pass that is the entrance to the Central Asiatic world. Their enchanting sound called forth memories and lured me on to new adventures. The caravan drivers sang of the freedom of the steppes, the solemnity of the desert and the purity of the mountains.

> When the flames of sunset gild my hair—I remember thee.
> When the eternal snows change to purple and gold—I remember thee.
> When the first star gleams to call the herdsmen home,
> When the pallid moon is coloured red—I remember thee.
> When there is nothing else but all that is—and me—I remember thee,
>
> and so

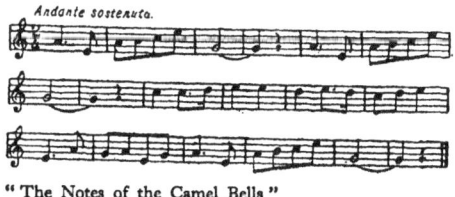

"The Notes of the Camel Bells" (Mongolian Melody)

I followed the caravans.

NOTES

Obo, a structure consisting of tree-trunks piled against one another, or a pyramid formed of heaped stones or of various objects. The people of Central Asia regard them as sanctuaries for the spirits of nature in bad weather, especially for those spirits that are important to the well-being of the herds.

Each district has its chief *obo* at which the whole population of the district assemble once a year for a great feast in honour of the local spirits and for their own enjoyment. At this festival, *obo takhilna*, they bring rich offerings to the spirits, and competitions are held in manly sports such as horse-racing, archery, wrestling—*bokh barildena* —and the like. This festival as a rule takes place in June and lasts three days. During the last two days the mood is generally pretty wild, since the assembled *harhung* (non-lamas), and many lamas too, get gloriously drunk on *arik* and *arihi*.

Harhung. The Mongolian word *harhung* (*hare hung*) signifies " black man " and describes a person who is not a lama (lamaistic monk). A *harhung* is recognized by his dress and hair which differ from the lama's. While the latter shaves off all hair from his head, the *harhung* carries a long pigtail on his neck. A lama's robe is always red or yellow, while a *harhung* chooses other gay colours, but never black or grey.

Arik and arihi. Arik is better known under the name of *koumiss*. This remarkable drink mainly consists of mare's milk which contains abundance of milk sugar. In the Mongol's tent hangs a horse-hide bag containing sour milk. Every day as much is taken out as is needed by the family. In the evening it is filled up with new milk which sours during the night and together with the residue is transformed into an alcoholic ferment. At weddings, when a new family is to be founded, such a bag of *koumiss* is an important and invariable wedding gift.

When such a leather bag is filled with new milk, the fermentation must be induced by artificial means, that is to say by frequently stirring and whipping it with a stick. When it is in this way brought into contact with the air, acid elements arise in the milk. Treated in this manner the new milk becomes not only sour but also alcoholic and thus intoxicating.

But if one lets this drink become more than three days old, one gets a beverage even more strongly alcoholic and comparable in its intoxicating properties with brandy. It contains, moreover, so much

NOTES

carbonic acid, that it effervesces violently when poured out, and it possesses an ether-like bouquet.

Finally *koumiss* can be converted into real spirits with an alcohol content of about 80 per cent by distillation, which the Mongols know how to carry out in a very effective manner with their primitive wooden apparatus. This distilled liquor is called in Mongolian *arihi*.

Shabi is a Mongolian word signifying a person or community under orders or instruction from another person or community. A *shabi* may be a little disciple in his novitiate at a monastery and assigned a particular lama as a teacher (*baksh*) from whom he receives instruction and orders. The *baksh* is responsible for his pupil's conduct and progress in knowledge.

But *shabi* may also denote a monastery or territory directly subordinate to a particular divinity or his reincarnation on earth.

Aimak. Mongolia is divided into *aimaks* (tribes); these again into *hosyun* (banners, standards) which in their turn are divided into *sumon* (arrows).

Dugun. The individual temples within the precincts of a *Kure* are called *duguns*.

Kure. Monastery.

Ambar. This Russian word has been adopted by the population of Mongolia and denotes a building in which provisions are stored.

Hashanda. A yard enclosed by palisades.

Tsaran tsar. The words signify " the white month " and denotes the first month after the Mongolian New Year, which occurs at the beginning of our February. The Mongolian year has as a rule twelve months, or moons, since they observe the lunar reckoning. In certain years an extra month has consequently to be inserted and these leap-years accordingly contain thirteen months. The four seasons are called *habehr* (spring), *zung* (summer), *namehr* (autumn) and *obyl* (winter), and each consists of three months which are called *turun tsar* (first month), *donder tsar* (middle month) and *sulde tsar* (last month). In leap year the extra month is inserted in the winter period.

Kilitai shobo, " the talking bird ", as the Mongols call the raven, may bring the traveller good or ill omen. Some of the auguries attributed to the bird are:

If a raven crosses you in its flight from left to right, the omen is good; if from right to left, it is evil.

If a raven croaks behind you when you are on your way, the omen is good.

If it flaps its wings and croaks, you are approaching a great danger.

NOTES

If it pecks at its feathers with its beak and croaks, it signifies death.

If it pecks food and croaks at the same time, you will find food for yourself and your horse on the journey.

If many ravens gather at sunrise, it signifies difficulties on the journey.

If a raven croaks at sunrise it foretells a fortunate journey during the day and that you are about to reach your goal.

Soyotes. It is supposed that the aboriginal population of the region along the present boundary between Mongolia and Siberia were a peaceful agricultural people who were annihilated by the incursion of the warlike Uighurs from the South. These were supposed to have come from what is now Inner Mongolia and were possibly of Turkish race. They should, however, according to the Chinese historians, have had fair hair and blue eyes. The palmy days of the Uighurs lay between the tenth and twelfth centuries. Their descendants are supposed to be the peoples whom we now call Finnish Ugrians and Ugro-Samoyedes. All these peoples have thus Uighur, and so probably Turkish blood in them.

In the fifth century a new people again penetrated from the south. These were " old Kirghiz " or Haka tribes, who are considered by most people to be a branch of the original Uighurs. The Haka tribes thrust out the population which had arisen from the fusion of the Uighurs with the aboriginal population of the country, or mingled with them. The Haka tribes were in their turn driven out by the Mongols who under Jenghiz Khan chased them to the north. One tribe took refuge in the wild forest tract between the Sayan mountains and Tannu Ola, where they have since remained isolated and unremarked. These are the Soyotes.

INDEX

Academic Protection Society, 8
Ado (herds of horses), 40
Adochin, district of Chahar, 40; signification of name, 40
Aicha Nor, 81
Aichen Nor (Lake), 81
Aimaks, Mongolian tribes, 338
Albertsen, K. P., Superintendent of Chinese Telegraphs, 7
Alpino Serai (Trading Station): life at, 217 *et seq.*; entertainment of trappers at, 218, 219; rules of, 219; extensive purchases of squirrel fur at, 219, 220; snowing-up of, 232, 233; hoisting of Danish flag at, 236
Altai Mountains, 4, 199
Ambar (warehouse), 130, 185, 338; Russian word adopted by Mongolians, 338
Ambulance Service (Danish) in Poland, 9
American Club, Ilo-Ilo, 16
— Consulate at Kalgan, 28
Andersen and Meyer, 67
Andersen, H. C., story of Kronborg, 2
Andrews, chasing with motor-car to ascertain speed of antelope of steppes, 52
Andrews Expedition, discovery of Dinosaurus in Gobi Desert by, 55
Animal life, preservation within radius of two miles of Igagården, 147
Antelope foot and drum, manipulations by female Shaman, 301

Antelopes, pair of, sculptured, on roof of temple, legend attaching to symbol, 284
— of Mongolian steppes: first sight of, 52; grazing among herds of camels, 52; search for water-holes, 52; species of, 52; speed of, how ascertained, 52
Apple trees, sole specimens seen in Mongolia, 190
Aratin nome, 251
Arbai (Siberian barley), 129
Aremark Gol, River, 197
Arihi, *koumiss* distilled into real spirits, 337, 338
Arik, drink consisting of mare's milk, 337. *See also* Koumiss
Arol (kind of cheese), 113, 114
Arrows (*sumon*), 338; of Heaven (*Tenggerin sumon*), 288
Arselang, name given to Mongol boy adopted by author, 145
Asia, Central, 70, 288, 335; caravan routes of, 30; plateau of, 32; fossils found in, 56; expense of sweetmeats in, 132; tyranny of Bolsheviks in, 203
Asses, riders upon, held in contempt by Mongols, 210
Attree, Mr., 154, 156; Larson's English manager, 154; advances capital to Expedition by order of Larson, 162
Australia, 332
Autumn (*namehr*), 338
Avalokita Buddha, reincarnation of, 289
Avyos, oats, 317

INDEX

Badmasiapov, supporter of Mongolia's independence, 74
Baikal Cossacks, privations of, on return journey from Great War, 203
— Lake, waters of Northern Mongolia discharging into, 190
Baksh (teacher), 338
Balalaika, Russian melody harmonized for strings of, 189
Baldan, hunter, 222
Balder (Chinese and Mongolian half-caste), 37
Bandits (*t'u-fei*), 37
Banners (*hosyun*), 338
Barley, Siberian (*arbai*), 129
Barter of butter for flour, 308
Barun, meaning of word, 53
Barun Sunit, Mongols belonging to race called, 53
Baslik (kind of cheese), 113, 114
Bater, 217, 218, 241, 242, 279, 280, 282, 284, 285, 286, 290, 292, 295, 296, 297, 306, 312, 319, 320; male assistant to Krebs Expedition, 114; arrival with mail from Borgström, 214; journey of, 222; mystic consultation of bones by, 222; return in company with *Ole'en Lama*, 224, 226; superstitious belief regarding Siberian wolves, 244, 245; superstitious belief regarding ravens, 246, 247; capture of, by Soviet Buriats, 254, 255; imprisonment of, 266; release from Shinkish prison, 274; recounts legend relating to symbol on roof of temple, 284; recounts legend as to origin of Lake Hubso Gol, 286, 287
Battle-song, Mongolian, sign of modernity of, 306
Bavasan (Secretary to Kalka Mongolian Government), murder of, 155

Bayard (Mongol), camp of, 116, 117, 119
Bazaars, Mongolian, measurements used in, diagrams of, 209, 212, 213
Bear: lair of, discovery, 315; tracking down and killing of, described, 316
Beef, Mongolian cattle good producers of, 113
Bellman, 24
Bible, Christian, events recorded in known to Dangsurong, 308
Birck, Tage, 10, 20, 46, 47, 48, 49, 66; selection as pioneer for Krebs Expedition, 8; training for Expedition, 9
Bird-life at Bulgun Tal, 148
Biscay, Bay of, voyage through, 13
Black, S., head of Great Northern Telegraph Company, Tientsin, 7; assistance rendered to Expedition by, 18
Black doctrine (Shamanism), 297; professors of, 196. *See also* Shamanism
Black man (*Harhung*), 337
Blackgame, 135
Bogdo Gegen (the Living Buddha), 203; and four Khans, supreme power of, 71; erection of Bogdo Kure begun by, 74; death of, 154, 203; horses belonging to, 196
Bogdo Khan, Emperor of China, 32; legend relating to, 71, 72, 73, 74
Bogdo Kure (God's Cloister), 70, 74; erection of, 74; change of name to Ulan Bator Khoto, 154; increase in number of Mongolian soldiers in Soviet uniform at, 154
— Ola (Mountain of the Gods), 51; wooded steeps of, 66; pilgrimages to, 70, 71

INDEX

Boldikov, 168, 173, 174; trade with, 108; religious devotion of, 174, 175
Boldon, 89
Bolsheviks, 3, 58; campaign of Baron von Ungern-Sternberg and White Guards against, 7; persecution of colonists by, 90, 91; tyranny of, in Central Asia, 203; danger to Sava from, 236; slaughter by, of Chinese at Uri Gol, 306
Bomberja, 207, 208
Bones: consultation of, divination practised by Mongols, 222; position of, female Shaman's augury from, 300
Borgström ("Buffalo"), 2, 12, 28, 66, 80, 81, 82, 85, 88, 89, 95, 101, 103, 104, 105, 106, 107, 114, 149; popularity of, 42; physical development of, 42, 43; Yalserai and author, school kept by, 91; conjuring tricks of, 94; watch of, 94; house-building of, 97, 98; stock of consignment of goods brought from Urga taken by, 185; mail from, brought to Kiäkt, 214; becomes merchant in Copenhagen, 335
Borildje Kure, monastery of, 81; description, 82, 83
Boxer Rising, valiant action of cavalry of Chahar Guards during, 41
Boxing lessons on journey to Shanghai, 42
— rounds on voyage, 13
Brändström, Elsa, 3
Brandy, intoxicant qualities of alcoholic *Koumiss* comparable with those of, 337
Brick-making, 147
Brick-tea, 29, 162; different kinds of, described, 30,—purposes for which severally adapted, 30; failure of firm of Lipton to produce, 30; site of production, 30; packets of, purchase of house in exchange for, 208
British American Tobacco Company, representatives of, at Kalgan, 24
Bronze weapons in desert dating from past ages, 288; Mongols' name for, 288
Buddha, gilded image of, at monastery of Borildje Kure, 82; the Living (Bogdo Gegen), 203
Buffalo. *See* Borgström
Bulgun Tal, 3, 42, 81, 82, 85, 86, 87, 108, 127, 144, 190, 203, 222, 308, 318, 320, 323, 326, 327, 333, 334; expedition to, 76 *et seq.*; steam baths at, 96; winter cold of, 107; arrival at, 129; spring season at, 129; distance from to Khathyl, 136; water-birds and fowl at, 147, 148; introduction of pigs and poultry to, 148; summer heat at, 148; potato-growing at, 148; Danish hoisted flag at, 149; plan of homestead at, 151; arrival at, after journey from Urga, 185; district north of, 187; Krebs' stay at, 335. *See also* Sable Plateau
Bure Gol, River, 197; tributary of Uri, 195
Buriat, 48
— ex-officer in Russian Army, adventures of, recounted, 202, 203
— hunters, threatened treatment of Russian smugglers by, 314
Buriats, 30, 96, 99, 101, 104, 186; dress of, 31; three, inciting rebellion against ruler of Mongol tribe, punishments of, 204, 205
Burkhan, meaning of, 179
Burkhani nome, 251
Business colony of Kalgan, 27

343

INDEX

Butter ; yield of Mongolian cows, 113 ; storage in ice-cellar, 149 ; barter of, for flour, 308 ; *krupchatka* in exchange for, 320 ; scarcity and dearness of, in Kiäkt, 307

Camel caravan, manœuvre adopted by driver of, 29
— dead, found in water-hole, 57
— transport of brick tea to Khirghiz steppes, 30
Camel-drivers from Tartary, described, 21
Camel-droppings used as fuel in desert, 64
Camels (*teme*), 40 ; herds of, antelopes grazing among, 52 ; Bactrian, period in year of transport through desert by, 60
Canada, 332 ; research stations in, wheat seed from, 131 ; Tot's emigration to, 335
Candy, Chinese, 132
Capercailzie, 135
Caravan bells, rhythm of, 61
— drivers : dread of journey to Outer Mongolia, 59 ; Chinese : dread of Mongol soldiers, 63, sacrifice of goat by, 59, 60
— life, in desert, privations and dangers of, 57, 58
— route from Kalgan to Urga, importance of, 58
— routes of Central Asia, 30
— transport : across River Selenga under difficulties, 184, 185 ; from Urga to Van Kure, difficulties of, recounted, 168 *et seq.*
Caravans of Krebs Expedition, difficulties in progress of, 28
— ravage and plunder by *t'u-fei* (brigands), 45
Carlsberg Fund, support of Krebs Expedition by, 10
Catherine II, Empress, work of Russian Boundary Commission during reign of, 4, 5 ; coins stamped with head of, in *Obo* of Uri Hangrän, 196
Cattle (*ugher*), 40 ; purchased at low prices by Chinese from Mongols, 37 ; herds of, on Mongolian steppes, 65 ; Mongolian, qualities of, 113 ; destruction from effects of Mongolian winter, 120
Cattle-census (1918–19) in Mongolia, 110
Chahar, abolition of *Dsasak Darog* (law of succession of princes) in, 40 ; districts into which divided, 40 ; extermination of princes and hereditary dignitaries in, 40 ; present government of, 40 ; military constitution of, 41
— Guards, cavalry of, valiant fighting during Boxer Rising, 41 ; disbanding of, coincident with fall of Manchu Dynasty (1912), 41
— Mongols, 36 ; former history of, 39 ; regiments of, on guard against Russian aggression, 40
Chang-chia K'ou, Kalgan now named, 41
Cheese, kinds of, made from skimmed milk, 113, 114
Cheka, the, 205
Ch'ieng Dynasty, 35
"Chikherli bodena" (Mongolian war song), theme of, 211
China, 67, 70, 74, 99 ; and Russian Dominions in Asia, point of boundary between, 4 ; exchange of Empire for Republic (1912), 35 ; military resources of, princes of Inner Mongolia dependent on, 35 ; Mongolians' sale of horses to, 112 ; political events in Mongolia following deliverance from yoke of, 154, 155 ; fragment of, in Urga, 169 ; trade in horses with, 330

INDEX

China, Emperor of : claim for possession of Urianhai, 6 ; war with Lekdan Khan, 39
— Sea, 16
Chinese, 35 ; wall and watchtower of, 32 ; aggression of, causing retreat of Mongols into desert, 36 ; purchase of cattle from Mongols by, at low prices, 37 ; and Mongolian half-caste (*balder*), 37 ; and Mongolian administration, mixed, of Chahar, 40 ; and Mongols, guerilla warfare between, 58 ; settlement in Mongolia (Sheng-Wat-Sin), 38 ; encouragement by, of wolves, by show of fear, 242 ; slaughter of, at Uri Gol, 306
— caravan drivers : dread of Kalka Mongols by, 59 ; dread of Mongol soldiers, 63
— coins, in *obo* of Uri Hangrän, 196
— coolies : attack on Foreign Settlement, Hong Kong, how repulsed (1846), 16
— habits and acquirements of Nils Poulsen, 22, 23
— immigrants, Mongolian girls sold to, for wives, 37
— irregular soldiers (*gam-min*), force of, annihilated by small troop of Mongols, 210, 211
— merchants and nomadic traders, market place for, 29
— pedlars paying tribute to Uri Hangrän, 196
— Republic, uprising of Mongols against, 35
— Scientific Mission to the North-West, The, 280
— silver dollar (*yenshan*), 188
— soldiers, extermination of, by Kalka Mongols, 54, 55 ; skeletons of, in desert, 59
— spirit (Chiu), 36
— " Tatar General " : arms sent from, to Mongol tribes in East, by whom carried, 158
— " Tatar General " at Kalgan, adviser to, 156
— Telegraphs, 7
— temple, worship at, 34
— town of Kalgan, 21, 22
— traders : method of inducing debt among Mongols, 36 ; in Van Kure, 175 ; and Mongolian trappers, monastery as centre of exchange for, 192 ; settled at Kiäkt : disappointment of, 210, 221, expert knowledge of pelts possessed by, 213, inducement to trappers to become sole vendors to them, 213, offer of purchase of furs made to, 215 ; capable men of business, 211 ; tolerated but despised by Mongols, 211
Chiu, 36
Chomut of Russian harness, 170
Chononi bobo (wolf cakes), 311, 315
Christian, King, birthday of, 76
Citadel Church, Copenhagen, 11
Cloud-shapes seen on Mongolian steppes, 116
Coins, Chinese and Russian in *obo* of Uri Hangrän, 196
Copenhagen, 67, 103, 104 ; Borgström becomes merchant in, 335, 336
Cossacks, 186 ; assistance in horse-capture, 137, 139, 140 ; paying tribute to Uri Hangrän, 196 ; difficulties of, upon Eastern Front in Great War, 203
Cotton stuff (*dalimba*), 30, 31
Cows, Mongolian, and yak bulls, product of, 113
Crane, Mongolian : eaten as game, 51 ; shooting of, 51
Cream (*urum*), 113
Customs examination : at Urga, escape through with packages

INDEX

Customs examination (*contd.*)—
of strychnine, 164 ; at Van Kure, 176, 177, 178, 179
Customs officers, discovery of packets of strychnine by, how evaded, 179, 180

Dägerli, cloak, in Kiäkt dialect, 201
Daichin Wang (Mongol prince) : imprisonment of, 175 ; dispersal of soldiers and adherents of, 175
Dain Derchen Kure, Mongolian Monastery : built of wood, 190, 191, 192 ; centre for exchange of goods, 192 ; lamas of, 192
Da Kulen (Great Cloister), 70 ; *see also* Urga, Westerner's
Dalai Lama, 73, 74 ; significance of name, 289
Däle, Mongolian for " cloak," 201
Dance, Mongolian, 251
Dalimba (cotton stuff), 162 ; mode in which produced, 30, 31
Dandiade (Master), 314
Dangsurong, 307, 312, 313, 314, 315, 318, 319, 320, 327, 328 ; Mongolian traveller, 187 ; past history and adventures of, 308, 309 ; formerly a monk, 308 ; events in Christian Bible known to, 308 ; amorous escapades of, 309, 310 ; composite character of, how illustrated, 315 ; repetition of prayer by, 315 ; description of tracking down and killing of bear, 316
Danish Army, mobilization, without action during Great War, 3
— flag (Dannebrog) : flying at Bulgun Tal, 149 ; hoisting of at house at Kiäkt, 208 ; hoisting of, at Alpino Serai, 236 ; waving of, 307
— Legation : service of Carl and Ove Krebs under, 3 ; Moscow, 274 ; Peking, 276

Danish Mess at Peking, 18
Danzan (Kalka Mongolian War Minister), 74 ; speech of, denouncing closer relations with Soviet, 155 ; murder of, by Rintjino and Bolsheviks, 155
Darkhat Kure, Monastery of, 186
Davids, Mr., 334
Debt collection from hunters in form of furs, 318
Deer, herd of, nocturnal camp of, how indicated, 305
Denmark, 105, 134 ; postal communications of members of Krebs Expedition with, improved, 136
Deri (powder), sale of, 31
Dinosaurus, discovery of, at Ehrlien (Gobi Desert), 55, 56
Disciple in monastery (*Shabi*), 338
Diseases, use of fossils by Mongolians for cure of, 56
Divination practised by Mongols by examination of bones, 222
Dog's hour (8–10), 231, 300
Dogs, Mongolian : exceptions to usual savagery of, 191 ; attacks of, manœuvre adopted to ward off, 309, 310 ; attracted by human excrement, 309, 310
— wild, of Gobi Desert, 57
Dollar, silver, Chinese (*yenshan*), 188
Donder-tsar, middle month of season, 338
Drum and antelope foot, manipulation of female Shaman with, 301
Dsasak Darog (law of succession of princes), abolition in Chahar, 40
Duche (butterflies), Mongolian name for columns of snow, 232
Duga, of Russian harness, 170, 188, 220
Duguns, temples within a cloister, 190, 308

INDEX

Dunjur Mani, prayer, countless repetition of, 315
Dunsa, tobacco used on steppes, 30 ; where produced, 30
Dysentery, Haslund's attacks of, 20, 44
Dzungaria, 207

Eagles, attacks of, method of warding off in desert, 58
East Asiatic Company, support of Mongolian Expedition by, 10
Egin Gol, 8, 130, 132, 308, 309
— — River, 149, 150, 286 ; flowing through Bulgun Tal, 83, 85, 88 ; course of, 189, 190 ; confluence of Uri River with, 190 ; union with Selenga, 190
Erebugher Wang, Mongol prince, legend relating to, 71, 72, 73
Ermine, 305 ; price of : at Urga, 125, dispute regarding, 126
Europe, main overland route of transference of tea consumed in, 58
Evil spirits, expulsion from body of Zerang, 297, 300–2, by female Shaman, ceremony described, 300–2
Exchange centre, Mongolian monastery as, 192
Excrement, human, Mongolian dogs attracted by, 309, 310

Famine in Russia (1922), 9
Farmers and agriculturists, Danish, settled in Siberia before Russian Revolution, 7
Felt, manufacture of, Russian prohibition on, 334 ; necessity of, to Mongolians, 334
— stockings (*oimus*), 114
Field work, hours of, during spring season, 130
Finnish Ugrians, 339
Fish, storage in ice-cellar, 149
Fish-nets, setting of, 131
Flag Battery, Helsingör, 1

Flagstaff, selection of, 91, 92
Flour : abundance in Kiäkt, 307 ; barter of butter for, 308
Fossils : found in Central Asia, 56 ; Mongolian name for, 56 ; used by Mongolians for cure of diseases, 56
Fox fur, price of goods paid in exchange for, 209
Fox, silver, 305
Freightage, price of commodity mainly determined by, in regions difficult of access, 317
Friend of China and Hong-Kong Gazette, 16
Friendship, difficult act of, 161 *et seq.*
From Peking to Moscow (Sven Hedin), 278
Fuel in desert, sole means of obtaining, 64
Fur campaign in winter, 188 *et seq.* ; equipment for, 188, 189
— supply of, diminished by fatal disease attacking young squirrels, 194
— transport of, under difficulties, 116 *et seq.*
Furs : cargo of,—obtained by Krebs and Ping, 115, rescued from frozen river, 118 ; purchased, agreement with Russian-American firm regarding, 125 ; price of, at Urga : dictated by Russian-American firm, 125, no official quotation regarding, 125 ; disposal of, to Russian-American firm, 125, result, 126 ; application for new contract for supply of, 152, 156 ; used as currency by Mongols, 185, 186 ; expert in, long experience required to become, 211 ; prices excessive at Turuk, 307 ; debt collection from hunters in form of, 318

347

INDEX

Future events, prediction of, from appearances produced by heating shoulder - blade of sheep, 228

Fykes, setting of, 131

Galathea, Danish frigate, Captain of, repelling attack on Foreign Settlement, Hong Kong, 17

Gam-min (Chinese irregular soldiers), force of, annihilated by small troop of Mongols, 210–211

Ganjur (Holy), by Gautama Buddha, translated into Mongolian, 39

Gautama Buddha : Holy *Ganjur*, written by, translated into Mongolian, 39 ; priests of, reverencing Uri Hangrän (God of Nature), 195

Gazella gutterosa (Yellow Antelope, *Share gurus*), 52

— *subgutterosa* (Tailed Antelope, *Sultei gurus*), 52

Geographical Society, see Royal Danish Geographical Society

Ger (tent), 114

Gobi Desert, 35, 36, 42, 48, 53, 55, 94, 100, 156 ; journey of Krebs Expedition through, 55 *et seq.* ; difficulty of obtaining water in, 56 ; wild animal life of, 57 ; marmots of (*Tarbagan*), 64 ; storms and whirlwinds of, 61, 62 ; sole means of obtaining fuel in, 64 ; treelessness of, nearly total, 64

God's Cloister (Bogdo Kure), 154

Gold, obtained by Mr. Riefestahl in Urianhai, 6

— coins, old Russian, used for ornamentation, 201

— prospectors, Russian, in Urianhai, 5

Great Northern Telegraph Company, 7 ; at Tientsin, 18 ; office at Irkutsk, 136, 274

Great Wall of China, 21, 35 ; tunnel through, passage of, 29 ; no longer a barrier, 36

— War, difficulties of Cossacks on Eastern Front during, 203

Gudenaa, 107

Guntse Lama, prior of Monastery of Odagna Kure, 326

Habehr (spring), 338

Hadak, silk material (footnote), 115 ; used in presentation to gods or venerated persons, (footnote), 115 ; presentation to female Shaman, 299, 300

Haka tribes, 339 ; driven out by Mongols under Jenghiz Khan, 339

Hamburg, 10, 12 ; unemployment in, 12

Hamsters (*Cricetulus*) in Gobi Desert, 57

Hanga, 141, 261, 286

— Kure, temple of, 284 ; sculptured symbol on roof of, 284, legend attached to, 284

Hankow district, production of brick tea in, 30

" Hao " (desert horse), capture and breaking to harness described, 136–40

Hares, white, 305

Harhung, how distinguished from lama, 337 ; Mongolian word for " black man ", 337

Harhung, Mongolian, prayer of, 314

Harness, Russian : advantages of, 170, proved, 197 ; *chomut* and *duga* of, 170 ; description of, 170 ; difficulty of management single-handed, 170

Hartman, 24

Hashanda (dwelling-place), 138 ; contraband strychnine buried in, 162 ; yard enclosed by palisades, 338

Haslund, H. : illness of, 19 ; departure from Peking, 20 ;

INDEX

Haslund, H. (*continued*)—
house-building by, 97, 98; difficulties of fur transport experienced by, 116 *et seq.*; adoption of Mongol boy (Gongerer), 145, 146; why wrongly placed on Soviets' black list, 205; knowledge of furs acquired by, 212, 213; self-assumption of Mongol habit of mind, 227; capture of, by Soviet Buriats, 254, 255; abandoned by Soviet Buriats, 255, 256; trial of, by Soviet Buriats, 257 *et seq.*; false accusations of, by Soviet Buriats, 259; interrogation of, by Russians in Shinkish, 264; imprisonment of, by Soviet Russians, 265; prison life in Shinkish, 268 *et seq.*; revolt of in Shinkish prison, 273; release from Shinkish prison, 274; permission to witness female Shaman's contest with spirits granted, 300; return to Kiäkt, 306, 307; assistance rendered to, by Tibetan prayer formularies, 309; deliverance of Russian smugglers effected by, 314; personal stock of strychnine exchanged for horse with Shara Geling, 319; departure from Kiäkt, 320; and Isager, journey to Urga, 327; difficulties of, in Urga, 331
Haymaking, hitherto unknown to Mongols, 147
He, 35
Hedin, Sven, *From Peking to Moscow*, 278
Helsingör, 1
Hishik, Boyan, a Young Mongol, 306; adventures and past history of, 306; dress and appearance of, 306; linguistic capabilities of, 306; arrival of, at Kiäkt, 318; go-between in negotiating strychnine, 319; departure from Kiäkt, 320; treachery of, 321, 322; account of criminality of, 323; end of, 324
" Holy Russia ", *taiga* of, 187
Hong Kong, 16
Horse: carcase of, used as bait in hunting wolves, 222, 223; ridden on journey to Tunka, qualities of, 239
— -breaking in Mongolia, 111
— -capture, account of, 136–40
— caravans, limited possibility of employment in desert, 60
— herd (*Tabun*), 294
— racing in Mongolia, 112
Horses: herds of (*ado*), 40; Mongolians' wealth represented by, 111, 112; destruction from severity of Mongolian winter, 120; belonging to Bogdo Gegen (living God), 196
Hosyun (banners, standards), 338
Honichin: district of Chahar, 40; signification of name, 40
House, purchase of, in exchange for packets of brick-tea, 208
Hsi-chih-men, 20, 333
Hsi-pei, 21
Hsü, General, fate of soldiers of, 54
Hubso Gol, 102; Dalai, 287; significance of prefix " Hubso ", 289
Hubso Gol, Lake, 136, 141, 142, 292; dimensions and situation of, 286; legend as to origin of, 286, 287; ice-covered, difficulty of gaining shore, 289, 290; strychnine buried near to, 319; wild mountains north of, 325
" Hudcha ", 100, 101
Hunters, account of Tunka obtained from, 238; plight of Zerang discovered by, 294, 295; reason for not rescuing Zerang, 295; collection of debts from, in form of furs, 318

349

INDEX

Hunting grounds of primitive Soyotes, 187
Hutuktu, new, forbidden by Soviet to be elected in Kalka Mongolia; 154; deceased, incarnation of, 226
Hutuktu Bogdo Gegen, legend relating to, 71
Hutuktu Gegen, 112; proclaimed Emperor of Kalka Khanates, 70
Hypsometer, aid of, in making map of route, 45

Ice-accident to transport wagon on Selenga river, 117-20, 124
Ice-cellar, storage of fish and butter in, 149
Ice-formation, unique example of, 117
Igagården, 109, 128, 146, 175, 335; name of Danish property at Bulgun Tal, 87; return to, 128; preservation of animal life within radius of two miles of, 147
Ili River, 40
Ilo-Ilo, capital of Panay, 15
Indian Ocean, voyage across, 14, 15
Indians, North American, wigwams of, similarity of summer camping places of Soyotes to, 292
Inn (*serai*), 219
International Red Cross, service of Carl Krebs under, 3
Irkutsk, 3, 88, 101, 102, 104, 105, 133, 202, 263, 308; Russian mining department at, support of gold prospectors in Urianhai by, 5; office of Great Northern Telegraph Company at, 136, 274
Iron Horse, year of (1930), 145
Irrigation, system of: adopted for experimental planting, 131; from canal, construction of, 132

Isager, Erik, 102, 103, 105, 106, 107, 135, 152, 185, 186, 307, 308, 326, 331; selection as pioneer for Krebs Expedition, 8, 10; training for Expedition, 9; acts as medical assistant to Krebs, 115; return from Turuk, 307; in charge of station at Kiäkt, 307; illness of, 327; cure of, by Mongolian lama, 327, 328; and Haslund, H., journey to Urga, 327; farming of, in Jylland, 335
Ivan, Russian prisoner in Shinkish prison, murders committed by, 269, 270, 279

Jade from Khotan, sale of, 31
Jakob, killed by Bolsheviks, 325
Japan, 74; attack by Mongols of Kublai Khan, after crossing sea, 289
Jenghiz Bogdo Khan: route of armies of, from highlands to plains, 32; immemorial law (*Yassa*) laid down by, for Mongols, 204
Jenghiz Khan, 77, 138; ordinance regarding use of water, 115; warriors of, leading horses to wells, 289; Haka tribes driven out by Mongols under, 339
Jirem plateau, snowstorm on, 328, 329
Jomsborg (Viking stronghold), 150
Jun, meaning of word, 53
Jun Sunit, 53
— Prince of, 49
Jylland, 8, 10, 335
— North, 9

Kalgan, 7, 20, 42, 48, 63, 70, 324, 326, 330, 331, 332, 334, 335; arrival of Expedition at, 21; first meeting with Mongols at, 21, 22; Western

INDEX

Kalgan (*continued*)—
  firms with outposts at, 24; business colony of, 27; departure of Krebs Expedition from, 27, 28; American Consulate at, 28; now named Chang-chia K'ou, 41; caravan route from, to Urga, 58; escape of Kelley to, 158
Kalgan and Urga: mode of communication between, 25; possibility of constructing railway between, 45; caravan journey between, 60
Kalka, 53, 110
— women, married, description of dress of, legendary reason for, 69, 70
— Mongolia, 30; Khans and Princes of, fate of, 154; new *hutuktu* forbidden by Soviet to be elected in, 154; predominance of Soviet influence in, 154, 155; new government of, why displeasing to Russians, 155
— Mongols, 36; extermination of Chinese soldiery by, 54, 55; dread of, by Chinese caravan drivers, 59; official entrance to country of, 62; legend relating to, 69, 70
Kangaroo rats (Dipus) in Gobi Desert, 57
Karakorum, camp of Kha Khan at, 207
Kasagrenin, General, persecution of Shiskin and family at Bulgun Tal, 90, 91
Kashgar, rugs from, 31
Kattegat, the, 1
Kedr, cedar (?) growing in Siberia, 102
Kelley: adviser to Chinese " Tatar General " at Kalgan, 156; mixed parentage of, 156; United States Representative at Urga, 156; adventurous and many-sided career of, 156, 157; amorous intrigue of, 156, 157; business undertakings of, 157; scandal connected with, 157; detected in carrying arms to Mongol tribes, 158; escape of, to Kalgan, 158
Kha Khan, camp of, at Karakorum, 207
Khainak: as milk and meat producer, 113; product of yak bulls and Mongolian cows, 113; qualities of, 113
— oxen, weight of, 113
Khalagan and *Ude*, difference between in meaning explained, 62
Khans, legendary, of Mongols, rulers over all waters, 289
— four, legend relating to, 71, 72, 73
Khathyl, 141, 286; distance from Bulgun Tal to, 136; small Russian colony, 136
Khitat (Slav), epithet of contempt used by trappers, 210
Khotan, jade from, 31
Khuduks (wells), 289
Kiachta, 7, 58; capture of Baron Ungern by Bolsheviks near, 91; telegraph line to, 120
Kiäkt, 197, 199, 216, 217, 236, 242, 285, 320; river valley of, 187, and Mongolian steppes in south, means of communication between, 187; journey to, described, 193, 194; government of, 203; population of, 203; hoisting of flag at, 208; house at, purchase of, 208; mountains round, 209; disappointment of Chinese traders settling at, 210; high-class squirrelpelts brought to, by Tunka Buriats, 215; return to, 306, 307; abundance of flour in, 307; scarcity and dearness of butter in, 307; station at,

INDEX

Kiäkt (*continued*)—
  Isager in charge of, 307;
  Haslund's departure from, 320
— Buriat women, dress of, 201
— Buriats, 249; inmates of house of, described, 200, 201; language of, compared with that of Mongols and of Torguts, 201; skin coats of, compared with those of Mongols, 201; oppression of, by soldiers (Red and White), 307
Kiäkt River, 199, 241
Kiel, 12
Kilitai shobo ("talking bird"), Mongol name for raven, 338
Kipling, R., 83
Kirghiz: dress of, 31; similarity of Soyote language to that of, 292; Old, or Haka tribes, 339
— steppes, camel transport of brick-tea to, 30
Kites, predatory, in Gobi Desert, 57
Kobdo, 30, 308, 310
Kolchak, 275
Konsulstvo, Russian quarter of Urga, 162
Koslov, General, expedition to Mongolia, 278
Kosogol, Russian corruption of Mongol name of lake, Hubso Gol Dalai, 287
Koumiss, bag of, important wedding present, 337; drink consisting of, 337; distillation into real spirits, 338; *see also Arihi*
— alcoholic, 337; intoxicant qualities comparable with those of brandy, 337
Kowloon Promontory, 17
Kronborg, 1, 2
Krebs, Carl, 2, 3, 9, 10, 21, 28, 48, 74, 75, 76, 78, 79, 81, 82, 83, 85, 86, 87, 88, 89, 91, 93, 94, 98, 99, 100, 101, 103, 104, 106, 108, 148, 186, 327, 334; assistance rendered by, to Queen Maria Feodorovna, 3; journey to Peking, 3; service under Danish Legation, 3; attached to International Red Cross, 3; assistance of distress in Siberian war-prisons, 3; in Mongolia and Urianhai (1919–20), 4; promotion of Expedition by, 6; lecture before Royal Danish Geographical Society, 6, 7; selected as leader of Expedition, 8; ambulance and Red Cross work of (1922), 9; accident to, 18; return of, from Irkutsk, 102, 103; cargo of furs obtained by, in company with Ping, 115; medical treatment of sick Mongols by, 115; astonishment of Mongols at surgical operation carried out by, 115; presentation of *hadaks* to, by cured Mongols, 115; co-operation with lama-doctor, 115; method of disposal of consignment of potatoes, 133; departure for Shanghai, 134; arrangement for better postal communications with Denmark, 136; marriage of, 150; in pursuit of Hishik, 323; journey through mountains north of Lake Hubso Gol, 325; behaviour towards Russian Frontier Guard, 326; remains at Bulgun Tal, 335
Krebs, Ove, 2, 3, 66, 68, 326, 327; Danish Chargé d'Affaires at Peking, 3; return from Peking, 6; active part taken by, in planning Expedition, 6; self-training in mining undertaken by, 9, 10; harbour building in Portugal, 335

INDEX

Krebs, Mrs., arrival at Bulgun Tal, 150

Krebs Expedition to Mongolia: origin of, 1 *et seq.*; promotion of, 6, 7; applications to take part in, 7; selection of pioneers for, 8; agreement drawn up for, 8; shares of profits to be assigned to members of, 8; subscription of members to funds of, 8; leader of, 8; object of, 9; share to be paid to retiring member, 9; forbidden by Soviet Government to travel through Russia, 9, 10; embarkation of members on M.S. *Malaya*, 12; route of, from start to finish, map showing, 14; means of land transport used by, 25, 27; departure from Kalgan, 28; arrival at Sheng-Wat-Sin, 38; victualling and rationing during desert journey described, 41, 43, 44; sleeping arrangements, 44; journey through Gobi Desert, 55 *et seq.*; arrival in Outer Mongolia, 60; arrival at Ude, 62; Mongol family in service with, 114; postal communications of members of, with Denmark, improved, 136; false news as to fate of, sent by telegram from Shanghai to *Vossische Zeitung*, 155, contradicted by telegram, 155; final dispersal of members of, 335; *see also under names of members* (Borgström, Haslund, Isager, Krebs, etc.)

Krupchatka in exchange for butter, 320

Kublai Khan, Mongols of, crossing sea to attack Japan, 289

Kuko Gol, River, tributary of Uri, 195

Kuku Khoto (Blue Town), present name of, 41; ancient capital of Tumut Mongols, 41

Kultuk, 141, 261

Kure (monastery), 338

Kwei-hua-ch'eng, Kuku Khoto (Blue Town) now named, 41

Lakes in Mongolia, supernatural legends attached to all, 289

Lama and *harhung*, distinguishing points between, 337

— Mongolian, dress of, 193

Lama-doctor, Krebs' co-operation with, 115

Lamaism, literature of Uri Hangrän not included in, 196

Lamas: forbidden by Soviet to elect new *hutuktu* in Kalka Mongolia, 154; in temple quarter of Urga, retirement to bed at sun-down, 165; of Van Kure, 175; of Mongolian Monastery (Dain Derchen Kure), 192

— Buddhistic, paying tribute to Uri Hangrän, 196

— Mongolian, prophecies of, regarding Bulgun Tal, 93

Lange-Müller, 24

Langelinie, 11

Larson, F. A., 63, 66, 67, 74, 123, 154, 326, 327, 329, 331, 334; hunting dog of, 100; work done by Tot for, 124; services of Tot let out to, 125; compound of, 125, arrival at, 123; authorization of advance of capital to Expedition, 162; arrest of, for gambling, 330

Larson, F. A., & Company, Inc., 22, 75; compound of, near Kalgan, 224

Lead (*tolegon*), sale of, 31

Leguminous plants, thriving on lime in soil, 129

Leipzig, 5, 27

INDEX

Lekdan Khan: translation of holy *Ganjur* by Gautama Buddha into Mongolian language authorized by, 39; war with Emperor of China, 39; written language of Mongols improved by, 39; defeat and death of, 40

Lemberg, 202

Lhasa, legendary mission to, 73

Ligget & Mayer Tobacco Company, representatives of, at Kalgan, 24

Li Hung Chang, services rendered to, by Nils Poulsen, 23

Lime in soil, leguminous plants thriving on, 129

Lipton, firm of, failure to produce brick-tea, 30

Livestock, methods of increase, 134

Log House in Bulgun Tal, description of, 99

London, 27

Love-song, Mongolian, 207, 208; music of, 207

Lynxes, 305

Mai-mai-cheng, 69

Malaya, M.S., 10; embarkation on, 12

Manchu Dynasty, fall of (1912), disbanding of Chahar Guards coincident with, 41

Manchuria, 68

Manchus, government of, reason for Mongols acquiescing in, 35

Manila, 16

Mare's milk, drink consisting of (*koumiss*), 337

Maria Feodorovna, Queen, assistance rendered to, by Karl Krebs, 3

Market-place for Chinese merchants and nomadic traders, 29; wares sold at, 29, 30

Marmots (*tarbagan*) of Gobi Desert, 64

Master (*dandiade*), 314

Meat-producer, *khainak* as, 113

Medicine, practice of, by Krebs among Mongols, 115

Merchandise, in market-place, description of, 31

Meteorological station of Krebs Expedition, 131

Military constitution of Chahar, 40

Milk producer, *khainak* as, 113

Misha, 150, 185; account of, 108, 109; horse-breaker to Expedition, 137

Mogensen, G., 18; meeting with Haslund, 333

Monastery (*kure*), Mongolian, 338; of Darkhat Kure, 186; Dain Derchen Kure, built of wood, 190, 191, 192; disciple (*shabi*) in, 338

Mongol boy (*Gongerer*), adoption of, 144, 145
— family in service with Krebs Expedition, 114
— mode of life adopted by Swede (Söderbom), 159
— soldiers, dreaded by Chinese caravan drivers, 63
— tribe at Uri, ruler of: incitement of rebellion against, by three Buriats, 204; murdered through agency of Soviet Government at Urga, 205
— tribes in East, Kelley's attempt to carry arms to, 158

Mongols, 35; first meeting with, at Kalgan, 21, 22; attirement and weapons of, 31; reason for acquiescing in government of Manchus, 35; uprising against Chinese Republic, 35; cause of perpetual retreat into desert, 36; Chinese traders' method of incurring debt among, 36; daughters of, sold to Chinese immigrants for wives, 37; purchase of cattle of, by Chinese, at low prices, 37; written language of, by whom

INDEX

Mongols (*continued*)—
improved, 39; appreciation of beauties of nature by, 51; of race called Barun Sunit, 53; and Chinese, guerilla warfare between, 58; attack of, on Chinese in Turin, 65; method of warfare of, 65; dairy-farming methods of, 113; sheep indispensable to, 114; sick, medical treatment of, by Krebs, 115; hospitality of, 120; frozen to death, discovery of, 121, 122; tending of livestock by requiring supervision, 134; haymaking hitherto unknown to, 147; labour supplied by, during hay harvest, 147; inability of, to swim, 183; furs used as currency by, 185, 186; critical of accepting silver in payment, 188; language of Soyotes understood by, 197; language of Kiäkt Buriats compared with that of, 201; skin coats of Kiäkt Buriats compared with those of, 201; immemorial law (*Yassa*) laid down for, 204; annihilation by, of force of *gam-min* (Chinese irregular soldiers), 210, 211; riders upon asses held in contempt by, 210; Chinese traders tolerated but despised by, 211; extraordinary skill in attack and in planning onslaught, 211; unerring aim in shooting, 211; divination by consulting bones, 222; name of, for bronze weapons in desert dating from past ages, 288; conception of immensity of sea, how shown, 289; legendary Khans of, rulers over all waters, 289; no present knowledge of sea, 289; silence of, in neighbourhood of running or great still waters, 289; observation and interpretation of nature by, 304; *see also* Chahar Mongols, Kalka Mongols, Tumut Mongols, Young Mongols

Mongolia, 7, 74, 75; visit of Carl Krebs to (1919–20), 4; depredations and outrages committed by forces of Ungarn-Sternberg in, 25; scenery of, described, 34; Chinese settlement in (Sheng-Wat-Sin), 38; hills in, beauty of, 51; supposed tropical climate of, six million years ago, 55, 56; products of, route of transference to seaport of Tientsin, 58; seat of principal monastery of, at Urga, 70; cattle census in, 110; chief industries of, 110; horse-racing in, 112; effects of Soviet Revolution on, 154 *et seq.*; deliverance from China, political changes following, 154, 155; importation of strychnine into, why profitable, 161; sole specimens of apple-trees seen in, 190; return to, after release from prison, 283 *et seq.*; privations in, after imprisonment in Shinkish, 285; supernatural legends attached to all lakes in, 289; divisions of, 338; and Siberia, aboriginal population of region along boundary between, supposed fate of, 339; *see also* Kalka Mongolia

— Inner, 35, 36; princes of, dependent on military resources of China, 35; and Outer, boundary between, 59; winter season of, time of commencement, 60

— Northern, 274; waters of, discharging into Lake Baikal, 190

355

INDEX

Mongolia, Outer, 36; dread of journey to, shown by caravan drivers, 59; arrival of Krebs Expedition in, 60
Mongolian and Chinese administration, mixed, of Chahar, 40
— battle song, 306
— bazaars, measurements used in, diagrams of, 209, 212, 213
— *harhung*, 314
— Minister of Justice, B., pretext of farewell visit to, 162
— method of reckoning time, 231, 234, 300, 302
— name for columns of snow (*duche*, butterflies), 232; for lake (*nor*), 289
— New Year, 338
— soldiers in Soviet uniform, increase of, in Bogdo Kure, 154
— songs, 206, 207, 208
— trappers and Chinese traders: monastery as centre of exchange for, 192
— year, 338
Mongolian-Chinese War (1912), 6
Mongolians, use of fossils by, for cure of diseases, 56; wealth of, how represented, 111, 112
— in Urga, murder of, 334
Monks, Mongolian, massacre of, 54
Months of Mongolian year, 338; three, each Mongolian season divided into, 338
Moscow, 275; Danish Legation in, 274
Motor-car chasing, ascertaining speed of antelope of steppes by means of, 52
Motor-cars (*muhor teleg*), 306; unsuitable as means of transport for the Expedition, 25
Mountain ponies, representing Uri Hangrän, 196
Mouse's hour (12–2), 231, 234
Muhammedans, dress of, 31
Muhor teleg (motor cars), 306

Mundi, 261, 282
Munku Sardyk, peak of, 283, 284; legend as to creation of, 287
Murin Kure, Monastery of, 307, 308, 326
Mus-dawan Pass, 217, 241
Music, perception of, varying capacities for, 227
Mynter, Mr., chief of Great Northern Telegraph Company, Tientsin, 18, 19
Mystical, the, perception of, varying capacities for, 227

Naamogon, Prince, legend relating to, 73
Namehr (autumn), 338
Nankow Pass, 20
Nature, observation and interpretation by Mongols, 304
New Year, Mongolian: first month of (*Tsaghan sar*, white month), 307, 308, 338
New York, 27
Nikolai (Kao-Wen Pu), history of, 275, 276; aid of, to Haslund, 276, 277
Nomadic traders and Chinese merchants, market place for, 29
Nor, Mongolian name for lake, 289
Noyan (Noble, high official) (footnote), 204
Noyan Bogdo (Divine Prince), 52

Oats (*avyos*), purchase for a brick of tea the pood (36 lb.), 317; pood of (36 lb.), transport cost of equal to that of eight bricks of tea, 317
Obo, heaps of stone in desert, 59; of Uri Hangrän (God of Nature), described, 195, 196, 296; gifts offered at, 296
Obos, raising of, by Soyotes, 294, 295

INDEX

Obyl (winter), 338
Odogna Kure, 115; monastery of, 95, 320, 326
Odin, 246
Odsha, 294
Ogier the Dane, 2
Oimus (felt stockings), 114
Oka Buriats, 325
Oka Valley, 325
Ole'en Lama : a lama not attached to monastery, 237; account of past life of, 237; appearance of, described, 225, 226; ceremony connected with sheep's shoulder-blade performed by, 228, 229, 230; prediction as to shooting of roebuck verified, 228, 229; prediction as to occurrence of snowstorm, 230, 231, verification of, 232 et seq.
Olufsen, E. V.: biographical account of, 67; marriage of, 67; tragic fate of, 67, 68
Omsk, 269
Orchon Valley, sportsmen's paradise, 78
Orenburg Cossacks, 202
Oros, 314
— *posta* (Russian post office), 141
Osun Lozang Khans, 289
Ox caravans, traffic with, slowness of, 61
Oxen, Mongolian, excellency of, as draught cattle, 113

Panchen Bogdo, 35
P'ang-chiang, 331; desert city of, 53, 54
Pasque-flowers, 129
Passports obtained from *yamen* (chancery), 162
Peking, 175, 332; journey of Carl Krebs to, 3; Ove Krebs Danish Chargé d'Affaires at, 3; "Danish Mess" at, 18; stay at, 18, 19, 20; government of Chahar administered under, 40; tribute paid by Mongolian tribes summoned to, 71; Danish Legation at, 276
Pelts: kinds of, obtained by trappers enumerated, 208; examination of, 211, 212; classification of, 212, difficulties in, 212; expert knowledge of, possessed by Chinese traders settling at Kiäkt, 213
Pig, wild, traces of, how indicated, 305
Ping, 81, 85, 86, 94, 97, 98, 103, 104, 105, 108, 109, 110, 116, 117, 121, 122; expert on furs, 75; cooking abilities of, 92; wonderful shop of (*p'u-tse*), 92, 93, 103; cargo of furs obtained by, in company with Krebs, 115
Ploughing and sowing of virgin soil on steppe, 130, 131
Poland, 9; Danish Red Cross in, 75
Poplar, solitary, found on Gobi Desert, 64
Port Said, 13, 14
Portugal, Ove Krebs' work in, 335
Post-office, Russian (*Oros posta*), 141
Postal communications of members of Krebs Expedition with Denmark, improvement in, 136
Potato-growing at Bulgun Tal, 133, 148
Poulsen, Nils, 21; Chinese acquirements and habits of, 22, 23; Scandinavian rather than Danish sympathies of, 23; services rendered to Li Hung Chang by, 23
Poultry-keeping at Bulgun Tal, 148
Prayer, "*Dunjur Mani*", 315
— formularies, Tibetan, assistance rendered by knowledge of, 309
— Tibetan, repetition of, 313, 314

INDEX

Price of commodity, how determined in regions difficult of access, 317

Prisoners in Shinkish, description of, 266, 270, 271

Pub, Island of, in Lake Hubso Gol, 286, 287 ; reputed holiness of, 286

Puntsuk, Mongolian woman in service of Krebs Expedition, 114

Rationing during desert journey of Krebs Expedition, 43

Raven, Mongol name for (*kilitai shobo*, " talking bird "), 338

Ravens : predatory, in Gobi Desert, 57 ; important rôle played by, for Mongols, 246 ; prognostications from, 295, 338, 339

Red Cross Relief Expedition to Russia, 9

Resin pellets containing strychnine, preparation of, 311

Resin-chewing, object of, 310, 311

Riefestahl, Herr : gold obtained by, in Urianhai, 6 ; mine of, 325

Rintjino, Russian Buriat : Communist Party established by, 155 ; murder of Danzan (War Minister) and Bavasan, Secretary to Kalka Mongolian Government, 155

River birds at Bulgun Tal, 148

Robber Princess : meeting of Expedition with, 47 ; attirement of, 47, 48

Roebuck, shooting of, prediction of *Ole'en Lama* as to, verified, 228, 229

— deer : defensive instincts of, how indicated, 305 ; shooting for food, 130

Rosshafen, 12

Royal Danish Geographical Society, lecture before by Carl Krebs promoting Expedition, 6, 7 ; support of expedition by, 10

Rugs from Kashgar, sale of, 31

Russia, 74 ; famine in (1922), 9 ; Expedition forbidden to travel through, 10

Russian aggression, regiments of Chahar Mongols on guard against, 40

— bath, 173

— baths at Bulgun Tal, 96, 103

— Boundary Commission, work of, during reign of Catherine II, 4, 5 ; loss of Urianhai to Imperial Crown through action of, 5

— chauffeur, information against Wilson given by, 161

— coins in *obo* of Uri Hangrän, 196

— Dominions in Asia and China, line of boundary between, 4

— Frontier Guard, 326

— gold coins, old, used for ornamentation, 201

— harness, description of, 170 ; see also Harness, Russian

— immigrants, settlement just within Urianhai, 5

— melody harmonized for strings of balalaika, 189

— post-office (*Oros posta*), 141

— quarter of Urga (Konsulstvo), 162

— smugglers from Tunkinski Trakt, 313, 314

— song, theme of, 189

— territory, hunting with strychnine not prohibited in, 319

Russian-American firm : disposal of furs to, 125, result, 126 ; price of furs dictated by, at Urga, 125 ; agreement regarding purchased furs with, 125

Russians, anti-Soviet policy of new government of Kalka Mongolia displeasing to, 155

INDEX

Russo-Japanese War, fall of Russian prestige in Asia following, 6
Sable Plateau, 3, 4, 74, 76, 79; establishment of Shishkin family on, 4
Sacrifice of goat by Chinese caravan drivers, 59, 60
Sain Noyan Khanate, 53
Salmon-fishing, commencement of, 135
Salsarai, 110
Sanagen Buriats, 214, 235
Sanagen Mountains, 320
Sand rats (*Meriones*) in Gobi Desert, 57
Sarhöj, mine situated in, 325
Sava (Cossack), 196, 197; account of, 108, 109; companion and attendant during winter fur campaign, 188; departure of from Kiäkt, 214; return of, 234; visit to old home recounted, 235; danger to, from Bolsheviks, 236; hunting expedition undertaken by, 240; recounts expedition among Sanagen Mountains, 321
Sayan Mountains, 199, 283, 287, 339; range of, 4, 5
Scandinavian colony at Tientsin, 18
Scottsberg, Prof. Carl, 102
Sea: crossed by Mongols of Kublai Khan to attack Japan, 289; immensity of, Mongols' conception of, how shown, 289; no present knowledge of, among Mongols, 289
Seasons of Mongolian Year, 338; each divided into three months, 338
Selba, River, 70
Selenga, 8
— River, 79, 80, 175; ice-accident to transport wagon on, 117–20, 124; dangerous crossing of, accomplished, 183; transport of caravan across, under difficulties, 184, 185; union of Egin Gol with, 190; with tributaries, discharging into Lake Baikal, 190
Sepailov, Colonel: murder of Olsen by, 68; death of, in prison in Manchuria, 68
September, snowstorm in, 152
Serai (inn), 219
Shabi: (dependency), 203; disciple of lama, 192, 193; disciple in monastery, 338; general signification of word, 338
Shaman (the) as driver-out of spirits, 297, 298; miracles performed by, 298; female, 299, presentation with a *hadak*, 299, 300, augury from position of bones, 300, investment with sorcerer's robe, 300, supposed expulsion of evil spirits by, ceremony described, 300, manipulations with antelope foot and drum, 301
Shamanism (Black doctrine), 297; professors of, 196; official faith of whole population of Urianhai, 297
Shanghai, 12, 18, 42; boxing lesson on journey to, 42; departure of Krebs for, 134; false news sent from, by telegram as to fate of Krebs Expedition, 155, contradicted by telegram, 155
Shantung, tobacco used on steppes (*dunsa*) produced at, 30
Shara Geling, headquarters and avocations of, 318
Share gurus (yellow antelope, *Gazella gutterosa*), 52
Shaslik, 235; grilling of, 218

359

INDEX

Sheep: (*honi*), 40; attacks of wolves on, 134; indispensable to Mongols, 114; milk of, 114; tails of: self-nutriment derived from, 114, fat of, food value of, 114; in exchange for strychnine, 319, 320
— Mongolian, wool of, quantity and quality, 114
Sheng-Wat-Sin: arrival of Krebs Expedition at, 38; Chinese settlement in Mongolia, 38
Shinkish, 260, 261, 275, 276, 279; interrogation of Haslund at, 262
— Prison: Haslund's cell in, description, 267
Shishkin and family, persecution of, at Bulgun Tal, 86, 87, 90, 91
— family, establishment on Sable Plateau, 4
Shivert Pass: description of 245; crossing of, 246 *et seq.*, time for, 245; tempests on, 246, 247; boundary between two ancient empires, 248
Shooting, unerring aim of Mongols in, 211
Shoulder-blade of sheep; examination of, ceremony connected with performed by *Ole'en Lama*, 228, 229, 230; heating of, prediction of future events from appearances produced by, 228
Siasting, Michail, supporter of Mongolia's independence, 74
Siberia, 110; war-prisons of, alleviation of distress in, by Carl Krebs, 3; Danish farmers and agriculturists settled in, before Russian Revolution, 7
— and Mongolia, aboriginal population of region along present boundary between, supposed fate of, 339

Siberian barley (*arbai*), 129
Silver in payment, Mongols critical of accepting, 188
Silver coins, method of testing used by Mongols, 188
Singapore, stay at, 15
Skimmed-milk, kinds of cheese made from, 113, 114
Skin coats of Kiäkt Buriats and of Mongols compared, 201
Skylark, 129
Slav (*Khitat*), epithet of contempt used by trappers, 210
Sleeping arrangements of members of Krebs Expedition, 44
Smugglers, Russian, from Tunkinski Trakt: threatened fate of, 313; deliverance of, 314
Snow, columns of, Mongolian name for (*duche*, butterflies), 232
Snowstorm: in September, 152; prediction as to occurrence of, by *Ole'en Lama*, 230, 231, 233, verification of, 232, 233; description of, 232, 233
— Mongolian, violence and severity of, 121
Söderbom, 76; born and brought up in East, 158; Swede by nationality, 158; lover of Mongolian steppe-life, 158, 159; settlement among Mongols and adoption of Mongol mode of life, 159; death of, 159
Soldiers (" Red " and " White "), oppression of Kiäkt Buriats by, 307; *see also* Chinese soldiers; Mongolian soldiers
Songs, Mongolian, 206, 207, 208; themes of, 207
Sorcerer's robe, investment of female Shaman with, 300
South Sea Islands, 332
Soviet, 67; new *hutuktu* forbidden by, to be elected in Kalka Mongolia, 154

INDEX

Soviet Army, soldiers of, 276
— authorities, oppressive treatment of Tunka Buriats by, 215, 216
— Buriats, capture of Haslund by, 254 et seq.
— Government: permission for Expedition to travel across Russia not granted by, 9, 10; at Urga: chief of Mongol tribe at Uri murdered through agency of, 204, black list of, 205
— influence in Kalka Mongolia, predominance of, 154, 155
— power, Young Mongols representatives of, 203
— Revolution, effects on Mongolia, 154 et seq.
— Russians, imprisonment of Haslund by, 265
— uniform, Mongolian soldiers in, increase in Bogdo Kure, 154
Soyote camp, stay at, 292–303
— hunters professing black doctrine (Shamanism) paying tribute at *obo* of Uri Hangrän, 196
— Pass, 222
Soyotes: abandoned summer camping-places of, 292; characteristics of, 292; friendliness of, 292; language of: similarity to that of the Kirghiz, 292, understood by Mongols, 197; living east of Lake Hubso Gol, winter dwelling-places of, 292; origin of, 339; primitive, hunting grounds of, 187; raising of *obos* by, 294, 295; reports of miracles performed by the Shaman, 298, 299; tents of, 197
Spiegel, cattle of, robbed by Bolsheviks, 91; fate of, at hands of Bolsheviks, 91
Spiegel, Madame (Russian widow): local knowledge of, 186; farm of, used as base for hunting and buying journeys, 186
Spirits: driver-out of, the Shaman as, 297, 298; released, of dead person, superstition regarding, 295; *see also* Evil Spirits
Spring (*habehr*), 338; season at Bulgun Tal described, 129
Squirrel fur: difficulty of obtaining, 208; price of goods paid in exchange for, 209; profitable nature of, 208; extensive purchases at Alpino Serai (Trading Station), 219, 220
— pelts, high-class, brought to Kiäkt by Tunka Buriats, 215
Squirrels: winter coats of, 305; young, attacked by fatal disease, diminution of fur supply from, 194
Standard Oil Company: compound of, near Kalgan, 22, 24; representatives of, at Kalgan, 24
Steppe, ploughing and sowing of virgin soil on, 130, 131
Steppes, Mongolian: deserted state of, cause of, 45; antelopes of, 52; vast herds of cattle in, 65; cloud-shapes seen on, 116; in south, means of communication with Kiäkt, 187
— snow-covered, difficulties of travel across, 290, 291
Stockholm, 8
Storms of the desert, 61, 62
Stronghold of the Red Power (Ulan Bator Khoto), 154
Strychnine: poisoning of wolves with, 161; importation of, into Mongolia, why profitable, 161; smuggling of, imprisonment of Wilson on

361

INDEX

Strychnine (*continued*)—
suspicion of, 161; hunting with, 310, not prohibited in Russian territory, 319; resin-pellets containing preparation of, 311; pills: for destroying wolves, method of depositing, 312, destruction of wolf by, 315; traffic in, by private persons forbidden in Urga, 319; sheep in exchange for, 319, 320
— contraband: buried in *hashanda*, 162, abstraction of, 164; escape through customs at Urga without discovery of, 164; removal from Urga, 165, 166; risk entailed by conveyance of, 176; discovery of, by customs officers, how evaded, 179, 180; packages of, not discovered at customs examination at Van Kure, 180; final hiding-place of, 186
Sugar-beet, sowing of, 132
Sulde-tsar, last month of season, 338
Sultei gurus (Tailed Antelope, *Gazella subgutterosa*), 52
Sulu Sea, passage through, 15
Summer (*zung*), 338
— camping-places of Soyotes, similarity to Indian wigwams, 292
Sumon (arrows), 338
Sund, the, 1
Suni (night), 53
Superstition regarding released spirits of dead person, 295
Surong, maid-servant to Krebs Expedition, 114
Sweetmeats, expense of, in Central Asia, 132
Swede (Söderbom) adopting Mongol mode of life, 159
Swimming, Mongols incapable of, 183

Tabun (horse herd), 294
Taiga, 308; of "holy Russia", 187
Ta-lien-pu (*dalimba*), 30
Tang chia-ti, Chinese for "Master" (footnote), 314
Tannu Ola, 339; mountain chain of, boundary between China and Russia in Asia, 4
Tarbagan (marmots), 64
Tartary, 22
Tashi Lama, 35
Tea: sold along caravan routes by Chinese, 30; consumed in Europe, main overland route of transference, 58; eight bricks of, transport cost of pood of oats same as that of, 317; one brick of, pood of oats (36 lb.) bought for, 317; *see also* Brick-tea
Telegraph line from Urga to Kiachta, 120; guiding value in snow, 123
Telegraphs, Chinese, 7
Teme (camels), 40
Temechin: district of Chahar, 40; signification of name, 40
Temperature of air, figures showing fall in, 44
Temples within a cloister (*duguns*), 190
Tengger (heaven), 35
Tenggerin losang yasa (bones of the Dragons of Heaven), Mongolian name for fossils, 56
— *sumon* (arrows of heaven), 288
Terje Vigenfärd, 313
"Three trees of Gobi", The, 63
Tibet, 70
Tibetan prayer formularies, assistance rendered by knowledge by, 309; repetition of, 313, 314
Tichang River, 85
Tientsin, 7, 43, 175, 331, 334; delay of Expedition at, 18;

INDEX

Tientsin (*continued*)—
Scandinavian colony at, 18 ; route of transference of products of Mongolia to, 58
Tiestiakov, executioner of Sepailov, 68
Tiger's hour, 302
Timbuktoo of the Gobi Desert, Ude misnamed, 62
Time, Mongolian method of reckoning, 231, 234, 300, 302
Timur, warriors of, leading horses to wells, 289
Titiang River, irrigation with water of, 132
obacco used on steppes (*dunsa*), 30
Tola River, 165, 167 ; encircling Urga, 66, 74 ; first permanent Buddhist temple at, 70, 74
— Valley, arrival at, 123
Tolegon (lead), sale of, 31
Torguts, language of Kiäkt Buriats compared with that of, 201
Tot, 75, 123, 124, 127, 138, 152, 168, 171 ; work done by, for Larson, 124 ; property of Expedition, let out to Larson, 125 ; removal of contraband strychnine from Urga by, 165, 166 ; emigration to Canada, 335
Trading station (Alpino Serai), life at, 217 *et seq.*
Transbaikalia, 202
Transport by land, means of, used by Expedition, 25, 27
— price of pood of oats same as that of eight bricks of tea, 317
Transport-wagon, ice-accident to, on Selenga River, 117-20, 124
Trappers, entertainment at Alpino Serai (Trading Station), 218, 219 ; kinds of pelts obtained by, enumerated, 208
Trappers, Mongolian : entertainment of, 209 ; how induced to become sole vendors to Chinese traders, 213

Travel, awakening of lust for, 194
Treelessness, general, of Gobi Desert, 64
Trees, fallen, impediment to travelling, 194
Troikas, 170
Tsaghan sar (white month), 325, celebration of, by Mongols, 307
Tsaghan tos : substance formed from cream, 113 ; storage of, 113
Tsasaktu, Prince, legend relating to, 73
Tsetsen Khan, *see* Erebugher
Tsong Kapa, priests of, reverencing Uri Hangrän (God of Nature), 195
T'u-fei (bandits, brigands), 59 ; ravaging caravans and settlements, 37, 45 ; protection against attacks of, 47, 48, 49
Tumut Mongols, ancient capital of (Kuku Khoto), 41
Tunka, 241, 248, 249 ; accounts of, obtained from hunters, 238 ; journey to, resolved upon and undertaken, 239 ; outpost of European civilization, 238 ; treatment of Haslund by Soviet Buriats in, 257 *et seq.*
— Buriats : family of, skill of, in building, 89 ; high-class squirrel pelts brought to Kiäkt by, 215, reason explained, 215, 216 ; oppressive treatment of, by Soviet authorities, 215, 216
— Valley, 270
Tunkinski Buriats, 249 ; " Red " atmosphere prevailing among, 249–52 ; impious picture in house of, 250
" Tunkinski Trakt ", 261 ; Russian smugglers from, 313, 314
Turansk, 277, 280

INDEX

Turin, attack of Mongols on Chinese at, 65
Turkestan, Chinese capital of (Urumchi), 280
Turuk, prices of furs excessive at, 307; return of Isager from, 307
Turunt-tsar, first month of season, 338
Tushetu Khan, Prince, legend relating to, 73

Ude : arrival of Krebs Expedition at, 62; misnamed " the Timbuktoo of the Gobi Desert ", 62; official entrance to country of Kalka Mongols, 62; and *Khalagan*, difference between, in meaning explained, 62
Ugher (cattle), 40
Ugherchin, district of Chahar, 40; signification of name, 40
Ugrians, Finnish, 339
Ugro-Samoyedes, 339
Uighurs : supposed origin of, 339; supposed descendants of, 339
Ulan Bator Khoto, name of Bogdo Kure changed to, 154
Uliassutai, wool campaign at west of, 75
Ungern-Sternberg, Baron, 58, 67, 259, 306, and White Guards, campaign against Bolsheviks, 7; depredations and outrages committed by forces of, in Mongolia, 25; guerillas of, 90; capture of, by Bolsheviks near Kiachta, 91
United States, 67; research stations, wheat seed from, 131
Unti, 218, 224
Urga, 42, 43, 44, 60, 73, 74, 75, 76, 81, 100, 108, 112, 120, 134, 152, 154, 157, 188, 203, 259, 277, 324, 326, 327, 328, 330, 332, 333, 334; caravan route from Kalgan to, 58; city of Mongols, 66, 67, 68; description of, 68, 69; fragment of China in, 69; Westerner's, history of, 70, 74; arrival and stay at, 123; price of ermine at, 125; price of furs in, no official quotation regarding, 125; departure of Expedition from, 127, 128, privations endured following, 127, 128; United States Representative at (Kelley), 156; Russian quarter of (Konsulstvo), 162; removal of contraband strychnine from, 165, 166; caravan transport from, to Van Kure, difficulties recounted, 168 *et seq.*; Daichin Wang incarcerated in Soviet prison at, 175; arrival at Bulgun Tal after journey from, 185; traffic in strychnine by private persons forbidden in, 319
— and Kalgan : mode of communication between, 25; possibility of constructing railway between, 45
Urga Dawn (Urga's only newspaper), 74
Uri, 318
— River, 195; confluence with Egin Gol, 190
Uri Gol, 306
Uri Hangrän (God of Nature) : highest worship paid to, 195; how offended and penalties exacted, 195; reverence paid to, by priests of other deities, 195; supposed dwelling-place of, 195; *obo* of, described, 195, 196; mountain ponies representing, 196; no place in literature of lamaism, 196; offerings to : kind presented, 196, requisite, 195; tribute to, paid by members of different nationalities and religions, 196

INDEX

Urianhai, 4; visit of Carl Krebs to (1919–20), 4; how excluded from Russian territory, 5; Russian gold prospectors in, 5; gold obtained by Mr. Riefestahl in, 6; settlement of Russian immigrants just within, 5; Shamanism, official faith of whole population of, 297

Urtoni (relays), 207

Urtoni-rider, 207

Urum (cream), 113

Urumchi: capital of Chinese Turkestan, 280; banquet in, to distinguished visitors by Chinese Governor-General, 280, 281, 282

Utgård Loki, 86

Vallov, Mr., Russian telegraphist at Ude, 63

Van Kure, 75, 90, 94, 108, 109, 120, 128, 188; monastic town of, 78, 79; caravan transport to, from Urga, difficulties recounted, 168 *et seq.*; inhabitants of: nationality, 175, peaceful character of, 175; customs examination at, 176, 177, 178, 179, contraband strychnine escapes detection, 180; monastery of, 323

Vasilev, Comrade (Soviet Consul in Urga), opinion as to effect of murder of Danzan and Bavasan, 155

Vegetables: successful growing of, 132; storage underground, 133

Victualling and rationing during desert journey of Krebs Expedition described, 41, 43, 44

Viking stronghold (*Jomsborg*), 150

Volga, River, 75

Vossische Zeitung, false news as to fate of Krebs Expedition sent to, by telegram from Shanghai, 155, contradicted by telegram, 155

War song, Mongolian ("Chikherli bodena"), theme of, 211

War-prisons, Siberian, alleviation of distress in, by Carl Krebs, 3

Warder in Shinkish prison, behaviour of, 269

Warsaw, 202

Watch (Borgström's), magical powers of, 94, demonstration of, to lamas, 95

Water: difficulty of obtaining, in Gobi Desert, 56; polluted, boiled for drinking, 57; use of, Jenghiz Khan's ordinance regarding, 115

Water-birds and fowl at Bulgun Tal, 147, 148

Water-holes, search of antelopes for, 52

Water-wheels, irrigation by means of, 131

Waters: all, legendary Khans of Mongols rulers over, 289; running or great still, silence of Mongols in neighbourhood of, 289

Weapons, concealment of, purpose of, 28

Wedding present, bag of *koumiss* important as, 33

Wells (*khuduks*), 289; reverence paid by Mongols to, 289

Wheat: experimental cultivation of, 131; seed, sources whence obtained, 131

Whirlwinds of the desert, 61, 62

White Guards, 306; campaign against Bolsheviks, 7

White month (*Tsaran tsar*), 338; first month of Mongolian New Year, 307, 308

Wigwams, Indian, similarity of summer camping-places of Soyotes to, 292

Wild boar hunt, 221

INDEX

Wild cats, 305

Wilson, William: account of Olufsen's death given by, 68; imprisonment of, on suspicion of smuggling strychnine, 159, 161; treachery of Russian chauffeur of, 161

Wilson, Mrs., difficult act of friendship toward, 161 *et seq.*

Winter (*obyl*), 338; season of Inner Mongolia, time of commencement, 60; fur campaign in, 188 *et seq.*; outfit on steppes, necessity for, proved, 171
— Mongolian, fatal effect on horses and cattle, 120

Wives, Mongolian, of Chinese immigrants, 37

Wolf, destruction of, by strychnine, 315
— cakes (*chononi bobo*), 311, 315
— fur, price of goods paid in exchange for, 209

Wolves, attacks on sheep, 134; predatory, poisoning with strychnine, 161; hunting of, carcase of horse used as bait in, 222, 223; legend of transformation into human beings, 226; method of baiting to take strychnine pills, 312; mystical, 227
— Siberian: adventure with, on journey to Tunka, 241–4; characteristics of, 244

Women, Mongolian, uncleanliness of, 114

Wood, Mongolian monastery built of, 190

Wulf, Dr., 19

"*Yabonah*": cry of, significance, 32, 34; summons to break camp, 288

Yak bulls and Mongolian cows, product of (*khainak*), 113
— cattle: Mongolian, 113, qualities of, 113

Yalserai, 89, 90, 95, 96, 97, 98, 101; pressing of, into ranks of White Guards, 91

Yamen (Chancery), passports obtained from, 162

Yassa, immemorial law laid down for Mongols by Jenghiz Bogdo Khan, 204

Year, Mongolian, months and seasons of, 338

Yenshan (Chinese silver dollar), 188

Yetom (Mongol), 138

Young Mongol Party, pro-Russian political activities of, 175
— — rider (Boyan Hishik), 30
— Mongols, 177; pro-Russian, official interference of, 176; representatives of Soviet power, 203

Yurts, winter dwelling-places of Soyotes east of Lake Hubso Gol, 292

Zerang, 298, 299; accident to, 294; plight of, discovered by hunters, 294, 295; reason for hunters not rescuing, 295; rescue of, alive, 296; expulsion of evil spirits from body of, 297 *et seq.*; daughter of, 294–6, 298, 302, 303

Zung (summer), 338

For Product Safety Concerns and Information please contact our EU representative GPSR@taylorandfrancis.com
Taylor & Francis Verlag GmbH, Kaufingerstraße 24, 80331 München, Germany

www.ingramcontent.com/pod-product-compliance
Lightning Source LLC
Chambersburg PA
CBHW071233300426
44116CB00008B/1023